Turning Point

Selected Messages of
the Universal House of Justice
and Supplementary Material
1996–2006

Palabra Publications

Palabra Publications
7369 Westport Place
West Palm Beach, Florida 33413
U.S.A.
1-561-697-9823
1-561-697-9815 (fax)
palabrapub@aol.com
www.palabrapublications.com

Cover photographs: *Masoud Emadén*

Contents

Contents

PART II
Global Plans: Fundamental Concepts
a document dated 29 October 2005 prepared
by an ad hoc committee for a workshop
conducted at the Bahá'í World Centre

PART III
Additional Documents

Preface

ALMOST NINETY YEARS AGO, 'Abdu'l-Bahá revealed the Tablets of the Divine Plan, a plan "divine in origin," the "grand design for the spiritual conquest of the planet," which holds within it "the seeds of the world's spiritual revival and ultimate redemption." 'Abdu'l-Bahá presented in "graphic" language and "definite terms" guidance that originated with the Báb and was reinforced by Bahá'u'lláh for the expansion and consolidation of the Faith throughout the world, ultimately leading to the establishment of the Kingdom of God on earth. The Divine Plan unfolds through a series of stages—first under the direction of Shoghi Effendi and then the Universal House of Justice—that will stretch "as far as the fringes" of the Golden Age.

To initiate the systematic implementation of the Divine Plan, Shoghi Effendi directed Bahá'í communities to formulate national plans of action, beginning with the first Seven Year Plan in North America in 1937. Country after country gradually reached the point where each could adopt its own plan. This led to the international collaboration of six nations in the African Campaign of 1951–1953 and, eventually, to the first global plan, the Ten Year Crusade, which began in 1953 and involved the combined efforts of the existing twelve National Spiritual Assemblies. As a result of these plans, the Faith spread to villages, towns, cities, and provinces within countries and throughout the world, raising the number of Local Spiritual Assemblies and strengthening the foundations of the Administrative Order. The size and diversity of the membership of the community greatly increased, particularly through the emergence in Uganda, Indonesia, and other countries of the process of entry by troops—where people began to enter the Faith not merely as a steady flow of fresh recruits, but by hundreds, thousands, and eventually, tens of thousands.

Shoghi Effendi foresaw "the launching of world-wide enterprises destined to be embarked upon, in future epochs . . . by the Universal House of Justice, that will symbolize the unity and co-ordinate and unify the activities of these National Assemblies." After the end of the Ten Year Crusade, the plans conducted under the direction of the House of Justice maintained the objectives of spreading the Faith to new areas and establishing local and national institutions, while gradually adding new objectives to diversify and strengthen the capacities of the Bahá'í world. The Nine Year Plan (1964–1973) included the objectives of a vast expansion in membership and universal participation by individuals in the life of the Cause. The Five Year Plan (1974–1979) gave particular attention to developing Local Assemblies and activities of Bahá'í community life, such as regular observance of the Feast and Holy Days. The Seven Year Plan (1979–1986) underscored the importance of involvement in the affairs of society and introduced the pursuit of projects of social and economic development. Bringing together seven major objectives for the progress of the Bahá'í world, the Six Year Plan (1986–1992) instituted a procedure whereby national plans were formulated in consultation between the Counsellors and National Assemblies, while the Three Year Plan (1993–1996) called for three developments that would contribute to the seven objectives, that is, enhancing the vitality of the faith of the individual believer, developing human resources, and fostering the proper functioning of institutions.

Over this period of some three decades, the process of entry by troops that began during the ministry of Shoghi Effendi continued to gather momentum in other countries. Many had tens of thousands of new believers; a few surpassed one hundred thousand, while the Indian community grew by hundreds of thousands to some two million. Such rapid growth, however, often carried out by a relatively small core of dedicated believers, could not be matched by a pattern of consolidation that would adequately deepen such vast numbers, educate their children, raise institutions, and lay the foundations of community life. Although large-scale expansion was initiated in country after country, it could not be sustained. The challenge was not simply to place emphasis on activities for consolidation, which, alone, would lead to an inward-looking orientation and the potential stagnation of the Bahá'í community. Rather, what was needed was a capacity to maintain the balance between expansion and consolidation in a pattern of systematic action over time.

This broad historical sketch provides the backdrop for the decade from 1996 to 2006 that is the focus of the present book. Beginning with the Four Year Plan (1996–2000), the Universal House of Justice set the Bahá'í world on an unprecedented course of action. "The next four years will represent an extraordinary period in the history of our Faith, a turning point of epochal magnitude," it stated. "This Plan acquires a special place in the scheme of Bahá'í and world history." "[T]he Bahá'í community is engaged in an immense historical process that is entering a critical stage." The Plan had but a single aim of "accelerating the process of entry by troops," which the House of Justice described as "a necessity at this stage in the progress of the Cause and in the state of human society." The designated protagonists of this effort—the individual, the community, and the institutions—were charged with demonstrating "more tangibly than ever before their capacity and willingness to embrace masses of new adherents, to effect the spiritual and administrative transformation of thousands upon thousands, and, above all, to multiply the army of knowledgeable, consecrated teachers of a Faith whose emergence from obscurity must be registered on the consciousness of countless multitudes throughout the earth."

What began in 1996 as an imperative need became, by 2006, a dawning reality. Over the course of the decade that opened with the Four Year Plan, and included both the Twelve Month Plan (2000–2001) and the Five Year Plan (2001–2006), the capacity to promote the process of entry by troops had been distinctly enhanced. In setting the ten-year period in perspective, the Universal House of Justice offered a vision of possibilities for the future. "The elements required for a concerted effort to infuse the diverse regions of the world with the spirit of Bahá'u'lláh's Revelation," it wrote, "have crystallized into a framework for action that now needs only to be exploited." The Bahá'í world stands poised to make an unprecedented, systematic advance in the process of entry by troops during the series of Plans unfolding over the next fifteen years until the year 2021, the end of the first century of the Formative Age.

This book traces the evolution of thought in the Bahá'í world over the critical last decade. While it provides insights into many aspects of the Faith, there are two observations of particular significance that can be drawn from its pages. One concerns the nature of the process of the growth itself. That human resources are required at different levels of capacity to sustain progress, that these human resources must be prepared through formal programs of training, that they are to be deployed in accordance with plans of action focused on geographic areas of a manageable size—these are some of the distinguishing features of the pattern of growth that has emerged in the past ten years. A rich description of its dynamics and the means for promoting it, one that employs phrases such as "two essential movements," "stages of development," "cycles of activity," unfolds in the book. What is striking is the pace at which such a high degree of understanding on the subject was achieved among Bahá'ís everywhere. "Never before," the House of Justice noted, "have the means for establishing a pattern of activity that places equal emphasis on the twin processes of expansion and consolidation been better understood."

A second observation, inseparable from the first, relates to the shift in culture that occurred during the period under review. The collective acknowledgement that there were no easy formulas for accelerating the process of entry by troops and the willingness to adopt a posture characterized by learning opened the way for so many rapid advances to be made in such a relatively short span of time. A mode of operation in which the friends study the guidance, consult on the best alternatives before them, step into the field of action, and reflect on their experience to improve their understanding and adjust their efforts became pervasive. It is this culture of learning that is, perhaps, the most noteworthy development of the decade, for it will ensure that the Bahá'í community can continually adapt its actions to the organic needs of the Faith and to the circumstances of an ever-changing society.

The book is divided into three parts. Part I includes a selection of thirty-eight messages from the Universal House of Justice covering the period from 26 December 1995 to Riḍván 2006. Part II consists of a document dated 29 October 2005 prepared by an ad hoc committee for a workshop presented as part of the Serving the Divine Plan Program at the Bahá'í World Centre. This section, which explores themes related to the current series of global Plans, provides helpful commentary but, apart from the copious extracts taken from letters written by or on behalf of the Guardian and the House of Justice, should not be considered a statement of authoritative guidance. Part III contains a number of well-familiar documents that systematize the learning of national communities in their efforts to advance the process of entry by troops; the first was prepared for and approved by the House of Justice, while the next three were written at its request by the International Teaching Centre. We hope that this compilation of messages and documents will serve as a valuable resource, outlining the essential concepts that will inform future activities for the expansion and consolidation of the Faith worldwide.

Palabra Publications
November 2006

PART I
Selected Messages of
the Universal House of Justice

26 December 1995

To the Conference of the Continental Boards of Counsellors

Beloved Friends,

The Four Year Plan

Our deliberations on the Four Year Plan have benefited 1.1
enormously from the analysis the International Teaching Centre
prepared for us of conditions in the Bahá'í world, based on its
constant interaction with the Counsellors in the field, and from
our subsequent consultations with that body. It gives us great
pleasure to share with you at the outset of this conference the
general features of the Plan. We invite you to turn your attention in the coming days to issues related to implementation,
drawing on the insights and knowledge gained from decades of
experience around the world.

Certain elements of our decisions and comments on the Plan 1.2
will have a direct bearing on your labors throughout your present term of service. These are: the principal focus of the coming
Plan; the process we envisage for the elaboration of the Plan and
your part in this process; developments in the mode of functioning of the Continental Boards of Counsellors; the formulation
of plans at the national, regional and local levels; the vital need
for institutes to train believers and develop human resources;
the intimate involvement of Counsellors and Auxiliary Board
members in the establishment and operation of these institutes;
effective approaches to the raising up and consolidation of
Local Spiritual Assemblies and the development of local Bahá'í
communities; and the allocation of limited financial resources to
the many challenges before the Bahá'í community.

At Riḍván 1996, the Bahá'ís of the world will embark 1.3
on a global enterprise aimed at one major accomplishment:
a significant advance in the process of entry by troops. This

is to be achieved through marked progress in the activity and development of the individual believer, of the institutions, and of the local community. That an advance in this process depends on the progress of all three of these intimately connected participants is abundantly clear. The next four years must witness a dramatic upsurge in effective teaching activities undertaken at the initiative of the individual. Thousands upon thousands of believers will need to be aided to express the vitality of their faith through constancy in teaching the Cause and by supporting the plans of their institutions and the endeavors of their communities. They should be helped to realize that their efforts will be sustained by the degree to which their inner life and private character "mirror forth in their manifold aspects the splendor of those eternal principles proclaimed by Bahá'u'lláh." An acceleration in the tempo of individual teaching must necessarily be complemented by a multiplication in the number of regional and local teaching projects. To this end the institutions should be assisted in increasing their ability to consult according to Bahá'í principles, to unify the friends in a common vision, and to use their talents in service to the Cause. Furthermore, those who enter the Faith must be integrated into vibrant local communities, characterized by tolerance and love and guided by a strong sense of purpose and collective will, environments in which the capacities of all components—men, women, youth and children—are developed and their powers multiplied in unified action.

Planning Process

1.4   At the close of this conference, we intend to announce to the Bahá'í world our decision to launch a Four Year Plan at Riḍván 1996. The formulation of national plans is to begin in each country after Riḍván, allowing the friends to concentrate their energies in the intervening months on bringing the Three Year Plan to a successful conclusion.

1.5   The ideas expressed in the initial announcement will be elaborated further in the forthcoming Riḍván message. Moreover, we have decided to address messages to the believers in each continent of the globe, or parts thereof, exploring the implications of the Four Year Plan in the light of the particular conditions of their countries. Following Riḍván, it should be feasible to hold consultative meetings among the institutions and with active supporters of the Faith in every country and to formulate national plans within a period of a few months. Once consultations between the Counsellors and a National Spiritual Assembly on the provisions of a plan have reached fruition, its implementation can begin. Approval of these plans from the Bahá'í World Centre will not be necessary; copies should, nonetheless, be forwarded to it.

The seven objectives specified for the Six Year and Three Year Plans describe interacting processes that must advance simultaneously over many decades.† They will guide the institutions as they set goals in various areas of activity to further the aim of the Four Year Plan. National plans, however, will need to go beyond the mere enumeration of goals to include an analysis of approaches to be adopted and lines of action to be followed, so that the friends will be able to set out on their endeavors with clarity of mind and decisiveness.   1.6

Continental Level

In the discharge of their vital responsibilities during the Four Year Plan, the Continental Boards of Counsellors will have a wide range of possibilities available to them. The flexibility inherent in their functioning must be fully exploited at this time when events both within and outside the Bahá'í community are moving at an accelerated rate.   1.7

Certain Counsellor functions, including the supervision and guidance of the Auxiliary Board members in an area, are generally best performed by one Counsellor on behalf of the Board. However, in the performance of other functions, there   1.8

---

† "For ease of reference, the objectives as originally stated are repeated here: 1. Carrying the healing Message of Bahá'u'lláh to the generality of mankind; 2. Greater involvement of the Faith in the life of human society; 3. A worldwide increase in the translation, production, distribution and use of Bahá'í literature; 4. Further acceleration in the process of the maturation of local and national Bahá'í communities; 5. Greater attention to universal participation and the spiritual enrichment of individual believers; 6. A wider extension of Bahá'í family life; and 7. The pursuit of projects of social and economic development in well-established Bahá'í communities." The Universal House of Justice, from a letter dated 30 September 1992 to all National Spiritual Assemblies introducing the Three Year Plan.

is great value in a diversity of approaches and in consultation among several Counsellors. For example, in providing stimulus to National Assemblies, in promoting teaching among various strata of the population, and in counseling different components of the Bahá'í community, better results are achieved when the abilities of a number of Counsellors are used in a complementary fashion. Further ways and means should be devised by each Continental Board of Counsellors to enable the Assemblies and communities to benefit, to the extent feasible, from the varied talents of the Counsellors. This may well involve periodic in-depth consultation among a group of Counsellors on the conditions and needs of countries in a specific part of the continent since, in general, circumstances do not allow such consultations to occur frequently among all members of the Board.

1.9   Fundamental to the work of the Counsellors is the understanding that all members of the Continental Board are responsible for the entire continent, and should, to the degree possible, endeavor to familiarize themselves with the conditions of the Cause in the countries therein. Through periodic reports from individual Counsellors, the Board is kept abreast of developments in all areas of the continent and is able to offer guidance to assist its members in the execution of their duties. Whereas no Counsellor should be regarded as having exclusive responsibility for any one territory, the detailed familiarity acquired by each through close interaction with the National Spiritual Assembly and Auxiliary Board members in a particular area is in fact a valuable asset to all the Counsellors on the Board.

1.10   Another aspect of the work of the Counsellors which merits further attention is the interaction between Counsellors of different Boards who serve adjacent areas or areas which have a special relationship. Among the examples which come to mind are the Russian Federation, located partly in Europe and partly in Asia; the circumpolar national Bahá'í communities; the countries bordering the Mediterranean Sea; the communities of Northeastern Asia and the Antipodes, referred to by the Guardian as constituting a spiritual axis; the Arabic-speaking countries of North Africa and the Middle East; and French-speaking territories in various continents.

1.11   We hope that, while in the Holy Land, each Board will be able to give consideration to its mode of operation and explore effective means of interaction among the Counsellors. In this way, between the close of the conference and Riḍván, groups of Counsellors will be able to consult together about the planning process in a number of related countries and the role they and their auxiliaries are to play in it.

National and Regional Levels

In most countries, once the major elements of the national   1.12
plan have been identified, it is desirable that the planning process move quickly to the regional level. The resulting plans should include provisions for the promotion of individual teaching, the launching of campaigns of various kinds, the holding of conferences, the establishment of local and regional projects, the strengthening of local communities, and the movement of traveling teachers. Moreover, the widespread distribution of literature and audiovisual materials must be given urgent attention, and, particularly in areas of large-scale expansion, human resource development must be a key component of national and regional plans.

During the Nine Year Plan, the Universal House of Justice   1.13
called upon National Spiritual Assemblies in countries where large-scale expansion was taking place to establish teaching institutes to meet the deepening needs of the thousands who were entering the Faith. At that time, the emphasis was on acquiring a physical facility to which group after group of newly enrolled believers would be invited to attend deepening courses. Over the years, in conjunction with these institutes, and often independent of them, a number of courses—referred to, for example, as weekend institutes, five-day institutes, and nine-day institutes—were developed for the purpose of helping the friends gain an understanding of the fundamental verities of the Faith and arise to serve it. These efforts have contributed significantly to the enriching of the spiritual life of the believers and will undoubtedly continue in the future.

With the growth in the number of enrollments, it has be-   1.14
come apparent that such occasional courses of instruction and the informal activities of community life, though important, are not sufficient as a means of human resource development, for they have resulted in only a relatively small band of active supporters of the Cause. These believers, no matter how dedicated, no matter how willing to make sacrifices, cannot attend

to the needs of hundreds, much less thousands, of fledgling local communities. Systematic attention has to be given by Bahá'í institutions to training a significant number of believers and assisting them in serving the Cause according to their God-given talents and capacities.

1.15   The development of human resources on a large scale requires that the establishment of institutes be viewed in a new light. In many regions, it has become imperative to create institutes as organizational structures dedicated to systematic training. The purpose of such training is to endow ever-growing contingents of believers with the spiritual insights, the knowledge, and the skills needed to carry out the many tasks of accelerated expansion and consolidation, including the teaching and deepening of a large number of people—adults, youth and children. This purpose can best be achieved through well-organized, formal programs consisting of courses that follow appropriately designed curricula.

1.16   As an agency of the National Spiritual Assembly, the training institute should be charged with the task of developing human resources in all or part of a country. The requirements of expansion and consolidation in the country or region will dictate the complexity of its organization. In some instances, the institute may consist of a group of dedicated believers with a well-defined program and some administrative arrangement that enables it to offer regular training courses. In many cases, in addition to a group of teachers associated with it, the institute will require part- and full-time staff, for whom assistance from the funds of the Faith may be necessary. The institute needs access to some physical facilities in which it can conduct courses and, at some stage of its development, may require a building of its own. Irrespective of whether or not an institute has its own physical facilities, its teachers must offer courses both at a central location and in the villages and towns so that an appreciable number of believers can enter its programs. The complexity and number of courses offered by an institute, as well as the size of its staff and the pool of teachers from which it draws, may call for the appointment of a board to direct its affairs. When the region under the influence of an institute is large, it may have branches serving specific areas, each with its own administration.

1.17   For the new thrust in the establishment of institutes to succeed, the active involvement of the Counsellors and

Auxiliary Board members in their operation is essential. Such involvement will help the Counsellors to kindle "the Fire of the Love of God in the very hearts and souls of His servants," "to diffuse the Divine Fragrances," "to edify the souls of men," "to promote learning," and "to improve the character of all men." These institutes will provide the Counsellors and Auxiliary Board members with immediate access to a formal means of educating the believers, in addition to other avenues available to them such as conferences, summer schools, and meetings with the friends. Institutes should be regarded as centers of learning, and since their character harmonizes with, and provides scope for the exercise of, the educational responsibilities of the Auxiliary Board members, we have decided that intimate involvement in institute operations should now become a part of the evolving functions of these officers of the Faith. The Counsellors and National Spiritual Assemblies will need to consult on the details of the collaboration between the two arms of the Administrative Order in overseeing the budget and functioning of an institute and in planning program content, developing curricula, and delivering courses. If a board of directors is named, its membership should be decided upon by the National Spiritual Assembly in consultation with the Counsellors and with their full support; Auxiliary Board members may serve on these bodies.

1.18 In addition to having a working relationship with Auxiliary Board members, the institute must necessarily collaborate closely with Local Assemblies and committees in charge of administering plans and projects of expansion and consolidation. This will ensure that the institute's programs are designed to help raise up individuals who can contribute effectively to such plans. However, even if these administrative bodies have not yet developed the capacity to utilize the talents of those being trained, the programs of the institute should be regularly carried out. After all, the strengthening of the institutions in a region depends, as do all other matters, on skilled and confirmed supporters of the Faith.

1.19 In developing its programs, the institute should draw on the talents of a growing number of believers and should also take advantage of its institutional links to have access to resources worldwide. A newly established institute will often utilize materials created by institutes in other parts of the world. Gradually, those designing and delivering courses will learn how these materials might be supplemented to better suit their specific needs and will decide what new ones should be created. The curriculum of the institute at any given time, then, may well use a combination of materials created locally and those that have proven successful elsewhere. As institutes begin to flourish, a wide variety of curricula will be developed for various training needs. We hope that, with the assistance of the International Teaching Centre, you will be able to assess the materials available from time to time and help the institutes in the communities you serve to select those most appropriate for their needs.

1.20   We are placing at the disposal of the Teaching Centre funds specifically designated for the operation of institutes and intend to call on National Spiritual Assemblies, according to their circumstances, to pay particular attention to the development of institutes in their countries. It is our hope that significant progress in this direction will constitute one of the distinguishing features of the Four Year Plan.

Local Level

1.21   The development of the local community and the functioning of the Local Spiritual Assembly have been ongoing challenges to the Bahá'í world through successive Plans. At present, a few thousand Local Spiritual Assemblies have attained at least a basic level of functioning. National and regional plans will clearly have to include provision for the adoption by such Assemblies of local plans of expansion and consolidation. To ensure that local plans contribute to the advancement of the process of entry by troops, you will need to call upon your Auxiliary Board members and their assistants to work closely with these Assemblies, both in the formulation of plans and in their execution, helping them to shoulder the responsibility of systematic growth in their own communities and in localities adopted as extension goals. The community must become imbued with a sense of mission and the Assembly grow in awareness of its role as a channel of God's grace not only for the Bahá'ís but for the entire village, town or city in which it serves.

1.22   However, in those many communities where no organized activities are taking place, whether or not a Local Spiritual Assembly has been elected, more basic challenges have to be addressed, and in this the Auxiliary Board members and their assistants must play a fundamental role. Concerted effort must be made to help the individual believers, men and women alike, increase their love for Bahá'u'lláh and His Cause and to bring them together in the Nineteen Day Feast as well as periodic meetings aimed at raising their awareness of their identity as a community. In those localities where the participation of women in community affairs is lagging, determined steps have to be taken to foster such participation. Effective measures have to be adopted so that the Local Spiritual Assembly is properly elected year after year and consistent progress in its functioning is made. The regular holding of Bahá'í children's classes should be given high priority. Indeed in many parts of the world this is the first activity in a process of community building, which, if pursued vigorously, gives rise to the other developments. In all this, particular attention needs to be given to the youth, who are often the Faith's most enthusiastic supporters. The establishment of these activities defines a first stage in the process of community development, which, once attained, must be followed by subsequent stages until a community reaches a point where it can formulate its own plans of expansion and consolidation.

In this context, we feel that the Auxiliary Board members 1.23 should take further advantage of the possibility of naming, where appropriate, more than one assistant to a given community, with the intention of assigning each to promote one or more of these fundamental community activities. We also urge you to consult with National Spiritual Assemblies on the experience of past endeavors to assist such communities. Arrangements can then be made for the lessons learned from this experience to be discussed with the active supporters of the Faith in each region, helping them to identify the approaches and methods applicable to their specific conditions and to set in motion a systematic process of community development. This process should be one in which the friends review their successes and difficulties, adjust and improve their methods accordingly, and learn, and move forward unhesitatingly.

In general, we feel the functions of the Auxiliary Board 1.24 members for Protection have to be clarified and their influence augmented. The deepening of the friends and the proper functioning of the Local Spiritual Assembly are essential to the healthy growth of the community and should be important concerns of the Auxiliary Board members for Protection. We are contemplating an increase in the membership of Protection Boards to make the number equal to that of the Propagation Boards. It is our hope that Protection Board members will, in turn, name more assistants to focus on issues related to community development.

Election of Local Spiritual Assemblies

1.25   In developing the Administrative Order, the Guardian established the First Day of Riḍván as the day when all Local Spiritual Assemblies should be elected. During his own lifetime, this practice was followed as the number of Local Assemblies steadily grew to over one thousand.

1.26   In the subsequent two decades the Faith expanded greatly, especially in the rural areas of the world, often remote and difficult to reach. In view of this development, the Universal House of Justice decided in 1977 that, in certain cases, when the local friends failed to elect their Spiritual Assembly on the First Day of Riḍván, they could do so on any subsequent day of the Riḍván Festival. This permission did not apply to all localities, but to those that, in the judgment of the National Spiritual Assembly, were particularly affected by such factors as illiteracy, remoteness, and unfamiliarity with concepts of Baháʼí Administration. The House of Justice also gave permission at the beginning of the Five Year Plan for Assemblies being formed for the first time to be elected at any point during the year.

1.27   These provisions have enabled the believers in a large number of localities to receive assistance in electing their Local Spiritual Assemblies, and much experience has been gained in strengthening Local Assemblies under diverse conditions in a vast array of cultural settings. Nevertheless, in principle, the initiative and responsibility for electing a Local Spiritual Assembly belong primarily to the Baháʼís in the locality, and assistance from outside is ultimately fruitful only if the friends become conscious of this sacred responsibility. As progress is made in the training of human resources and in the development of the entire range of Baháʼí community life, the capacity of the friends to elect their Local Spiritual Assemblies on their own will certainly grow.

1.28   With these thoughts in mind, we have decided that, beginning at Riḍván 1997, the practice of electing all Local Spiritual

Assemblies on the First Day of Riḍván will be reinstituted. We recognize that the immediate result may be a reduction in the number of Local Spiritual Assemblies at Riḍván 1997, but we are confident that subsequent years will witness a steady increase.

The National Spiritual Assemblies and their agencies on   1.29 the one hand, and the Counsellors and their auxiliaries on the other, clearly have a duty to foster the establishment and development of Bahá'í communities, including their divinely ordained local institutions. This duty can be discharged mainly through sustained educational programs which create in the believers the awareness of the importance of the Teachings in every area of their individual and social lives and which engender in them the desire and determination to elect and support their Local Spiritual Assemblies. These programs should take full advantage of the provision that has been made for the temporary formation of administrative committees of three or more members in localities where Local Assemblies are not elected, or where the members of a Local Assembly fail to meet.

Financial Needs

The magnitude of the tasks the Bahá'í community is being   1.30 summoned to perform during the Four Year Plan will call for a considerable outlay of funds. The pressing demands of the Arc Projects will continue to place severe constraints on the International Funds of the Faith. Yet, the Universal House of Justice will do its utmost to make available to the Counsellors and the National Spiritual Assemblies the financial means necessary for the discharge of the tasks of expansion and consolidation in areas requiring assistance. This will include funds for the all-important work of the Auxiliary Boards.

As experience has shown, however, the expenditure of   1.31 money does not, by itself, bring results. The challenge before you is to help develop in the various institutions and agencies involved in the execution of the Plan the capacity to expend funds in a judicious and effective manner. In addition, you must redouble your efforts to educate every member of the Bahá'í community—the new and the old believer, the youth and the adult—on the spiritual significance of contributing to the Fund. We are confident that you will give special attention to this twofold challenge as you set out to help the friends in every continent to win victories for the Cause during these crucial years in the history of humanity.

1.32   Dear Friends, the few short years that separate us from the close of the century are a period of both spiritual potency and immense opportunity. Great responsibilities rest on your shoulders. During the first months of the Plan you will be making a decisive contribution to the formulation of plans that will inspire the friends to action and will guide them in their individual and collective endeavors. Throughout the Plan, you and your auxiliaries will encourage the friends, stimulate the spiritual powers latent in their hearts, and assist them in fulfilling their duties towards a Cause so dear to them. As you take up these manifold tasks, you must constantly bear in mind that the realization of the aim of the Four Year Plan will depend on the rapid increase in the number of teachers of the Cause who will bring in the multitudes, nurture them, and infuse in them "so deep a longing" as to impel them "to arise independently" and devote their energies "to the quickening of other souls."

1.33   Be assured that we will remember each and all of you in the Holy Shrines.

THE UNIVERSAL HOUSE OF JUSTICE

2

31 December 1995

To the Bahá'ís of the World

Dearly loved Friends,

In the wake of the dynamic spirit animating the six-day-long   2.1
Counsellors' Conference at the World Centre, now in its final
session as we address you, we take the occasion to announce
our decision which has been the subject of their deliberations:
At Riḍván 1996 a global plan of expansion and consolidation
will be launched, to end four years later at Riḍván 2000.

It is this anticipation that has focused the thoughts of the   2.2
seventy-eight Counsellors from the five continents, who have
been conferring together in the presence of the Hands of the
Cause of God Amatu'l-Bahá Rúḥíyyih Khánum, 'Alí-Akbar
Furútan and 'Alí-Muḥammad Varqá, the members of the
Universal House of Justice and the Counsellor members of
the International Teaching Centre. Their consultations on the
challenges and prospects facing the Bahá'í world community
have been of such caliber and content as to have emboldened
our expectations of a mighty thrust in the growth and development of that community during the crucial years immediately
ahead.

The whole Plan will be announced at Riḍván. However, we   2.3
wish you to have some information about it now within the
measure of the discussions which have been taking place at the
Counsellors' Conference.

The Four Year Plan will aim at one major accomplishment: 2.4
a significant advance in the process of entry by troops. This
is to be achieved through marked progress in the activity and
development of the individual believer, of the institutions,
and of the local community. Keen attention to all three will
ensure a greatly expanded, visibly united, vibrant and cohesive
international community by the end of the twentieth century.
The basic requisites can be summarized as follows.

2.5   The first calls for a vitality of the faith of each believer that is expressed through personal initiative and constancy in teaching the Cause to others, and through conscientious, individual effort to provide energy and resources to upbuild the community, to uphold the authority of its institutions, and to support local and regional plans and teaching projects. The second requires that local and national Bahá'í institutions evolve more rapidly into a proper exercise of their responsibilities as channels of guidance, planners of the teaching work, developers of human resources, builders of communities, and loving shepherds of the multitudes. The third, the flourishing of the community especially at the local level, demands a significant enhancement in patterns of behavior by which the collective expression of the virtues of the individual members and the functioning of the Spiritual Assembly is manifest in the unity and fellowship of the community and the dynamism of its activity and growth.

2.6   Towards these ends, the work of the Continental Counsellors must assume new dimensions. Thus, at their conference, they have been deliberating on such matters as:

2.7   ▪ Developments in the mode of the functioning of the Continental Boards of Counsellors.

2.8   ▪ The process for the elaboration of the Plan through the formulation of derivative plans and strategies at the national, regional, and local levels. Joint consultations between the Continental Counsellors and National Spiritual Assemblies will begin immediately after Riḍván, and the planning process will move quickly to the regional level, involving Auxiliary Board members, Local Spiritual Assemblies and committees.

2.9   ▪ The development of human resources to meet the needs of a rapidly expanding community. Large-scale growth necessitates sustained measures of consolidation. The urgent requirement is for formally conducted programs of training through institutes and other centers of learning, in the establishment and operation of which the Counsellors and Auxiliary Board members will become more intimately involved.

2.10   ▪ Effective approaches to the raising up and consolidation of Local Spiritual Assemblies. In accordance with the objective of fostering the maturation of these Assemblies, a greater effort is required to uphold a vital principle, which is that the responsibility for electing a Local Spiritual Assembly rests primarily on the Bahá'ís in the locality. The Auxiliary Board members and their assistants are to increase their efforts to improve the general understanding of this principle and will devote more attention to assisting the development of Local Assemblies. As of Riḍván 1997, all Local Spiritual Assemblies throughout the world will have to be elected on the First Day of Riḍván.

- Further means for the development of local Bahá'í communities. The needs in this respect will be met in part by an immediate increase in the membership of the Auxiliary Boards for Protection to equal that of the Auxiliary Boards for Propagation, so that Protection Board members can directly and systematically assist on a wide scale the fundamental activities of the community, such as the spiritual nurturing of individual believers, the participation of women in all aspects of community life, the observance of the Nineteen Day Feasts and Holy Days, the holding of children's classes, the fostering of youth activities.   2.11

The seven objectives specified in previous Plans describe essential, interacting directions that must advance simultaneously into the foreseeable future. The Four Year Plan's aim at accelerating the process of entry by troops identifies a necessity at this stage in the progress of the Cause and in the state of human society. With this perspective, the three inseparable participants in the evolution of the new World Order—the individual, the institutions, and the community—must now demonstrate more tangibly than ever before their capacity and willingness to embrace masses of new adherents, to effect the spiritual and administrative transformation of thousands upon thousands, and, above all, to multiply the army of knowledgeable, consecrated teachers of a Faith whose emergence from obscurity must be registered on the consciousness of countless multitudes throughout the earth. These are among the detailed considerations that have occupied the deliberations of the Continental Counsellors, who, upon their return home and in the course of their work, will have occasion to share the results of their conference with the friends.   2.12

2.13   An auspicious beginning for the new Plan will largely depend on the results of the current one, which will end in just a few months. The adequacy of these results will owe much to the degree to which the Local Spiritual Assemblies and the friends carry out the directions of their National Spiritual Assemblies, the generals of every Plan. Time is slipping away. This reality should prod us all to maximum action. Hence, in preparation for what beckons us on the near horizon, we cannot, we must not, hesitate to expend every energy to bring the Three Year Plan to a successful conclusion. The urgency which intensifies our desire for such an outcome is not merely pride of victory, gratifying as that may be. There are divine deadlines to be met. Our work is intended not only to increase the size and consolidate the foundations of our community, but more particularly to exert a positive influence on the affairs of the entire human race. At so crucial a moment in world affairs, we must not fail in our duty to take timely action on the goals set before us in the Three Year Plan.

2.14   With the full fervor of our expectant hearts, we call upon you all, individually and collectively, to arise to the summons of the Lord of Hosts to teach His Cause. Do so with love, faith and courage; and the doors of heaven will open wide to pour forth benedictions upon your efforts.

THE UNIVERSAL HOUSE OF JUSTICE

3

3 January 1996

To the Friends Gathered at the International
Youth Conference in Santa Cruz, Bolivia

Dear Friends,

We send our loving greetings to each and all of you. Your 3.1
conference opens at an auspicious time. But three days ago,
the Conference of the Continental Boards of Counsellors
came to a close in the Holy Land, while the Bahá'í world was
being informed of our decision to initiate a Four Year Plan at
Riḍván 1996. You may well take advantage of the energies
released through these momentous events by focusing your
attention during the next few days on the opportunities available to the Bahá'í youth, both individually and collectively, to
contribute to the successful conclusion of the Three Year Plan
and to ensure that the victories won will lend a substantial
impetus to the work of the Faith during the last years of the
Twentieth Century.

At every stage of the growth of the Faith, young people have 3.2
played a pivotal role in its propagation and consolidation. You
have the bounty of being youth at a unique time in history. Like
the generations before you, you must seize the opportunities
that the hour has thrust upon you. These are the years during
which the Bahá'í community must make a significant advance
in the process of entry by troops. Now is the time to teach. It
is imperative that you take up your responsibility to lead not
only your peers but all people towards the world civilization
of Bahá'u'lláh.

You must equip yourselves for the tasks you are being 3.3
summoned to perform. Turn for your guidance to the Sacred
Writings and dedicate yourselves to their systematic study. As
they permeate your hearts and minds, so may they strengthen
you in your efforts to carry forth the Teachings of Bahá'u'lláh.

Do not hesitate; put your complete trust in Him and enter the field of service armed with the power of His Word.

3.4   We shall remember you in our prayers in the Holy Shrines.

THE UNIVERSAL HOUSE OF JUSTICE

4

Riḍván 1996

To the Bahá'ís of the World

Dearly loved Friends,

Our hearts overflowing with gratitude to the Blessed Beauty, we acknowledge the abundant manifestations of His grace during the Three Year Plan, which has run its course with the advent of this Riḍván Festival. The animating spirit of the Holy Year, which lent impetus to the launching of the Plan at Riḍván 1993, pervaded this period of concentrated endeavor, rendering our world community more consolidated, more resilient, more mature, and more confident than before. At the same time, the community's prestige attained new heights. While this Plan has not ended on a note of dramatic, numerical expansion, even though significant growth of membership occurred in various countries, it has nonetheless resulted in a qualitatively enriched community—one prepared to exploit the immediate prospects for the advancement of the Faith.

4.1

The magnificent progress of the projects on Mount Carmel is preeminent among the measurable achievements of this period. Indeed, despite numerous difficulties, the stage of accomplishment anticipated in our message announcing the Three Year Plan is entirely evident. All phases of construction have been initiated. The structural framework of the Centre for the Study of the Texts and the Extension to the International Archives Building has been raised up and the work on these buildings has advanced towards initiation of the exterior and interior finishing work. The erection of the permanent seat of the International Teaching Centre, the third structure currently being built on the Arc, is progressing rapidly. Seven terraces below the Shrine of the Báb are now completed, foreshowing the unfolding splendor from the foot to the ridge of God's Holy Mountain. A watchful public is awed at the tapestry of beauty spreading over the mountainside.

4.2

4.3   The physical reality of the progress thus far so marvelously realized is proof of an even more profound achievement, namely, the unity of purpose effected throughout our global community in the pursuit of this gigantic, collective enterprise. The intensity of the interest and support it has evoked has expressed itself in an unprecedented outpouring of contributions, reflecting a level of sacrifice that bespeaks the quality of faith and generosity of heart of Bahá'u'lláh's lovers throughout the planet. That contributions towards the Mount Carmel Projects have met the three-year goal of seventy-four million dollars marks yet another measurable and exceptional achievement, inspiring confidence that the necessary financial support for these projects will continue until their completion by the end of the century.

4.4   The signs of progress during the past three years were evident in a wide and varied field. The remarkable efforts to expand and consolidate the community, the increased ventures in social and economic development, and the unprecedented thrust of the external affairs work combine to portray a community endowed with new capacities.

4.5   In the arena of teaching, there was a general increase of activity as indicated by the formation of twelve new National Spiritual Assemblies during the course of the Plan and by the surge of pioneering and travel-teaching. Believers in many countries were galvanized by the fresh approach suggested in the pioneer call released during the Plan. The number of pioneers from and to various countries was high, and there was a veritable flood of traveling teachers operating both at home and abroad. Systematic approaches to collective teaching activities and well-focused long-term teaching projects were fruitful and were more evident than ever before in a number of countries.

4.6   The energy and creativity attendant to the various developments in expansion and consolidation owed much to the spirit of enterprise shown by the International Teaching Centre. Its constant direction and encouragement of the Continental Boards of Counsellors; its recommendation of new methods for the deployment of pioneers, as endorsed by the Universal House of Justice in the pioneer call released in the early months of the Plan, and its regular assistance to the Continental Pioneer Committees placed in its charge; its unflagging attention to the educational needs of the community as expressed in its interactions with Counsellors concerning the inclusion in teaching projects of deepening programs for new believers, the devising of courses and workshops for training in different capacities, the training of children's teachers, and the multiplication of children's classes; its stimulation of efforts to establish training institutes in different parts of the world—all have produced resounding results. Major credit must also go to the Teaching Centre for the influence it exerted through the Counsellors on the adoption of core literature programs in an increasing number of countries. Through such programs a few titles essential to the propagation of the Faith and the deepening of the believers were selected, printed in large quantities and made available at reduced prices. The outstanding progress in the evolution of this vital institution operating at the World Centre was palpable in its preparation and conduct of the Counsellors' Conference last December which set the course for the work of these high-ranking officers of the Faith during the immediate years ahead.

A relevant development was the notable rise in the assump- 4.7 tion of responsibility by indigenous believers for the teaching and consolidation work in their own countries. In greatly troubled areas, such as Angola, Cambodia, Liberia, Sierra Leone, the friends claimed important victories, whether in pursuing teaching activities which resulted in numerically significant enrollments, or in establishing and reactivating Bahá'í Assemblies, or in initiating and sustaining development projects. In places with recently formed National Spiritual Assemblies, such as countries of the former Eastern Bloc, the friends have shown an admirable capacity for administering the affairs of the Cause. A highlight of this period was the upsurge of vigor, courage and creativity in Bahá'í island communities throughout the world. The categories of activity were wide-ranging, involving the raising up of local teachers, the training and dispatch of scores of traveling teachers to neighboring islands, the inauguration of primary schools, the multiple occasions for proclamation of the Faith, the sponsorship of events attended by high-ranking officials and influential persons. The fact that in recent years a number of government leaders of island nations have visited the Bahá'í World Centre is indicative of the vitality of the activities of the believers in these small lands scattered throughout the seven seas. Taken together, all the foregoing examples of the attitudes and efforts of the friends in different settings demonstrate a heightened commitment to the teaching work and a growing maturity and resilience reflective of the depth of faith motivating Bahá'ís from diverse populations.

4.8 Consonant with these observations were the outstanding contributions of the youth to expansion and consolidation. Their activities took on added dimensions during the three-year period. Actuated by youth conferences and other gatherings attentive to their interests, youth throughout the world invested immense amounts of time, energy and zeal in the teaching work as traveling teachers within and outside their countries and as teams in collective teaching projects and, in so doing, they stimulated hundreds of new enrollments and the formation of many Local Spiritual Assemblies; involvement of youth in music and the arts as a means of proclaiming and teaching the Cause distinguished their exertions in many places; the spread of dance and drama workshops was particularly effective; participation of youth in external affairs opened new possibilities for the Faith in this field; commitment to a year of service was more widely demonstrated; at the same time there was a notable increase in the number of youth acquiring formal training and achieving academic, professional and vocational excellence—altogether an indication that the youth are doing more in direct service to the Faith while at the same time contributing to the general development of society.

4.9 Signs of the consolidation of the community were also discernible in the greater involvement of the friends in social and economic development, particularly in the field of education. In one outstanding instance, a government asked the Bahá'ís to take responsibility for the management of seven public schools, and they did so with the backing of the Office of Social and Economic Development at the World Centre. Worthy of note is that in Africa Bahá'í communities in exile because of political unrest in their home country continued to develop farming and other projects that went far towards ensuring self-sufficiency. Efforts at improving the status of women gathered momentum in a number of countries where, in addition to Bahá'í participation in projects sponsored by other organizations, the Bahá'í institutions set up committees and offices to attend to the interests of women. The Bahá'í International Community's Office for the Advancement of Women emerged as a symbol of this upswing.

In a number of countries, too, there was significant Bahá'í 4.10
participation in government-sponsored programs to improve
health; in other instances Bahá'í groups initiated such programs
and carried them out. The work in social and economic
development was also distinguished by the firm establishment
and consolidation of a number of major projects and organizations. Three pilot literacy projects were begun as a first step in
a literacy campaign which the Office of Social and Economic
Development intends to extend throughout the world. The
Bahá'í initiation and involvement in development projects
also resulted in proclamation of the Faith as they attracted the
participation of the public and the interest of mass media.

A thrust in the external affairs work exceeding all previous 4.11
records for a similar period boosted the proclamation of the
Cause. A prodigy of effort in all parts of the world redounded
to a much greater visibility of the Faith than obtained before
and to a consequent rise in the prestige of the Bahá'í international community. The broad lines of progress were evident
in the ease with which Bahá'í communities, large and small,
sponsored or participated in public events; in the emergence
of the Bahá'ís as a force in society recognized by governmental
and nongovernmental organizations and many prominent
persons; in the ready accessibility of the media. Indeed, the wide
coverage accorded Bahá'í events and interests by the print and
electronic communications media was beyond calculation.

In the sweep of activities throughout the world, certain 4.12
specific developments stood out: the frequency with which high
public officials would invite Bahá'ís to participate in or assist
with events or projects; the successful initiatives of Bahá'ís in
influencing government action; the establishment of Bahá'í
academic programs and courses in colleges and universities
and the adoption of curricular material for public schools; the
use of the arts by Bahá'í institutions, groups and individuals in
proclamation events.

During 1995, two major United Nations events exemplified 4.13
the gathering momentum of an emerging unity of thought in
world undertakings, and these engaged the active attention and
participation of the Bahá'í community. First, the World Summit
for Social Development in Copenhagen during March involved
250 friends from more than 40 countries who mounted an
impressive effort to acquaint the summit participants and the
related NGO Forum with the Teachings. It was on this occasion

that the statement "The Prosperity of Humankind," produced by the Bahá'í International Community's Office of Public Information, was first distributed and discussed. Follow-up activities all over the world included the holding of conferences and seminars, as well as the distribution of the statement. Second, the Fourth World Conference on Women and the concomitant NGO Forum held in Beijing during September drew the attendance of more than 500 Bahá'ís from around the world, in addition to the official delegation of the Bahá'í International Community. In that same year, a third event, the observance of the Fiftieth Anniversary of the United Nations, prompted the Bahá'í International Community's United Nations Office to produce and distribute a statement, entitled "Turning Point for All Nations," containing proposals for the development of that world organization.

4.14 Also of particular note among the external affairs activities were two occasions involving the prominent participation of Amatu'l-Bahá Rúḥíyyih Khánum. Last spring she headed the delegation of the four official Bahá'í representatives to the Summit on the Alliance between Religions and Conservation, patronized by His Royal Highness Prince Philip and held at Windsor Castle. During October Rúḥíyyih Khánum was the keynote speaker at the Fourth International Dialogue on the Transition to Global Society held under the auspices of the United Nations Educational, Scientific, and Cultural Organization (UNESCO) and organized by the Bahá'í Chair for World Peace and the Department of History at the University of Maryland.

4.15 Nor can we neglect to mention certain other significant marks of the period under review. An edition of the Kitáb-i-Aqdas in the original Arabic was published with, for the first time, notes in Persian, supplementing the text as in the English edition. The Law of Ḥuqúqu'lláh became more deeply rooted in the hearts of the believers throughout the world, and during the final year of the Plan, the Trustee of Ḥuqúqu'lláh, Hand of the Cause of God 'Alí-Muḥammad Varqá, took up residence in the Holy Land. This significant step also means that all three Hands of the Cause of God—Amatu'l-Bahá Rúḥíyyih Khánum, Mr. 'Alí-Akbar Furútan, and Dr. Varqá—are now residing at the World Centre, bringing inspiration to pilgrims and visitors, and to the friends serving at the World Centre.

It is against such a background of heartening developments   4.16
that we embark at this Riḍván upon a Four Year Plan that will
carry us to Riḍván 2000. We earnestly and lovingly call upon
our brothers and sisters of every land to join us in a mobilization
of effort that will ensure to generations of the fast-approaching
twenty-first century an abundant and lasting legacy.

The Four Year Plan aims at one major accomplishment: 4.17
a significant advance in the process of entry by troops. As
we have stated earlier, such an advance is to be achieved
through marked progress in the activity and development of
the individual believer, of the institutions, and of the local
community.

The phrase "advance in the process of entry by troops"   4.18
accommodates the concept that current circumstances demand
and existing opportunities allow for a sustained growth
of the Bahá'í world community on a large scale; that this
upsurge is necessary in the face of world conditions; that
the three constituent participants in the upbuilding of the
Order of Bahá'u'lláh—the individual, the institutions, and the
community—can foster such growth first by spiritually and
mentally accepting the possibility of it, and then by working
towards embracing masses of new believers, setting in motion the means for effecting their spiritual and administrative
training and development, thereby multiplying the number
of knowledgeable, active teachers and administrators whose
involvement in the work of the Cause will ensure a constant
influx of new adherents, an uninterrupted evolution of Bahá'í
Assemblies, and a steady consolidation of the community.

Moreover, to advance the process implies that that process   4.19
is already in progress and that local and national communities
are at different stages of it. All communities are now tasked to
take steps and sustain efforts to achieve a level of expansion
and consolidation commensurate with their possibilities. The
individual and the institutions, while operating in distinctive
spheres, are summoned to arise to meet the requirements of this
crucial time in the life of our community and in the fortunes of
all humankind.

The role of the individual is of unique importance in the   4.20
work of the Cause. It is the individual who manifests the vitality of faith upon which the success of the teaching work and the
development of the community depend. Bahá'u'lláh's command
to each believer to teach His Faith confers an inescapable

responsibility which cannot be transferred to, or assumed by, any institution of the Cause. The individual alone can exercise those capacities which include the ability to take initiative, to seize opportunities, to form friendships, to interact personally with others, to build relationships, to win the cooperation of others in common service to the Faith and society, and to convert into action the decisions made by consultative bodies. It is the individual's duty to "consider every avenue of approach which he might utilize in his personal attempts to capture the attention, maintain the interest, and deepen the faith, of those whom he seeks to bring into the fold of his Faith."

4.21   To optimize the use of these capacities, the individual draws upon his love for Bahá'u'lláh, the power of the Covenant, the dynamics of prayer, the inspiration and education derived from regular reading and study of the Holy Texts, and the transformative forces that operate upon his soul as he strives to behave in accordance with the divine laws and principles. In addition to these, the individual, having been given the duty to teach the Cause, is endowed with the capacity to attract particular blessings promised by Bahá'u'lláh. "Whoso openeth his lips in this Day," the Blessed Beauty asserts, "and maketh mention of the name of his Lord, the hosts of Divine inspiration shall descend upon him from the heaven of My name, the All-Knowing, the All-Wise. On him shall also descend the Concourse on high, each bearing aloft a chalice of pure light."

4.22   Shoghi Effendi underscored the absolute necessity of individual initiative and action. He explained that without the support of the individual, "at once wholehearted, continuous and generous," every measure and plan of his National Spiritual Assembly is "foredoomed to failure," the purpose of the Master's Divine Plan is "impeded"; furthermore, the sustaining strength of Bahá'u'lláh Himself "will be withheld from every and each individual who fails in the long run to arise and play his part." Hence, at the very crux of any progress to be made is the individual believer, who possesses the power of execution which only he can release through his own initiative and sustained action. Regarding the sense of inadequacy that sometimes hampers individual initiative, a letter written on his behalf conveys the Guardian's advice: "Chief among these, you mention the lack of courage and of initiative on the part of the believers, and a feeling of inferiority which prevents them from addressing the public. It is precisely these weaknesses that he wishes the friends to overcome, for these do not only paralyze their efforts but actually serve to quench the flame of faith in their hearts. Not until all the friends come to realize that every one of them is able, in his own measure, to deliver the Message, can they ever hope to reach the goal that has been set before them by a loving and wise Master. . . . Everyone is a potential teacher. He has only to use what God has given him and thus prove that he is faithful to his trust."

As for the institutions, entry by troops will act upon them as much as they will act upon it. The evolution of local and national Bahá'í Assemblies at this time calls for a new state of mind on the part of their members as well as on the part of those who elect them, for the Bahá'í community is engaged in an immense historical process that is entering a critical stage. Bahá'u'lláh has given to the world institutions to operate in an Order designed to canalize the forces of a new civilization. Progress towards that glorious realization requires a great and continuous expansion of the Bahá'í community, so that adequate scope is provided for the maturation of these institutions. This is a matter of immediate importance to Bahá'u'lláh's avowed supporters in all lands. 4.23

For such an expansion to be stimulated and accommodated, the Spiritual Assemblies must rise to a new stage in the exercise of their responsibilities as channels of divine guidance, planners of the teaching work, developers of human resources, builders of communities, and loving shepherds of the multitudes. They can realize these prospects through increasing the ability of their members to take counsel together in accordance with the principles of the Faith and to consult with the friends under their jurisdiction, through fostering the spirit of service, through spontaneously collaborating with the Continental Counsellors and their auxiliaries, and through cultivating their external relations. Particularly must the progress in the evolution of the institutions be manifest in the multiplication of localities in which the functioning of the Spiritual Assembly enhances the individual believers' capacity to serve the Cause and fosters unified action. In sum, the maturity of the Spiritual Assembly must be measured not only by the regularity of its meetings and the efficiency of its functioning, but also by the continuity of the growth of Bahá'í membership, the effectiveness of the interaction between the Assembly and the members of its community, the quality of the spiritual and social life of the community, and 4.24

the overall sense of vitality of a community in the process of dynamic, ever-advancing development.

4.25 The community, as distinguished from the individual and the institutions, assumes its own character and identity as it grows in size. This is a necessary development to which much attention is required both with respect to places where large-scale enrollment has occurred and in anticipation of more numerous instances of entry by troops. A community is of course more than the sum of its membership; it is a comprehensive unit of civilization composed of individuals, families and institutions that are originators and encouragers of systems, agencies and organizations working together with a common purpose for the welfare of people both within and beyond its own borders; it is a composition of diverse, interacting participants that are achieving unity in an unremitting quest for spiritual and social progress. Since Bahá'ís everywhere are at the very beginning of the process of community building, enormous effort must be devoted to the tasks at hand.

4.26 As we have said in an earlier message, the flourishing of the community, especially at the local level, demands a significant enhancement in patterns of behavior: those patterns by which the collective expression of the virtues of the individual members and the functioning of the Spiritual Assembly are manifest in the unity and fellowship of the community and the dynamism of its activity and growth. This calls for the integration of the component elements—adults, youth and children—in spiritual, social, educational and administrative activities; and their engagement in local plans of teaching and development. It implies a collective will and sense of purpose to perpetuate the Spiritual Assembly through annual elections. It involves the practice of collective worship of God. Hence, it is essential to the spiritual life of the community that the friends hold regular devotional meetings in local Bahá'í centers, where available, or elsewhere, including the homes of believers.

4.27 To effect the possibilities of expansion and consolidation implied by entry by troops, a determined, worldwide effort to develop human resources must be made. The endeavor of individuals to conduct study classes in their homes, the sponsorship by the institutions of occasional courses of instruction, and the informal activities of the community, though important, are not adequate for the education and training of a rapidly expanding community. It is therefore of paramount importance that systematic attention be given to devising methods for educating large numbers of believers in the fundamental verities of the Faith and for training and assisting them to serve the Cause as their God-given talents allow. There should be no delay in establishing permanent institutes designed to provide well-organized, formally conducted programs of training on a regular schedule. Access of the institute to physical facilities will of course be necessary, but it may not require a building of its own.

This matter calls for an intensification of the collaboration between the Continental Counsellors and National Spiritual Assemblies. For the success of these training institutes will depend in very large measure on the active involvement of the Continental Counsellors and the Auxiliary Board members in their operation. Particularly will it be necessary for Auxiliary Board members to have a close working relationship with institutes and, of course, with the Local Spiritual Assemblies whose communities will benefit from institute programs. Since institutes are to be regarded as centers of learning, and since their character harmonizes with, and provides scope for the exercise of, the educational responsibilities of the Auxiliary Board members, the intimate involvement in institute operations should now become a part of the evolving functions of these officers of the Faith. Drawing on the talents and abilities of increasing numbers of believers will also be crucial to the development and execution of institute programs. 4.28

As the term "institute" has assumed various uses in the Bahá'í community, a word of clarification is needed. The next four years will represent an extraordinary period in the history of our Faith, a turning point of epochal magnitude. What the friends throughout the world are now being asked to do is to commit themselves, their material resources, their abilities and their time to the development of a network of training institutes on a scale never before attempted. These centers of Bahá'í learning will have as their goal one very practical outcome, namely, the raising up of large numbers of believers who are trained to foster and facilitate the process of entry by troops with efficiency and love. 4.29

"Center your energies in the propagation of the Faith of God," Bahá'u'lláh thus instructs His servants, adding, "Whoso is worthy of so high a calling, let him arise and promote it. Whoso is unable, it is his duty to appoint him who will, in 4.30

his stead, proclaim this Revelation. . . ." Just as one deputizes another to teach in one's stead by covering the expenses of a pioneer or traveling teacher, one can deputize a teacher serving an institute, who is, of course, a teacher of teachers. To do so, one may make contributions to the Continental Bahá'í Fund, as well as to the Local, National and International Funds, earmarked for this purpose.

4.31   In all their efforts to achieve the aim of the Four Year Plan, the friends are also asked to give greater attention to the use of the arts, not only for proclamation, but also for the work in expansion and consolidation. The graphic and performing arts and literature have played, and can play, a major role in extending the influence of the Cause. At the level of folk art, this possibility can be pursued in every part of the world, whether it be in villages, towns or cities. Shoghi Effendi held high hopes for the arts as a means for attracting attention to the Teachings. A letter written on his behalf to an individual thus conveys the Guardian's view: "The day will come when the Cause will spread like wildfire when its spirit and teachings will be presented on the stage or in art and literature as a whole. Art can better awaken such noble sentiments than cold rationalizing, especially among the mass of the people."

4.32   While the friends and institutions everywhere bend their energies to implementing the requirements of the Plan, work on the great projects on Mount Carmel will continue towards their anticipated completion at the end of the century. By the end of the Plan at Riḍván 2000, the buildings for the Centre for the Study of the Texts and the Extension of the Archives Building will become operational; the International Teaching Centre building will have advanced to the final finishing stage. The section of the public road which now interrupts the path of the terraces above the Shrine of the Báb will have been lowered and a broad connecting bridge with its own gardens will have been built; five of the upper terraces will also have been completed. The remaining four upper terraces and the two at the foot of the mountain will be in an advanced stage of development. Other particular efforts will be pursued at the World Centre as well. Attention will be given to such matters as the universal application of additional laws of the Kitáb-i-Aqdas, the preparation of a new volume in English of selected Writings of Bahá'u'lláh, the further development of the functions of the International

Teaching Centre, and the devising of measures for increasing the number of pilgrims and visitors to the World Centre.

The Bahá'í world community will expand its endeavors in 4.33 both social and economic development and external affairs, and thus continue to collaborate directly with the forces leading towards the establishment of order in the world. By improving its coordinating capacity, the Office of Social and Economic Development will assist in building, as resources and opportunity permit, on the progress already made with hundreds of development projects around the world. In the arena of external affairs, efforts will be aimed at influencing the processes towards world peace, particularly through the community's involvement in the promotion of human rights, the status of women, global prosperity, and moral development. In the pursuit of these themes, the Bahá'í International Community's United Nations Office will seek ways to reinforce the ties between the Bahá'ís and the United Nations. Similarly, the Office of Public Information will assist the Bahá'í institutions to utilize these themes towards greater proclamation of the Faith. Defense of the rights of the Bahá'ís in Iran and increased efforts to emancipate the Faith in that country and other countries where it is proscribed will constitute a vital part of our dealings with governments and nongovernmental organizations. In all such respects the Bahá'í friends and institutions are urged to be alert to the importance of activities in external affairs and to give renewed attention to them.

The formation this Riḍván of two National Spiritual 4.34 Assemblies lends a propitious beginning to the Four Year Plan. We are delighted to announce that our two representatives to the inaugural National Conventions are the Hand of the Cause of God Amatu'l-Bahá Rúḥíyyih Khánum, Moldova; and Mr. Fred Schechter, Counsellor member of the International Teaching Centre, Sao Tome and Principe. Regrettably, due to circumstances entirely beyond their control, the National Spiritual Assemblies of Burundi and Rwanda cannot be re-elected this year. The number of these institutions worldwide will consequently remain at 174.

Riḍván 2000, the point at which the Four Year Plan is to be 4.35 concluded, will come many months before the end of the twentieth century. At that juncture in time, the Bahá'í world will look back in appreciation at the extraordinary developments and dazzling achievements that will have distinguished the annals of the Cause of Bahá'u'lláh during that eventful period—a period which 'Abdu'l-Bahá called the "century of light." Not the least of the accomplishments then to be recognized will be the completion of the current projects on Mount Carmel which, together with the other edifices on that holy mountain, will stand as a monument to the progress which the Administrative Order will have attained by that time in the Formative Age. The highlight of such appreciations will, God willing, be the holding at the World Centre of a major event to mark the completion of the buildings on the Arc and the opening of the Terraces of the Shrine of the Báb to the public.

4.36   Beloved Friends, we enter this Plan amid the turbulence of a period of accelerating transition. The twin processes prompted by the impact of Bahá'u'lláh's Revelation are fast at work, gathering a momentum that will, in the words of Shoghi Effendi, "bring to a climax the forces that are transforming the face of our planet." One is an integrating process; the other is disruptive. Out of the "universal fermentation" created by these processes, peace will emerge in stages, through which the unifying effects of a growing consciousness of world citizenship will become manifest.

4.37   Towards that end, recent world developments have, para- doxically, been both shocking and reassuring. On one hand, the disarray of human affairs produces a daily diet of horrors that benumb the senses; on the other, world leaders are often taking collective actions that, to a Bahá'í observer, signify a tendency towards a common approach by nations to solving world prob- lems. Consider, for instance, the unusual frequency of the global occasions on which these leaders have gathered since the Holy Year four years ago, such as the one in observance of the Fiftieth Anniversary of the United Nations, at which the attending heads of state and heads of government asserted their commitment to world peace. Noteworthy, too, are the promptitude and spon- taneity with which these government leaders have been acting together in responding to a variety of crises in different parts of the world. Such trends coincide with the increasing cries from enlightened circles for attention to be given to the feasibility of achieving some form of global governance. Might we not see in these swiftly developing occurrences the workings of the Hand of Providence, indeed the very harbinger of the monumental occasion forecast in our Writings?

Even though the establishment of the Lesser Peace is not   4.38
dependent on any Bahá'í plan or action, and although it will not
represent the ultimate goal humanity is destined to reach in the
Golden Age, our community has a responsibility to lend spiritual
impetus to the processes towards that peace. The need at this
exact time is to so intensify our efforts in building the Bahá'í
System that we will attract the confirmations of Bahá'u'lláh
and thus invoke a spiritual atmosphere that will accrue to the
quickening of these processes. Two main challenges face us: one
is to mount a campaign of teaching in which the broad membership of our community is enthusiastically, systematically and
personally engaged, and in which the activation of an extensive
training program will ensure the development of a mass of human resources; the other is to complete the construction projects
on Mount Carmel towards which every sacrifice must be made
to provide a liberal outpouring of material means. These twin
foci, if resolutely pursued, will foster conditions towards the
release of pent-up forces that will forge a change in the direction
of human affairs throughout the planet.

However short the path to peace, it will be tortuous;   4.39
however promising the anticipated event that will set its course,
it must mature through a long period of evolution, with its
attendant tests, setbacks and conflicts, towards the moment
when it will have emerged, under the direct influences of
God's Faith, as the Most Great Peace. In the meantime, people
everywhere will often face despair and bewilderment before
arriving at an appreciation of the transition in progress. We
who have been enlightened by the new Revelation have the
sacred Word to assure us, a Divine Plan to guide us, a history
of valor to encourage us. Let us therefore take heart not only
from the Word we treasure, but also from the deeds of heroism
and sacrifice which even today shine resplendent in the land in
which our Cause was born.

For some seventeen years our persecuted brethren in Iran   4.40
have demonstrated a constancy of faith and courage that has
produced a vast proclamation of the Faith, forcing it out of
obscurity. Here then is living evidence in our own time of the
potencies of crisis and victory. Please God, it may not be too
long before our Iranian brethren are relieved of the yoke they
bear and are ushered into the glories and wonders of a victory
that only the Blessed Beauty can bestow. Their experience is a

signal and an example to us all wherever we may live; for eventually, opposition, as the Master has told us, will rear its head on all the continents. Though it may be of a different character from place to place, it will no doubt be intensive. But, thanks to the strengthening grace of Bahá'u'lláh and the demonstration of steadfastness by these noble friends, we shall know how to meet the shafts of the enemy without fear. Indeed, the Lord of Hosts has promised to deliver to His people an overwhelming and decisive triumph.

4.41 As humanity is tossed and tormented by the ravages inflicted upon it by a civilization gone out of control, let us keep our heads and hearts focused on the divine tasks set before us. For amid this turmoil opportunities will abound that must be exploited "for the purpose of spreading far and wide the knowledge of the redemptive power of the Faith of Bahá'u'lláh and for enlisting fresh recruits in the ever-swelling army of His followers." This Plan to which we are now committed is set at one of the most critical times in the life of the planet. It is meant to prepare our community to cope with the accelerating changes that are occurring in the world about us and to place the community in a position both to withstand the weight of the accompanying tests and challenges and to make more visible a pattern of functioning to which the world can turn for aid and example in the wake of a tumultuous transition. Thus, this Plan acquires a special place in the scheme of Bahá'í and world history. Those of us who are alive to the vision of the Faith are particularly privileged to be consciously engaged in efforts intended to stimulate and eventually enhance such processes.

4.42 May you all arise to seize the tasks of this crucial moment. May each inscribe his or her own mark on a brief span of time so charged with potentialities and hope for all humanity. Lest you become distracted or preoccupied with the drastic happenings of this age of transition, bear ever in mind the advice of our infallible guide, Shoghi Effendi: "Not ours, puny mortals that we are, to attempt, at so critical a stage in the long and checkered history of mankind, to arrive at a precise and satisfactory understanding of the steps which must successively lead a bleeding humanity, wretchedly oblivious of its God, and careless of Bahá'u'lláh, from its calvary to its ultimate resurrection. . . . Ours rather the duty, however confused the scene, however dismal the present outlook, however circumscribed the resources we dispose of, to labor serenely, confidently, and unremittingly to lend our share of assistance, in whichever way circumstances may enable us, to the operation of the forces which, as marshaled and directed by Bahá'u'lláh, are leading humanity out of the valley of misery and shame to the loftiest summits of power and glory."

THE UNIVERSAL HOUSE OF JUSTICE

5

Riḍván 1996

To the Followers of Bahá'u'lláh in Africa

Dear Bahá'í Friends,

5.1 You come to the Four Year Plan with an extraordinary history of achievement, which indicates that you are well equipped spiritually and administratively, and in the inherent potential of your people, to respond successfully to the Plan's central aim to advance the process of entry by troops. In whatever direction south of the Sahara one may look—whether to the eastern, western, central or southern region of the continent —portents of great, imminent expansion are evident. The torch of faith burns brightly in your hearts, setting our spirits aglow with gladness at the scale of your attainments and the magnificent possibilities that are now yours.

5.2 The bright hope inspired by such observations is justified by thrilling facts. The spiritual endowments of Africa derive naturally from the creative forces universally released by the Revelation of Bahá'u'lláh, but these have been marvelously enhanced by the continent's direct associations with the Channels of such forces: the ship transporting the Blessed Beauty on His exile to the Holy Land touched briefly its northern shores; the Center of the Covenant spent extended periods in Egypt before and after His historic visit to the West. The continent was also twice crossed from south to north by the beloved Guardian. Bahá'u'lláh favored the black peoples by making a specific reference to them when, as the Master testified, He compared them to the "black pupil of the eye" through which "the light of the spirit shineth forth."

5.3 African Bahá'í history had its beginnings in Egypt, which was opened to the Faith during the period of the ministry of Bahá'u'lláh; it gathered momentum during the ministry of 'Abdu'l-Bahá when Bahá'í localities were established in South Africa and Tunisia. But the early effects of these spiritual endowments became more obvious with the remarkable success of the two-year Africa Project (1951-53) when 16 territories were opened, bringing to 25 the total number of countries and islands in which Bahá'ís resided; this preceded the opening of the 33 virgin territories called for in the beloved Guardian's Ten Year Global Crusade, a period of astonishing development in Africa that evoked the admiration and praise of Shoghi Effendi as many people from different tribes entered the Cause, a number of administrative institutions were formed, and it became possible to raise up the Mother Temple of Africa in the heart of the continent. During the course of these rapid developments, the African believers themselves, through sacrificial effort as teachers and pioneers, arose to champion the Cause of God, manifesting the profundity of their response to the Message of the New Day.

5.4   In the countries lying to the north where programs of public teaching cannot now be pursued, the friends have continued for many years to maintain their posts with circumspection and heroic fortitude. Not only have they kept the flame of faith alive in their hearts, they also endeavor to transmit the fire of the love of God to members of their families, including their children and youth, in anticipation of the day when freedom to openly proclaim their religion and conduct their community affairs is secured.

5.5   With immense gratification we now look back over just a few decades during which Africa attained the largest number of National Spiritual Assemblies of any continent; moreover, Africa's Local Spiritual Assemblies amount to a substantial percentage of the world's total. The prodigious output of energy devoted to expansion and consolidation has included major endeavors to train the believers and to mount and maintain development projects. As a result the African Bahá'í community can boast of notable progress in the establishment of a number of primary and secondary schools and training institutes. A source of much of this energy in recent times has been the African youth, who have increasingly demonstrated exemplary dedication and vigor in their Bahá'í activities. In the field of external affairs, the African community, whether in small or large states, has shown a boldness, a creativity, and a tenacity that have resonated in the worldwide proclamation of the Faith and the promotion of its vital interests.

Clearly, then, Africa is poised to register a victory for the   5.6
Cause that will reaffirm its position among the front ranks
of our world community. The time is critical, and you must
act promptly to realize this prospect. We therefore urge our
African brothers and sisters to take immediate account of their
strengths, needs and opportunities, and then resolve to turn the
challenge posed by these conditions into the means of success.
You will of necessity give concentrated attention to various
plans and programs of activity if you are to advance to new
stages of entry by troops, but simultaneously certain underlying
requisites will claim your special vigilance and exertion. These
are the elimination of tribal prejudice, the transformation of
prevailing social practices, and the fostering of education.

Tribal conflict is one of the most pressing issues facing   5.7
Africa. This must be dealt with in the heart of every faithful
follower of Bahá'u'lláh and resolutely overcome through the
collective will of every local and national Bahá'í community.
Indeed, how can the lovers of the Blessed Beauty allow tribal
prejudice and rivalry to be practiced in their midst when He has
made unity the pivotal principle and goal of His Faith? Hatred
and animosity based on tribe, like those based on race, blight
the human spirit and arrest the development of the society that
accommodates them. If outside the Bahá'í community in recent
years influential persons and public officials have been able to
see the practical benefit of bringing diverse groups together
towards unity, how much more should it be possible for those
imbued with the spirit of our Teachings to strive to eliminate
within the Bahá'í fellowship the unsavory characteristics of
tribal division and disunity. It is imperative and urgent in the
current state of society for the Bahá'ís so to practice genuine
unity among themselves and in their relations to others that
they may become renowned as a new people in the eyes of all
Africans. Such a demonstration will attract divine confirmations and greatly reinforce their power to succeed in spreading
the Teachings.

Much of what distinguishes African life is to be found in   5.8
patterns of behavior displayed in the tribe and particularly
in the family. Increasingly, urban life threatens to destroy the
positive qualities of such patterns. Since change is inevitable if
progress is to be made by any African society, a primary challenge to Bahá'ís is to preserve and improve those wholesome
aspects of tribal and family custom that are in accord with the

Bahá'í Teachings and to dispense with those that are not. Such a challenge must be embraced with the understanding that the Book of God is the standard by which to weigh all forms of behavior. While unwavering action is necessary, wisdom and tact and patience must, of course, be exercised. Let it be understood, too, that Africans are not alone in the struggle to change certain age-old practices. People everywhere have customs which must be abandoned so as to clear the path along which their societies must evolve towards that glorious, new civilization which is to be the fruit of Bahá'u'lláh's stupendous Revelation. Indeed, in no society on earth can there be found practices which adequately mirror the standards of His Cause. His own truth-bearing Words clarify the matter: "The summons and the message which We gave were never intended to reach or to benefit one land or one people only. Mankind in its entirety must firmly adhere to whatsoever hath been revealed and vouchsafed unto it. Then and only then will it attain unto true liberty. The whole earth is illuminated with the resplendent glory of God's Revelation."

5.9   The acute inadequacy of plans and programs to educate Africa's people poses a particular challenge to the followers of Bahá'u'lláh in that continent, for He has emphasized the importance of education for all; and individuals ought to be taught at least to read and write. The education of which Bahá'u'lláh spoke includes both spiritual and material aspects. The lack of such education affects the ability of people to achieve true progress. This matter should be of the keenest interest to all segments of the community. Parents have a special responsibility to see that their children, both boys and girls, receive an education; and they must take care that the girls are not left behind, since well-educated girls are a guarantee of the excellence of future society; indeed, preference should, if necessary, be given to their education. Closely linked to this concern is the principle of the equality of men and women taught by Bahá'u'lláh. It is also highly desirable for adults, both men and women, who are illiterate to participate in literacy programs, so that gradually all Bahá'ís will be able to read the Word of God for themselves. The Bahá'í community is not fully equipped to undertake what responsible authorities have neglected to do for the education of the people; however, the Bahá'í institutions at all levels are urged to give attention to these critical needs, as circumstances permit.

Bearing in mind these three foregoing considerations, you 5.10
can move vigorously and wisely to tackle the manifold tasks implied by the Plan's emphasis on advancing the process of entry
by troops. An extension of your efforts to effect both expansion
and consolidation on a wholly new scale is imperative. The one
suggests a powerful outward thrust of your teaching activities
to cover the length and breadth of your countries, reaching the
remotest areas with the Divine Message. The other indicates a
drive to consolidate and multiply your gains through an ever-
deepening penetration of spiritual knowledge of the Faith into
the hearts of the believers, a systematic development of human
resources, and a marked improvement in the functioning of
your national and, particularly, your local institutions.

In all this exertion, the three components of the process—the 5.11
individual, the institutions and the community—must assume
their respective responsibilities. We especially expect you all
to pursue every means at your disposal that will bring about
the realization of an organic unity between the Local Spiritual
Assembly and the community, and thereby establish a sharp
contrast to the fragmentation of present-day social life. Thus,
we long to see the individual African believers arise in greater
numbers to claim the Faith of Bahá'u'lláh as their own and to
take on the requisite tasks of teaching and administering a rapidly expanding Faith. And we look for accumulating evidence
that the Spiritual Assemblies are taking to heart their God-given
mandate and are conscientiously fulfilling their obligations to
Bahá'u'lláh to foster the growth and development of vibrant
communities in which adults, youth and children are more
and more integrated and active. To fulfill these expectations is
to demonstrate to a skeptical world the power of the Faith to
hold aloft a new standard for the guidance of the nations, and
eventually to attract the disillusioned masses to the security of
God's Faith.

What specific actions, you may well ask, would indicate that 5.12
you are fulfilling the basic requirement of the Plan in Africa?
A reply would include mention of the following. Whatever
the state of expansion in a community, take the next steps to
increase enrollments, deepen the believers and strengthen the
teaching force. Where entry by troops is in progress, intensify
your efforts to stimulate further increase in the number of believers, while at the same time conducting a program of training
that will deepen the new believers and raise up new teachers

on a continuing basis. Maximize action to bring families into the Faith by encouraging individuals in their duty to endeavor to lead as many of their family members as possible to the light of divine guidance. Regularize efforts to teach among the sub-Saharan Muslims. Proliferate the publication of Bahá'í literature and audio-cassette tapes, especially in vernacular languages. Swell the number of Local Spiritual Assemblies elected by their communities without help from outside. Support more abundantly the Funds of the Faith. Orient believers from among the traditional rulers to the Teachings, so that they will find appropriate ways to serve the Faith.

5.13   Moreover, extend provisions for children regularly to attend Bahá'í classes for their spiritual training. Give consistent attention to involving the youth in the expansion and consolidation work and to opening channels of activity suited to their talents and necessary for their development into mature Bahá'ís. Increase the number and effectiveness of observances of Nineteen Day Feasts. Expand the use of music and drama in the proclamation and teaching work, an effort in which Africa has already distinguished itself. Multiply plans and programs to raise the status of women and to encourage the active support of men in such endeavors. Extend the range of your exertions in the fields of external affairs and social and economic development.

5.14   You will readily appreciate, then, the emphasis placed on multiplying the number of training institutes; for without them it will be impossible to meet the needs of hugely expanding communities. In some places, the friends may find it possible to offer sites and facilities for these essential operations, which must be located in as many areas as necessary to provide regular and well-organized training to increasing numbers of believers. The programs of the institutes must be designed to instill in the participants a good understanding of the fundamental verities of the Faith and to help them acquire skills and abilities that will enable them to serve the Faith effectively.

5.15   Immediately after Riḍván your National Spiritual Assemblies will initiate efforts to formulate, in consultation with the Counsellors, the details of the Four Year Plan, country by country. To ensure that the Plan is broadly based and responsive to the needs of all areas of a country, the participation of the Local Spiritual Assemblies and individuals, in evolving their own local plans and in following the lines of action to be clearly laid down, will be essential.

Dear Friends, we are acutely conscious of the crushing difficulties that afflict life in Africa: the conditions that have caused a flood of refugees on the continent, the horrors created by ethnic conflict, the political unrest, the economic distress, the high incidence of hunger and disease, the horrendous natural disasters. But, paradoxical as it may seem, there exist in all of these the very possibilities of your success. Your ability to endure and forge ahead is reinforced in the assurance given by the Divine Physician, Who anticipated all these conditions and prescribed a sure remedy. His prescriptions have been placed in your hands. 5.16

Therefore, we remind you of the noble ambitions the beloved Guardian held for you as a people in a continent that has "a great contribution to make to the advancement of world civilization." May such memories resound afresh in your hearts, quickening your will to fulfill the major aim of the Plan before you, and setting a pace for your actions like the urgent rhythm of drums pulsating throughout your immensely potent, far-stretching land. 5.17

Our ardent prayer at the Holy Threshold on your behalf is that the divine storehouses of heaven may pour out their bounties upon you all, healing your ills, magnifying your powers, and enabling you to achieve victory upon victory. 5.18

THE UNIVERSAL HOUSE OF JUSTICE

6

Riḍván 1996

To the Followers of Bahá'u'lláh in Europe

Dearly loved Friends,

Forty-three years ago, when the European Bahá'ís gathered 6.1
at the conference in Stockholm called by the beloved Guardian
for the launching of the mighty Ten Year Crusade in your continent, you had but three National Spiritual Assemblies—those
of the British Isles, of Germany and Austria, and of Italy and
Switzerland—together with slowly developing local communities in the other countries of western Europe. In the east, cut off
by political barriers, were tiny remnants of communities which
had been raised up in earlier years and, in neighboring Turkey,
was a small, struggling national community. As the European
believers of that time contemplated the awe-inspiring tasks before them, they heard the words of the Guardian, illuminating
the historical significance of the continent in which they were to
build the institutions of Bahá'u'lláh's embryonic World Order:

> A continent, occupying such a central and strategic 6.2
> position on the entire planet; so rich and eventful in its
> history, so diversified in its culture; from whose soil sprang
> both the Hellenic and Roman civilizations; the mainspring of
> a civilization to some of whose features Bahá'u'lláh Himself
> paid tribute; on whose southern shores Christendom first
> established its home; along whose eastern marches the
> mighty forces of the Cross and the Crescent so frequently
> clashed; on whose southwestern extremity a fast-evolving
> Islamic culture yielded its fairest fruit; in whose heart the
> light of the Reformation shone so brightly, shedding its rays
> as far as the outlying regions of the globe. . . .

This, your continent, whose soil was blessed by the 6.3
footsteps of Bahá'u'lláh Himself, which was twice visited by
'Abdu'l-Bahá in His epoch-making journeys following His

47

release from imprisonment, whose travelers and scholars early responded to the dawning light of the Bábí Revelation, two of whose governments extended the hand of succor during the Heroic Age of the Faith, and whose nations, in recent years, have intervened so effectively in defense of the persecuted Bahá'ís in Iran, has amply demonstrated the capacity of its people to rally to the banner of the Cause of God, once their hearts are touched and their minds awakened to its Message.

6.4   In the course of these forty-three years the European Bahá'í communities have shown great vitality. The number of National Spiritual Assemblies has risen to thirty-four, covering the entire continent and embracing, in the case of Russia, vast territories as far as the Pacific Ocean. Great victories have been won for the Faith by European pioneers in Africa, the Pacific, the Caribbean region and Greenland. Your institutions have distinguished themselves in external affairs. Your communities include outstanding scholars of the Faith, musicians, artists, scientists and those concerned with the application of Bahá'í Teachings to economics and business. You have exerted special efforts for the advancement of women and the strengthening of family life. The European Bahá'í Youth Council provides a focal point and a source of stimulation to the youth in all parts of Europe, complemented by a network of National and Local Youth Committees closely linked to and supported by their National and Local Spiritual Assemblies. Now is the time to build on these achievements, clearly focusing all efforts on the central purpose of taking the Message of Bahá'u'lláh to a spiritually famished population.

6.5   The first task of your National Spiritual Assemblies immediately after Riḍván will be to formulate, in consultation with the Counsellors, the details of the Four Year Plan, country by country. The participation of the Local Spiritual Assemblies and individual believers in evolving their own local plans, and in following the lines of action to be clearly laid down, will be essential for the successful achievement of the high aims of this stage of the implementation of the Divine Plan of 'Abdu'l-Bahá.

6.6   Europe is a continent of great variety, and each of your National Assemblies will be studying with care the processes and achievements required for the advancement of the Cause of God in its area during the coming four years. Each must consider the current condition of its community, the territory within which it is working, and areas of potential collaboration with other Bahá'í communities. Special attention will need to be paid to the attainment of official recognition in those countries where the institutions of the Faith are not yet legally incorporated, and to raising up National Spiritual Assemblies in certain of those independent countries and major islands, such as the Faroes, which have not yet attained them. There are, however, certain elements of an even wider vision which must be considered as they apply to specific countries, groups of countries and the entire continent.

There are areas which cry out for pioneers and traveling teachers; the mind turns, for example, to the work among the Sami and the other peoples of the arctic and sub-arctic areas as far north as Spitsbergen. We contemplate the significance of teaching the Faith in the islands of the Mediterranean, the Atlantic and the North Sea; the continent-wide importance of the Romany peoples, who have begun to show such receptivity to the call of Bahá'u'lláh; the opportunity for the European Bahá'í communities to demonstrate the salutary nature of the Teachings in relation to minorities of every kind; the specific tasks described by the beloved Guardian as the destiny of certain communities, and their responsibilities in far-flung lands where their languages are spoken; the implications of the advancement of the Faith in Italy where is to be found "the heart and stronghold of the leading, the most ancient and powerful Church of Christendom"; the need to rapidly increase the number of Bahá'í centers in the vast areas of the Ukraine and European Russia; and, beyond this, the special responsibilities and opportunities of the Bahá'í community of the Russian Federation, the larger part of whose area lies in Asia and must continue to benefit from collaboration with neighboring communities of central, southern and eastern Asia as well as Alaska, Canada and the United States. All these are but some examples of the challenges which you face in the years ahead.

The central aim of the Four Year Plan, a significant advance in the process of entry by troops, is of especial significance for Europe. You should have no misgivings—it is a process that can advance in all parts of Europe, in the west as well as in the east. All should recognize that entry by troops is an inevitable stage in the development of the Cause. The nature of the process is clarified in the compilation on the subject, whence it becomes

6.7

6.8

49

apparent that the desired outcome, a sustained entry by troops, cannot be achieved by a mere series of spasmodic, uncoordinated exertions, no matter how enthusiastic. Confidence; unity of vision; systematic, realistic, but audacious planning; acceptance of the fact that mistakes will be made, and willingness to learn from this mistakes; and, above all, reliance on the guidance and sustaining confirmations of Bahá'u'lláh will advance this process.

6.9   The establishment of training institutes in various locations is emphasized in the Four Year Plan because current methods, valuable though they are, are not adequate by themselves to meet the challenges of this new stage in the growth of the Cause. The character and structure of the training institutes must be adapted to the conditions of each country and region; clearly their form in Europe will not be identical with that of training institutes in the rural areas of India. Their essential functions, however, will be the same. They will foster a firm acceptance of Bahá'í identity in those who take part: the capacity to look upon the world and its conditions from the point of view of the Teachings rather than from the standpoint of one's nationality or non-Bahá'í background. They will help to develop in each participant a deep love for Bahá'u'lláh, a good understanding of His essential Teachings and an awareness of the importance of developing the spiritual life of each individual through prayer, meditation and immersion in the Sacred Writings. They will also cover such practical matters as how to teach the Faith, for there are too many who, for lack of confidence in their ability to do so, are hesitant to convey the Message. The transformation that such deepening in the Faith produces will surely inflame the hearts of the individual friends with the longing to share this Message with those around them, and this is the seed of all success in teaching. Those who have attended training institutes will be able to help the other Bahá'ís, new and old, to increase their potential for teaching, and so to greatly increase the human resources of the Cause, in which every believer is a teacher.

6.10   The teaching of the Faith by the friends in Europe must increase in range; it must be varied, spontaneous and individual on the one hand, and focused, united and mutually supportive on the other. It must be both inspiring and practical and must, above all, be informed with serene faith in the power of Bahá'u'lláh. You should widen the field of your teaching work to include the country people and the masses laboring in the cities; people of little education as well as intellectuals in university towns. You should consciously approach every stratum of society, adapting your methods, literature and audio-visual materials to each audience. Both the heart and the mind need to be fed; both spiritual force and intellectual clarity must be recognized as vital elements of the teaching work. You have excelled in the use of the arts for the proclamation, expansion and consolidation of the Faith; this is a key to opening many doors and should be encouraged and developed. Your unity, enthusiasm, confidence and perseverance, strengthened and guided by the power of prayer, cannot fail to act as a channel for divine confirmations, which will be a magnet to seeking souls.

For our part, we shall pray ardently at the Sacred Threshold   6.11
that you, who have won such historic victories in your homelands and throughout the world, will enter during the Four Year Plan into a stage of even greater achievement, presaging the as yet unimaginable glories destined to unfold during the twenty-first century.

THE UNIVERSAL HOUSE OF JUSTICE

Riḍván 1996

To the Followers of Bahá'u'lláh in Latin America
and the Caribbean

Dearly loved Friends,

As you contemplate the challenges awaiting you during
these closing years of the century, you may draw confidence
from the knowledge that your past endeavors have been
abundantly blessed by divine confirmation. Some sixty years
ago, when the Guardian had called for the establishment of
at least one center in each of the Central and South American
Republics, he wrote of "the strenuous and organized labors
by which future generations of believers in the Latin countries must distinguish themselves." Addressing the friends
in the Caribbean some years later in a letter written shortly
after the formation of the Spiritual Assembly of the Greater
Antilles, he urged them to exert "continuous and systematic
effort," to evince "unyielding determination" and to display
"whole-hearted consecration." Your achievements during the
intervening decades have amply demonstrated your capacity to
meet his expectations. You have proved by the spirit animating
your efforts to be well deserving of such tributes as "staunch,"
"warm-hearted," "eager," "spiritually minded."

7.1

The central concern of the plans that will guide your
endeavors during the coming four years will be to effect a
significant advance in the process of entry by troops. This challenge you will not be facing as novices. You have accumulated
through successive plans valuable experience which must now
be brought to bear on the aim of the Four Year Plan with clarity
and single-mindedness. Your success will depend on the degree
to which you can, on the one hand, intensify activity in the
areas that have already witnessed large-scale expansion and, on
the other, exploit the fresh opportunities presented to you as a
result of your growing involvement in the affairs of society.

7.2

7.3   Your numerical strength lies in those many regions where, over the decades, intense teaching activities have been undertaken among diverse populations. Through these exertions, large numbers from most of the indigenous tribes—singled out by 'Abdu'l-Bahá to be the recipients of special favors and promises—as well as people of the African, Asian and European races, have enlisted under the banner of the Faith. As a result, your community now boasts of a harmonious blend of groups from various ethnic and cultural backgrounds.

7.4   Plans focusing on these areas of large-scale expansion will necessarily seek to mobilize an appreciable number of believers within each population not only to labor diligently in their own local communities, but also to serve as long- and short-term pioneers and visiting teachers in other localities. Training programs, with which many of your communities have considerable experience, constitute a most potent instrument for the accomplishment of such a vast mobilization. We call upon you, then, to support the work of the training institutes in your countries, the more experienced among you giving generously of their time as teachers so that courses can be offered widely and consistently. As you acquire new knowledge and skills through these programs, you will be able to put into practice with enthusiasm and zeal what you have learned, and arise to shoulder the manifold responsibilities that accelerated expansion and consolidation demand.

7.5   This mobilization will greatly facilitate the development of local communities, a task that in the past has not been an easy one to accomplish. Your labors in this field of endeavor must now be systematically and vigorously multiplied, utilizing the valuable methods and approaches that have been devised in many of your countries in recent years. A host of dedicated workers is needed within each population who, supported by Auxiliary Board members, regional committees and institutes, focus their energies on the strengthening of community after community. Let those of you who arise, even when you can find but a handful of believers in a locality, gather them together, broaden their vision, and raise their awareness of the greatness of the Cause they have embraced. Help the Local Spiritual Assembly to launch the community on a path of systematic expansion and consolidation, bringing in new recruits or revitalizing those who, having accepted the Faith years ago, have seen their enthusiasm wane. Remember, moreover, that in this process of community building the education of children—without which the victories of a whole generation may be lost—must be given due emphasis.

While paying close attention to areas of large-scale expansion, you should not lose sight of the fact that your nations have undergone profound change over the past decades, resulting in increased receptivity to the Faith in many sectors of society. You have, in each of your national communities, developed remarkable capacity to interact with society at large. Through your extensive work in social and economic development, especially in the area of education, through your discourse on issues such as the preservation of the environment and the organization of social action, through your substantive interactions with leaders of thought, you are developing a keen understanding of the needs and aspirations of your peoples which enhances your ability to present the Faith to a wide range of interests. 7.6

Together with your increased involvement in the affairs of society, you will need to make a concerted effort to attract receptive souls from diverse groups, teaching them and confirming them in the Faith. In this respect, the climate of search prevailing among both the leaders and the masses in your countries, which has emerged following the ideological upheaval of recent years, is of special significance. Two sectors have been particularly and differently affected and are athirst for the life-giving waters of Bahá'u'lláh's Revelation: on the one hand, the teachers in the national school systems and, on the other, university students and their professors. Historically, both have exerted widespread influence in your societies, and should you teach them systematically, you will certainly reap abundant fruits. 7.7

In all of this great endeavor—pursuing large-scale expansion and consolidation, furthering the work of external affairs and carrying out activities of social and economic development —you must be driven by a passion to teach the Faith. Let regular study of the Writings feed the flame of your enthusiasm. Let His Words so shape your thoughts that the most pressing obligation of your lives becomes the sharing of His Message with others. The designation given to the Latin American communities by the Guardian as the associates of the chief executors of the Divine Plan has defined for you a vast arena of service. As you take up the tasks of the Four Year Plan, keep in mind the words of the Guardian calling on the individual 7.8

believer to ". . . shed, heroically and irrevocably, the trivial and superfluous attachments which hold him back, empty himself of every thought that may tend to obstruct his path, mix, in obedience to the counsels of the Author of His Faith, and in imitation of the One Who is its true Exemplar, with men and women, in all walks of life, seek to touch their hearts, through the distinction which characterizes his thoughts, his words and his acts, and win them over tactfully, lovingly, prayerfully and persistently, to the Faith he himself has espoused."

7.9   We shall remember each and all of you in our prayers in the Holy Shrines and shall beseech Bahá'u'lláh to vouchsafe to you His unfailing protection and guidance, as you boldly go forth to conquer the hearts of men.

THE UNIVERSAL HOUSE OF JUSTICE

8

Riḍván 1996

To the Followers of Bahá'u'lláh in North America:
Alaska, Canada, Greenland, and the United States

Dearly loved Friends,

As members of the North American Bahá'í community, you 8.1
enter the Four Year Plan with a brilliant record of progress in
fulfilling the mandate issued by 'Abdu'l-Bahá in the Tablets of
the Divine Plan. In the eight decades since you received this
mandate, your prodigious exertions have carried the Message
of Bahá'u'lláh to all parts of your continent, and throughout the
length and breadth of the planet. You have played a critical role
in the establishment of the framework of the Administrative
Order and in the sustained proclamation of the Faith. These
Tablets launched you on a worldwide enterprise which you, and
the generations to succeed you, are called upon to continue during the vast period of time stretching throughout the Formative
Age and into the Golden Age of the Bahá'í Dispensation.

In your pursuit of the provisions of the Four Year Plan 8.2
on national, regional and local levels, in conformity with the
detailed plans to be formulated in the weeks ahead, you should
constantly bear in mind the one central aim of the Plan: advancing the process of entry by troops. There can be no doubt that
this process, propelled by mysterious spiritual forces beyond
the ken of the skeptic, will in due course quicken the souls of a
multitude from every background in North America and dramatically increase the numerical strength of your communities.

Training institutes and other centers of learning are an 8.3
indispensable element of a sustained endeavor to advance this
process, and to ensure that the essential deepening of new
believers is not neglected, that they develop the necessary
skills to effectively teach the Faith, and that an opportunity
is provided for all Bahá'ís, new and veteran, to embark on a
systematic study of the fundamental verities of the Revelation

of Bahá'u'lláh. We look to your communities to make an energetic response to the call for such institutes, and to develop a wide variety of approaches fitted to the needs of the diverse components of your population.

8.4   In one of the Tablets of the Divine Plan, 'Abdu'l-Bahá, exhorting the North American believers to strive to attain the exalted station of Apostles of Bahá'u'lláh, specifies firmness in the Covenant to be a prerequisite for this achievement. We urge you to manifest unwavering adherence to the provisions of the Covenant, while ever striving for a deeper understanding of its challenging features and of its implications, which far transcend the familiar arrangements of present society.

8.5   You are in a most enviable position to provide a mighty impetus to the teaching work. Through the alertness and perseverance of your institutions and the effect of your exertions, there is now a general awareness of, and respect for, the Cause in your region, and the Faith has acquired a reputation for universality and liberality of thought. Well may you rejoice at this remarkable achievement, and well may you contemplate the present needs of the Cause with eagerness and confidence.

8.6   Your accomplishments have prepared the way for even more spectacular successes in the years immediately ahead. Now as never before should you strive mightily to free yourselves from the obstacles of apathy, attachment to worldly pursuits, and lethargy, which stand in the way of so glorious a realization. As the people around you yearn increasingly for a society in which rectitude of conduct prevails, which is animated by a nobility of moral behavior, and in which the diverse races are firmly united, your challenge is to demonstrate the efficacy of the Message of Bahá'u'lláh in ministering to their needs and in recreating the very foundation of individual and social life. The whole of North America stands in desperate need of the inspiring vision, the dynamic sense of purpose and the idealism, which can be provided only by those who are imbued with the spirit and truths of the Bahá'í Writings.

8.7   The community of the Greatest Name must increasingly become renowned for its social cohesion, and for the spirit of trust and confidence which distinguishes the relationship between believers and their institutions. In the earliest years of his ministry, the Guardian stated, ". . . I hope to see the friends at all times, in every land, and of every shade of thought and character, voluntarily and joyously rallying round their local and in particular their national centers of activity, upholding and promoting their interests with complete unanimity and contentment, with perfect understanding, genuine enthusiasm, and sustained vigor. This indeed is the one joy and yearning of my life, for it is the fountainhead from which all future blessings will flow, the broad foundation upon which the security of the Divine Edifice must ultimately rest." Realization of this longing requires that you commit yourselves to the wholehearted support of your institutions. In turn, those of you called upon to serve as members of such bodies should ever be mindful of the attitude and manner prescribed for the conduct of their duties, and should strive continually to approach the exalted standard set out in the Teachings.

In the Divine Plan bequeathed to you by 'Abdu'l-Bahá is 8.8 disclosed the glorious destiny of those who are the descendants of the early inhabitants of your continent. We call upon the indigenous believers who are firmly rooted in the Bahá'í Teachings to aid, through both deed and word, those who have not yet attained that level of understanding. Progress along the path to their destiny requires that they refuse to be drawn into the divisiveness and militancy around them, and that they strive to make their own distinctive contribution to the pursuit of the goals of the Four Year Plan, both beyond the confines of North America and at home. They should be ever mindful of the vital contribution they can make to the work of the Faith throughout the American continent, in the circumpolar areas and in the Asian region of the Russian Federation.

We direct the attention of the believers of African descent, 8.9 so beloved by the Master, to the pressing need for pioneers, who will contribute to the further development of the Cause in distant areas, including the continent of Africa for which they were assigned a special responsibility by the Guardian when the first systematic campaign was launched for its spiritual illumination. Although their contributions to all aspects of Bahá'í service on the home front and elsewhere will be of great value, they can be a unique source of encouragement and inspiration to their African brothers and sisters who are now poised on the threshold of great advances for the Faith of Bahá'u'lláh.

Increasingly over the years, the Bahá'í community in North 8.10 America has been augmented by the addition of a substantial number of believers who have come from the Cradle of the Faith. We urge all the friends of Persian background, who constitute a most valuable source of ability and experience, to dedicate themselves, to an extent surpassing their past services, to the accomplishment of the goals of the Four Year Plan, under the leadership and guidance of the institutions of the Faith in North America. The unity of thought and endeavor between the friends from East and West will offer a shining example of the power of Bahá'u'lláh to demolish traditional barriers and will be a powerful source of attraction to the Cause.

8.11   The Alaskan Bahá'ís are privileged to live in an area described by the Guardian as "a region destined to play an important role in shaping the spiritual destinies of the great Republic of the West of which it forms a part, and to contribute, in no small measure, to the establishment of the institutions of His World Order throughout the American continent." The invaluable contribution they have made to the establishment of the Faith in Siberia in recent years, together with their significant advances in strengthening the home front, provide compelling evidence of their capacity to take full advantage of the opportunities before them in the Four Year Plan.

8.12   The valiant Canadian Bahá'í community was praised by the Guardian for "the staunchness of the faith of its members, their unyielding resolve, their ceaseless efforts, their willingness to sacrifice, their exemplary loyalty, their steadfast courage," a description fully confirmed by the record of its achievements during the Three Year Plan. It has played a disproportionately great and much-appreciated role in the defense of the Faith, in its propagation to all corners of the earth, and in the establishment of its institutions in other lands, both near and far, and is in an enviable position to build upon these successes in the new Plan on which it now embarks.

8.13   Our thoughts turn often to the Bahá'í community of Greenland, whose staunchness of faith and dogged perseverance have won our admiration and praise, and have resulted in the Faith's becoming firmly established in that distant land. Inspired by the promise set out in the Tablets of the Divine Plan that "if the hearts be touched with the heat of the love of God, that territory will become a divine rose-garden and a heavenly paradise, and the souls, even as fruitful trees, will acquire the utmost freshness and beauty," let them now go forth to claim new victories on the home front and to transform their nation through the power of the Divine Teachings.

Some four decades ago, Shoghi Effendi described the   8.14
members of the United States Bahá'í community as "the outstanding protagonists of the Cause of God; the stout-hearted
defenders of its integrity, its claims and its rights; the champion-
builders of its Administrative Order; the standard-bearers of its
crusading hosts; the torchbearers of its embryonic civilization;
the chief succorers of the down-trodden, the needy and the fet-
tered among its followers. . . ." Any survey of the distinguished
accomplishments of these dearly loved friends during the past
three years provides striking evidence of the continuing applicability of this description, and of the immense contribution
they are making to the advancement of the Cause. We look to
the members of the Bahá'í community in the United States to
perform, during the Four Year Plan, heroic deeds of service to
the Cause, which will astonish and inspire their fellow-believers
throughout the world.

In North America, there are opportunities for the advance-   8.15
ment of the process of entry by troops, the like of which
presently exist in no other place on earth. Three unique
characteristics combine to give rise to this condition: the
unparalleled strength of your local communities, particularly
evident in the activity of your Local Spiritual Assemblies and in
the consecration of the Bahá'í youth; the positive impression of
the Faith which has been conveyed, not only to the generality
of the population, but also to leaders of thought and people
of influence; and the composition of your nations, which have
welcomed to their shores immigrants, students and refugees
from all parts of the planet, drawn from all the major racial,
ethnic and religious backgrounds of humanity. You, who live
in a continent described by 'Abdu'l-Bahá as "the land wherein
the splendors of His light shall be revealed, where the mysteries
of His Faith shall be unveiled, the home of the righteous, and
the gathering-place of the free," are called upon to take full
advantage of these favorable circumstances.

Dear Friends, now must you commit yourselves to the work   8.16
of the Cause afresh, liberated from any doubts, uncertainties
or hesitations which may have impeded you in the past. Every
stratum of society must be brought within your embrace, as you
vigorously advance toward the goal of entry by troops at this
time when powerful spiritual forces are at work in the hearts
of the people. Neither the affluent nor the indigent should be
excluded from your purview. Receptive souls should be sought

in the sophisticated circles of urban society, on the campuses of colleges and universities, in centers of industry and commerce, on the farms and villages of the mountains, plains and prairies —wherever are to be found human beings in search of the divine Truth. You should strive to create a Bahá'í community which will offer to the entire world a vibrant model of unity in diversity. The influence of your exertions can extend well beyond the confines of North America; in particular, French Canadian believers can perform an invaluable service to the Faith in the French-speaking nations and islands throughout the world, the Bahá'ís dwelling in the Arctic and sub-Arctic regions can powerfully reinforce the work of the Cause in the circumpolar areas, and the friends of Hispanic background have fertile fields before them throughout Latin America. Let all believers consider the extent to which they can use familial and ethnic ties to other regions of the world for the fulfillment of the global mission conferred on the recipients of the Tablets of the Divine Plan.

8.17   At this critical hour in the fortunes of humanity, our eyes turn with eagerness and hope to the Bahá'ís of all parts of North America, who constitute a reservoir of human and material resources unmatched elsewhere in the Bahá'í world. As you proceed along your prescribed path, you should be ever mindful of these words addressed to you by the Author of the Tablets of the Divine Plan: "I fervently hope that in the near future the whole earth may be stirred and shaken by the results of your achievements. The hope which 'Abdu'l-Bahá cherishes for you is that the same success which has attended your efforts in America may crown your endeavors in other parts of the world, that through you the fame of the Cause of God may be diffused throughout the East and the West, and the advent of the Kingdom of the Lord of Hosts be proclaimed in all the five continents of the globe."

8.18   Our ardent prayers at the Sacred Threshold will surround and accompany you at every step of the momentous under-taking to which you are now summoned.

THE UNIVERSAL HOUSE OF JUSTICE

9

Riḍván 1996

To the Followers of Bahá'u'lláh in Australia, the Cook
Islands, the Eastern Caroline Islands, the Fiji Islands,
French Polynesia, the Hawaiian Islands, Indonesia,
Japan, Kiribati, Korea, the Mariana Islands, the
Marshall Islands, New Caledonia and the Loyalty
Islands, New Zealand, Papua New Guinea, the
Philippines, Samoa, the Solomon Islands, Tonga,
Tuvalu, Vanuatu, and the Western Caroline Islands

Dearly loved Friends,

You are privileged to live in a region of the world unique in   9.1
the opportunities it offers to advance the interests of the Faith
during the course of the Four Year Plan. You constitute Bahá'í
communities within, or on the fringe of, the vast Pacific Ocean,
with which is associated this promise of Bahá'u'lláh: "Should
they attempt to conceal His light on the continent, He will
assuredly rear His head in the midmost part of the ocean and,
raising His voice proclaim: 'I am the lifegiver of the world.'"
At a time when the dear Bahá'í friends in the Cradle of the
Faith yearn for the yoke of oppression to be lifted from their
shoulders, you can compensate for their present and temporary
inability to propagate the Faith if you undertake a sustained
endeavor to convey the Divine Message to the peoples of your
countries and multiply Bahá'í institutions throughout these
lands.

Within your region is to be found a vast diversity of races,   9.2
cultures, languages and religious traditions, illustrative of the
major influences which have shaped the affairs of humanity
throughout history. One of this region's distinguishing features
is described by the Guardian as "a spiritual axis, extending from
the Antipodes to the northern islands of the Pacific Ocean—an
axis whose northern and southern poles will act as powerful
magnets, endowed with exceptional spiritual potency, and

towards which other younger and less experienced communities will tend for some time to gravitate." This emphasizes the vital role to be played by the Bahá'í communities of Northeastern Asia and of the Antipodes in the spiritual illumination of the surrounding areas.

9.3   Every country of the region must witness, in the course of the Four Year Plan, a significant advance in the process of entry by troops. It is essential that the plans formulated on national and local levels reflect this vital aim. The advancement of this process will require that greater attention be given not only to fostering individual initiative in the teaching work, but also to developing human resources through the establishment and efficient operation of training institutes and other centers of learning, and to vastly increasing the strength and quality of the functioning of the Local Spiritual Assemblies.

9.4   We direct a special appeal to the indigenous believers in all parts of the Pacific region, men and women alike, to intensify their efforts to acquire a deeper understanding of the Revelation of Bahá'u'lláh, and to strive for a position in the forefront of the promoters of the Faith through their teaching endeavors on the home front and their international cooperation in programs of the Ocean of Light. As the tensions and divisions of a declining social order increase, the believers throughout the Pacific Islands should provide compelling testimony to the potency of the Bahá'í Teachings through their manifest unity transcending tribal, national or ethnic barriers. The desperate search for solutions to the social and economic problems afflicting these countries is tempting people, in increasing numbers, to indulge in partisan political activities; the indigenous Bahá'ís should refuse to be drawn into such divisive pursuits and should strive to acquire a more profound insight into the nature of the World Order of Bahá'u'lláh, which offers a pattern for a future society distinguished by justice and unity, far removed from the contention of competing political interests.

9.5   In many of the nations of your area, women have traditionally been restricted to a secondary role in the life of society. We call upon the Bahá'í women of these countries, assured of the support and encouragement of all elements of the Bahá'í community, to demonstrate the transforming power of this Revelation by their courage and initiative in the teaching work and their full participation in the administrative activities of the Faith.

In much of the region, insufficient attention has been given   9.6
to the education of children. Far more extensive programs
should be initiated in those countries where the need exists,
to ensure that Bahá'í children are nurtured, encouraged to
acquire trained minds, illumined with a sound knowledge of
the Divine Teachings, well-equipped to participate in the work
of the Cause at all levels and to contribute to the arts, crafts
and sciences necessary for the advancement of civilization.
Such programs, when open to all children, Bahá'í or not,
offer a potent means of extending the beneficial influences of
Bahá'u'lláh's Message to the wider society.

In Northeastern Asia, the progress of the Faith has been   9.7
most encouraging, and a good foundation has been laid for the
Bahá'ís of Japan and Korea to magnify the size of their communities substantially during the Four Year Plan, while making
a notable contribution to the work of the Faith in neighboring
countries. Special attention should be given to the development
of the Faith in the Ryukyu Islands and also to the exploration
of any opportunities which might arise to carry the healing
Message of Bahá'u'lláh to all parts of the Korean peninsula.

The dedication and vitality of the Bahá'í community in the   9.8
Philippine Islands is a constant source of joy to us. We look to
the Filipino believers to make a significant advance in the process of entry by troops during the Four Year Plan, while giving
renewed attention to the strengthening of their Local Spiritual
Assemblies and the development of community life. This will
necessitate the intensive use of training institutes throughout
the country, and the involvement of a larger number of believers
in these training programs. The members of this devoted Bahá'í
community provide a welcome source of manpower for the
reinforcement of Bahá'í endeavors elsewhere, particularly in the
Asian and Pacific regions.

We are well aware of the restrictions which have long af-   9.9
flicted the members of the Indonesian Bahá'í community. Their
staunchness of faith, and their initiative in taking full advantage
of whatever opportunities are open to them, attract our admiration and gratitude. We urge them to continue their endeavors
throughout the whole of Indonesia, with full confidence that
their hopes will be fulfilled in the future.

A special responsibility must rest upon the believers in   9.10
Papua New Guinea, constituting the largest body of Bahá'ís in
Australasia, to strive unceasingly to build a vibrant community

which embraces all strata of society and which is renowned as a dynamic and enlightened segment of their nation. We look forward, in the course of the Four Year Plan, to a greater participation of the Bahá'í men and women of this country in the development of the Faith in other parts of Melanesia and elsewhere throughout the Pacific Islands.

9.11   In Australia, New Zealand and Hawaii, there are well-established and soundly functioning Bahá'í communities, each characterized by an admirable record of accomplishments on the home front and by a notable contribution to the work of the Faith in other parts of the Pacific and beyond. We call upon the believers in these countries to strive for a fuller realization of their duty to advance the interests of the Faith on the home fronts and throughout the length and breadth of the Pacific region. In their own countries, they should aspire to far greater attainments, marked by a substantial increase in the number of adherents and an enhanced public awareness of the distinctive character of the Bahá'í Faith and its followers. They can render invaluable assistance to other Bahá'í communities, not only in the Pacific region but in Southeast Asia and beyond, because of the experience they have acquired in the teaching and adminis-trative fields and the resources to which they have access. The believers from the Pacific Islands who have taken up residence in these three countries should be mindful of the responsibili-ties which rest upon them to devise means by which they can contribute to the strengthening of the Bahá'í communities in the island nations from which they have come.

9.12   Many of the valiant Bahá'í communities of the Pacific Islands are distinguished by the fact that they constitute sig-nificant percentages of the populations of their countries. The believers in these island nations need to direct their attention, more than ever, to the propagation of the Faith. They should also concentrate on the development of a distinctive community life, based on an uncompromising adherence to the precepts of the Faith, and guided by well-functioning Local Spiritual Assemblies, which will demonstrate to the entire populations of their countries the unifying and transforming power of the Faith, and will attract to the Cause a multitude of new believ-ers. Through this effort, they can make a vital contribution to enhancing the worldwide prestige of the Faith, and can lay the foundation for even more outstanding victories in the future. We urge them to give attention to sharply increasing their level of international cooperation in pursuit of the goals of the Four Year Plan, including support of the establishment of a strong Bahá'í community in French Polynesia as a basis for the future election of a National Spiritual Assembly there.

Almost four decades have passed since Shoghi Effendi   9.13 described the Pacific region in which you live as "that vast area of the globe, an area endowed with unimaginable potentialities, and which, owing to its strategic position, is bound to feel the impact of world-shaking forces, and to shape to a marked degree through the experience gained by its peoples in the school of adversity, the destinies of mankind." Since that time your nations have come ever more fully under the influence of the forces which are causing turmoil and disorder to human society, while the followers of Bahá'u'lláh have labored, undeterred and with admirable dedication, to advance the Cause of their Lord and to establish His institutions. The Pacific area, where, as the Guardian stated, "Bahá'í exploits bid fair to outshine the feats achieved in any other ocean, and indeed in every continent of the globe," now stands at the threshold of victories far greater than any yet won. We call upon you to go forward now as never before, assured of our ardent prayers in the Holy Shrines on your behalf, confident of your ultimate triumph.

THE UNIVERSAL HOUSE OF JUSTICE

10

Riḍván 1996

To the Followers of Bahá'u'lláh in Cambodia,
Hong Kong, Lao People's Democratic Republic,
Macau, Malaysia, Mongolia, Myanmar,
Singapore, Taiwan, Thailand, and Vietnam

Dearly loved Friends,

Some four decades ago, in a message to the first Regional 10.1
Convention of the Bahá'ís of Southeast Asia, the Guardian
wrote of the "far-reaching influence" that area would exercise
on the "future destinies of the world Bahá'í community." He
referred to the area's "heterogeneous character" and "geographical position," underscored "the spiritual receptivity of
many of its inhabitants," and drew attention to "the role they
are destined to play in the future shaping of the affairs of mankind." The remarkable progress of the Faith in Southeast Asia
since that time, in a period of social and political upheaval, is
but a prelude to the fulfillment of the Guardian's promise. This,
taken together with the recent accomplishments of the believers
in the neighboring territories as far north as Mongolia, gives
rise to a brilliant vision of future triumphs in the entirety of
that vast region.

You now embark on the next stage of your endeavors, a 10.2
Four Year Plan whose aim is to effect a significant advance
in the process of entry by troops. Among your peoples, the
majority of whom have been influenced by noble and high-
minded teachings of Buddhism, are many who possess a
profound sense of spirituality, which is reflected in the practices
of their daily lives and in the quality of their relationships with
one another, with nature, and with their social institutions.
They have a keen understanding of the need for coherence
between the material and the spiritual, and are disturbed by the
effects of gross materialism on their societies in recent years.
Your region represents a vast reservoir of potential promoters

of the Cause waiting to be tapped. The number and quality of the active supporters of the Faith with which it is already blessed bespeak the richness of that reservoir.

10.3 Systematic training programs constitute the most potent instrument at your disposal for realizing the potential of that highly promising region to contribute significantly to the human resources of the Faith. To this end, the establishment and strengthening of institutes will undoubtedly be a central component of the plans of all your countries. Your participation in institute programs, through which you will deepen your knowledge of the Faith, cultivate your inner spiritual lives and develop abilities of service, will enable you to intensify your individual and collective exertions in the teaching field and will result in a commensurate acceleration in the expansion of your communities. Varying patterns of growth, of course, will evolve according to the particular conditions in each country.

10.4 In Malaysia, large numbers of believers from among the Chinese, Indian and indigenous populations can be mobilized, and their energies directed towards the stimulation of activity at the local level. Many of the local communities are in a position to implement plans and projects under the direction of their Local Spiritual Assemblies, and they should be encouraged and aided in their efforts to do so. The capacity to achieve rapid and simultaneous expansion and consolidation exists in Malaysia, but needs to be fully exercised. Such an undertaking must be complemented by concrete measures to broaden the range of activities in areas such as the advancement of women, the spread of literacy, and the promotion of moral education —areas in which the Malaysian community already has an impressive record. In addition to contributing to the progress of society, such activities will go far in winning the admiration and respect of the enlightened in government circles and, beyond that, in drawing the attention of leaders of thought throughout the region to the Teachings of the Faith.

10.5 The Bahá'í community of Myanmar, which traces its roots back to the time of Bahá'u'lláh, has in recent years been able to pay increasing attention to the expansion of the Faith. The results have been encouraging indeed. The large body of believers in Myanmar, faithful to the Covenant and with hearts filled with love for Bahá'u'lláh, who stand ready to serve His Faith, can be helped by the institute program now being established there to enter the field of teaching with confidence. The effects such an endeavor will have, in a land so receptive to the Divine Message, are incalculable.

The friends in Thailand may draw courage from the success of their efforts to help reestablish the Bahá'í community of Cambodia and resolve to turn with the same vigor and determination to the tasks of expansion and consolidation in their homeland. There they have proved themselves capable of teaching among many strata of society and of bringing into their ranks people of diverse cultural and educational backgrounds. Setting aside all hesitation, and with unity of thought and purpose, let them dedicate the coming four years to the unflagging pursuit of a clearly defined course of action traced for them by their institutions. 10.6

In Vietnam, Laos and Cambodia, where possibilities for growth exist in varying degrees, the sorely tried, steadfast and devoted friends need to demonstrate to the authorities and leaders of their countries that Bahá'ís, obedient and loyal to their governments, desire but the prosperity of their nations and the upliftment of their peoples. Through the spiritual enrichment of families in Vietnam, through the program of deepening in small groups now initiated in Laos, and through systematic plans for expansion and consolidation and for social and economic development in Cambodia, where the friends enjoy greater freedom, each of these communities can achieve substantial progress within the parameters defined for them by prevailing social and political conditions. 10.7

The manner in which the Bahá'í community of Mongolia, so young and so full of vitality, has taken its affairs in hand is exhilarating. In the span of seven years, the friends have ranged methodically across that vast land and have established the Faith on solid and enduring foundations. At the national level, they are becoming known for their high ideals, particularly as champions of the rights of children. At the same time, their Bahá'í classes, open to children from Bahá'í and non-Bahá'í families alike, are being received with great enthusiasm, presenting them with extensive teaching opportunities. There is a spirit in the Mongolian people which must needs manifest itself in the efflorescence of a numerically strong, vibrant community. 10.8

The Bahá'í community of Singapore is energetic and dedicated. Its past experience demonstrates that focused attention on expansion invariably brings good results. What is required at this stage of the community's development is an accelerating 10.9

increase in the number of individual enrollments. Such an influx of new souls will continually strengthen the community which, although comparatively small, has demonstrated its ability to play an important role in the affairs of the Faith in the region.

10.10 Dear Friends, any attempt to present, no matter how briefly, an overview of the potentialities of your region must necessarily take into account the preponderating influence that the Chinese people are to exert on the destiny of humankind. To them, 'Abdu'l-Bahá has referred as "truth-seeking" and "prompted with ideal motives." From among them, He declared, can be raised "such divine personages that each one of them may become the bright candle of the world of humanity." The progress of the Faith in Hong Kong, Macau and Taiwan, and the labors of the Chinese believers resident in other parts of the region, are early indications of that which is yet to come. We turn our expectant eyes towards the Chinese people, confident in their ability to become illumined with the light of Bahá'u'lláh's Revelation and to apply His Teachings, with characteristic diligence, to the advancement of spiritual and material civilization. As larger and larger numbers become imbued with heavenly qualities, and as they make sincere exertions for the progress of their people, they shall, God willing, win the trust of fair-minded leaders and be able to broaden the scope of their endeavors in a land that 'Abdu'l-Bahá has designated "the country of the future."

10.11 We shall pray ardently at the Sacred Threshold that the blessings of Bahá'u'lláh may sustain you and guide you in your noble services to His Cause.

THE UNIVERSAL HOUSE OF JUSTICE

11

Riḍván 1996

To the Followers of Bahá'u'lláh in the Andaman and Nicobar
Islands, Bangladesh, India, Nepal, and Sri Lanka

Dearly loved Friends,

With bright hopes and high expectations, we turn our 11.1
thoughts towards you, who, serving in a region at the forefront
of large-scale expansion, find yourselves poised to make a
significant advance in the process of entry by troops, the central
aim of the Four Year Plan. Your region, which claims a substantial percentage of the world's people, has a Bahá'í population
that already exceeds by far that of any other area of the globe.

By virtue of its immense natural and human resources, its 11.2
magnificent history and the rich cultural diversity of its inhabitants, India plays a prominent role in the shaping of human
affairs. Throughout the history of the Faith, it has been the
recipient of countless blessings and the arena of unparalleled
triumphs. Mentioned by the Báb in the first of His Writings,
India is eternally honored to have had one of its native sons
numbered among the Letters of the Living, privileged to behold
the first rays of the Dawn of a New Day. Bahá'u'lláh Himself
selected and dispatched emissaries to propagate His Faith in
India, and, under the direction of 'Abdu'l-Bahá and Shoghi
Effendi, streams of teachers from both Iran and the West continued to flow to that land to help the believers carry forward
the standard of Divine guidance.

In response to the bountiful favors conferred upon them 11.3
over the decades, the friends in India have made sacrificial efforts
for the progress of the Cause of Bahá'u'lláh and have achieved
splendid victories in His Name. They first demonstrated their
ability to initiate entry by troops as early as the closing years of
the Ten Year Crusade when they enlisted thousands of receptive
souls into the ranks of His followers. The sudden influx of
new adherents to the Cause from all castes and creeds—clear

73

evidence of the receptivity of that great nation—transformed a small body of believers into a vibrant and broadly based community which gradually learned to shoulder immense and inescapable responsibilities. Its valiant members, relying on the unfailing grace of Bahá'u'lláh, surmounted the obstacles before them, persevered, and sustained their efforts until India came to occupy a privileged place in the eyes of the Bahá'ís of the world.

11.4   The Indian Bahá'í community has gone from strength to strength. It has established the institutions of the Faith throughout the length and breadth of that vast country, including suitable agencies to administer the affairs of the Cause in each state; has undertaken countless projects and campaigns of expansion and consolidation; has produced and disseminated literature in a wide array of languages; has pursued numerous projects of social and economic development, especially in the field of education; and, aided by the power of attraction of its House of Worship, has proclaimed the Faith to many millions of people. From every standpoint—its administrative structure, its relations with the government, its experience in large-scale expansion, and the devotion of the active supporters of its programs and projects—the Indian community stands in an enviable position at the beginning of this, the Four Year Plan.

11.5   The Bahá'í community of Bangladesh, flourishing in the midst of a Muslim society, is a source of joy to the entire Bahá'í world. In recent years and with astonishing rapidity, that community began to achieve extraordinary success in the teaching field, and throughout the Three Year Plan it has sustained consistently large-scale expansion. Its institutions have demonstrated their capacity to mobilize the human resources at their disposal, and those who have responded to the call for action have sacrificially and with the utmost devotion spread the Divine Teachings among the Muslim, Hindu and tribal populations of that country. The purity of their motives and the sincerity of their efforts to address the needs of society have won them recognition from government officials in the highest circles. Their exertions to promote love and unity among the majority Muslim and minority Hindu populations are bearing increasing fruit, a striking testimony to the potency of Bahá'u'lláh's Revelation.

11.6   In the Himalayan Kingdom of Nepal, the believers have, through the integrity of their character and the excellence of their conduct, overcome in recent years restrictions on the expansion of the Cause. They are now held in high regard and are successfully engaged in presenting the Faith to the people as a unifying force which can contribute to the progress of the nation. As they grow in strength, they can begin to look beyond their own borders and assist in the propagation of the Faith in those areas to which they have such easy access.

In the Indian Ocean, the Bahá'í community of Sri Lanka, a 11.7
nation with a predominantly Buddhist population, is addressing diligently the challenges of growth. In spite of a number of set-backs in the past, the friends have persevered and are using the power of their hard-won unity to respond to the needs of that sorely tried country, whose suffering people thirst for the vivifying waters of Bahá'u'lláh's Revelation. Farther to the east, the Bahá'í community of the Andaman and Nicobar Islands has steadily grown over the years and is blessed with sincere and devoted believers, whose efforts won them the distinction of having their own National Spiritual Assembly.

Dear Friends, the receptivity of your peoples and the 11.8
extraordinary advances you have already made enable you to approach the challenges of entry by troops with vigor and optimism, and to give systematic attention to the tasks that must be diligently carried out to ensure accelerated growth.

Your past exploits were largely the result of the incessant 11.9
labors of a comparatively few consecrated believers who devoted their time and resources to the spread of the Cause in locality after locality. If you are to sustain rapid expansion and consolidation in the coming years, it is imperative that far greater numbers of dedicated and committed souls arise to promote these twin processes. Training courses—widespread, regular and well-organized—constitute the most effective means to mobilize believers on the scale required. Depending on the conditions of your countries, such courses will be conducted by teachers associated with national, state or regional institutes, some of which may well have several branches. Although the programs of the institutes may vary according to the character-istics of the populations they serve, their essential functions will be the same. They should seek to develop in the participants a good understanding of Bahá'u'lláh's essential Teachings and to help them acquire those skills and abilities that will enable them to serve the Faith effectively. They should also strive to imbue their hearts with a deep love for Bahá'u'lláh—a love from

which stems a desire to submit oneself to His Will, to obey His laws, to heed His exhortations and to promote His Faith.

11.10   While all the participants in these courses will naturally be directed to the field of teaching, a sufficient number will also have to acquire the ability to assist with the development of local communities. In a region of the world where villages constitute a major component of every nation, a concerted effort must be made to establish in them the patterns of Bahá'í community life on a firm basis. This can only be achieved through perseverance and constancy in working with the local communities. The friends in each locality must be helped to raise their awareness of the efficacy of the Teachings they have accepted and to broaden their vision of the tasks and opportunities before them. The Local Spiritual Assembly must be helped to take up the challenges of community development and of expansion.

11.11   In this respect, we call upon you to give special attention to the advancement of women. In almost all of your region, women have traditionally played a secondary role in the life of society, a condition which is still reflected in many Bahá'í communities. Effective measures have to be adopted to help women take their rightful place in the teaching and administrative fields. By teaching entire families, you can ensure that increasing numbers of women enter the Faith, thereby improving the balance in the composition of your communities and beginning in each family, from the moment of acceptance, a process through which the fundamental principle of the equality between men and women can be realized.

11.12   Of course, your successes in the teaching field and in the development of local communities will only yield lasting results if you ensure the proper education of children and youth. Youth will undoubtedly be the most enthusiastic supporters of the programs of your institutes. They are eager to make a significant contribution to the progress of their communities and have shown, time and again, their capacity to respond to the call to service. They can be trained to help shoulder the manifold responsibilities demanded by rapid expansion and consolidation. But it is especially important for large numbers of them to become capable teachers of Bahá'í children's classes. As you are well aware, without the education of children it is impossible to maintain victories from one generation to the next.

All these tasks will require your concentrated attention. 11.13
It is important, too, that you maintain the momentum which
the activities of social and economic development have gained,
especially in India. Within their own sphere of competence,
the specialized institutes, the schools and other projects are
each engaged in work critical to the development of human
resources. We hope that those who benefit from such programs
will generously offer their talents to the institutions of the Faith
in furthering the interests of the Four Year Plan.

As you respond to the requirements of the plans soon to 11.14
be formulated by your institutions, you must ever bear in mind
that you will contribute to the central aim of the Four Year Plan
only if you teach persistently, prayerfully, lovingly and wisely.
You should endeavor to bring into your ranks individuals from
every stratum of society as you vigorously advance in the process of entry by troops. Receptive souls should be sought among
the affluent and the indigent, in the various circles of urban
society and in schools and universities, in centers of industry
and commerce and in the vast rural areas of your countries.
You should also remember that your exertions are not to be
limited to your own home fronts, but that from among you
must continue to arise an increasing number of souls to serve as
pioneers and traveling teachers in the international field.

In the coming years, enormous spiritual forces will be 11.15
acting upon your peoples. You should be confident that your
exertions will have a powerful effect on the course of their
destinies. Let the words of the Guardian written during the first
of the systematic plans to be launched in your region guide your
endeavors: "You should at all times fix your gaze on the promise of Bahá'u'lláh, put your whole trust in His creative Word,
recall the past and manifold evidences of His all-encompassing
and resistless power and arise to become worthy and exemplary
recipients of His all-sustaining grace and blessings."

May the confirmations of the Blessed Beauty be ceaselessly 11.16
showered upon you, and His All-Powerful Spirit inspire and
sustain you throughout the collective enterprise on which you
now embark.

THE UNIVERSAL HOUSE OF JUSTICE

12

Riḍván 1996

To the Followers of Bahá'u'lláh in Western and Central Asia

Dearly loved Friends,

As a turbulent yet luminous century draws to a close, the Bahá'í community is embarking on another campaign in the progressive unfoldment of the Divine Plan. The global enterprises thus far executed by the consecrated adherents of His Cause have systematically spread the light of Bahá'u'lláh's Revelation to every corner of the earth and have firmly established the institutions of His Administrative Order. The Four Year Plan, whose primary aim is to effect a significant advance in the process of entry by troops, is being launched at a time when the Cause of God has emerged from obscurity, when its contributions to society are being increasingly acknowledged, and when humanity's prolonged and continuous suffering has created an atmosphere of search for spiritual values and has raised the level of receptivity to the Cause.

12.1

We call upon our much-loved coworkers in the western and central parts of the Asiatic continent, the home of the oldest and most venerable Bahá'í communities, to rally round their divinely ordained institutions and to arise during these years to demonstrate once again the devotion, valor and determination which have already conferred matchless distinction upon them. You have the honor of serving the Faith in a region above whose horizon the dawn of the Great Day of the Lord appeared, in whose bosom the infant Cause of God was nurtured, on whose soil so much sacred blood was shed, on whose western shores the Qiblih of the people of Bahá is established, within whose embrace the first Mashriqu'l-Adhkár was raised, and from which hosts of devoted and committed Bahá'ís have, in the past decades, set out to bear the banner of the Faith to every part of the globe.

12.2

12.3   Our thoughts turn first to the community of Bahá'u'lláh's lovers in the land where His Faith was born. Although they are still denied the freedom to resume direct participation in the series of campaigns by which the Cause is steadily advancing throughout the world, their achievements constitute irrefutable proof of the creative power of the daily sacrifices they are making for the vindication of the Faith. What is becoming apparent, as this new global Plan opens, is that the build-up of spiritual strength within the Iranian Bahá'í community—purified by suffering and steeled by adversity—represents a reservoir of energy that will, in God's good time, bring incalculable benefits to the Cause. "Say: The springs that sustain the life of these birds are not of this world. Their source is far above the reach and ken of human apprehension."

12.4   In the lands to the south and west of Iran, Bahá'ís live under restrictions which prevent them from teaching the Cause to their fellow-countrymen. Yet, by the outstanding contributions they have made to the progress of the Faith in other parts of the world, they have proved that their enthusiasm to spread the Divine Message cannot be dampened. It has been particularly heartening to witness the eagerness and rapidity with which, as soon as the barriers to teaching in the republics of Central Asia and the Caucasus were removed, they rushed to the aid of the small bands of believers who had persevered there for so many decades and helped them to build the vibrant communities now flourishing in these regions today. No doubt they will continue to lend valuable assistance to the communities in Central Asia and the Caucasus during the Four Year Plan.

12.5   In these republics, through the combined efforts of native and visiting teachers, extraordinary advances can be expected. A pattern for the rapid growth of the Cause has already been established in the region: locality after locality has been opened to the Faith and, because of the high receptivity of the people, the number of believers in each place has quickly risen, resulting in the election of a Spiritual Assembly to guide the affairs of the nascent community. Integral to this pattern, almost from the very outset, has been the holding of regular institute courses, which have assisted the friends in becoming strong promoters of the Cause. If the expansion and consolidation activities are vigorously pursued according to this same pattern in the coming years, the growth of the Faith will accelerate, greatly increasing the number of believers and centers.

To effect such accelerated growth, the friends in these 12.6
countries must become so deepened in their understanding of
the Faith as to take up, on their own initiative, the torch of
guidance that will enlighten the multitudes. They should not
be content with small communities, nor allow the tasks of
administering their own community affairs to divert them from
the essential purpose of bringing new members into their ranks.
Each community, from the earliest phases of its development,
should be fired by a vision of the glory of the Cause and imbued
with the zeal to achieve rapid and sustained expansion both in
the locality itself and in the nearby towns and villages.

In Pakistan, where a well-grounded community traces its 12.7
roots back some hundred years, the friends must make a mighty
effort to increase their numbers significantly among people of
every walk of life. The will and determination needed to sustain
large-scale expansion and consolidation can be created through
a consistent and widespread institute program aimed at exposing growing contingents of believers to the Creative Word, thus
enhancing their spiritual capacities to diffuse the light of the
Faith and to further the development of its institutions. Such a
rapid process of growth requires that more and more women be
enabled to move to the forefront of Bahá'í activity, in both the
teaching and administrative fields. While rising to the challenge
of entry by troops in their homeland, the friends in Pakistan
need also to pay special attention to their long-suffering Afghan
neighbors, who cry out for the Healing Message of Bahá'u'lláh,
the one true balm for their afflictions.

In all your countries, you must continue to give the highest 12.8
priority to the education of children. Having seen the effects
of the Teachings of Bahá'u'lláh on generation after generation,
you well understand the value of Bahá'í education and of a
proper spiritual upbringing. In those areas where activities
are restricted, you are nevertheless able to teach the children
of your own communities and help them to grow to become
pillars of strength. In other areas, you have the possibility, nay
the obligation, to open your classes to children of non-Bahá'í
families and to become known as the educators of the coming
generations of your peoples.

Dear Friends, the time is short, and weighty responsibilities 12.9
have been placed on the shoulders of each and every Bahá'í. In
His Most Holy Book, the Kitáb-i-Aqdas, the Blessed Beauty
states:

12.10   Verily, We behold you from Our realm of glory, and will aid whosoever will arise for the triumph of Our Cause with the hosts of the Concourse on high and a company of Our favored angels.

12.11   Be confident that your dedicated services will, like a magnet, attract the promised confirmations and that your hearts will be gladdened as you witness the successive triumphs of the Cause you hold so dear. We shall remember all of you in our prayers in the Holy Shrines and shall beseech Bahá'u'lláh to guide and assist you, as you face the many challenges of these spiritually potent closing years of the century.

THE UNIVERSAL HOUSE OF JUSTICE

13

Riḍván 1997

To the Bahá'ís of the World

Dearly loved Friends,

We acclaim with grateful hearts the eager response on all continents to the Four Year Plan launched last Riḍván.

13.1

Consultations of the Continental Counsellors and National Spiritual Assemblies started an extensive planning process, also involving Auxiliary Board members and Local Spiritual Assemblies. Through such a process the national and regional character of the derivative plans took shape. But this world-encompassing exercise did more than yield distinctive schemes for the different countries; it also boosted the collaborative relationship of the two arms of the Administrative Order, a most welcome portent of the victories yet to come.

13.2

A sign of the immediate impact of the Plan was the speed with which steps were taken to establish nearly two hundred training institutes during the last twelve months. Many of these have gone far beyond the point of designing their organization; they are actually in operation and have offered their first courses. Moreover, in the movement of homefront and international pioneers and traveling teachers; in the increased attention given by individuals to deputizing teachers; in the preparations made to ensure the formation of Local Spiritual Assemblies only on the first day of Riḍván; in the increasing endeavors to hold regular devotional meetings; in the widening efforts to make use of the arts in the teaching work and community activities—in all these respects could be discerned the friends' keen awareness of the importance of concentrating on the requirements of the major aim of the Plan, which is to effect a significant advance in the process of entry by troops.

13.3

Nor can we neglect to recognize other developments during the past year which confirmed the high merit of the manifold efforts being exerted by our world community and the results

13.4

83

being achieved. Among these, to mention a few, were: the acquisition of the apartment at 4 Avenue de Camoëns in Paris where the beloved Master, 'Abdu'l-Bahá, resided during His historic visit to the city; the special session on 14 August of the Federal Chamber of Deputies in Brazil to mark the 75th anniversary of the introduction of the Bahá'í Faith into that country—a unique, official occasion at which Amatu'l-Bahá Rúḥíyyih Khánum was present as the honored guest; the launching last July of the Bahá'í International Community's site on the World Wide Web, entitled "The Bahá'í World," which to date has received from more than 90 countries and territories over 50,000 visits, averaging some 200 per day.

13.5   Hardly outpaced by such accomplishments, the construction projects on Mount Carmel maintained a dazzling momentum highlighted by the completion of the marble colonnade of the Centre for the Study of the Texts, by the rise of the International Teaching Centre building towards its seventh level, and by the ongoing emergence of the far-stretching features of the Terraces of the Shrine of the Báb. In this connection must be mentioned the partial lowering of the section of the public road over which the line of terraces will pass, and the acquisition and subsequent demolition of the building at the foot of the mountain which stood as the last obstruction that had to be overcome to make possible the completion of the lower terraces through which the glorious pathway rises up towards the sacred Edifice and beyond it to the crest of the Hill of God.

13.6   Also of acute relevance to the progress thus described was the maintenance of a level of contributions to the Arc Projects Fund which fulfilled the goal for the last year. Clearly, the financial demands in this regard are being met with incessant heroism by rich and poor alike, and must be sustained over the remaining years. At the same time, however, a parallel effort, equally strenuous and sustained, should be simultaneously exerted by the Assemblies and friends throughout the world to fill the critical needs of the Bahá'í International Fund.

13.7   Such an auspicious beginning to the Four Year Plan as has been experienced cannot but inspire confidence in the hearts of the members of our worldwide community that they are fully equipped to execute its requirements as outlined in the messages that launched it, and as elaborated in the plans adopted by their respective Assemblies. A further and especially appreciated encouragement as we enter this second year is that circumstances have made it feasible for the reestablishment this Riḍván of the National Spiritual Assembly of Rwanda. This victory over crisis will bring to 175 the number of National Spiritual Assemblies that will be eligible to participate in the Eighth International Bahá'í Convention to be held next Riḍván at the Bahá'í World Centre. How dearly we hope that by then, at the very midpoint of the Plan, the Bahá'í world will have made a major leap forward in the multiplication of its human resources, the maturation of its Spiritual Assemblies, and the evolution of its local communities!

The opportunity offered by the brief span of time before   13.8
the century ends is precious beyond all telling. Only a united and sustained effort by the friends everywhere to advance the process of entry by troops can befit such a historic moment. Responsibilities urgent and inescapable press upon every institution, every member of a community striving towards its God-promised destiny. As there is only a short period in which to achieve a great deal, no time must be spared, no opportunity lost. Rest assured, dear friends, that the hosts of the Abhá Kingdom stand ready to rush to the support of anyone who will arise to offer his or her acts of service to the unfolding, spiritual drama of these momentous days.

THE UNIVERSAL HOUSE OF JUSTICE

14

30 May 1997

To National Spiritual Assemblies

Dear Bahá'í Friends,

The expansion of the Bahá'í community and the growing 14.1
complexity of the issues which are facing National Spiritual
Assemblies in certain countries have brought the Cause to a
new stage in its development. They have caused us in recent
years to examine various aspects of the balance between
centralization and decentralization. In a few countries we have
authorized the National Spiritual Assemblies to establish State
Bahá'í Councils or Regional Teaching and Administrative
Committees. From the experience gained in the operation of
these bodies, and from detailed examination of the principles
set forth by Shoghi Effendi, we have reached the conclusion
that the time has arrived for us to formalize a new element of
Bahá'í administration, between the local and national levels,
comprising institutions of a special kind, to be designated as
"Regional Bahá'í Councils."

Regional Bahá'í Councils will be brought into being only 14.2
with our permission and only in countries where conditions
make this step necessary. Nevertheless, we find it desirable to
inform all National Spiritual Assemblies of the nature of this
historic development, and to make clear its place in the evolution of national and local Bahá'í institutions.

The institutions of the Administrative Order of Bahá'u'lláh, 14.3
rooted in the provisions of His Revelation, have emerged
gradually and organically, as the Bahá'í community has grown
through the power of the divine impulse imparted to humankind
in this age. The characteristics and functions of each of these
institutions have evolved, and are still evolving, as are the relationships between them. The writings of the beloved Guardian
expound the fundamental elements of this mighty System and
make it clear that the Administrative Order, although different

in many ways from the World Order which it is the destiny of the Bahá'í Revelation to call into being, is both the "nucleus" and "pattern" of that World Order. Thus, the evolution of the institutions of the Administrative Order, while following many variants to meet changing conditions in different times and places, should strictly follow the essential principles of Bahá'í administration which have been laid down in the Sacred Text and in the interpretations provided by 'Abdu'l-Bahá and the Guardian.

14.4 One of the subtle qualities of the Bahá'í Administrative Order is the balance between centralization and decentralization. This balance must be correctly maintained, but different factors enter into the equation, depending upon the institutions involved. For example, the relationship between a National or Local Spiritual Assembly and its committees is of a different nature from that between National and Local Spiritual Assemblies. The former is a relationship between a central administrative body and "its assisting organs of executive and legislative action,"† while the latter is a relationship between national and local levels of the House of Justice, each of which is a divinely ordained institution with clearly prescribed jurisdiction, duties and prerogatives.

14.5 Regional Bahá'í Councils partake of some, but not all, characteristics of Spiritual Assemblies, and thus provide a means of carrying forward the teaching work and administering related affairs of a rapidly growing Bahá'í community in a number of situations. Without such an institution, the development of a national committee structure required to cover the needs in some countries would run the danger of over-complexity through adding a further layer of committees under the regional committees, or the danger of excessive decentralization through conferring too much autonomy on committees which are characterized by the Guardian as "bodies that should be regarded in no other light than that of expert advisers and executive assistants."

14.6 The distinguishing effects of the establishment of Regional Bahá'í Councils are the following:

14.7 ▪ It provides for a level of autonomous decision making on both teaching and administrative matters, as distinct from

---

† Letter of 18 October 1927 to the National Spiritual Assembly of the Bahá'ís of the United States and Canada.

merely executive action, below the National Assembly and above the Local Assemblies.

- It involves the members of Local Spiritual Assemblies of the area in the choice of the members of the Council, thus reinforcing the bond between it and the local believers while, at the same time, bringing into public service capable believers who are known to the friends in their own region. 14.8

- It establishes direct consultative relationships between the Continental Counsellors and the Regional Bahá'í Councils. 14.9

- It offers the possibility of forming a Regional Bahá'í Council in an ethnically distinct region which covers parts of two or more countries. In such a situation the Council is designated to work directly under one of the National Assemblies involved, providing copies of its reports and minutes to the other National Assembly. 14.10

- The greater degree of decentralization involved in the devolution of authority upon Regional Bahá'í Councils requires a corresponding increase in the capacity of the National Spiritual Assembly itself to keep fully informed of what is proceeding in all parts of the territory over which it has ultimate jurisdiction. 14.11

For those National Spiritual Assemblies which have already established Regional Bahá'í Councils or Regional Teaching and Administrative Committees, we enclose a document which outlines the various policies governing the formation and functioning of Regional Bahá'í Councils. For the sake of simplicity, we have used the designation "Regional Bahá'í Councils" throughout, but the actual name used will, as heretofore, vary from country to country, including such names as "State Bahá'í Councils," "Provincial Bahá'í Councils" or, when referring to an individual Council, "The Bahá'í Council for . . . ," etc. To avoid the confusion of thought which seems to have been caused by referring to "Regional Teaching and Administrative Committees," we have decided to cease using this designation and to refer to these bodies as Bahá'í Councils formed by appointment rather than election. We shall be writing separately to these National Spiritual Assemblies, indicating what modifications, if any, they should now make to the existing structures. 14.12

14.13   It is our ardent prayer at the Sacred Threshold, that the establishment of Regional Bahá'í Councils will greatly enhance the ability of the Administrative Order to deal with the complex situations with which it is confronted in a number of countries at the present time, and thus carry forward, with increased vigor, the propagation of the Cause of God.

THE UNIVERSAL HOUSE OF JUSTICE

*The establishment of Regional Bahá'í Councils in
certain countries, their characteristics and functions*

1. The Formation of Regional Bahá'í Councils:

   1.1 Authority for the formation of Regional Bahá'í   14.14
   Councils: The formation of Regional Bahá'í Councils
   in any country, and the choice of the regions to be
   assigned to them are dependent upon the approval of
   the Universal House of Justice in each case.

   1.2 Conditions indicating a need for the formation of   14.15
   Regional Bahá'í Councils: Regional Bahá'í Councils
   will be formed only in certain specific situations where
   this kind of decentralization is judged by the Universal
   House of Justice to be appropriate.

2. The Characteristic Features of Regional Bahá'í Councils:

   2.1 Mode of Establishment and Membership: 14.16

       2.1.1 Regional Bahá'í Councils are not necessarily
   established universally throughout a country,
   but rather in those regions where the condition
   and size of the Bahá'í community indicate that
   such a development would be beneficial. In
   such cases, all other parts of the country remain
   under the well-established pattern of national
   committees, including a national teaching committee and its regional teaching committees.

       2.1.2 The number of members of a Regional Bahá'í
   Council is nine or, in certain cases, seven or
   even five, depending upon the decision of the
   National Spiritual Assembly in each case.

       2.1.3 In accordance with local requirements and
   the condition of the Bahá'í community, the
   Universal House of Justice will decide which
   Regional Bahá'í Councils are to be formed by
   election and which by appointment.

       2.1.4 It is within the discretion of the National
   Spiritual Assembly to decide, case by case,
   whether its members may also serve on

Regional Bahá'í Councils. In general the preference is for members of National Assemblies not to serve on Councils, whether these be elected or appointed bodies.

14.17   2.2   Regional Bahá'í Councils formed by election:

2.2.1   The members of an elected Regional Bahá'í Council, who shall be nine in number, are elected from among all the adult believers in the region by the members of the Local Spiritual Assemblies in that region every year on 23 May, the anniversary of the Declaration of the Báb according to the Gregorian calendar, or on a weekend immediately before or after that date.†

2.2.2   Owing to the large number of voters involved and the brief interval between the National Convention and the elections of the Regional Bahá'í Councils, these elections are to be conducted primarily by mail, through methods to be decided by the National Spiritual Assembly. The voting is to be by secret ballot. The members of the Local Spiritual Assemblies may send in their ballots individually or they may be collected by the Secretary of the Local Spiritual Assembly and mailed together.

2.2.3   If feasible and desirable, an electoral meeting, or several electoral meetings, may be held in the region for those voters able to attend, in order to provide an occasion for members of Local Spiritual Assemblies in the region to consult about the progress of the Cause. Other believers may attend, but would not take part in the voting.

---

† A letter dated 12 March 2000 to all National Spiritual Assemblies written on behalf of the Universal House of Justice explained: "In view of the experience gained over a period of several years, the House of Justice has recognized that it would be more practical to set a new date for the formation of these institutions. Henceforth, then, the election or appointment of Regional Councils will take effect every year on 26 November, the Day of the Covenant. The formation processes will, of course, have to be set in motion in sufficient time to be concluded on this date."

2.2.4 If there is a tie vote, the tie is to be broken by lot, in view of the impracticability of holding a revote in such a situation.

2.2.5 Any vacancy on a Regional Bahá'í Council should be filled by the person who had the next highest number of votes on the ballot in the preceding election.

2.2.6 Auxiliary Board members are not eligible for service on a Regional Bahá'í Council.

2.2.7 The result of the election is to be confirmed by the National Spiritual Assembly.

2.3 Regional Bahá'í Councils formed by appointment: 14.18

2.3.1 It is left to the National Spiritual Assembly to decide whether the number of members is to be five, seven or nine.

2.3.2 Balloting takes place among members of Local Spiritual Assemblies in the region, similarly to that for the election of a Regional Bahá'í Council, but the outcome of the voting constitutes a confidential list of nominations for the National Spiritual Assembly, which appoints the members of the Council from among these nominees and others, including persons proposed by the members of the Auxiliary Boards within whose areas of responsibility the region lies.

3. The Functions of Regional Bahá'í Councils:

The functions of a Regional Bahá'í Council and the degree 14.19 of authority conferred upon it are within the discretion of a National Spiritual Assembly. However, they should not be limited to those of a national or regional committee for, in such a case, there would be no justification for bringing into being a Regional Bahá'í Council rather than appointing a national or regional committee. The functions and responsibilities generally envisaged for a Regional Bahá'í Council are as follows:

3.1 To carry out the policies of the National Spiritual 14.20 Assembly and to supervise, on behalf of the National Assembly, the smooth and efficient execution of the plans and projects for its region.

14.21   3.2 To keep the National Spiritual Assembly regularly informed of the Council's activities and of the conditions of the Faith throughout the region. Regional Bahá'í Councils are allowed to develop their own strategies and programs, and to carry out their day-to-day work without having to obtain further approval from the National Spiritual Assembly. However, through their frequent reports and the minutes of their meetings, the National Assembly is kept informed of their activities and maintains its overall supervision of the affairs of the Cause in all parts of the country.

14.22   3.3 To take initiative in the promotion of the Faith in the region and to carry out its decisions within the range of authority vested in it by the National Assembly. The National Assembly allows the Council a wide latitude for autonomous action, intervening in its work only in matters which the Assembly regards as being of major importance. The main task of a Regional Bahá'í Council is to devise and execute expansion and consolidation plans in close collaboration with the Local Spiritual Assemblies and the believers within its area of jurisdiction. Its goal is to create strong Local Spiritual Assemblies which will be the focal centers of Bahá'í activity, will exercise their vitally important role in the development of the Faith and will demonstrate their ability to regulate the affairs of their local communities.

14.23   3.4 To deal with both teaching and administrative matters within the region including the appointment of committees for issues within its terms of reference, such as external affairs and the translation, publication and distribution of Bahá'í literature.

3.4.1   In the area of teaching, a Regional Bahá'í Council may be given authority by the National Assembly to appoint, direct and supervise the work of a number of area or district teaching committees. In those cases where a Regional Bahá'í Council has to carry out a wide range of functions, it may also be authorized by the National Spiritual Assembly to appoint a regional teaching committee to be responsible to it for the teaching work in the region as a whole and for the direction and supervision of the area or district teaching committees.

3.4.2 A Regional Bahá'í Council may be asked by the National Spiritual Assembly to arrange and supervise the unit elections for delegates to the national convention.

3.4.3 The working relationship between the Local Spiritual Assemblies and the National Spiritual Assembly in an area where there is a Regional Bahá'í Council will depend upon the range of functions and responsibilities conferred by the National Assembly upon the Council. In any case the authority to deprive a believer of his or her administrative rights, or to restore them, remains with the National Assembly. The right of direct access to the National Assembly by a Local Spiritual Assembly is preserved.

3.5 To be responsible, under the general guidelines and policies established by the National Spiritual Assembly, for conducting, on behalf of the National Assembly, the external affairs of the Faith at the level of the region, representing the Bahá'ís of the region in relation to the civil authorities of that region. 14.24

3.6 To take part, under the guidance of the National Spiritual Assembly and in consultation with the Counsellors or their deputies, in the formulation of a plan for its region as part of the national plan within the framework of each worldwide Plan. 14.25

3.7 To devise, for the approval of the National Assembly, its own expansion and consolidation programs for the achievement of the plan for its region, within the overall framework of the national plan. 14.26

3.8 To formulate an annual budget for the region, in consultation with the Counsellors or their deputies when advisable, and to submit this budget to the National Spiritual Assembly for its approval. 14.27

3.8.1 Alternatively, should the conditions indicate the advisability of such a method, the annual budgets of Regional Bahá'í Councils may be specified by the National Spiritual Assembly.

14.28   3.9 To administer the budget for the region, sending regular reports and financial statements to the National Spiritual Assembly.

14.29   3.10 A Regional Bahá'í Council can be authorized by the National Spiritual Assembly to act as its agent in operating a regional branch of the national Bahá'í fund. In this respect the Council may perform the following functions.

            3.10.1 It encourages believers within its region to contribute to various funds of the Cause, including the regional branch of the national fund, with the aim that, in due course, the entire expenditure for the region would be provided by the believers in the region.

            3.10.2 If the whole of the budgeted expenditure for a year cannot be met by contributions from the believers in the region, the Council may apply to the National Spiritual Assembly for an allocation from the national Bahá'í fund.

            3.10.3 It is also within the discretion of the Counsellors to allocate financial assistance to a Regional Bahá'í Council from the funds at their disposition.

14.30   3.11 Under normal conditions, correspondence between Regional Bahá'í Councils and the Bahá'í World Centre should be addressed to the National Spiritual Assembly, which would then convey the communication to its intended recipient.

            3.11.1 If, because of local conditions, the Universal House of Justice authorizes certain Regional Bahá'í Councils to correspond directly with it, copies of all such correspondence should be sent to the National Assembly.

            3.11.2 Copies of the *Bahá'í International News Service* and of certain circular letters may be mailed from the Bahá'í World Centre directly to all Regional Bahá'í Councils.

            3.11.3 When Regional Bahá'í Councils publish Bahá'í literature or regional newsletters, copies of such publications should be sent directly to the

Bahá'í World Centre under the same guidelines as apply to national Bahá'í publications.

3.11.4 Although, in general, Regional Bahá'í Councils can be authorized to correspond directly with the World Centre in order to share current information about the activities of their respective communities, this should not be misconstrued as a means to bypass the institution of the National Spiritual Assembly in matters requiring guidance or decision.

3.12 In most countries the legal status of Regional Bahá'í Councils would seem to be adequately covered by the National Assembly's incorporation. 14.31

3.13 Just as Counsellors have direct consultative relations with National and Local Spiritual Assemblies, so they also have direct relations with Regional Bahá'í Councils. 14.32

3.13.1 Whenever the Counsellors feel it necessary or desirable, they are free to deputize one or more Auxiliary Board members to represent them in consultations with a Regional Bahá'í Council. Also, occasional meetings should be arranged between a Regional Bahá'í Council and the Auxiliary Board members responsible for areas within its region, for the discussion of the vision and strategies for the work. A regular and free exchange of information between Auxiliary Board members on the one hand and Regional Bahá'í Councils on the other is encouraged.

4. National Committees in the New Structure:

It is advisable for a National Spiritual Assembly to have a National Teaching Committee even if Regional Bahá'í Councils are formed in every part of a country. The functions of the National Teaching Committee in a country in which Regional Bahá'í Councils have been established are as follows. 14.33

4.1 The Guardian has referred to national committees as expert advisers and executive assistants of a National Spiritual Assembly. This suggests that, rather than diminishing the role of its National Teaching Committee 14.34

when Regional Bahá'í Councils are formed, a National Spiritual Assembly would develop further the advisory and executive aspects of its responsibilities in certain respects. The capacity of the National Teaching Committee to monitor the effectiveness of the teaching work throughout the country could be enhanced. Through its knowledge of the progress of the work, it should be able to bring to the National Assembly's attention strengths and needs in any region. There are also a number of specific matters, such as the analysis of opportunities for expansion and consolidation in rapidly changing conditions, the identification of successful approaches to teaching, and the dissemination of promising teaching methods, which would benefit from the constant attention of a vibrant and competent National Teaching Committee. Issues related to teaching among minorities and specific groups who reside in more than one region of the country present another area which would benefit from a National Teaching Committee's attention.

14.35   4.2   The work of the National Teaching Committee in relation to Regional Bahá'í Councils is one of service and assistance, rather than direction and supervision as it is in relation to regional teaching committees. A parallel can be seen in the work of a national training institute, to which the National Assembly assigns the task of developing human resources: the institute assists the Councils by offering them programs for the training of the human resources needed to carry out their plans in each region. The National Teaching Committee would, similarly, offer services to the Councils in support of the teaching work.

14.36   4.3   In countries where Regional Bahá'í Councils have been introduced only for certain areas, the National Teaching Committee is expected to perform not only the functions outlined above, but also to remain responsible, both directly and through its Regional Teaching Committees, for serving those areas not under the care of a Council. In carrying out such functions there must, of course, be close collaboration between the National Teaching Committee and its

Regional Teaching Committees on the one hand, and the Regional Bahá'í Councils on the other.

4.4 In the case of all national committees, it is important to ensure that legitimate national programs do not run counter to the process of decentralization, except in special emergency situations.

14.37

15

6 January 1998

To the Friends Gathered at the Latin American
    Youth Congress in Chile

Dear Friends,

As the Cause of God advances resistlessly along the path 15.1
traced out for it by its Divine Founder, each stage of the process
opens up to a new generation of Bahá'í youth challenges unique
to the historical moment. Building on the accomplishments
of the generations before, youth must devise ways to take
advantage of the opportunities presented to them. A discourse
in consonance with the requirements of the time has to be
refined, and activities aimed at transforming society have to be
pursued with vigor.

To accomplish such tasks during the brief span of time 15.2
afforded youth requires resolve, spiritual discipline, energy, reliance on the power of divine assistance, and constant immersion
in the Word of God. These efforts, which constitute an integral
part of the growth processes of the Bahá'í community itself,
nevertheless possess characteristics distinctly their own. In
recent years, and in many parts of the world, Bahá'í Youth have
referred to their collective endeavors as a "youth movement,"
a reminder that the energy being generated will not only bring
new recruits from among their peers, but will move an entire
generation one step closer to the World Order of Bahá'u'lláh.

Over the next few days you will be contemplating the 15.3
special opportunities which the Hand of Providence has laid
before you. An essential component of any strategy you devise
is training. In all your countries, this question is being enthusiastically addressed as institutes learn to operate with increasing
effectiveness. You yourselves are participating, as students and
as teachers, in building capacity in your communities to train
thousands and thousands of believers, many of whom will
be young people. With this vision in mind, you should devise

actions, characteristic of your youth movement, in which your swelling numbers will engage. How will you teach the Cause and advance the process of entry by troops? How will you contribute to the establishment of a distinctly Bahá'í life? And how will you accelerate the transformation of Latin American society to achieve its high destiny? As you contemplate these questions, be assured that our prayers will surround you.

THE UNIVERSAL HOUSE OF JUSTICE

16

Riḍván 1998

To the Bahá'ís of the World

Dearly loved Friends,

At this halfway mark in the Four Year Plan, we affirm   16.1
with uplifted hearts that the worldwide Bahá'í community is
breaking new ground at a dynamic stage in its evolution. The
process of entry by troops, upon which its energies are focused,
is clearly advancing.

Three developments brighten our expectations. One is in   16.2
the solid results being produced wherever training institutes
are in operation. Tens of thousands of individuals have over
the last two years completed at least one institute course. The
immediate effects upon them have been a greatly strengthened
faith, a more conscious spiritual identity, and a deepened commitment to Bahá'í service. The second pertains to the notable
improvement in the conditions affecting the establishment and
renewal of Local Spiritual Assemblies. The decision to form
these institutions only on the first day of Riḍván, and to do so
principally at the initiative of the communities to which they
belong, was put into effect in 1997. While there was an immediate but not unexpected drop in the number of Local Assemblies
worldwide, the decrease was not very large; in fact, increases
were recorded in some countries. This outcome indicates that
the process of maturation of these divinely ordained institutions
is on course. The third is that a new confidence in teaching
is stirring the friends, yielding impressive results in various
regions. The potential for a steady and ever-expanding influx
of new believers has always been great, and we are able to say
with assurance that the capacity to actualize it is methodically
being developed more than ever before with the prosecution of
the current Plan.

Further to these signs of progress, we are gratified by the   16.3
marvelous speed with which the construction projects on Mount

Carmel proceeded to fulfill the schedule which had been set for the year just ended. Immediately ahead are the establishment in May of three new National Spiritual Assemblies—Sabah, Sarawak, and Slovakia—and the reestablishment of the National Spiritual Assembly in Liberia, raising to 179 the pillars of the Universal House of Justice. In contemplating the divine favors being bestowed on our community, we acknowledge with deep gratitude the constancy of the acts of service being performed by the individual Hands of the Cause of God, by the International Teaching Centre, and by the Counsellors and their auxiliaries on all continents. The increasing strength of National Spiritual Assemblies also bolsters our certitude in the imminence of resounding victories.

16.4 Against this salutary picture of the community's prospects is the confused background of a planet at odds with itself. And yet, amid the widespread desolation of the human spirit, it is apparent that at some level of consciousness there is among the peoples of the world a growing sense of an irresistible movement towards global unity and peace. This sense is being aroused as the physical barriers between peoples are being virtually eliminated by breathtaking advances in science and technology. Nevertheless, a mixed catalogue of world-shaking tribulations and world-shaping developments keeps humanity concurrently dazed and dazzled. The storms and stresses battering the social fabric are incomprehensible to all except the relatively few of the planet's inhabitants who recognize God's purpose for this Day.

16.5 Our fellow human beings everywhere are insensibly subjected at one and the same time to the conflicting emotions incited by the continuous operation of simultaneous processes of "rise and of fall, of integration and of disintegration, of order and chaos." These Shoghi Effendi identified as aspects of the Major Plan and Minor Plan of God, the two known ways in which His purpose for humankind is going forward. The Major Plan is associated with turbulence and calamity and proceeds with an apparent, random disorderliness, but is, in fact, inexorably driving humanity towards unity and maturity. Its agency for the most part is the people who are ignorant of its course and even antagonistic towards its aim. As Shoghi Effendi has pointed out, God's Major Plan uses "both the mighty and the lowly as pawns in His world-shaping game, for the fulfillment of His immediate purpose and the eventual establishment of His Kingdom on earth." The acceleration of the processes it generates is lending impetus to developments which, with all the initial pain and heartache attributable to them, we Bahá'ís see as signs of the emergence of the Lesser Peace.

Unlike His Major Plan, which works mysteriously, God's Minor Plan is clearly delineated, operates according to orderly and well-known processes, and has been given to us to execute. Its ultimate goal is the Most Great Peace. The four-year-long campaign, at the mid-point of which we have arrived, constitutes the current stage in the Minor Plan. It is to the achievement of its purpose that we must all devote our attention and energies. 16.6

At times it may seem that the operation of the Major Plan causes a disruption in the work of the Minor Plan, but the friends have every reason to remain undismayed. For they recognize the source of the recurrent turbulence at play in the world and, in the words of our Guardian, "acknowledge its necessity, observe confidently its mysterious processes, ardently pray for the mitigation of its severity, intelligently labor to assuage its fury, and anticipate, with undimmed vision, the consummation of the fears and the hopes it must necessarily engender." 16.7

Even a cursory survey of the global scene in recent years cannot but lead to observations fraught with special significance for a Bahá'í viewer. For one thing, amid the din of a society in turmoil can be discerned an unmistakable trend towards the Lesser Peace. An intriguing inkling is provided by the greater involvement of the United Nations, with the backing of powerful governments, in attending to long-standing and urgent world problems; another derives from the dramatic recognition by world leaders in only recent months of what the interconnectedness of all nations in the matter of trade and finance really implies—a condition which Shoghi Effendi anticipated as an essential aspect of an organically unified world. But a development of even greater moment to the Bahá'í community is that a massive number of people are searching for spiritual truth. Several recently published studies have been devoted to this phenomenon. The ideologies that dominated the larger part of this century have been exhausted; at their waning in the century's closing years, a hunger for meaning, a yearning of the soul, is on the rise. 16.8

This spiritual hunger is characterized by a restlessness, by a swelling dissatisfaction with the moral state of society; it is also evident in the upsurge of fundamentalism among various 16.9

religious sects, and in the multiplication of new movements posing as religions or aspiring to take the place of religion. Here are observations that enable one to appreciate the interaction between the two divinely propelled processes at work on the planet. The manifold opportunities thus providentially provided to present the Message of Bahá'u'lláh to searching souls create a dynamic situation for the Bahá'í teacher. The implications for the task at hand are immensely encouraging.

16.10 Our hopes, our goals, our possibilities of moving forward can all be realized through concentrating our endeavors on the major aim of the Divine Plan at its current stage—that is, to effect a significant advance in the process of entry by troops. This challenge can be met through persistent effort patiently pursued. Entry by troops is a possibility well within the grasp of our community. Unremitting faith, prayer, the promptings of the soul, Divine assistance—these are among the essentials of progress in any Bahá'í undertaking. But also of vital importance to bringing about entry by troops is a realistic approach, systematic action. There are no shortcuts. Systematization ensures consistency of lines of action based on well-conceived plans. In a general sense, it implies an orderliness of approach in all that pertains to Bahá'í service, whether in teaching or administration, in individual or collective endeavor. While allowing for individual initiative and spontaneity, it suggests the need to be clear-headed, methodical, efficient, constant, balanced and harmonious. Systematization is a necessary mode of functioning animated by the urgency to act.

16.11 Towards ensuring an orderly evolution of the community, a function of Bahá'í institutions is to organize and maintain a process of developing human resources whereby Bahá'ís, new and veteran alike, can acquire the knowledge and capacity to sustain a continuous expansion and consolidation of the community. The establishment of training institutes is critical to such effort, since they are centers through which large numbers of individuals can acquire and improve their ability to teach and administer the Faith. Their existence underscores the importance of knowledge of the Faith as a source of power for invigorating the life of the Bahá'í community and of the individuals who compose it.

16.12 The facts at hand confirm that the Four Year Plan works where a systematic approach is understood and applied. These same facts show that the institutions of the Faith, in their collaborative efforts at national, regional, and local levels, have clearly been adhering to this understanding. However, with individuals, on whom rests the ultimate success of the Plan, this understanding is less clear. For this reason, we must emphasize to our fellow-believers the importance to their individual effort of this prerequisite of success in teaching and in other undertakings.

As translated into programs and projects by national and 16.13 local institutions, the Plan, among other things, gives direction, identifies goals, stimulates effort, provides a variety of needed facilities and materials to benefit the work of teachers and administrators. This is of course necessary for the proper functioning of the community, but is of no consequence unless its individual members respond through active participation. In so responding, each individual, too, must make a conscious decision as to what he or she will do to serve the Plan, and as to how, where and when to do it. This determination enables the individual to check the progress of his actions and, if necessary, to modify the steps being taken. Becoming accustomed to such a procedure of systematic striving lends meaning and fulfillment to the life of any Bahá'í.

But beyond the necessity of responding to the call of the 16.14 institutions, the individual is charged by Bahá'u'lláh Himself with the sacred duty of teaching His Cause, described by Him as the "most meritorious of all deeds."

So long as there are souls in need of enlightenment, this 16.15 duty must surely remain the constant occupation of every believer. In its fulfillment, the individual is directly responsible to Bahá'u'lláh. "Let him not wait for any directions," Shoghi Effendi urgently advises, "or expect any special encouragement, from the elected representatives of his community, nor be deterred by any obstacles which his relatives, or fellow-citizens may be inclined to place in his path, nor mind the censure of his critics or enemies." The writings of the Central Figures and of our Guardian are replete with advice and exhortations concerning the individual's irreplaceable role in the advancement of the Cause. So it is inevitable that we should feel impelled, at this particular time in the life of humanity as a whole, to appeal directly to each member of our community to ponder the urgent situation facing us all as the helpers of the Abhá Beauty.

Our lot, dear brothers and sisters, is to be consciously 16.16 involved in a vast historic process the like of which has not ever before been experienced by any people. As a global community, we have, thus far, attained a unique and magnificent success in being representative of the full spectrum of the human race— thanks to the inestimable expenditure of life, effort and treasure willingly made by thousands of our spiritual forebears. There is no other aggregation of human beings who can claim to have raised up a system with the demonstrated capacity to unite all of God's children in one world-embracing Order. This achievement places us not only in a position of incomparable strength, but more particularly in one of inescapable responsibility. Does not every one of us therefore have a divine obligation to fulfill, a sacred duty to perform towards every other one who is not yet aware of the call of God's latest Manifestation? Time does not stop, does not wait. With every passing hour a fresh affliction strikes at a distracted humanity. Dare we linger?

16.17   In a mere two years the Four Year Plan will be concluded, just some months before the end of an unforgettable century. Looming before us, then, is a twofold date with destiny. In extolling the unprecedented potential of the twentieth century, the beloved Master averred that its traces will last forever. Seized with such a vision, the mind of the alert follower of the Blessed Beauty must undoubtedly be astir with anxious questions as to what part he or she will play in these few fleeting years, and as to whether he or she will, at the end of this seminal period, have made a mark among those enduring traces which the mind of the Master perceived. To ensure a soul-satisfying answer, one thing above all else is necessary: to act, to act now, and to continue to act.

16.18   Our heartfelt plea at the Holy Threshold on behalf of us all is that we may be divinely aided and richly confirmed in whatever we do towards meeting the urgent aim of the Divine Plan at so fate-laden a moment in human history.

THE UNIVERSAL HOUSE OF JUSTICE

17

3 May 1998

To the Conference of the Continental Counsellors

Beloved Friends,

It has been barely two years and four months since you came together here at the outset of your current term of service. In our message to your conference at that time, we described in detail not only the purpose and structure of the Four Year Plan but the form in which it would have to be pursued if it was to realize its ambitious aim. You were then given the mandate to go forth and prepare the Bahá'í world to take on the challenges that lay ahead. 17.1

The extraordinary events of the Convention we have all just witnessed bear eloquent testimony to the ardor and effectiveness of your response. All of the institutions of the Faith have most certainly played their parts in moving our beloved Cause a giant step forward in this brief period. The clarity and vigor with which the National Spiritual Assemblies are addressing the tasks of the Plan reflect that dramatic advance in maturity that the Guardian encouraged us to expect in these closing years of the century. We feel compelled, however, to pay special tribute to the selfless, inspiriting and intelligent contributions which you have made to this collective enterprise. Your work has brought honor to your institution and immense joy to our hearts. 17.2

As a result of your unceasing activity during the months immediately following the conference, the Bahá'í world had been made ready, by the time it received our Riḍván 1996 message, to enter into intensive detailed planning. And once national plans were formulated your efforts did not slacken; with equal vigor you and your auxiliaries galvanized the believers into systematic action and helped them to remain focused on the central aim of the Plan. We hope that you will convey to your Auxiliary Board members and their assistants our heartfelt gratitude. 17.3

17.4   The challenge which now faces the Bahá'í world is to take advantage of the momentum thus achieved. It has within its grasp the opportunity to multiply its human resources on a scale far beyond anything heretofore attained. Every measure must be taken to ensure that this possibility becomes a reality. Training must be offered widely, to contingents of newly enrolled and veteran believers alike. It is also imperative that the energies being generated and the skills being developed through training institute programs be channeled to serve directly the needs of the Plan. In short—without any delay—the work should move to the higher tempo that recent accomplishments make possible.

17.5   Your consultations this week need to be eminently practical. You come to them with a wealth of experience that the Bahá'í community has never before enjoyed. You are well aware of the diverse strengths of the communities you serve and of the efficacy of the methods being employed in the field. The lessons of these past two years need to be examined and correlated, and their implications for advancing the process of entry by troops must be understood. In this context, you will also have to consider the increased capacity of your own institution, the work of the Auxiliary Board members, and your interaction with them, with Spiritual Assemblies, and with the International Teaching Centre, whose concern it is to reinforce your efforts with advice, perspectives and resources.

17.6   Dear friends! You represent an army of able and highly motivated servants of the Cause throughout the world. Yours is an institution which, in one respect, has a particularly intimate relationship with the Universal House of Justice; in another, it is able to exercise an influence that penetrates the very grassroots of the community. Its nature fits it, uniquely, to serve as a river of encouragement, example and love whose waters can refresh and invigorate the spirit of every believer they touch.

17.7   We will follow your consultations this week with the heightened hope and confidence which your impressive achievements to date have awakened. For your part, be sure of our ardent prayers that Bahá'u'lláh will bless your deliberations and confirm your efforts to help bring about the massive increase in resources which the mission of our beloved Cause so urgently requires.

THE UNIVERSAL HOUSE OF JUSTICE

18

Riḍván 1999

To the Bahá'ís of the World

Dearly loved Friends,

Our hearts are aglow with hope as we survey what has been accomplished in the year preceding the fateful, final stretch toward the consummation of the Four Year Plan. From the year's momentous beginning with the Eighth International Bahá'í Convention, the Baha'í world has sustained a rising pace of activity that has significantly advanced the process of entry by troops. Our community has grown appreciably, its human resources have been richly enhanced. From projects of expansion to endeavors at consolidation, from social and economic development to external affairs, from services of the youth to expressions in the arts, from the World Centre of the Faith to remote villages and towns—in fact, from whatever angle the community is viewed—progress has been made. The prospects for the Plan are impelling. 18.1

The momentum generated at the International Convention pervaded the Counsellors' Conference that immediately followed it, further galvanizing the indefatigable participants; and it charged the proceedings of the National Conventions held in May, including those of Sabah, Sarawak, and Slovakia which met for the first time to form their National Spiritual Assemblies. That same energy infused the International Teaching Centre, which has been displaying a remarkable potency in the short time since its sixth term began on the anniversary of the Declaration of the Báb. Concentrating on refining and consolidating their organization, the Counsellor members have refrained from their usual travels during this first year, but they can be expected after this to resume their visits to various parts of the world, so as to reinforce their vitalizing influence on the successful conclusion of the Four Year Plan. 18.2

18.3   Further to these happenings in the Holy Land, the construction projects on Mount Carmel, beheld with such thrilling astonishment by the delegates to the International Convention, press onward towards their scheduled completion at the end of the century. With the opening since last Riḍván of all remaining areas of construction, the speed of work has reached a new peak. The Centre for the Study of the Texts and the Extension to the Archives Building are being readied for occupancy within a few weeks; the exterior of the International Teaching Centre building is fully clad in marble, while finishing work at all levels of its interior is proceeding. The lowering of Hatzionut Avenue, to accommodate the bridge which now connects the Terraces of the Shrine of the Báb on both sides of the road, has been completed and normal traffic restored. The unfolding magnificence of the Terraces has so captured public attention that the nineteenth terrace at the top of the mountain has already been opened to visitors on a daily schedule, evoking the enthusiastic response of a grateful populace. As part of a campaign to attract international attention to the city, the Municipality of Haifa has published a pictorial brochure on the Shrine of the Báb and the Terraces, available in five major languages besides Hebrew.

18.4   We feel compelled to mention at least two other developments at the World Centre of a wholly different order: First, the decision to raise the number of pilgrims in each group to 150 from 100—this to take effect when the revamping, now in progress, of the newly acquired building, situated across the way from the resting place of the Greatest Holy Leaf, has been completed and use can be made of its provision of a pilgrim hall and other facilities for the administration of an expanded pilgrimage program. Second is the notable headway being made, despite the inevitable slowness of the process, in the plan to translate texts from the Writings of Bahá'u'lláh with a view to publishing a new English volume of His works. Effort is being devoted to providing full versions of such major Tablets as the Súriy-i-Mulúk and the Súriy-i-Haykal, as well as complete texts of Tablets addressed to individual kings and rulers. Also scheduled for inclusion are the Súriy-i-Ra'ís, the Lawḥ-i-Ra'ís and the Lawḥ-i-Fu'ád.

18.5   The Cause of Bahá'u'lláh marches on resistlessly, quickened by the increasing application of an approach to the development and use of human resources that is systematic. The further creation of national and regional training institutes, now numbering 344, has pressed this development forward, with the result that, apart from North America and Iran where numerous courses have been given, some 70,000 individuals have already completed at least one institute course. All of this is contributing to a growing body of confirmed, active supporters of the Cause. The untold potential of this progression is illustrated in such reports as the one received from Chad, where in an area served by an institute more than 1,000 people embraced the Faith through the individual efforts of those who had received training. Understanding of the necessity for systematization in the development of human resources is everywhere taking hold.

Collateral with the demonstrated efficacy of training institutes is the pragmatic emergence of Regional Bahá'í Councils in selected countries where conditions have made the establishment of these institutions necessary and viable. Where there is close interaction between a Council and a training institute, the stage is set for a galvanic coherence of the processes effecting expansion and consolidation in a region, and for the practical matching of the training services of institutes to the developmental needs of local communities. Moreover, the operational guidelines whereby the Continental Counsellors and the Regional Councils have direct access to each other give rise to a further institutional relationship which, along with that connecting the Councils to the National and Local Spiritual Assemblies, effectuates a dynamic integration of functions at the regional level. 18.6

The ever-expanding work in social and economic development is also benefiting from the operation of those training institutes that give attention to such subjects as literacy, primary health care and the advancement of women. The more widespread efforts of the Office of Social and Economic Development to promote a global process of learning about relevant Bahá'í principles are enhanced by the work of these institutes, as well as by the rise of Bahá'í-inspired organizations scattered throughout the planet. Clearly, then, the institutional capacity to administer development programs is gaining in strength. This is apparent in projects sponsored by Bahá'í institutions or initiated by individuals through the inspiration of the Faith. An outstanding example of the latter is Unity College, which was created by a family in Ethiopia as the first, 18.7

and since late 1998, the only private college in the country, with a student body that swelled to 5,000 during this past year. Another example, on a smaller scale but of significance nonetheless, is the initiative taken by a family in Buffalo, New York: here, in their home, they have been assisting tens of children and youth from the inner city to develop, through Bahá'í spiritual and moral teachings, patterns of behavior that will enable them to overcome self-destructive attitudes bred by poverty and racism.

18.8   In the area of external affairs, the most energetic actions have been prompted by two tragic happenings in Iran. The sudden execution in Mashhad last July of Mr. Rúḥu'lláh Rawḥání, the first such official action in six years, registered a shock that provoked a worldwide and unprecedented outcry by governments and United Nations agencies. In late September the government's intelligence agency launched an organized attack on the Bahá'í Institute of Higher Education, involving the arrest of 36 members of the faculty and raids on more than 500 homes across the country. The latter incident inspired a global campaign of protest, still in progress, in which academic institutions and associations, educators, and student groups have been participating, and in which the press has taken a special interest, as reflected in the appearance of substantial articles in *Le Monde*, *The New York Times* and other major newspapers. The successful passage in the United Nations General Assembly last December of yet another resolution on Iran, in which the Bahá'ís are distinctly mentioned, must surely have been influenced by these two conspicuous manifestations of an unrelenting religious persecution.

18.9   But intensive as has been the demand upon the friends in all parts of the world to defend our beleaguered brethren, much attention was devoted as well to a wide range of external affairs endeavors. The four-month-long mission undertaken by an emissary of the House of Justice, Mr. Giovanni Ballerio, to islands of the Pacific Ocean where he met with 22 heads of state, 5 heads of government and more than 40 other high-ranking officials; the efforts pursued by a number of National Assemblies, at the urging of the Bahá'í International Community's United Nations Office, to promote human rights education; the participation, by invitation, of representatives of South Africa's Bahá'í community in the proceedings of the Truth and Reconciliation Commission, at which they were able to recount their record of unflinching support of racial unity throughout the years of apartheid; the recent success of communities in Australia, Brazil, Finland and Portugal in obtaining the decision of educational authorities to include courses on the Bahá'í Faith in the curricula of primary and secondary schools—these, not to mention the public information projects that generated publicity through all forms of the media, are examples of the broadly based enterprises in external affairs that engaged the energies of the community.

A corollary spate of activities involved the use of the arts, 18.10 of which the musical and other artistic performances associated with the celebration in Paris of the centenary of the establishment of the Faith in Europe were an outstanding instance. The Voices of Bahá Choir, composed of 68 members drawn from Europe and the Americas, delighted audiences in eight European cities and introduced the Faith to many. "Light and Fire," the completed part of an opera/ballet being written by Bahá'í composer Lasse Thoresen of Norway, was successfully performed last September at the prestigious music festival in Poland known as the Warsaw Autumn, which was opened by the Queen of Sweden. The work is based on recent heroic acts of the martyrs in Iran, a fact that exposed the audience to knowledge of the Faith. Europe's apparent lead in these particular endeavors was also marked by the occasion of the Austrian Chamber Music Festival when the Austrian Cross for Sciences and Arts, the highest award of its kind for Austria, was presented by the President of the Republic to Mr. Bijan Khadem-Missagh, a Bahá'í violinist and conductor. A program at that same Festival featured the recitation of extracts from Bahá'í and other sacred scriptures. But a word, too, must be said in recognition of the prominent part being played by youth all over the world in their employment of the arts in the teaching work; renditions by their dance workshops, in particular, have acquired renown within and outside the Bahá'í community.

We therefore enter this Riḍván season, as a community in a 18.11 dynamic state of transformation, enjoying a coherence of vision and activity consonant with the aim of advancing the process of entry by troops. And we begin the final year of the Plan with a boost in administrative strength, as three countries in Europe—Latvia, Lithuania and Macedonia—convoke their first Conventions to form National Spiritual Assemblies and thus raise the number of pillars of the Universal House of Justice to 182. But beyond this festive moment is a chronology of expectations that lists, first and foremost, the conclusion of the Four Year Plan at Riḍván 2000. This will be followed by the commencement on the Day of the Covenant of that very year of a new term of office for the Continental Boards of Counsellors, whose members will soon thereafter be called to the Bahá'í World Centre for a conference at which, among other matters, the features of the next global teaching and consolidation plan will be discussed. The Counsellors' Conference will mark the occupation by the International Teaching Centre of its permanent seat, an occasion for which Auxiliary Board members throughout the world will be invited to join the Counsellors in the Holy Land. The Mount Carmel projects will have been completed by this time and the preparations will have been well advanced for dedicatory events, scheduled to take place on 22 and 23 May 2001, to which a number of representatives from each national Bahá'í community will be invited. The details concerning these events are to be announced in due course.

18.12   This projection of portentous happenings cuts across the divide in time between the twentieth century and the new millennium, according to the reckoning of the common era. It is a projection that underscores the contrast between the confident vision that propels the constructive endeavors of an illumined community and the tangled fears seizing the millions upon millions who are as yet unaware of the Day in which they are living. Bereft of authentic guidance, they dwell on the horrors of the century, despairing over what these could imply for the future, hardly appreciating that this very century contains a light that will be shed on centuries to come. Ill-equipped to interpret the social commotion at play throughout the planet, they listen to the pundits of error and sink deeper into a slough of despond. Troubled by forecasts of doom, they do battle with the phantoms of a wrongly informed imagination. Knowing nothing of the transformative vision vouchsafed by the Lord of the Age, they stumble ahead, blind to the peerlessness of the new Day of God.

18.13   The pitiful conditions implied by such a state of heart and mind cannot but prompt us all to action, unabating action, to fulfill the intentions of a Plan whose major aim is to accelerate that process which will make it possible for growing numbers of the world's people to find the Object of their quest and thus to build a united, peaceful and prosperous life.

Dear Friends: The days pass swiftly as the twinkle of a star.   18.14
Make your mark now, at this crucial turning point of a juncture,
the like of which shall never return. Make that mark in deeds
that will ensure for you celestial blessings—guarantee for you,
for the entire race, a future beyond any earthly reckoning.

THE UNIVERSAL HOUSE OF JUSTICE

19

26 November 1999

To the Bahá'ís of the World

Dearly loved Friends,

On this special day, when our hearts and thoughts are focused on the immortal example set by the life of the Center of the Covenant, we pause to note, with feelings of deep gratitude, the current progress of the Divine Plan which He conceived, and to glance at the future beyond the four-year stage now rapidly coming to an end. 19.1

The accomplishments during this period are encouraging indeed. An impressive network of training institutes on a scale but dimly imagined at the start of the Plan has been established throughout the world. These nascent centers of learning have made significant strides in developing formal programs and in putting into place effective systems for the delivery of courses. Reports indicate that the number of believers benefiting directly from training courses has climbed to nearly 100,000. Without question, the capacity of the worldwide community to develop its human resources has been distinctly enhanced. 19.2

The effects of this systematic approach to human resource development are making themselves felt in the lives of all three protagonists of the Plan—the individual believer, the institutions, and the local community. There has been an upsurge in teaching activities undertaken at the initiative of the individual. Spiritual Assemblies, Councils, and committees have grown in their ability to guide the believers in their individual and collective endeavors. And community life has flourished, even in localities long dormant, as new patterns of thought and behavior have emerged. 19.3

As we survey the Bahá'í world, we see a greatly strengthened community, internally sound and notably reinforced. Its achievements in reaching the general public, governments and organizations of civil society and in winning trust in all these 19.4

circles are striking. Agencies specialized in external affairs, following a well-defined strategy, have broadened the range of the Faith's influence nationally and internationally, and projects of social and economic development, which seek the spiritual and material upliftment of entire communities, are penetrating society at the grassroots.

19.5   The two stages in the unfoldment of the Divine Plan lying immediately ahead will last one year and five years respectively. At Riḍván 2000 the Bahá'í world will be asked to embark on the first of these two stages, a twelve-month effort aimed at concentrating the forces, the capacities and the insights that have so strongly emerged. The Five Year Plan that follows will initiate a series of worldwide enterprises that will carry the Bahá'í community through the final twenty years in the first century of the Faith's Formative Age. These global Plans will continue to focus on advancing the process of entry by troops and on its systematic acceleration.

19.6   It is essential that, during the one-year effort, national and regional institutes everywhere bring into full operation the programs and systems that they have now devised. National communities should enter the Five Year Plan confident that the acquisition of knowledge, qualities and skills of service by large contingents of believers, with the aid of a sequence of courses, will proceed unhindered. Ample attention must also be given to further systematization of teaching efforts, whether undertaken by the individual or directed by the institutions. In this respect, the International Teaching Centre has identified certain patterns of systematic expansion and consolidation for relatively small geographical areas consisting of a manageable number of localities. Through the collaboration of Counsellors and National Spiritual Assemblies, several "Area Growth Programs" are being established in each continent. They will be carefully monitored during the Twelve Month Plan and their methods will be refined so that this approach can be incorporated into subsequent Plans.

19.7   Strategies to advance the process of entry by troops cannot ignore children and junior youth, if the victories won in one generation are not to be lost with the passage of time. It is imperative, then, that at this point in the process of systematization of the teaching work, definite steps be taken to ensure that the vision of the community fully embraces its younger members. The education of children, an obligation enjoined on both parents and institutions, requires special emphasis so as to become thoroughly integrated into the process of community development. This activity should be taken to new levels of intensity during these twelve months and then be further raised in the years immediately after. That the programs of most institutes in the world provide for the training of children's class teachers represents an element of strength. Spiritual Assemblies and Auxiliary Board members will need to mobilize these newly trained human resources to meet the spiritual requirements of children and junior youth.

The period of the Twelve Month Plan will be marked by great activity in society at large as the twentieth century draws to a close. Already keen interest is being shown by leaders of thought in the destiny of the coming generations, and we hope that the fervor of the Bahá'í community, both in its internal operation and its interactions with society, will convey a sense of confidence in the future of humanity. 19.8

We will pray ardently in the Holy Shrines that Bahá'u'lláh will bless your exertions to bring the Four Year Plan to a triumphal conclusion. 19.9

THE UNIVERSAL HOUSE OF JUSTICE

20

8 January 2000

To the Friends Gathered at the Youth Congress in Paraguay

Dear Friends,

You have come together to examine the progress of a youth 20.1
movement which embraces larger and larger numbers of participants from generation to generation. As you deliberate on the
issues before you, you can take pride in the accomplishments of
the community of the Greatest Name in your continent. Youth
have played a key role in the impressive unfoldment of the Four
Year Plan throughout Latin America, and you can look forward
with confidence to the harvest you are destined to reap.

As we recently stated, advancing the process of entry by 20.2
troops will remain the focus of the global Plans that will carry
the Bahá'í community to the end of the first century of the
Formative Age. You and those who will be attracted to the
Faith through your teaching efforts will bring about signal
developments that will mark this twenty-one year period. As a
result of recent endeavors to consolidate the work of institutes,
your communities are now endowed with the capacity to address the training needs of your rapidly growing ranks. This
training will help you exploit the opportunities offered you at
this crucial moment in history. In the face of these opportunities, you need to examine and shape the discourse in which you
will engage.

At the end of the twentieth century, the majority of the 20.3
population of Latin America is under the age of 30. As this
generation of youth assumes the responsibilities of conducting
the affairs of society, it will encounter a landscape of bewilder-
ing contrast. On the one hand, the region can justly boast
brilliant achievements in the intellectual, technological and economic spheres. On the other, it has failed to reduce widespread
poverty or to avoid a rising sea of violence that threatens to
submerge its peoples. Why—and the question needs to be asked

plainly—has this society been impotent, despite its great wealth, to remove the injustices that are tearing its fiber apart?

20.4 The answer to this question, as amply evidenced by decades of contentious history, cannot be found in political passion, conflicting expressions of class interest, or technical recipes. What is called for is a spiritual revival, as a prerequisite to the successful application of political, economic and technological instruments. But there is a need for a catalyst. Be assured that, in spite of your small numbers, you are the channels through which such a catalyst can be provided.

20.5 Be not dismayed if your endeavors are dismissed as utopian by the voices that would oppose any suggestion of fundamental change. Trust in the capacity of this generation to disentangle itself from the embroilments of a divided society. To discharge your responsibilities, you will have to show forth courage, the courage of those who cling to standards of rectitude, whose lives are characterized by purity of thought and action, and whose purpose is directed by love and indomitable faith. As you dedicate yourselves to healing the wounds with which your peoples have been afflicted, you will become invincible champions of justice.

20.6 We assure you of our loving prayers for the success of your deliberations.

THE UNIVERSAL HOUSE OF JUSTICE

21

Riḍván 2000

To the Bahá'ís of the World

Dearly loved Friends,

We bow our heads in gratitude to the Lord of Hosts, our hearts brimming with joy, as we witness how marvelous a difference four years have made since the launching of the global Plan now concluded at this Festival of Splendors. So marked was the progress achieved during this period that our world community attained heights from which bright new horizons for its future exploits can clearly be discerned.

The quantitative difference resulted mainly from a more critical qualitative difference. The culture of the Bahá'í community experienced a change. This change is noticeable in the expanded capability, the methodical pattern of functioning and the consequent depth of confidence of the three constituent participants in the Plan—the individual, the institutions and the local community. That is so because the friends concerned themselves more consistently with deepening their knowledge of the divine Teachings and learned much—and this more systematically than before—about how to apply them to promulgating the Cause, to managing their individual and collective activities, and to working with their neighbors. In a word, they entered into a learning mode from which purposeful action was pursued. The chief propellant of this change was the system of training institutes established throughout the world with great rapidity—an accomplishment which, in the field of expansion and consolidation, qualifies as the single greatest legacy of the Four Year Plan.

In the increased capacity of individuals to teach the Faith, as shown in the thrust of individual initiatives; in the improved ability of Spiritual Assemblies, Councils and committees to guide the endeavors of the friends; in the introduction of new patterns of thought and action which influenced the collective

21.1

21.2

21.3

behavior of the local community—in all such respects the system of training institutes demonstrated its indispensability as an engine of the process of entry by troops. By extending their operation through local study circles, many institutes magnified their capacity to cover wide regions with their programs. Mongolia, for instance, set up 106 study circles and, as a result, recorded a significant rise in the number of new believers. Concurrent with these kinds of developments, the members of our worldwide community also gave more attention to drawing on the power of prayer, to meditating on the sacred Word, and to deriving the spiritual benefits of participation in devotional gatherings. It is through the workings of these elements of an intensified individual and collective transformation that the size of the community is increasing. Although the number of new believers has as yet only slightly surpassed those of recent years, it is immensely gratifying to see that this increase is now geographically widespread, is engaging ever-larger segments of the community, and is successful in integrating new declarants into the life of the Cause.

21.4 So salutary, so promising a condition of the Faith also owes much, beyond measure, to the advisory influence, collaborative role and practical work of the institution of the Counsellors which were amplified with respect to the formation and operation of institutes—an amplification that reflected the timely stimulation imparted by a vibrant and ever alert International Teaching Centre.

21.5 The central theme of the Four Year Plan—that of advancing the process of entry by troops—produced a high degree of integration of thought and action. It focused attention on a major stage of the evolution of the Bahá'í community that must be attained during the Formative Age; for until entry by troops is more widely sustained, the conditions will not be ripe for mass conversion, that breakthrough promised by Shoghi Effendi in his writings. The thematic focus of the Plan bore implications for all categories of Bahá'í activity; it called for a clarity of understanding which made possible systematic and strategic planning as a prerequisite of individual and collective action. The members of the community came gradually to appreciate how systematization would facilitate the processes of growth and development. This raising of consciousness was a huge step that led to an upgrading of teaching activities and a change in the culture of the community.

The integrative aspects of the theme were evident in the   21.6
efforts at planning, building institutional capacity, and developing human resources. The threads connecting all these can be
traced from the outset of the Plan to its very end. The December
1995 Conference of the Continental Boards of Counsellors in the
Holy Land marked the beginning. There the Counsellors were
oriented to the features of the Plan. This was followed by their
consultations with National Spiritual Assemblies in national
planning sessions that moved subsequently to the regional level,
involving Auxiliary Board members, Local Spiritual Assemblies
and committees. Thus, at all levels, elements of the Bahá'í
administration became involved in the planning process, and
reached beyond this stage to that of implementation, at which
the institutional capacity to cope with entry by troops had to be
created. Two major steps were taken in this regard: one was the
establishment of training institutes; the other was the formal
establishment and widespread introduction of Regional Bahá'í
Councils as a feature of the administration between the local
and national levels to strengthen the administrative capacity of
certain communities where the growing complexity of the issues
facing National Spiritual Assemblies required this development.
Equally of relevance to integrating the essentials of the process
were the strategies defined for the work in social and economic
development, which is a critical part of consolidation, and in
external affairs, which is a vital factor in enabling the Faith to
manage the consequences of its emergence from obscurity. The
combined effect produced resounding results, the enumeration
of which would far exceed the compass of these pages. We are
moved, however, to cite certain highlights that illustrate the
scope of the Plan's achievements.

In the Holy Land, the construction of the Terraces and   21.7
the buildings on the Arc forged ahead with every assurance
of meeting the announced deadline for their completion at the
end of this Gregorian year. Moreover, the building in Haifa to
which we referred in our last Riḍván message in connection
with the expanded size of pilgrimage groups is ready for use
as of this Riḍván. In this same connection, architectural plans
were approved for the much-needed facility to be built at Bahjí
to accommodate pilgrims and other Bahá'í and non-Bahá'í visitors. The translation of the Texts for the expected new volume
of Bahá'u'lláh's Writings has been completed and preparations
are under way for its publication.

21.8   Strides in expansion and consolidation were manifest in ways other than those already mentioned: in pioneering, proclamation, the publication of literature, the use of the arts, the formation of Spiritual Assemblies, and advances of Bahá'í studies associations. Some 3,300 believers settled as long- and short-term international pioneers. That many countries usually on the receiving end had themselves dispatched pioneers abroad was a further indication of the maturation of national communities. True to the mandate addressed to their members, the Canadian and United States communities excelled in the number of pioneers that left their shores and in the much greater number of traveling teachers, including a significant representation of youth. Especially noteworthy, too, was the heartening response of believers of African descent in the United States to the call that Bahá'í teachers travel to Africa.

21.9   Proclamation of the Cause involved a variety of actions which included the sponsoring of a wide range of occasions —anniversaries, commemorations, discussion groups, exhibits, and the like—that made it possible for large numbers of people to become acquainted with the teachings of the Faith. The Houses of Worship were magnetic centers for visitors who entered their doors in increasing numbers, especially in India, where some five million people were received during the last year. Added to such activities were the multiple uses of the media to get the Bahá'í message across. In the United States, some 60,000 inquirers responded to a media campaign designed by the National Teaching Committee. Worldwide, knowledge of the Faith was spread through the appearance, more frequently than before, of unsolicited, sympathetic articles in the print media. There was a similar broadening of exposure through readiness on the part of radio and television stations to include regular Bahá'í programs; this was so in such countries as the Democratic Republic of the Congo and Liberia. Such fortunate developments were crowned by the independent choice of international media establishments to use the Shrine of the Báb and the Terraces as the site for the telecast of the Holy Land's segment of the worldwide media program celebrating the arrival of the year 2000.

21.10   The use of the arts became an important feature in the proclamation, teaching, deepening and devotional activities of the worldwide community. The arts attracted young people, who applied them to their teaching and deepening activities principally through the numerous drama and dance workshops active in many parts of the world. But the dynamics of the arts went far beyond singing and dancing to involve a range of imaginative activities that grounded people in the Cause. Where folk art was used, particularly in Africa, the teaching work was greatly enhanced. For example, Ghana and Liberia each mounted a Light of Unity Project for promoting the arts in teaching. In India, the Communal Harmony Group had a similar purpose.

Mostly at the urging of the Counsellors and with the support of the Continental Fund, a boost was given to the translation and publication of Bahá'í literature especially in Africa and Asia. Moreover, the Kitáb-i-Aqdas appeared in a complete Arabic edition and in other languages. 21.11

While the restriction of the formation of Local Spiritual Assemblies to the first day of Riḍván, which took effect in 1997, produced the anticipated decrease in the number of these institutions, the fall was not drastic. The number has since held its ground and a sound process of consolidation is in place. Seven new pillars of the Universal House of Justice were raised up, bringing the total of National Spiritual Assemblies to 181. 21.12

Particularly gratifying has been the gathering momentum, during these four years, of Bahá'í scholarly activity, which forged ahead with the vital task of reinforcing the intellectual foundations of the Faith's work. Two invaluable results have been the impressive enrichment of Bahá'í literature and the production of a body of dissertations examining various contemporary problems in the light of Bahá'í principles. The network of Associations of Bahá'í Studies, celebrating this year its twenty-fifth anniversary, welcomed five new affiliates during the Plan. Reflective of the diversity and creativity that this field of service is attracting were the holding of Papua New Guinea's first Bahá'í studies conference and the Japanese Association's ground-breaking focus on the spiritual origins of traditional Japanese scholarship. 21.13

Progress in the field of social and economic development was decidedly qualitative, although figures showing an increase of projects were also impressive. Annually reported activities grew from some 1,600 at the beginning of the Plan to more than 1,900 nearing its end. The movement towards a more systematic approach remained the dominant characteristic of the work during this period. To promote consultation and 21.14

action on the principles of social and economic development, the Office of Social and Economic Development at the Bahá'í World Centre sponsored 13 regional seminars in which an estimated 700 representatives from 60 countries participated. This Office also attended to the devising of pilot projects and materials suitable for the mounting of organized campaigns to foster youth empowerment and literacy, community health worker training, the advancement of women, and moral education. An example was the program in Guyana that trained more than 1,500 literacy facilitators; another was the completion in Malaysia of eight modules for the advancement of women, which became the basis for training sessions held in Africa, Asia and Latin America. A plan to integrate Bahá'í radio stations with the work of training institutes was initiated in the Guaymi region of Panama. As institutes have the potential to provide training for social and economic development, a movement in that direction involved a dozen institutes, which are currently experimenting with such efforts in areas including literacy, community health worker training, and vocational training. A number of Bahá'í-sponsored and Bahá'í-inspired agencies have devoted their energies to projects, such as the one which involved collaboration with the World Health Organization in combating river blindness in Cameroon; more than 30,000 individuals have received the needed medication through this Bahá'í project. Another instance is the private university in Ethiopia, Unity College, whose student body has risen to 8,000. Another is Landegg Academy in Switzerland, which, while expanding and consolidating its academic program, extended highly appreciated assistance in the ongoing quest for a remedy to the horrendous social consequences of conflict in the Balkans. Yet another is Núr University in Bolivia, which, in a collaborative project with Ecuador, offered training to more than 1,000 school teachers in its moral leadership program. In this field of social and economic development, such evidences of capacity building were a great benefit to the purposes of the Plan.

21.15   Guided by the external affairs strategy communicated to National Spiritual Assemblies in 1994, the community's capacity in the fields of diplomatic and public information likewise expanded at an astonishing rate, placing the Bahá'í community in a dynamic relationship with the United Nations, governments, nongovernmental organizations (NGOs) and the media.

The strategy focused activities at international and national levels on two key objectives: to influence the processes towards world peace, and to defend the Faith. Through the measures adopted for the defense of our dearly loved co-religionists in Iran, the Bahá'í International Community won a new measure of respect and support that created opportunities for other aims of the strategy to be pursued. To meet the challenge of the intractable situation in Iran, our institutions and external affairs agencies devised new approaches to activating available instruments of governments and the United Nations. The case of the persecutions in Iran occupied the attention of the highest authorities on the planet. Indeed, the news that an Iranian court had reaffirmed death sentences for two of the friends and imposed a similar sentence on a third evoked a sharp response from the President of the United States, who issued a clear admonition to Iran. As a consequence of the interventions of world leaders and the United Nations, the executions of Iranian Bahá'ís virtually stopped and the number of those sentenced to long-term imprisonment was drastically reduced.

21.16 While we have welcomed these interventions, we acclaim the self-sacrificing spirit, the fortitude, and the indomitable faith of our brothers and sisters in Iran that have invested such efforts with potency. These manifest qualities of the soul baffle their compatriots as to the stamina with which they withstand the assaults so viciously and so relentlessly unloosed against them. How else could one explain that so few have been able to stand up to so many for so long? How else could they have aroused the active concern of the world when even a single one of them faces the threat of death? Iran's tragedy is that the assailants have until now failed to see that the divine principles for which these persecuted ones have sacrificed their possessions and even their lives contain the very solutions that would satisfy the yearnings of a population in its hour of discontent. But there can be no doubt whatever that the systematic tyranny to which our Iranian friends have so cruelly been subjected will ultimately yield to the Almighty Power guiding the mysterious proceedings toward their assured destiny in all its promised glory.

21.17 With regard to the other objective of the external affairs strategy, the lines of action were guided by four themes—human rights, the status of women, global prosperity, and moral development. Our records show a huge step forward in the work on human rights and the status of women. With regard to the former, the United Nations Office prosecuted a creative program of human rights education which has, so far, served as a means of building the capacity of no fewer than 99 National Spiritual Assemblies for diplomatic work. Regarding the status of women, the existence of 52 national offices for the advancement of women, the contributions of numerous Bahá'í women and men to conferences and workshops at all levels, the selection of Bahá'í representatives to crucial positions on key NGO committees, including the one that serves the United Nations Development Fund for Women, show how the followers of Bahá'u'lláh assiduously promote His principle of the equality of women and men.

21.18   At the same time an array of initiatives are disseminating information about the Bahá'í Faith to various publics. These include such innovative undertakings as: the launching of "The Bahá'í World" Web site, which is already averaging 25,000 visits a month; the issuing of a statement entitled "Who Is Writing the Future?," which is helping the friends everywhere talk about contemporary issues; the airing since last November on the World Wide Web of "Payam-e-Doost," the Persian-language radio program broadcast for an hour weekly in the Washington, D.C., metropolitan area—a program which is available at all times throughout the world on the Internet; and the implementation of a highly original television program, applying moral principles to day-to-day problems, which has won the warm endorsement of government authorities in Albania, Bosnia-Herzegovina, Bulgaria, Croatia, Hungary, Romania, Slovenia, and the former Yugoslav Republic of Macedonia.

21.19   A phenomenon that has gathered force as the century draws to its end is that the people of the world have arisen to express their aspirations through what has come to be known as the "organizations of civil society." It must be a source of great satisfaction to Bahá'ís everywhere that the Bahá'í International Community as an NGO representing a cross-section of humankind has won such trust as a unifying agent in major discussions shaping the future of humankind. Our principal representative at the United Nations was appointed to co-chair a committee of nongovernmental organizations—a position that is giving the Bahá'í International Community a leading role in the organization of the Millennium Forum. This gathering, called by UN Secretary-General Kofi Annan and scheduled to be held in May, will give organizations of civil society an opportunity to formulate views and recommendations on global issues which will be taken up at the subsequent Millennium Summit in September of this year to be attended by heads of state and government.

Humanity's awakening to the spiritual dimensions of the 21.20 changes occurring in the world has a special significance for Bahá'ís. The interfaith dialogue has intensified. During the Four Year Plan it increasingly involved the Faith as a recognized participant. The Parliament of the World's Religions held in Cape Town last December brought together some 6,000 attendees, among whom was a strong Bahá'í delegation. Bahá'ís served on both the South African and International Boards of Directors that planned the event. For Bahá'ís, interest in the occasion arose particularly from the fact that the first mention of the Name of Bahá'u'lláh at a public gathering in the Western Hemisphere had occurred at the Parliament held in Chicago in 1893. Two inter-religious events held in Jordan last November included Bahá'ís as invited participants: a conference on conflict and religion in the Middle East, and the annual meeting of the World Conference on Religion and Peace. Bahá'í representatives attended events in Vatican City and New Delhi sponsored by the Roman Catholic Church; on the latter occasion, in the presence of Pope John Paul II, Counsellor Zena Sorabjee was one of the representatives of religions addressing the gathering. In the United Kingdom, the Faith was placed in the public arena when Bahá'í representatives joined members of eight other major religions for an interfaith celebration of the new millennium in the Royal Gallery of Westminster Palace, where, in the presence of Royalty, the Prime Minister, the Archbishop of Canterbury and other distinguished persons, reference was made to the gathering of the "nine major religions of the United Kingdom." In Germany, for the first time Bahá'ís were included in an interfaith dialogue. This reversed a longstanding attitude of Christian denominations which had avoided contact with the Faith owing to a book written by a Covenant-breaker and issued by a Lutheran publishing house in 1981. The remedy was provided in a 600-page scholarly rebuttal written by three Bahá'ís and published in 1995 by a leading non-Bahá'í firm, representing a signal victory for the German Bahá'í community. An English translation was published in the last year of the Plan. Interfaith dialogue took an unusual form when at Lambeth Palace in 1998 representatives of the World Bank and of nine major religions held a meeting which led to the formation of the World Faiths Development Dialogue. The announced aim of the Dialogue is to try to bridge the gap between the faith communities and the World Bank in order to enable them to work together more effectively to overcome world poverty. The frequency and wide embrace of interfaith gatherings represent a new phenomenon in the relations among the religions. It is apparent that the various religious communities are striving to achieve the spirit of friendliness and fellowship among themselves that Bahá'u'lláh urged His followers to show towards the followers of other religions.

21.21   The concentrated endeavor of the Bahá'í community in these four years occurred at a time when the wider society grappled with a torrent of conflicting interests. In this brief but intensely dynamic span, the forces at work in the Bahá'í community and throughout the world proceeded with relentless acceleration. In their wake were revealed more conspicuously than before the social phenomena to which Shoghi Effendi alluded. More than six decades ago, he had called attention to the "simultaneous processes of rise and of fall, of integration and of disintegration, of order and chaos, with their continuous and reciprocal reactions on each other." These twin processes did not continue in isolation from those specific to the Bahá'í community but at times proceeded in such a way as to invite, as has already been shown, the direct involvement of the Faith. They seemed to run at opposite sides of the same corridor of time. On one side, wars fomented by religious, political, racial or tribal conflict raged in some 40 places; sudden, total breakdown of civil order paralyzed a number of countries; terrorism as a political weapon became epidemic; a surge of international criminal networks raised alarm. Yet on the opposite side, attempts at implementing and elaborating the methods of collective security were earnestly made, bringing to mind one of Bahá'u'lláh's prescriptions for maintaining peace; a call was raised for an international criminal court to be established, another action that accords with Bahá'í expectations; to focus attention on the imperative need for an adequate system to deal with global issues, world leaders are scheduled to meet in a Millennium Summit; new methods of communications have opened the way for everyone to communicate with anyone on the planet. The economic disintegration in Asia threatened to destabilize the world economy, but it prompted efforts both to remedy the immediate situation and to find ways of bringing a sense of equity to international trade and finance. These are but a few examples of the two contrasting but interactive tendencies operating at this time, confirming Shoghi Effendi's inspired summation of the forces at work in God's greater plan, "whose ultimate objectives are the unity of the human race and the peace of all mankind."

21.22   At the conclusion of these four eventful years, we have arrived at a portentous convergence of ends and beginnings in measures of Gregorian time and the Bahá'í era. In one instance, this convergence entails the wrapping up of the twentieth century and, in the other, opens a new stage in the unfolding of the Formative Age. The perspective from these two frames of time prompts us to reflect on a vision of world-shaping trends that have synchronized, and to do so in the context of the insight so graphically projected by Shoghi Effendi at the inception of the Arc he conceived. During the course of the Plan, this vision assumed a brilliant clarity as the construction projects advanced on Mount Carmel, as world leaders took bold steps towards fashioning the structures of a global political peace, and as local and national Bahá'í institutions moved to new levels in their evolution. We carry with us a sacred and enduring memory of the twentieth century that stirs our energies even as it sets our path: It is of that seminal moment in the history of humankind when the Center of the Covenant of Bahá'u'lláh, during an unparalleled ministry, designed the architecture of a new World Order and when, subsequently during some of the most devastating years, the Guardian of the Faith devoted his utmost energies to raising up the structures of an Administrative System that, at the end of the century, stands before the gaze of the world in the wholeness of its essential form. We come thus to a bridge between times. The capacities developed through a century of struggle and sacrifice by a handful of intoxicated lovers of Bahá'u'lláh must now be applied to the inescapable tasks remaining to the Formative Age, whose many epochs of unremitting labor will lead to that Golden Age of our Faith when the Most Great Peace will envelop the earth.

21.23   We begin at this Riḍván with a Twelve Month Plan. Brief though it is, it must and will suffice to accomplish certain vital tasks and to lay the ground for the next twenty-year thrust of the Master's Divine Plan. What was so carefully begun four years ago—the systematic acquisition of knowledge, qualities and skills of service—must be augmented. Wherever they exist, national and regional institutes must activate to the full the programs and systems they have adopted. New institutes must be formed where such needs have been identified. Greater steps must be taken to systematize the teaching work undertaken through individual initiative and institutional sponsorship. It is partly for this purpose that in several areas of each continent the Counsellors and the National Assemblies have established "Area Growth Programs." The results will provide a body of experience for the benefit of future Plans. The individual, the institutions and the local community are urged to focus their attention on these essential tasks, so as to be fully prepared for the five-year enterprise to begin at Riḍván 2001—an enterprise that will take the Bahá'í world to the next phase in the advancement of the process of entry by troops.

21.24   But beyond giving attention to these tasks, there is a pressing challenge to be faced: Our children need to be nurtured spiritually and to be integrated into the life of the Cause. They should not be left to drift in a world so laden with moral dangers. In the current state of society, children face a cruel fate. Millions and millions in country after country are dislocated socially. Children find themselves alienated by parents and other adults whether they live in conditions of wealth or poverty. This alienation has its roots in a selfishness that is born of materialism that is at the core of the godlessness seizing the hearts of people everywhere. The social dislocation of children in our time is a sure mark of a society in decline; this condition is not, however, confined to any race, class, nation or economic condition—it cuts across them all. It grieves our hearts to realize that in so many parts of the world children are employed as soldiers, exploited as laborers, sold into virtual slavery, forced into prostitution, made the objects of pornography, abandoned by parents centered on their own desires, and subjected to other forms of victimization too numerous to mention. Many such horrors are inflicted by the parents themselves upon their own children. The spiritual and psychological damage defies estimation. Our worldwide community cannot escape the consequences of these conditions. This realization should spur us all to urgent and sustained effort in the interests of children and the future.

Even though children's activities have been a part of past   21.25
Plans, these have fallen short of the need. Spiritual education
of children and junior youth are of paramount importance to
the further progress of the community. It is therefore imperative
that this deficiency be remedied. Institutes must be certain to
include in their programs the training of teachers of children's
classes, who can make their services available to local communities. But although providing spiritual and academic
education for children is essential, this represents only a part
of what must go into developing their characters and shaping
their personalities. The necessity exists, too, for individuals and
the institutions at all levels, which is to say the community as a
whole, to show a proper attitude towards children and to take
a general interest in their welfare. Such an attitude should be
far removed from that of a rapidly declining order.

Children are the most precious treasure a community can   21.26
possess, for in them are the promise and guarantee of the future.
They bear the seeds of the character of future society which is
largely shaped by what the adults constituting the community
do or fail to do with respect to children. They are a trust no
community can neglect with impunity. An all-embracing love
of children, the manner of treating them, the quality of the
attention shown them, the spirit of adult behavior toward
them—these are all among the vital aspects of the requisite
attitude. Love demands discipline, the courage to accustom
children to hardship, not to indulge their whims or leave them
entirely to their own devices. An atmosphere needs to be maintained in which children feel that they belong to the community
and share in its purpose. They must lovingly but insistently be
guided to live up to Bahá'í standards, to study and teach the
Cause in ways that are suited to their circumstances.

Among the young ones in the community are those known   21.27
as junior youth, who fall between the ages of, say, 12 and 15.
They represent a special group with special needs as they are
somewhat in between childhood and youth when many changes
are occurring within them. Creative attention must be devoted
to involving them in programs of activity that will engage
their interests, mold their capacities for teaching and service,
and involve them in social interaction with older youth. The
employment of the arts in various forms can be of great value
in such activity.

21.28   And now we wish to address a few words to parents, who bear the primary responsibility for the upbringing of their children. We appeal to them to give constant attention to the spiritual education of their children. Some parents appear to think that this is the exclusive responsibility of the community; others believe that in order to preserve the independence of children to investigate truth, the Faith should not be taught to them. Still others feel inadequate to take on such a task. None of this is correct. The beloved Master has said that "it is enjoined upon the father and mother, as a duty, to strive with all effort to train the daughter and the son," adding that, "should they neglect this matter, they shall be held responsible and worthy of reproach in the presence of the stern Lord." Independent of the level of their education, parents are in a critical position to shape the spiritual development of their children. They should not ever underestimate their capacity to mold their children's moral character. For they exercise indispensable influence through the home environment they consciously create by their love of God, their striving to adhere to His laws, their spirit of service to His Cause, their lack of fanaticism, and their freedom from the corrosive effects of backbiting. Every parent who is a believer in the Blessed Beauty has the responsibility to conduct herself or himself in such a way as to elicit the spontaneous obedience to parents to which the Teachings attach so high a value. Of course, in addition to the efforts made at home, the parents should support Bahá'í children's classes provided by the community. It must be borne in mind, too, that children live in a world that informs them of harsh realities through direct experience with the horrors already described or through the unavoidable outpourings of the mass media. Many of them are thereby forced to mature prematurely, and among these are those who look for standards and discipline by which to guide their lives. Against this gloomy backdrop of a decadent society, Bahá'í children should shine as the emblems of a better future.

21.29   Our expectations are alive with the thought that the Continental Counsellors will gather in the Holy Land in January 2001 on an occasion that will celebrate the occupation by the International Teaching Centre of its permanent seat on the Hill of God. Auxiliary Board members from throughout the world will participate with them in what will undoubtedly turn out to be one of the historic happenings of the Formative

Age. The coming together of such a constellation of Bahá'í officers must by its very nature produce untold benefits for a community which will again be close to ending one Plan and embarking on another. As we contemplate the implications, we turn our hearts in gratitude to the very dear Hands of the Cause of God 'Alí-Akbar Furútan and 'Alí Muḥammad Varqá, who by their residence in the Holy Land hold aloft the torch of service which the beloved Guardian lit in their hearts.

21.30   With this Twelve Month Plan, we cross a bridge to which we shall never return. We launch this Plan in the earthly absence of Amatu'l-Bahá Rúḥíyyih Khánum. She remained with us to the virtual end of the twentieth century as a beam of the light that had shone during that incomparable period in the history of the human race. In the Tablets of the Divine Plan, the Master lamented His inability to travel throughout the world to raise the Divine call, and in the intensity of His disappointment He penned the hope: "Please God, ye may achieve it." Amatu'l-Bahá responded with boundless energy, touching far-flung spots of the earth in the 185 countries that were privileged to receive her inimitable gifts. Her example, which will retain forever its splendor, illumines the hearts of thousands upon thousands throughout the planet. Against the inadequacy of any other gesture, might we all not dedicate our humble efforts during this Plan to the memory of one for whom teaching was the primary purpose, the perfect joy of life?

THE UNIVERSAL HOUSE OF JUSTICE

22

9 January 2001

To the Conference of the Continental Boards of Counsellors

Dearly loved Friends,

Five years ago, we called on the body of Counsellors 22.1
assembled in the Holy Land to aid the Bahá'í world to understand and shoulder the challenges of systematic growth.
The brilliant achievements of the Four Year Plan testify to the
wholehearted response they made. Today, we ask for an equally
great effort on your part, this time to ensure the successful
launching of the Five Year Plan.

In your deliberations on the nature of this next stage in the 22.2
unfoldment of the Divine Plan, you need to take into account
the magnitude of the changes occurring in the fortunes of the
Faith. At the World Centre, the raising of the great edifices now
standing on the Arc represents a major step in the consolidation of a divinely appointed Administrative Order. The Four
Year Plan witnessed a remarkable increase in the institutional
capacity of Bahá'í communities in every continent. The evolution of National and Local Spiritual Assemblies has visibly
accelerated, and Regional Councils, where they have been
established, have brought a new energy and effectiveness to the
work of the Cause. With the birth and efflorescence of more
than 300 training institutes, the Faith now possesses a powerful instrument for developing the human resources needed
to sustain large-scale expansion and consolidation. Further,
the ability of the Bahá'í community to influence the course of
human affairs, both through its dealings with governments and
organizations of civil society and through its endeavors in social
and economic development, has been greatly enhanced. The
Cause of Bahá'u'lláh stands at the threshold of a new epoch, at
a moment in history when, despite confusion and outbursts of
fresh hostility, the world has made real strides towards peace.

One clearly sees an increasing receptivity to His all-pervasive and resplendent Spirit.

22.3   Advancing the process of entry by troops will continue as the aim of the Five Year Plan—indeed the aim of the series of Plans that will carry the community to the end of the first century of the Formative Age. The acceleration of this vital process will be achieved through systematic activity on the part of the three participants in the Plan: the individual believer, the institutions, and the community.

The Training Institute

22.4   A searching analysis of the Four Year Plan recently prepared for us by the International Teaching Centre demonstrates that the training institute is effective not only in enhancing the powers of the individual, but also in vitalizing communities and institutions. The continued development of training institutes in the diverse countries and territories of the world, then, must be a central feature of the new Plan.

22.5   Drawing on the wealth of experience now accumulated in this area of endeavor, institutes will have to provide their communities with a constant stream of human resources to serve the process of entry by troops. Elements of a system that can meet the training needs of large numbers of believers have already been tested worldwide and have proven themselves. Study circles, reinforced by extension courses and special campaigns, have shown their ability to lend structure to the process of spiritual education at the grassroots. The value of a sequence of courses, each one following the other in a logical pattern and each one building on the achievements of the previous ones, has become abundantly clear. Various models are emerging that provide insight into how such sequences can be used to create training programs. In one example the main sequence, much like the trunk of a tree, supports courses branching out from it, each branch dedicated to some specific area of training. In another, several tracks of courses, each with its own focus, run parallel. Institutes will do well to examine these elements and approaches and employ them in a manner that responds to the opportunities before them.

22.6   At the outset of the Twelve Month Plan we underscored the need for Bahá'í children to be nurtured spiritually and to be integrated into the life of the Cause. There is every indication from the response of the friends thus far that a raised awareness of the importance of child education will, in fact, be a hallmark of this brief yet significant Plan. A new impetus has been given to Bahá'í children's classes. Increased awareness has also brought to light opportunities to offer moral and spiritual education to children in general, as exemplified by the success of the efforts to introduce courses on the Bahá'í Faith into programs of official school systems.

That institutes are placing more and more emphasis on the   22.7
training of teachers for children's classes is a particularly en-couraging sign. Other measures are equally essential if regular classes for every age are to be offered in Bahá'í communities throughout the world. In some countries, national and regional committees have been established to assist Local Spiritual Assemblies in the discharge of their responsibility to educate children. In these, the relationship between the committees and the training institute will steadily evolve as experience is gained, each agency enhancing the work of the other. But there are many countries in which the institute is the only structure developing the capacity to organize and maintain courses in locality after locality. As this approach is working well with youth and adults, and increasingly for junior youth, there is no reason why the training institute should not also shoulder similar responsibility with respect to children, where necessary. As a general rule, institutes do not take on the administration of plans and programs for expansion and consolidation. Conducting children's classes, however, is a unique enterprise, of special urgency. In those countries where the task is given to it, the institute becomes a center of learning intensely engaged in the spiritual education of the friends from the tenderest age through adulthood.

Individual Initiative in Teaching

With the work of institutes growing in strength, attention   22.8
has now to be given everywhere to systematizing teaching ef-forts. In the document "The Institution of the Counsellors" just issued, we emphasize the role that the Auxiliary Board members and their assistants play in helping the friends to meet this chal-lenge, both at the level of individual initiative and of collective volition. As individuals progress through institute courses, they deepen their knowledge of the Faith, gain insights, and acquire

skills of service. Some of the courses devoted to teaching will no doubt treat the subject in general terms. Others will focus on various means of sharing Bahá'u'lláh's message with specific segments of society, incorporating the wisdom gleaned from the teaching endeavors of the friends. This combined process of action, learning and training will endow communities with an ever-increasing number of capable and eager teachers of the Cause.

22.9   Training alone, of course, does not necessarily lead to an upsurge in teaching activity. In every avenue of service, the friends need sustained encouragement. Our expectation is that the Auxiliary Board members, together with their assistants, will give special thought to how individual initiative can be cultivated, particularly as it relates to teaching. When training and encouragement are effective, a culture of growth is nourished in which the believers see their duty to teach as a natural consequence of having accepted Bahá'u'lláh. They "raise high the sacred torch of faith," as was 'Abdu'l-Bahá's wish, "labor ceaselessly, by day and by night," and "consecrate every fleeting moment of their lives to the diffusion of the divine fragrance and the exaltation of God's holy Word." So enkindled do their hearts become with the fire of the love of God that whoever approaches them feels its warmth. They strive to be channels of the spirit, pure of heart, selfless and humble, possessing certitude and the courage that stems from reliance on God. In such a culture, teaching is the dominating passion of the lives of the believers. Fear of failure finds no place. Mutual support, commitment to learning, and appreciation of diversity of action are the prevailing norms.

Systematic Programs of Growth

22.10   During the coming months, you will be helping national communities, whose circumstances differ widely, to formulate plans for systematic growth. There are many countries where increased institutional capacity, particularly at the level of the region, now makes it possible to focus attention on smaller geographic areas. Most of these will consist of a cluster of villages and towns, but, sometimes, a large city and its suburbs may constitute an area of this kind. Among the factors that determine the boundaries of a cluster are culture, language, patterns of transport, infrastructure, and the social and economic life of the inhabitants. The areas into which a region divides will fall into various categories of development. Some will not yet be open to the Faith, while others will contain a few isolated localities and groups; in some, established communities will be gaining strength through a vigorous institute process; in a few, strong communities of deepened believers will be in a position to take on the challenges of systematic and accelerated expansion and consolidation.

Once the appropriate categories have been identified, national plans in these countries will need to make provision for the progressive opening of virgin areas through the settlement of homefront pioneers. Such goals can be met with relative ease if pioneers are experienced in institute programs and are able to use their methods and materials in raising up a group of dedicated believers who can carry the work of the Faith forward in the area. Precious indeed will be the privilege of those who, in the remaining years of the first century of the Formative Age, place their trust in God and arise with fervor to take the lead in carrying the light of Divine guidance to every part of their countries. It is our hope that this call for homefront pioneers will generate great enthusiasm among the friends and open before their eyes a new vista of possibilities to serve the Faith.

22.11

According to this scheme, national plans will also need to include provision for the strengthening of other areas which, although open to the Faith, have yet to reach the level of development that prepares them for intensive activity. In those areas where strong communities with a corps of deepened believers exist, systematic programs for the expansion and consolidation of the Faith should be established forthwith. We have already indicated that the International Teaching Centre has identified certain patterns of growth appropriate for relatively small geographical areas. Since then, it has analyzed several pilot projects in various parts of the world, and its findings are highly encouraging. The lessons learned now provide a body of experience for the launching of programs for systematic growth in area after area. As you consult on this matter with National Spiritual Assemblies and Regional Councils, you will want to keep the Teaching Centre informed.

22.12

It is important that national communities not rush into establishing intensive programs in an area before conditions are propitious. These conditions include: a high level of enthusiasm among a sizeable group of devoted and capable believers who

22.13

understand the prerequisites for sustainable growth and can take ownership of the program; some basic experience on the part of a few communities in the cluster in holding classes for the spiritual education of children, devotional meetings, and the Nineteen Day Feast; the existence of a reasonable degree of administrative capacity in at least a few Local Spiritual Assemblies; the active involvement of several assistants to Auxiliary Board members in promoting community life; a pronounced spirit of collaboration among the various institutions working in the area; and above all, the strong presence of the training institute with a scheme of coordination that supports the systematic multiplication of study circles.

22.14   Programs initiated in such areas should aim at fostering sustainable growth by building the necessary capacity at the levels of the individual, the institution, and the community. Far from requiring grandiose and elaborate plans, these programs should focus on a few measures that have proven over the years to be indispensable to large-scale expansion and consolidation. Success will depend on the manner in which lines of action are integrated and on the attitude of learning that is adopted. The implementation of such a program will require the close collaboration of the institute, the Auxiliary Board members and their assistants, and an Area Teaching Committee.

22.15   At the core of the program must lie a sound and steady process of expansion, matched by an equally strong process of human resource development. A range of teaching efforts needs to be carried out, involving both activities undertaken by the individual and campaigns promoted by the institutions. As the number of believers in the area rises, a significant percentage should receive training from the institute, and their capabilities be directed towards the development of local communities.

22.16   Our message of 26 December 1995 delineating the features of the Four Year Plan made reference to the stages through which a community passes as it develops. The experience that has been gained in the ensuing years in working with communities at various stages will prove valuable to programs of growth. One of the first steps in implementing the program may well be a survey to determine the condition of each locality in the area. Among the initial goals for every community should be the establishment of study circles, children's classes, and devotional meetings, open to all the inhabitants of the locality. The observance of the Nineteen Day Feast has to be given due weight, and consistent effort should be made to strengthen the Local Spiritual Assemblies. Once communities are able to sustain the basic activities of Bahá'í life, a natural way to further their consolidation is to introduce small projects of social and economic development—for example, a literacy project, a project for the advancement of women or environmental preservation, or even a village school. As strength builds, the responsibility for an increasing number of lines of action is to be devolved onto the Local Spiritual Assemblies.

Throughout the endeavor, periodic meetings of consultation in the area need to reflect on issues, consider adjustments, and maintain enthusiasm and unity of thought. The best approach is to formulate plans for a few months at a time, beginning with one or two lines of action and gradually growing in complexity. Those who are actively involved in the implementation of plans, whether members of the institutions or not, should be encouraged to participate fully in the consultations. Other area-wide gatherings will also be necessary. Some of these will provide opportunity for the sharing of experience and further training. Others will focus on the use of the arts and the enrichment of culture. Together, such gatherings will support an intense process of action, consultation and learning. 22.17

The friends who participate in these intensive programs of growth should bear in mind that the purpose is to ensure that the Revelation of Bahá'u'lláh reaches the masses of humanity and enables them to achieve spiritual and material progress through the application of the Teachings. Vast numbers among the peoples of the world are ready, indeed yearn, for the bounties that Bahá'u'lláh alone can bestow upon them once they have committed themselves to building the new society He has envisioned. In learning to systematize their large-scale teaching work, Bahá'í communities are becoming better equipped to respond to this longing. They cannot withhold whatever effort, whatever sacrifice, may be called for. 22.18

A Spiritual Enterprise

Clearly, the scheme described here, while suitable to many national communities, cannot be applied in every situation. We count on the ability of the Bahá'í institutions to create plans which, if not reflecting the total scheme above, will incorporate elements of its vision, according to the circumstances of 22.19

each national community. Bahá'í communities are, of course, engaged in a range of indispensable endeavors such as public information activity, proclamation efforts, external affairs work, production of literature, and complex social and economic development projects. Most certainly, as plans are devised, they will also address these challenges.

22.20 The nature of the planning process with which you will be helping the friends is in many ways unique. At its core it is a spiritual process in which communities and institutions strive to align their pursuits with the Will of God. The Major Plan of God is at work and the forces it generates impel humanity towards its destiny. In their own plans of action, the institutions of the Faith must seek to gain insight into the operation of these great forces, explore the potentialities of the people they serve, measure the resources and strengths of their communities, and take practical steps to enlist the unreserved participation of the believers. The nurturing of this process is the sacred mission entrusted to you. We have every confidence in your ability to achieve it. May Bahá'u'lláh bless and sustain you through His unfailing grace and mighty confirmations.

THE UNIVERSAL HOUSE OF JUSTICE

23

14 January 2001

To the Conference Marking the Inauguration of
the International Teaching Centre Building

Dearly loved Friends,

We are filled with a sense of triumph as we reflect on the   23.1
significance of the occupation by the International Teaching
Centre of its permanent seat on the Mountain of the Lord. This
occasion marks the beginning of what future generations will
regard as a splendid chapter in the annals of our Faith.

What joy that the Hands of the Cause of God 'Alí-Akbar   23.2
Furútan and 'Alí-Muḥammad Varqá are able to participate in
these proceedings! We acknowledge the great debt of gratitude
owed to them and to the departed ones of their exalted rank for
so much of what we have come to celebrate.

And how fitting it is that the Continental Counsellors and   23.3
their deputies from the five continents are here to witness such
an auspicious beginning! The attendance of the Auxiliary Board
members is so unusual a feature of the gathering that we are
impelled to address our remarks particularly to them. Indeed, on
no occasion in the past have the major constituents of the institution of the Counsellors ever assembled in the Holy Land.

With joyous hearts, we extend to every member of the   23.4
Auxiliary Boards a special and loving welcome. We hail this
opportunity to greet and thank these officers of an institution
the crucial importance of whose vital role in the progress of
the Cause of Bahá'u'lláh is increasingly demonstrated as the
Divine Plan unfolds. May we not at such a moment invoke,
above all, the memory of him in whose divinely inspired mind
the conception of Auxiliary Boards took shape? Up until the
time of his passing in 1957, Shoghi Effendi had called for the
appointment of seventy-two such officers, who were evenly
divided between the two Boards on each of the five continents;

with the institutional evolution that has taken place since then, the number has increased to nearly one thousand.

23.5   With the International Teaching Centre having settled into its position at the heart of a ramified, global institution, we can readily recognize the fruition of the system set to extend into the future the specialized functions of propagation and protection originally assigned to the Hands of the Cause—a system that has derived impetus from the guidance and example of these irreplaceable appointees of Shoghi Effendi. This achievement is in itself a thrilling indication of how well the Cause is faring.

23.6   In you, the Auxiliary Board members here assembled, is reflected the whole world of humanity. You hail from far-flung geographic regions and cultural backgrounds that make you truly representative of a cross-section of the human family. Your coming here both reaffirms the existence of a dynamic, global community and signalizes the possibilities for an advance in the process of entry by troops far beyond any record yet established. In this latter regard, the value of your immediate future services cannot be overestimated.

23.7   The world's crying need for the divine prescriptions is made plain by the ills afflicting society at every level in all parts of the planet. We must be swift in ministering to this need. Doing so largely depends upon the revolutionary vision, the creative drive and systematic effort of Auxiliary Board members and their assistants, who prompt and encourage individuals, institutions and communities to act with dispatch, constancy and enthusiasm. Their operation at the grassroots, at the very wellspring, of individual and collective activity, makes manageable the fulfillment of this pressing need.

23.8   In contemplating the sublime purpose that has brought us together on this day, we find ourselves without words to describe adequately our wonderment at the evidences of Bahá'u'lláh's handiwork. We stand too close to the moment to comprehend the magnitude of what has been so amazingly accomplished. But to ponder the circumstances attending seminal happenings of the past is to awaken in us all some sense of appreciation for their wonderful consequences in our time. The revelation of the Tablet of Carmel, the interment of the remains of Bahá'u'lláh's martyred Forerunner in the mausoleum constructed by the beloved Master, the creation by our dear Guardian of the Arc on the Hill of God—reflections on just such historic landmarks illumine our understanding and evoke gratitude in our hearts.

The journeys that brought you to these sacred precincts have launched you on spiritual adventures that will be celebrated in times to come as having imparted a new impetus to the advancement of the Cause. This is the hope and expectation we cherish. For as you drink deep of the rarefied spirit of the Holy Shrines and imbibe the guidance that will flow from the consultations in which you will participate, there can be no doubt that you will find yourselves endowed with a new confidence, a new power. With so rich an endowment, how can your endeavors fail? Most surely, you will bring a rejuvenated fervor and a reconsecrated effort to the compelling civilizing tasks you have accepted to perform at this potent juncture in the evolution of our glorious Faith. 23.9

Our supplications are intermingled with yours that the Blessed Beauty may abundantly confirm you in His service. 23.10

THE UNIVERSAL HOUSE OF JUSTICE

24

16 January 2001

To the Bahá'ís of the World

Dearly loved Friends,

As we write you this message, the Conference of the   24.1
Continental Counsellors approaches a triumphant conclusion.

For eight days the Counsellors from all the continents have   24.2
consulted on the next phase of the process of entry by troops.
While they were meeting during the first five days, 849 members
of their Auxiliary Boards from 172 countries were arriving at
the Bahá'í World Centre and paying their respects at the Holy
Shrines in anticipation of the moment when they would all
come together in a series of soul-stirring events: ascent of the
newly built Terraces on Mount Carmel; circumambulation of
the Shrine of the Báb; procession along the Arc path for a visit
to the International Teaching Centre Building; a devotional
ceremony to mark the occupation by the Teaching Centre of its
permanent seat; and subsequent joint consultations concerning
their indispensable role in the Five Year Plan on which the
Bahá'í world will embark at Riḍván 2001.

The deliberations of the Counsellors themselves have   24.3
been the heart of these stupendous activities. Their consultations have been marked by a combination of sobriety and
effervescence that has refined the character of their discussions
and illumined understanding. It is clear from the confident
atmosphere in which they have conferred that their institution
has reached a new stage in its maturation. Even though they
function principally as individuals, the Counsellors across
all Boards have become of one mind. By internalizing and
integrating the lessons and experiences of systematization called
for in the Four Year Plan, they have indeed been transformed
into channels of unified thought. We appreciate that the new
height in the evolution of their institution is a reflection, too,
of the measure to which, with their wise and constant advice,

the Spiritual Assemblies and other institutions of the world community have evolved.

24.4   As the time for the Conference drew near, there were signs that the Faith had arrived at a point in its development beyond which a new horizon opens before us. Such intimations were communicated in our report last Riḍván of the change in culture of the Bahá'í community as training institutes emerged, as the construction projects on Mount Carmel approached their completion, and as the internal processes of institutional consolidation and the external processes towards world unity became more fully synchronized. They were elaborated in the message we addressed to the Conference of the Continental Boards of Counsellors a few days ago. But the extraordinary dynamics at work throughout the Conference crystallized these indications into a recognizable reality. With a spirit of exultation we are moved to announce to you: the Faith of Bahá'u'lláh now enters the fifth epoch of its Formative Age.

24.5   Recognition of this milestone falls within the patterns established by Shoghi Effendi for marking measures of time in the history of the Cause; he foresaw among these a succession of epochs occurring in the Formative Age. It must fill every devoted follower of Bahá'u'lláh with joy and wonder that His Administrative Order has reached so important a point at so crucial a time, when so many members of the institution of the Counsellors are gathered in splendid array at the World Centre of His Faith. They will return to the far corners of the earth as torches aflame with the spirit of service. That they will pour fresh energy into their activities, there can be no doubt. Their efforts will surely widen the path leading to the success of the Twelve Month Plan, and through that to the launching at Riḍván of the five year enterprise that will be the first in a series of Plans to be pursued until the centenary of the Formative Age.

24.6   The Counsellors will leave here anticipating their early consultations with National Spiritual Assemblies regarding the operation in their countries of the forthcoming Plan. With the involvement of their eager auxiliaries, they will assist, too, in quickly moving the requisite planning process to regional and local areas of the community in every land.

24.7   In the waning moments of these eventful days, our hearts are turned in humble gratitude to the Ancient Beauty for the abundance of the blessings He has bestowed. The very earth of Carmel is astir with the wonders of His grace as she responds to the redemptive call He raised in the Tablet bearing her name. His fervent wish expressed therein resounds in the souls of His lovers throughout the planet: "Oh, how I long to announce unto every spot on the surface of the earth, and to carry to each one of its cities, the glad-tidings of this Revelation. . . ." The friends now gathered amid the splendor at Carmel's heart have heard it with new ears and have reaffirmed their pledge to respond to this divine longing. May their exploits in the Name of Bahá scatter more widely the fragrance of His Revelation, strengthen more firmly the foundation of His institutions, and embolden more resolutely the activities of His worldwide community, impelling forward the process by which troop after troop will enter into the stronghold of the Ark of Salvation.

THE UNIVERSAL HOUSE OF JUSTICE

25

Riḍván 2001

To the Bahá'ís of the World

Dearly loved Friends,

With great joy in our hearts and high expectations, we come   25.1
to this Riḍván season at a change of time, when a new state of
mind is evident among us all. Abroad in our world community
there is a heightened awareness of the value of process, the
necessity of planning and the virtue of systematic action in
fostering growth and in developing the human resources by
which expansion can be sustained and consolidation assured.
The coherence of understanding about these prerequisites of
progress cannot be overvalued, nor can the importance of
perpetuating them through well-ordered training be overestimated. And so the arrival of our community at such a moment
of consciousness is an occasion of significance for us. We are
deeply grateful to the Blessed Beauty to be able to recognize and
acclaim it at the very beginning of the global enterprise being
launched during these festive days.

The power of will generated by this consciousness charac-   25.2
terized the conference of the Continental Counsellors and the
members of their Auxiliary Boards who gathered last January
in the Holy Land. The event produced so illuminating an
experience as to signalize the Faith's entry into a new epoch,
the fifth of its Formative Age. Such a freshness of vitality as
was displayed at this historic gathering came to be understood
as a manifestation of the rising quality of activity throughout
the community. Pursuit during the past year of the essentials
for advancing the process of entry by troops confirmed this
observation. The path was thus paved for the Five Year Plan,
the first venture being entered upon in the Fifth Epoch.

In augmenting major efforts of the previous Four Year   25.3
Plan that brought into being more than 300 training institutes,
the Twelve Month Plan achieved its purpose. It gathered

significance through the notable responses of institutions and individuals to the call for a greater focus on the spiritual nurturing of children and the involvement of junior youth in Bahá'í community life. The training of teachers of children's classes and the inclusion of junior youth in the institute process have become a regular part of Bahá'í activity in a number of countries. Despite its brevity, the Twelve Month Plan had an importance beyond the objectives specifically assigned. The Plan was a dynamic link between a highly eventful epoch in Bahá'í history and the immensely promising prospects of a new one, for which its achievements have so well prepared the community. It has been etched in our annals, too, for the enduring effects of the Faith's activities at the end of the twentieth century—a century that deserves to be reflected upon by any Bahá'í who wishes to understand the tumultuous forces that influenced the life of the planet and the processes of the Cause itself at a crucial time in humanity's social and spiritual evolution. As an aid to so worthy an effort, *Century of Light*, a review of the twentieth century, was prepared at our request and under our supervision.

25.4   On many occasions during this one-year endeavor, the external affairs activities of the Faith were especially visible. Consider, for example, the instances of Bahá'í representatives' having participated prominently in the millennial events that took place in May, August and September at the urging of the Secretary-General of the United Nations. The implications of so close and conspicuous an involvement of the Bahá'í International Community with the processes of the Lesser Peace will require the passage of time to be properly understood. Among other highlights was the continental colloquium organized in India by the Institute for Studies in Global Prosperity, a new agency operating under the aegis of the Bahá'í International Community. Adopting the theme of "science, religion and development," the conference featured the participation of leading nongovernmental organizations of India, as well as that of institutions of such renown as UNESCO, UNICEF, WHO and the World Bank. In October, the Bahá'í World News Service (BWNS) was launched on the Internet with the intention of reaching both Bahá'í and non-Bahá'í audiences with news stories about developments throughout the Bahá'í world.

25.5   The intensive activities at the Bahá'í World Centre during the last year were, for the most part, made known to the friends through previous reports that included references to such achievements as the occupation by the International Teaching Centre of its permanent seat on Mount Carmel; the Conference of Continental Counsellors and the members of their Auxiliary Boards held in the Holy Land last January; and the completion of the Mount Carmel projects, which are now receiving finishing touches in preparation for the celebratory events in May. Last October, for the first time, pilgrims and visitors were received at the new Reception Centre in Haifa, which became fully operational. At Bahjí the embellishment of the sacred site through the development of its gardens has proceeded continually; the effort has, however, received a boost from the new project initiated last year to construct a Visitors' Centre towards the northern end of the property beyond the Collins Gate. Scheduled for completion in the next few months, the structure is fully in place, and work is progressing in all areas, including finishing and landscaping. The new facilities will improve the ability of the World Centre to receive increasing numbers of pilgrims, short-term Bahá'í visitors, and special guests.

25.6   To conclude this summary of the year, we rejoice in informing you that, after the lapse of almost three decades, the National Spiritual Assembly of the Bahá'ís of Indonesia was restored at the National Convention held in Jakarta last Riḍván. A ban imposed on Bahá'í activities in August 1962 severely restricted the actions of the Indonesian Bahá'ís for all that time, but they remained steadfast and wise in their long-suffering until changed circumstances in that country resulted in the lifting of the ban. May we not venture to hope, then, that a similar happy report concerning our beleaguered co-religionists in Iran, Egypt and other countries will not be too far distant?

25.7   Dear Friends: Two decades from now the Bahá'í world will celebrate the centenary of the inception of the Formative Age. We look back at the dawning of the Age from the vantage point of attainments that could hardly have been imagined at the outset. Up ahead are horizons that urgently summon the community to even greater achievements in the short span separating it from that centennial. Those heights can and must be scaled. The Five Year Plan, to which we call the urgent and sustained attention of the friends throughout the world, is intended to meet this challenge. It constitutes the first of a series of campaigns

that will be pursued during these twenty years. This Plan marks
the next phase in the aim to accomplish a significant advance
in the process of entry by troops. It demands an acceleration of
this vital process and, furthermore, insists upon continuity in
systematic endeavor on the part of its three constituent participants: the individual, the institutions, and the community.

25.8   No need to elaborate on the requirements of the Plan,
for these were set out in our message to the assembled
Counsellors in the Holy Land and subsequently shared with
all National Spiritual Assemblies. Soon after their conference,
the Counsellors began consulting with the National Assemblies
about the execution of the Plan in their respective jurisdic-
tions. The Plan's direction is therefore known to the friends
everywhere, as regional and local preparations for pursuing
its major aim are under way. There is a general awareness by
now that efforts will be made to effect a deeper penetration
of the Faith into more and more regions within countries. For
example, where circumstances permit, local communities that
exist in close proximity to each other will be mobilized to participate in intensive programs of growth. Other approaches will
require methodical opening of new areas for which homefront
pioneers must be raised up in the same consecrated spirit that
prompted those who scattered abroad at earlier times to open
virgin territories across continents and seas. Suffice it to say
that the process animating this divinely driven enterprise will
eventually expand as related features are gradually introduced
and systematically integrated into its operation.

25.9   A feature of the Fifth Epoch will be the enrichment of
the devotional life of the community through the raising up
of national Houses of Worship, as circumstances in national
communities permit. The scheduling of these projects will be
determined by the Universal House of Justice in relation to
the advancement of the process of entry by troops within
countries. This development will unfold throughout successive
stages of 'Abdu'l-Bahá's Divine Plan. Upon the completion
of the Mother Temple of the West, the Guardian started a
program of constructing continental temples. The first among
these were the Mashriqu'l-Adhkárs in Kampala, Sydney and
Frankfurt, which were built in response to Ten Year Plan goals.
The Universal House of Justice continued along these lines with
the building of Temples in Panama City, Apia, and New Delhi.
But this continental stage has yet to be completed: one more

edifice remains to be built. It is with profound thankfulness and joy that we announce at this auspicious moment the decision to proceed with this last project. During the Five Year Plan, erection of the Mother Temple of South America in Santiago, Chile, will commence and thus fulfill a wish clearly expressed by Shoghi Effendi.

Meanwhile, the time is propitious that further steps 25.10 be taken at the World Centre to develop the functions of the institutions occupying the new edifices on the Arc. The International Teaching Centre having advanced significantly in its work, attention will be given particularly to organizing the work of the Centre for the Study of the Texts. Enriching the translations into English from the Holy Texts will be a special object of this attention. The purpose of the institution is to assist the Universal House of Justice in consulting the Sacred Writings and to prepare translations and commentaries on the authoritative texts of the Faith. Moreover, in the Holy Land, a continued effort will be devoted towards the devising of measures to make possible a further increase in the number of pilgrims and visitors to the Bahá'í World Centre.

In our Riḍván message five years ago, we announced the 25.11 holding of a major event at the World Centre to mark the completion of the projects on Mount Carmel and the opening of the Terraces of the Shrine of the Báb to the public. The moment is upon us, and we exult in the anticipation of welcoming friends from virtually all countries to programs that will extend over a five-day period, 21-25 May. We are also happy to say that steps are being taken to connect the Bahá'í world to the proceedings through live transmissions on the World Wide Web and by satellite, about which information is being provided. As the World Centre focuses on the preparations, excitement is building up among the public in Haifa, where municipal authorities have undertaken to publish a book entitled *Bahá'í Shrine and Gardens on Mount Carmel, Haifa, Israel: A Visual Journey* to coincide with the event. Moreover, the Israel Postal Authority is pursuing its decision to release at the same time a commemorative stamp featuring the Terraces. The significance of the occasion lies principally in the pause it will allow for a review of the remarkable distance the Cause has covered in its development during the twentieth century. It will be time, too, for considering the future implications of the phenomenal accomplishments symbolized by the rise of the monumental structures on God's holy mountain—a rise that opens the spiritual and administrative centers of our Faith to the gaze of the world.

25.12   As our community rejoices in these thrilling considerations, let every member bear in mind that there is no time for resting on laurels. Humanity's current plight is too desperate to allow for even a moment's hesitation in sharing the Bread of Life, which has come down from heaven in our time. Let there be no delay, then, in advancing the process that has every promise of success in ushering to the banquet table of the Lord of Hosts the souls of all that hunger after truth.

25.13   May He Who keeps watch over the destiny of His divine System guide and direct and confirm every effort you make towards the realization of the urgent tasks set before you.

THE UNIVERSAL HOUSE OF JUSTICE

26

24 May 2001

To the Believers Gathered for the Events Marking the
  Completion of the Projects on Mount Carmel

Dear Bahá'í Friends,

One hundred and forty-eight years have passed since the
moment in the darkness of the Síyáh-Chál when Bahá'u'lláh
received the Divine summons to rise and proclaim to all on
earth the dawning of the Day of God: 26.1

> Verily, We shall render Thee victorious by Thyself and by
> Thy pen. . . . Erelong God will raise up the treasures of the
> earth—men who will aid Thee through Thyself and through
> Thy Name, wherewith God hath revived the hearts of such
> as have recognized Him. 26.2

In terms of historical time, it is but the briefest of spaces
that separates that primal moment from the splendid victory
we celebrate here this week. You who have come together from
every corner of the earth and from every segment of the human
family represent a cross-section of those whom Bahá'u'lláh has
raised up to aid Him, and no one among us can hope to express
adequately the gratitude we feel at being in that company. 26.3

The majestic buildings that now stand along the Arc traced
for them by Shoghi Effendi on the slope of the Mountain of
God, together with the magnificent flight of garden terraces that
embrace the Shrine of the Báb, are an outward expression of
the immense power animating the Cause we serve. They offer
timeless witness to the fact that the followers of Bahá'u'lláh
have successfully laid the foundations of a worldwide community transcending all differences that divide the human race,
and have brought into existence the principal institutions of a
unique and unassailable Administrative Order that shapes this
community's life. In the transformation that has taken place
on Mount Carmel, the Bahá'í Cause emerges as a visible and 26.4

compelling reality on the global stage, as the focal center of forces that will, in God's good time, bring about the reconstruction of society, and as a mystic source of spiritual renewal for all who turn to it.

26.5   Reflection on what the Bahá'í community has accomplished throws into heartbreaking perspective the suffering and deprivation engulfing the great majority of our fellow human beings. It is necessary that it should do so, because the effect is to open our minds and souls to vital implications of the mission Bahá'u'lláh has laid on us. "Know thou of a truth," He declares, "these great oppressions that have befallen the world are preparing it for the advent of the Most Great Justice." "God be praised!" 'Abdu'l-Bahá adds, "The sun of justice hath risen above the horizon of Bahá'u'lláh. For in His Tablets the foundations of such a justice have been laid as no mind hath, from the beginning of creation, conceived." In the final analysis, it is this Divine purpose that all our activities are intended to serve, and we will advance this purpose to the degree that we understand what is at stake in the efforts we are making to teach the Faith, to establish and consolidate its institutions, and to intensify the influence it is exerting in the life of society.

26.6   Humanity's crying need will not be met by a struggle among competing ambitions or by protest against one or another of the countless wrongs afflicting a desperate age. It calls, rather, for a fundamental change of consciousness, for a wholehearted embrace of Bahá'u'lláh's teaching that the time has come when each human being on earth must learn to accept responsibility for the welfare of the entire human family. Commitment to this revolutionizing principle will increasingly empower individual believers and Bahá'í institutions alike in awakening others to the Day of God and to the latent spiritual and moral capacities that can change this world into another world. We demonstrate this commitment, Shoghi Effendi tells us, by our rectitude of conduct towards others, by the discipline of our own natures, and by our complete freedom from the prejudices that cripple collective action in the society around us and frustrate positive impulses towards change.

26.7   The standards set out by the Guardian apply to the entire Bahá'í community, both in its collective life and in the lives of its individual members. They hold, however, particular implications for Bahá'í youth, who are blessed with the enviable advantages of high energy, flexibility of mind and, to a great extent, freedom of movement. The world that Bahá'í youth are inheriting is one in which the distribution of educational, economic and other basic opportunities is grossly unjust. Bahá'í youth must not be daunted by such barriers. Their challenge is to understand the real condition of humanity and to forge among themselves enduring spiritual bonds that free them not only from racial and national divisions but also from those created by social and material conditions, and that will fit them to carry forward the great trust reposed in them.

Bahá'u'lláh encourages us to anticipate from the youth   26.8
of His community a much earlier advance to maturity than is characteristic of the rest of society. Clearly, that does not in any way diminish the importance of the pursuit of education, of economic realities, or of family obligations. It does mean that Bahá'í youth can accept—and should be encouraged to accept—a responsibility of their own for moral leadership in the transformation of society. In vindication of these words, we invoke the memory of the One Whose Shrine has today set the Mountain of God ablaze with light, and the memory of the band of youthful heroes and heroines whose greatness of soul and sacrifice of self launched on its course the enterprise in which we are engaged.

The achievement we are today celebrating brings into   26.9
focus two paradoxical realities. Within the Faith itself, the gathering strength of the Bahá'í community presages a great surge forward, intimations of which are already everywhere apparent. Inevitably, as Shoghi Effendi several times emphasized, this advance will excite even more intense opposition than the Cause has so far encountered, opposition that will in turn release the greater forces needed for the still more demanding tasks that lie ahead.

The world in which our efforts are taking place is likewise   26.10
undergoing profound changes. On the one hand, the vast network of agencies and individuals that promote understanding and cooperation among diverse peoples affirms ever more powerfully the growing recognition that the "earth is but one country, and mankind its citizens." On the other hand, it is equally clear that the world is moving through a period of social paralysis, tyranny and anarchy, a period marked by the widespread neglect of both governmental and personal responsibility, the ultimate consequences of which no one on earth can foresee. The effect of both developments, as Shoghi Effendi also

pointed out, will be to awaken in the hearts of those who share this planet with us a longing for unity and justice that can be met only by the Cause of God.

26.11   A long and arduous process of struggle, experimentation and construction has led to the victories that lift our hearts as a new century opens. Through the rapidly proliferating system of institutes and the energy being invested everywhere in area growth strategies, the Bahá'í community has moved swiftly to capitalize on what has been achieved. However deep may be the gloom enveloping the world, the future has never looked so bright for the prosecution of Bahá'u'lláh's mission. We who have been privileged to gather here this week have witnessed, with our own eyes, the dawning fulfillment of the words revealed by the Lord of Hosts on this mountain over a century ago, words which cause the very atoms of the earth to vibrate: "Verily this is the Day in which both land and sea rejoice at this announcement, the Day for which have been laid up those things which God, through a bounty beyond the ken of mortal mind or heart, hath destined for revelation."

26.12   Such a privilege carries with it an equally great responsibility, the responsibility to do our part, whatever the sacrifice, whatever the difficulty, to see that the poignant desire expressed by Bahá'u'lláh on that historic occasion is fulfilled: "Oh, how I long to announce unto every spot on the surface of the earth, and to carry to each one of its cities, the glad-tidings of this Revelation—a Revelation to which the heart of Sinai hath been attracted, and in whose name the Burning Bush is calling: 'Unto God, the Lord of Lords, belong the kingdoms of earth and heaven.'"

26.13   With all the fervor of thankful hearts, we will pray at the Holy Threshold that Bahá'u'lláh will bless and confirm every effort you make to advance His purpose for the redemption of humankind and the healing of its ills.

THE UNIVERSAL HOUSE OF JUSTICE

27

To the Friends Gathered at the Eighth ASEAN
    Youth Conference in Thailand

Dear Bahá'í Friends,

27.1   We send our loving greetings to all those gathered at the Eighth ASEAN Youth Conference.

27.2   The Five Year Plan, which will undoubtedly be the focus of your consultations over the next few days, requires concentrated and sustained attention to two essential movements. The first is the steady flow of believers through the sequence of courses offered by training institutes, for the purpose of developing the human resources of the Cause. The second, which receives its impetus from the first, is the movement of geographic clusters from one stage of growth to the next. That Bahá'í youth must be intensely involved in both of these—indeed, that they must be a driving force behind them—goes without saying. We urge you, then, to cast your deliberations in the framework of these two pressing requirements. Ask yourselves how, as individuals, as members of your local and national communities, and as the vanguard of an entire generation in your region, you can ensure that the advancement in the process of entry by troops, called for by the Five Year Plan, is achieved in each of your countries.

27.3   We shall remember you in our prayers in the Holy Shrines.

THE UNIVERSAL HOUSE OF JUSTICE

28

10 January 2002

To the Bahá'ís of the World

Dear Bahá'í Friends,

In the months since the launching of the Five Year Plan, 28.1
national communities have adopted measures that are giving
a dynamic thrust and added coherence to their activities. By
now, in most countries the National Spiritual Assembly, or its
Regional Councils, will have surveyed the territory under its
jurisdiction and divided it into small geographic clusters, in
keeping with the criteria set forth in our letter dated 9 January
2001. These clusters are being categorized according to their
current stage of development, and plans of action devised to
promote in them growth from one stage to the next. We could
not be more gratified by the eager response of the institutions
everywhere to the requirements of the Five Year Plan.

The clearly defined plans now in place multiply teach- 28.2
ing opportunities for those wishing to serve the Faith in the
international field as short- or long-term pioneers. Most of the
needs of the clusters in a given country should increasingly be
met by homefront pioneers as the Plan unfolds. But, given the
sheer number of geographic areas which require systematic
attention in order to advance, international pioneers will have
a notable role to play. Their participation will be especially
effective in the programs of growth spreading throughout the
world if they have developed abilities to foster the institute
process. Beyond this, international pioneers and traveling
teachers can contribute significantly to the work of the Faith
in such spheres of activity as administration, proclamation,
and social and economic development. A document has been
prepared by the International Teaching Centre which briefly
describes the conditions of national Bahá'í communities and
the endeavors that could benefit from outside assistance. It will

soon be available to you through National Spiritual Assemblies and the Counsellors and their auxiliaries.

28.3   The movement of pioneers and traveling teachers from one place to another is an indispensable feature of the Bahá'í community. In the Twelve Month Plan alone, over 1,800 believers from nearly 90 countries set out to serve the Faith in the international field. Apart from the services such staunch souls are able to render to the Cause of God, this intermingling of the peoples of the world is vital to the patterns of life that the followers of Bahá'u'lláh are striving to establish and which are destined to provide an example for the rest of humanity to emulate. As the Bahá'í community continues to grow in capacity, it should give increasing attention to bringing together the diverse members of the human race in ever closer association.

28.4   At this important juncture in the development of the Faith, when the systematization of the teaching work is gaining momentum in all parts of the globe and integrating forces are propelling society towards Bahá'u'lláh's design, every faithful servant of the Cause must be galvanized by the vision of splendid accomplishments ahead. We call upon you to consider your circumstances, examine the conditions of various countries, determine where you can best serve the needs of the Faith, and take resolute action. Let those who long to partake of the joy of such meritorious service go forth well assured that our prayers will accompany them, and fully expectant of Divine confirmations.

THE UNIVERSAL HOUSE OF JUSTICE

29

Riḍván 2002

To the Bahá'ís of the World

Dearly loved Friends,

The onrush of happenings within and without the Faith at 29.1
the beginning of the Fifth Epoch of the Formative Age presents
a spectacle that is awe-inspiring. Inside the Cause, the historic
importance of the events last May that marked the completion
of the edifices on Mount Carmel dazzled the senses as their
impact was instantly communicated throughout the planet by
satellite broadcasts and by the most extensive media coverage
ever accorded a Bahá'í occasion. As the latest evidences in the
tangible unfolding of the Tablet of Carmel were laid bare in
breathtaking splendor before the eyes of the world, the Cause
of Bahá'u'lláh leapt to new prominence in its continuing rise
from obscurity. An indelible impression was thus registered in
the annals of the Dispensation.

This outward manifestation of the vitality animating our 29.2
irrepressible Faith has had its counterpart in the thrust of the
internal processes at work since the inception last Riḍván of the
Five Year Plan. We are therefore moved to invite the delegates
assembled at National Conventions and all other followers of
Bahá'u'lláh throughout the world to join us in reflecting on a
few potent highlights of the operation of the Plan during its
first year—highlights that cannot but rejoice hearts and inspire
confidence in the incalculable potentialities of the course on
which the Plan is set.

In their eager response to its requirements, National 29.3
Spiritual Assemblies engaged in a series of planning sessions
with Continental Counsellors before and immediately after
Riḍván. These set the pace for a vigorous launching distinguished by the steps taken to effectuate a new feature of the
process of entry by troops. In each national community, Bahá'í
institutions began the task of systematically mapping their

171

country with the aim of sectioning it into clusters, each one being of a composition and size consonant with a scale of activities for growth and development that is manageable. Such a mapping, as has already been reported by some 150 countries, makes it possible to realize a pattern of well-ordered expansion and consolidation. Thus it creates as well a perspective, or vision, of systematic growth that can be sustained from cluster to cluster across an entire country. With this perspective, virgin clusters, like virgin territories identified in past campaigns, become goals for homefront pioneers, while opened clusters focus on their internal development mobilized by the mutually reinforcing work of the three constituent components of the Plan: the individual, the institutions and the community.

29.4   It is most encouraging to see that the progress of this work is being energized through the training institute process, which was considerably strengthened last year by the campaigns undertaken in many countries to increase the number of trained tutors. Where a training institute is well established and constantly functioning, three core activities—study circles, devotional meetings, and children's classes—have multiplied with relative ease. Indeed, the increasing participation of seekers in these activities, at the invitation of their Bahá'í friends, has lent a new dimension to their purposes, consequently effecting new enrollments. Here, surely, is a direction of great promise for the teaching work. These core activities, which at the outset were devised principally to benefit the believers themselves, are naturally becoming portals for entry by troops. By combining study circles, devotional meetings and children's classes within the framework of clusters, a model of coherence in lines of action has been put in place and is already producing welcome results. Worldwide application of this model, we feel confident, holds immense possibilities for the progress of the Cause in the years ahead.

29.5   These thrilling prospects were made the more viable by the enormous energy the International Teaching Centre invested in enriching the world community's understanding of systematic growth. Seizing the advantage afforded by the recent commencement of a new term of service for Auxiliary Board members, the Teaching Centre called for 16 regional orientation conferences to be held during the closing months of the year. To each of these it dispatched two of its members. In giving much focus to the theme "training institutes and systematic growth," the conferences, attended by all but a few of the Board members throughout the world, provided the participants with a wealth of information that will, through their tireless labors, suffuse the entire fabric of the community.

A community so richly endowed, so experienced, so focused   29.6
on a divinely-inspired plan of action looks outward to a world whose inhabitants have, since the May 2001 events in the Holy Land, sunk more deeply into a slough of multiple disorders. And yet it is precisely under these seemingly inhospitable conditions that the Cause is meant to advance, and will thrive. *The Summons of the Lord of Hosts*, the newly released volume containing English translations of the full texts of Bahá'u'lláh's Tablets to the kings and rulers of the world, has come as a propitious reminder of the dire consequences of ignoring His warnings against injustice, tyranny and corruption. The violent shocks being inflicted on the consciousness of people everywhere emphasize the urgency of the remedy He has prescribed. We, the scattered bands of His loyal servants, have thus come again to a time of irresistible opportunities—opportunities to teach His Cause, to build up His wondrous System, to provide sacrificially the urgently needed material means on which the progress and execution of spiritual activities inevitably depend.

Our inescapable task is to exploit the current turmoil,   29.7
without fear or hesitation, for the purpose of spreading and demonstrating the transformational virtue of the one Message that can secure the peace of the world. Has the Blessed Beauty not empowered and reassured us with potent words? "Let not the happenings of the world sadden you" is His loving counsel. "I swear by God," He continues; "The sea of joy yearneth to attain your presence, for every good thing hath been created for you, and will, according to the needs of the times, be revealed unto you."

Unhampered by any doubts, unhindered by any obstacles,   29.8
press on, then, with the Plan in hand.

THE UNIVERSAL HOUSE OF JUSTICE

30

To the Bahá'ís of the World†

Dearly loved Friends,

We have followed, with immense gratitude to Bahá'u'lláh, the unfoldment of the Five Year Plan in the two years since our message of 9 January 2001 to the Conference of the Continental Boards of Counsellors. It is heartening, indeed, to see the culture of learning that is taking root everywhere, as the Bahá'í world community focuses on advancing the process of entry by troops. At this juncture, when the collective experience of the community has taken so significant a step forward, we think it timely to review with you the insights thus far gained and to clarify issues that have arisen.   30.1

During the initial months of the Plan, National Spiritual Assemblies proceeded with relative ease to divide the territories under their jurisdiction into areas consisting of adjacent localities, called clusters, using criteria that were purely geographic and social and did not relate to the strength of local Bahá'í communities. Reports received at the World Centre indicate   30.2

---

† A cover letter to this message, dated 17 January 2003 to all National Spiritual Assemblies written on behalf of the Universal House of Justice stated: "The Bahá'í world community has made significant strides since the launching of the Plan, and the House of Justice is conscious of the role that the institutions of the Faith have played in keeping the friends focused on the vital work before them. It hopes that the attached message will offer them an exciting vision of the future unfoldment of the Plan and the tasks they are being called upon to accomplish. That through your wise leadership their efforts will reach the level of intensity required to bring about and sustain accelerated expansion and consolidation is the object of its most fervent prayers at the Sacred Threshold."

that there are now close to 17,000 clusters worldwide, excluding those countries where, for one reason or another, the operation of the Faith is restricted. The number of clusters per country varies widely—from India with its 1,580 to Singapore, which necessarily sees itself as one cluster. Some of the groupings are sparsely populated areas with only a few thousand inhabitants, while the boundaries of others encompass several million people. For the most part, large urban centers under the jurisdiction of one Local Spiritual Assembly have been designated single clusters, these in turn being divided into sectors, so as to facilitate planning and implementation.

30.3   With the various countries and territories divided into manageable areas, national communities moved quickly ahead to categorize clusters according to the stages of the development of the Faith mentioned in our 9 January message. The exercise afforded a realistic means for viewing the prospects of the community, but the task of refining the criteria needed for valid assessments is proving to be an ongoing challenge to institutions. To assign a cluster to one or another category is not to make a statement about status. Rather, it is a way of evaluating its capacity for growth, in order that an approach compatible with its evolving development can be adopted. Rigid criteria are obviously counterproductive, but a well-defined scheme to carry out evaluation is essential. Two criteria seem especially important: the strength of the human resources raised up by the training institute for the expansion and consolidation of the Faith in the cluster, and the ability of the institutions to mobilize these resources in the field of service.

30.4   Focus in almost every country has now turned to stimulating the movement of its priority clusters from their current stage of growth to the next. What has become strikingly clear is that progress in this respect depends largely on the efficacy of the parallel process aimed at helping an ever-increasing number of friends to move through the main sequence of courses offered by the institute serving the area. The rise in activity around the world testifies to the success of these courses in evoking the spirit of enterprise required to carry out the divers actions that growth in a cluster, at whatever stage, demands.

30.5   Particularly heartwarming to observe is a growing sense of initiative and resourcefulness throughout the Bahá'í world, along with courage and audacity. Consecration, zeal, confidence and tenacity—these are among the qualities that are distinguishing the believers in every continent. They are exemplified by, but are certainly not limited to, those who are arising to pioneer on the home front. As we had hoped, goals for the opening of virgin clusters are being readily met by enthusiastic participants of institute programs who, equipped with the knowledge and skills acquired through training courses, set out to establish the Faith in a new area and bring a fledgling community into being.

In most clusters, movement from one stage of growth to the next is being defined in terms of the multiplication of study circles, devotional meetings and children's classes, and the expansion they engender. Devotional meetings begin to flourish as consciousness of the spiritual dimension of human existence is raised among the believers in an area through institute courses. Children's classes, too, are a natural outgrowth of the training received early in the study of the main sequence. As both activities are made open to the wider community through a variety of well-conceived and imaginative means, they attract a growing number of seekers, who, more often than not, are eager to attend firesides and join study circles. Many go on subsequently to declare their faith in Bahá'u'lláh and, from the outset, view their role in the community as that of active participants in a dynamic process of growth. Individual and collective exertions in the teaching field intensify correspondingly, further fuelling the process. Established communities are revitalized, and newly formed ones soon gain the privilege of electing their Local Spiritual Assemblies. 30.6

The coherence thus achieved through the establishment of study circles, devotional meetings and children's classes provides the initial impulse for growth in a cluster, an impulse that gathers strength as these core activities multiply in number. Campaigns that help a sizeable group of believers advance far enough in the main sequence of courses to perform the necessary acts of service lend impetus to this multiplication of activity. 30.7

It is evident, then, that a systematic approach to training has created a way for Bahá'ís to reach out to the surrounding society, share Bahá'u'lláh's message with friends, family, neighbours and coworkers, and expose them to the richness of His teachings. This outward-looking orientation is one of the finest fruits of the grassroots learning taking place. The pattern of activity that is being established in clusters around the globe constitutes a proven means of accelerating expansion and consolidation. Yet this is only a beginning. 30.8

30.9   In many parts of the world, bringing large numbers into the ranks of Bahá'u'lláh's followers has traditionally not been a formidable task. It is therefore encouraging to see that, in some of the more developed clusters, carefully designed projects are being added to the existing pattern of growth to reach receptive populations and lift the rate of expansion to a higher level. Such projects accelerate the tempo of teaching, already on the rise through the efforts of individuals. And, where large-scale enrollment is beginning to result, provision is being made to ensure that a certain percentage of the new believers immediately enter the institute program, for, as we have emphasized in several messages, these friends will be called upon to serve the needs of an ever-growing Bahá'í population. They help deepen the generality of the Bahá'ís by visiting them regularly; they teach children, arrange devotional meetings and form study circles, making it possible to sustain expansion.

30.10   All of this opens thrilling opportunities for Local Spiritual Assemblies. Theirs is the challenge, in collaboration with the Auxiliary Board members who counsel and assist them, to utilize the energies and talents of the swelling human resources available in their respective areas of jurisdiction both to create a vibrant community life and to begin influencing the society around them. In localities where Spiritual Assemblies do not exist or are not yet functioning at the necessary level, a step-by-step approach to the development of communities and Local Spiritual Assemblies is showing excellent promise.

30.11   It is especially gratifying to note the high degree of participation of believers in the various aspects of the growth process. In cluster after cluster, the number of those shouldering the responsibilities of expansion and consolidation is steadily increasing. Meetings of consultation held at the cluster level serve to raise awareness of possibilities and generate enthusiasm. Here, free from the demands of formal decision-making, participants reflect on experience gained, share insights, explore approaches and acquire a better understanding of how each can contribute to achieving the aim of the Plan. In many cases, such interaction leads to consensus on a set of short-term goals, both individual and collective. Learning in action is becoming the outstanding feature of the emerging mode of operation.

30.12   Let there be no doubt that what we are witnessing is the gathering momentum of that process of the entry of humanity into the Cause by troops, foreshadowed in Bahá'u'lláh's Tablet to the King of Persia, eagerly anticipated by the Master, and described by the Guardian as the necessary prelude to mass conversion. In the vanguard of the process are those clusters which, although still relatively few in number, are now ready to launch intensive programs of growth. The scale of expansion that is to mark the next stage of growth in these clusters calls for an intensity of effort yet to be achieved. May the prodigious output of energy devoted to this mighty undertaking be reinforced by the power of Divine assistance.

Be assured of our heartfelt prayers in the Holy Shrines that 30.13 Bahá'u'lláh may bless and confirm your endeavors to realize, to the fullest, the extraordinary opportunities of these precious days.

THE UNIVERSAL HOUSE OF JUSTICE

31

10 April 2003

To the Friends Gathered at the Series of Youth Forums
   Called by the Regional Bahá'í Council
   of the Western States, U.S.A.

Dear Bahá'í Friends,

We were delighted to learn that the Regional Bahá'í Council 31.1
of the Western States has called upon selected Local Spiritual
Assemblies to conduct a series of youth forums at this juncture
in the unfoldment of the Five Year Plan. The Council is clearly
conscious of the weighty responsibilities with which it has
been entrusted and recognizes that the success of the efforts
to advance the process of entry by troops across the region
will depend, in no small measure, on your wholehearted and
sacrificial participation in the plans of action now in place. We
applaud the Council's decision and urge you to take advantage
of the opportunity to contribute to the progress of the Cause
in your communities.

From your study of our 17 January 2003 message to the 31.2
Bahá'ís of the world, you know that the challenge facing
the institutions of the Faith in every part of the globe is to
stimulate the movement of the clusters in their respective areas
of jurisdiction from one stage of growth to the next. You are
also well aware that this movement receives its impetus from
another, that is, from the steady flow of believers through the
sequence of courses adopted by their training institutes. In
those clusters where the institute process is well established,
three key activities—study circles, devotional meetings and
children's classes—tend to multiply with relative ease, creating
an initial pattern of growth, to which other elements must then
be added. Multiplying these activities ranks high among the
priorities of the institutions everywhere, and you should not
underestimate the importance of the part Bahá'í youth must
play in this mighty endeavor. Who more than the young people

of our communities can lend the collective energy needed to achieve so necessary an increase in the level of activity?

31.3   We hope, then, that you will become the most enthusiastic participants in the programs of growth in your clusters. You should take up with a true sense of responsibility, and in a spirit of joy that service to the Faith evokes, the task of rapidly increasing the number of study circles, devotional meetings and children's classes in the Western States. Your efforts to meet this challenge will be greatly enhanced if you constantly seek out receptive souls in your schools, at your universities, and in the workplace and invite them to join you in your systematic study of institute courses.

31.4   Now more than ever you should be attuned to the interests of your peers and be confident that many will welcome the opportunity to delve into the Writings with you. The widespread turmoil in the world, so graphically displayed by ongoing occurrences, brings with it a heightened degree of receptivity to the Cause, especially among young people. You should remain ever conscious of the forces at work in society and seize on the opening they provide for you to extend the influence of the Faith. Your peers long to make sense of the events they see unfolding around them, both at home and on the global scene. You alone have the Message that can soothe their troubled hearts and provide them with the clarity of thought they desire. Be assured of our prayers at the Sacred Threshold on your behalf.

THE UNIVERSAL HOUSE OF JUSTICE

32

Ridván 2003

To the Bahá'ís of the World

Dearly loved Friends,

As the Five Year Plan enters upon its third year, momentum is building: the record of achievement during the year just ended far outdistanced that of the previous twelve months. The thrust of this momentum owes as much to the increased coherence achieved in the Plan's constituent elements as to the animating effect of the spirit of unrest pervading the planet.

32.1

The circumstances attending the opening of this new administrative year are at once critical, challenging and extraordinary in their significance. The entire course of the previous year was agitated by a succession of crises that culminated in the outbreak of war in the Middle East. The implications are no less significant for the progress of the community of the Most Great Name than for the evolution of an increasingly global society in the throes of a turbulent transition. Of necessity, the timing, scale and tendencies of this transition have not been predictable. How swift indeed has been the current change in the tide of world conditions! In the resultant conflict, involving so conspicuously the countries in which the earliest history of the Cause took shape, we see a fresh reminder of Bahá'u'lláh's warning that the "world's equilibrium hath been upset through the vibrating influence of this most great, this new World Order." That the events of this crisis directly affect a territory with as rich a Bahá'í legacy as Iraq is particularly noteworthy.

32.2

The disruptions caused by this and other situations in the world have, in one instance, suggested the opening of a new chapter in the history of the highly prized but woefully oppressed Bahá'í community of a land in which the Manifestation of God for this Day resided for a whole decade. In another, they have dashed the preparations for the Ninth International

32.3

Convention at the World Centre of our Faith. But, however disappointing, this calls for no dismay. When the Major Plan of God interferes with His Minor Plan, there should be no doubt that in due course a way will providentially be opened to an opportunity of stellar possibilities for advancing the interests of His glorious Cause.

32.4   The sorrows, fears and perplexities evoked by this latest conflict in the unfoldment of the Lesser Peace have intensified the feelings of grievance and outrage at the recurrent crises agitating the planet. The anxieties of people across the globe are even now being played out publicly in angry demonstrations too overwhelming to be ignored. The issues they protest and the emotions they arouse often add to the chaos and confusion they hope by such public displays to resolve. For the friends of God, there is an unambiguous explanation for what is occurring; they have only to recall the vision and principles offered by the Faith if they are to respond effectively to the challenges posed by the spread of distress and dismay. Let them strive to understand more deeply the Teachings that are relevant by reviewing letters of Shoghi Effendi which have been published in *The World Order of Bahá'u'lláh,* particularly those entitled "The Goal of a New World Order," "America and the Most Great Peace," and "The Unfoldment of World Civilization."

32.5   While the world continues on its tumultuous course, the Five Year Plan has reached the operational capacity to enable our community to make giant strides towards its major aim of advancing the process of entry by troops. The details of so encouraging a state of affairs for the Faith on all five continents have already been given in our 17 January letter; to it we invite your further study. Only a few key details need now be underscored: The division of countries into clusters has been completed in 179 of them; there exist some 17,000 of these seedbeds of expansion. Reflection meetings at the level of clusters have become a powerful means of unifying thought and action across institutions and localities; they have lent a potent stimulus to institutional and individual initiatives in a mutually supportive spirit. The institute process has demonstrated even more prominently than before its influence as a generating force for expansion and consolidation. The core activities of the Plan have attained a scale far outstripping that of the past year. As a result, a growing number of friends are now active in the teaching and administrative work throughout the world, demonstrating the infectious spirit of confidence inspiring the enthusiasm of their efforts. Youth and children have been more systematically involved in the programs of the community, and non-Bahá'ís have been participating more numerously in study circles, devotional meetings and children's classes. It is indeed heartening to note that, in the brief period since the beginning of the Plan, where in many communities these three core activities had been sporadic they have become regular features and have multiplied. Here, then, is a snapshot of a world community focused and on the move as never before.

During the past year, as this pattern of growth became more firmly rooted in the operation of the Plan, other important developments were taking place. In the arena of external affairs, agencies of the Bahá'í International Community engaged in activities too numerous and varied to describe here, but of a collective effect too impressive to let pass without some mention. The highlight of such activities was the message we addressed last April to the world's religious leaders. This has given a fresh impulse to the approach being taken by the Bahá'í community to call the attention of the most influential elements of society to issues of critical importance to ensuring the peace of the world. Through the coordinating efforts of the Bahá'í International Community's Office of Public Information and the prompt efficiency of National Spiritual Assemblies, the message was distributed in a short time to the topmost ranks and other echelons of religious communities across the globe. The purpose of the initiative is to bring to the attention of all concerned the urgent need for religious leadership to address the problem of religious prejudice, which is becoming a steadily more serious danger to human well-being. The immediate reactions from many recipients indicate that the message is being seriously regarded and is even in some places lending new perspective to interfaith activities. 32.6

In the field of social and economic development a tempo has been attained that impresses ever more deeply the effects of institutional and individual effort on both the internal development of the community and the community's collaboration with others. The Office of Social and Economic Development reports that during the second year of the Plan eight new Bahá'í-inspired development agencies were established, operating in such diverse fields as the advancement of women, health, agriculture, child education and youth empowerment. 32.7

32.8   In the Holy Land, the English translation of Bahá'u'lláh's Arabic epistle known as Javáhiru'l-Asrár was released under the title *Gems of Divine Mysteries*. The restoration of the Cell of Bahá'u'lláh in the prison at 'Akká was completed, and work began on the remainder of the upper floor of the prison cell area. As of the next pilgrimage season, beginning in October 2003, the number of pilgrims in each group will be raised from 150 to 200.

32.9   Furthermore, efforts at fostering the development of institutions operating at the World Centre were especially evident in the continuing evolution of the institution of Ḥuqúqu'lláh under the distinguished leadership of the Trustee, the Hand of the Cause of God 'Alí-Muḥammad Varqá. Through his wise initiative and constant endeavor, Dr. Varqá has inspired the education of the friends everywhere concerning the law of Ḥuqúqu'lláh. In the decade since the law was universally applied, a network of national and regional boards of trustees has been brought into existence, which provides coordination and direction to the service of an increasing number of deputies and representatives. Knowledge of this great law has spread widely, and friends from all continents are responding to it with a spirit of devotion, which the Trustee hopes will touch those who have not yet availed themselves of the promised blessings flowing from adherence to this law.

32.10   In the nearly two years since we announced the special necessity for financial support to maintain, at a befitting standard, the buildings and gardens at the World Centre, the World Centre Endowment Fund has been established. The contributions have not yet reached a level equal to the annual need. However, we have felt obliged to set aside five million dollars of the contributions received as an earmarked fund towards building a corpus to provide a source of investment income dedicated to the original purpose. We have done so by drawing upon the Bahá'í International Fund to assist in covering the necessary expenditures, suspending activities in other fields that it would have been normal to pursue.

32.11   We are delighted to advise that, in response to the call issued by the National Spiritual Assembly of Chile, 185 design concepts have been received from architects and designers around the world for the Mother Temple of South America to be constructed in Santiago. A final choice will be announced in due course.

Dear Friends: Gratified by solid evidence of the progress being made far and wide, we trust in the continuing confirmations of our Supreme Lord upon the dedicated efforts you exert within the framework of the Five Year Plan—a Plan designed to fit the requirements of these times. May your persistence in its pursuit release those pent-up forces that, through the grace and favor of the Abhá Beauty, can advance by mighty thrusts the process of entry by troops in every land. 32.12

THE UNIVERSAL HOUSE OF JUSTICE

33

Riḍván 2004

To the Baháʼís of the World

Dearly loved Friends,

Three years of the Five Year Plan have passed. The processes set in motion in the Four Year Plan, strengthened through special attention to the Baháʼí education of children during the Twelve Month Plan, and followed up unflaggingly during these past years, are now fulfilling the high hopes with which they were launched. In every part of the world the three participants in the Plan—the individual, the community and the institutions—each playing a distinctive role, are reinforcing one another's actions. The core activities of study circles, children's classes and devotional meetings have become essential aspects and mutually enhancing achievements lending greater vigor and success to all the other elements of Baháʼí community life. Human resources are being augmented, and the Local Spiritual Assemblies are responding to the fresh demands of this rising vitality. 33.1

The capacity built for the Baháʼí education of children throughout the world is extraordinarily impressive. Initial efforts for the spiritual empowerment of junior youth are meeting with success. The movement of clusters from each level of activity to a higher one is well in hand and, as it proceeds, the kernel of avowed believers is being joined by a larger circle of people, still not Baháʼís but enthusiastically involved in core activities of the Plan. Structures for administering intensive growth are already appearing in certain advanced clusters. National Assemblies, while attending to the needs of all the clusters in their countries, have learned the value of concentrating special attention on certain priority clusters that show high promise, encouraging and developing them until the human resources they have raised up through the training institutes enable them to become centers of rapid, sustained growth. 33.2

33.3   As foreseen, the training institute is proving to be an engine of growth. On assessing the opportunities and needs of their respective communities, the great majority of National Spiritual Assemblies have chosen to adopt the course materials devised by the Ruhi Institute, finding them most responsive to the Plan's needs. This has had the collateral benefit that the same materials have been translated into many languages and, wherever Bahá'ís travel, they find other friends following the same path and familiar with the same books and methods.

33.4   A chaotic international society, torn by conflicting perceptions and interests, is assailed by rising terrorism, lawlessness and corruption, and eroded by economic failure, poverty and disease. In its midst the Bahá'í community is becoming increasingly visible, inspired by a divinely revealed vision, building on solid foundations, growing in strength through the processes that are now in place, and undaunted by seeming setbacks. An example of the capacity of the Bahá'í world to respond to unexpected conditions occurred a year ago, when multiple dangers required the cancellation of the International Bahá'í Convention; the election of the Universal House of Justice was duly held and the Plan went forward without a missed step. Concurrently, despite the disruption and chaos of life in Iraq, it was possible to contact the Bahá'ís in that land and reconstitute their Local Spiritual Assemblies. Now we announce with great joy the election, this Riḍván, of the National Spiritual Assembly of the Bahá'ís of Iraq, restored after more than thirty years of stifling oppression, to take its rightful place in the international Bahá'í community.

33.5   What the Divine Plan requires at this stage is for us to continue confidently and dynamically in the present direction, undeterred by storms battering the world of humanity. Be sure that the Blessed Beauty will guide your steps and the Hosts of the Supreme Concourse will reinforce your every effort for the progress of His Faith.

THE UNIVERSAL HOUSE OF JUSTICE

34

Riḍván 2005

To the Bahá'ís of the World

Dearly loved Friends,

The breakthroughs that have occurred in the Bahá'í world   34.1
since the beginning of the fifth epoch of the Formative Age
have brought us immeasurable joy. The past twelve months
have been no exception. The Bahá'í community has continued
its systematic advance and now, as it enters the final year of
the Five Year Plan, finds itself in a position of remarkable
strength—a strength acquired through strenuous, deliberate
exertion by the friends everywhere to promote the process of
entry by troops.

While inadequate to express the full significance of the   34.2
developments taking place, the statistics suggest something of
the scope of what is being achieved. The human resources of the
Faith have steadily multiplied. Altogether, more than 200,000
worldwide have completed Book 1 of the Ruhi Institute, and
many thousands have reached the level where they can effectively act as tutors of the study circles that, with increasing
frequency, are held in every part of the globe, over 10,000 at the
last count. The number of seekers engaged in the core activities
has continued to climb, crossing the 100,000 mark several
months ago. Meanwhile, some 150 clusters have developed to
the point that intensive programs of growth either have been
launched or stand ready to be initiated. There is every indication
that this number will be substantially surpassed by the end of
the Plan.

In celebrating these achievements, one should acknowledge,   34.3
equally, the advances in learning that have given rise to them.
Intensive institute campaigns, which pay due attention to the
practice required, have remained the vehicle for stimulating
growth at the cluster level. As the necessary conditions have
thus been created, systematic programs for the expansion and

consolidation of the Faith have been launched accordingly. A valuable body of knowledge about the nature of intensive programs of growth is accumulating, and certain features of these endeavors are now well understood. Such programs tend to consist of a series of cycles, each of several months' duration, devoted to planning, expansion, and consolidation. Human resource development proceeds uninterrupted from one cycle to the next, ensuring that the process of expansion not only is sustained but progressively gathers momentum. While undoubtedly many more lessons are still to be garnered, the experience already gained makes it possible to replicate the approach in an ever-increasing number of clusters around the world.

34.4 That the victories won have both quantitative and qualitative dimensions is gratifying indeed. At the heart of these accomplishments lies the continual enhancement of the spiritual life of Bahá'í communities everywhere. This new spiritual vitality accounts for the growing participation of people of divers backgrounds in devotional meetings, children's classes and study circles, which, in many cases, has resulted in their recognition of Bahá'u'lláh as God's Manifestation for this Day and in their declaration of faith.

34.5 New developments have, likewise, taken place at the World Centre. We have decided that the time is propitious to bring into being an International Board of Trustees of Ḥuqúqu'lláh to guide and supervise the work of Regional and National Boards of Trustees of Ḥuqúqu'lláh throughout the world. It will operate in close collaboration with the Chief Trustee, the Hand of the Cause of God Dr. 'Alí-Muḥammad Varqá, and will be able to benefit from his knowledge and counsel in carrying out its duties. The three members now appointed to the International Board of Trustees are Sally Foo, Ramin Khadem, and Grant Kvalheim. Their term of office will be determined at a later date. The members of the Board will not transfer their residence to the Holy Land but will utilize the services of the Office of Ḥuqúqu'lláh at the World Centre in performing their functions.

34.6 At all levels and in every direction the Cause is achieving marked progress—from gains in expansion and consolidation at the grassroots to institutional developments of an international scope. Such encouraging signs of the growing solidarity of the community come at a time when evidences of the decline in society are, alas, all too apparent. No need to review here the features of the breakdown in which a demoralized world is entrapped. Yet it should not be forgotten that it is precisely these circumstances which increase receptivity to the Teachings and create new opportunities for their diffusion.

In our message of 26 November 1999, we referred to a 34.7 series of global enterprises designed to carry the Bahá'í community through the final years of the first century of the Faith's Formative Age. Each Plan, we indicated, would focus on the central aim of advancing the process of entry by troops. The first in the series, the current Five Year Plan, will draw to a close in twelve short months, when we will call upon the followers of Bahá'u'lláh to embark on another Plan of five years' duration. What we ask the friends to do in the intervening period is to bend all their energies to put into resolute action the systematic learning being so vigorously promoted by the International Teaching Centre. No Bahá'í should lose the priceless opportunity afforded by the remaining days of the Plan to reinforce in this way the foundation for the launching next Riḍván of an even more ambitious undertaking. Our most fervent prayers in the Holy Shrines will surround you.

THE UNIVERSAL HOUSE OF JUSTICE

35

27 December 2005

To the Conference of the Continental Boards of Counsellors

Dearly loved Friends,

Over the past four and a half years, as the believers 35.1
throughout the world have striven to pursue the aim of advancing the process of entry by troops, it has become increasingly
clear that the close of the present Five Year Plan will mark a
decisive moment in the unfoldment of the historical enterprise
on which the community of the Greatest Name is embarked.
The elements required for a concerted effort to infuse the
diverse regions of the world with the spirit of Bahá'u'lláh's
Revelation have crystallized into a framework for action that
now needs only to be exploited.

Our 26 December 1995 message, which focused the Bahá'í 35.2
world on a path of intense learning about the sustained, rapid
growth of the Faith, described in general terms the nature of
the work that would have to be undertaken in meeting the challenges ahead. As a first step, Bahá'í communities were urged
to systematize their efforts to develop the human resources
of the Cause through a network of training institutes. While
every national community took measures to create institutional
capacity to perform this essential function, it was not until
the outset of the Five Year Plan that the significance of a well-
conceived program of training became widely appreciated. The
introduction of the concept of the cluster made it possible for
the friends to think about the accelerated growth of the community on a manageable scale and to conceive of it in terms of
two complementary, reinforcing movements: the steady flow
of individuals through the sequence of institute courses and
the movement of clusters from one stage of development to
the next. This image helped the believers to analyze the lessons
being learned in the field and to employ a common vocabulary
to articulate their findings. Never before have the means for

establishing a pattern of activity that places equal emphasis on the twin processes of expansion and consolidation been better understood. Indeed, so consistent has been the experience with intensive programs of growth, implemented on the basis of this understanding in divers clusters, that no cause for equivocation remains. The way forward is clear, and at Riḍván 2006 we will call upon the believers to steel their resolve and to proceed with the full force of their energies on the course that has been so decidedly set.

35.3   In presenting to you the features of the coming Five Year Plan, the subject of your deliberations in this conference, we will review the record of recent accomplishments of the Bahá'í world and indicate how current approaches, methods and instruments should be carried to this next stage. What the analysis will make evident is that the wholehearted response of the individual believer, the community and the institutions to the guidance they received five years ago has raised their capacity to new levels. The continued development of this capacity will remain essential to the aim of advancing the process of entry by troops—the focus of the Bahá'í world through the final years of the first century of the Formative Age.

The Individual

35.4   There is little need to describe in detail the achievements of the individual believer, for we have already noted these in our message of 17 January 2003 to the Bahá'ís of the world. In that message we highlighted the growing sense of initiative and resourcefulness, as well as the courage and audacity, that have come to characterize believers everywhere. Qualities such as consecration, zeal, confidence and tenacity attest to the enhanced vitality of their faith. We have also acknowledged the role played by the training institute in evoking the spirit of enterprise underlying the rise in activity observed around the world—the concrete expression of that vitality.

35.5   Developments since then have served only to demonstrate further the efficacy of a sequence of courses that seeks to build capacity for service by concentrating on the application of the spiritual insights gained through profound study of the Writings. Participants are exposed to a body of knowledge that fosters a set of related habits, attitudes and qualities and are assisted in sharpening certain skills and abilities needed to carry out acts of service. Discussions that revolve around the Creative Word, in the serious and uplifting atmosphere of a study circle, raise the level of consciousness about one's duties to the Cause and create an awareness of the joy one derives from teaching the Faith and serving its interests. The spiritual context in which specific deeds are addressed endows them with significance. Confidence is patiently built as the friends engage in progressively more complex and demanding acts of service. Yet, above all, it is reliance on God that sustains them in their endeavors. How abundant the accounts of believers who enter the teaching field with trepidation only to find themselves bolstered by confirmations on all sides. Seeing the possibilities and opportunities before them with new eyes, they witness first hand the power of Divine assistance, as they strive to put into practice what they are learning and achieve results far exceeding their expectations. That the spirit of faith born out of intimate contact with the Word of God has such an effect on souls is by no means a new phenomenon. What is heartening is that the institute process is helping such large numbers experience the transforming potency of the Faith. To extend this edifying influence to hundreds of thousands more should be the object of intense effort over the next five years.

A discernible outcome of the emphasis on capacity build-   35.6
ing has been a steady increase in the exercise of individual initiative—initiative that is disciplined by an understanding of the requirements of systematic action in advancing the process of entry by troops. Endeavors are pursued in a humble posture of learning within the framework defined by the Plan. As a result, activities that give expression to a diversity of talents become harmonized into one forward movement, and the stagnation caused by endless debate over personal preferences about approach is avoided. Commitment to long-term action grows, putting in context the initiatives undertaken by the believers at any particular moment.

Nowhere has the rise in individual initiative been more   35.7
clearly demonstrated than in the field of teaching. Whether in the form of firesides or study circles, individual efforts to teach the Faith are indisputably on the increase. Equipped with skills and methods, effective and accessible to all, and encouraged by the response their actions elicit, the believers are entering into closer association with people of many walks of life, engaging them in earnest conversation on themes of spiritual

import. With greater and greater spiritual perception, they are able to sense receptivity and recognize thirst for the vivifying waters of Bahá'u'lláh's message. From among all those they encounter—parents of neighborhood children, peers at school, colleagues at work, casual acquaintances—they seek out souls with whom they can share a portion of that which He has so graciously bestowed on humanity. Increased experience enables them to adapt their presentation to the seeker's needs, employing direct teaching methods that draw on the Writings to offer the message in a manner both forthcoming and inviting.

35.8   Most noteworthy in this regard is the spirit of initiative shown by believers who extend the range of their endeavors to assist others also striving to tread a path of service. Having acquired the capacity to serve as tutors of institute courses, they take up the challenge of accompanying participants in their initial attempts to perform acts of service until they, too, are ready to start their own study circles and help others do the same, widening in this way the scope of the institute's influence and bringing eager souls into contact with the Word of God. This particular aspect of the institute process, which serves to multiply the number of active supporters of the Faith in a self-perpetuating manner, holds much promise, and we hope that its potential will be realized in the coming Plan. "Let him not be content," are the words of the Guardian referring to every teacher of the Cause, "until he has infused into his spiritual child so deep a longing as to impel him to arise independently, in his turn, and devote his energies to the quickening of other souls, and the upholding of the laws and principles laid down by his newly adopted Faith."

The Community

35.9   The enhanced vitality that distinguishes the life of the individual believer is equally evident in Bahá'í community life. The degree to which this vitality manifests itself depends, of course, on the stage of development of the cluster. A cluster in an advanced stage of growth offers far greater insight into what can be achieved than one in an earlier stage, where the friends are still struggling to translate the provisions of the Plan into action. It is to these more advanced clusters, then, that we must look in analyzing the accomplishments of the community, convinced that their experience will be emulated by others as they continue to progress.

On several occasions we have made reference to the 35.10 coherence that is brought to the process of growth through the establishment of study circles, devotional meetings and children's classes. The steady multiplication of core activities, propelled by the training institute, creates a sustainable pattern of expansion and consolidation that is at once structured and organic. As seekers join these activities and declare their faith, individual and collective teaching endeavors gather momentum. Through the effort made to ensure that a percentage of the new believers enroll in the institute courses, the pool of human resources required to carry out the work of the Faith swells. When strenuously pursued in a cluster, all of this activity eventually brings about conditions favorable for launching an intensive program of growth.

What a close examination of clusters at this threshold 35.11 confirms is that the coherence thus achieved extends to various aspects of community life. The study and application of the teachings become a pervasive habit, and the spirit of communal worship generated by devotional meetings begins to permeate the community's collective endeavors. A graceful integration of the arts into diverse activities enhances the surge of energy that mobilizes the believers. Classes for the spiritual education of children and junior youth serve to strengthen the roots of the Faith in the local population. Even an act of service as simple as visiting the home of a new believer, whether in a village in the Pacific Islands or in a vast metropolitan area like London, reinforces ties of fellowship that bind the members of the community together. Conceived as a means for exposing believers to the fundamentals of the Faith, "home visits" are giving rise to an array of deepening efforts, both individual and collective, in which the friends are delving into the Writings and exploring their implications for their lives.

As the spiritual foundations of the community are fortified 35.12 in this way, the level of collective discourse is raised, social relations among the friends take on new meaning, and a sense of common purpose inspires their interactions. Little wonder, then, that a study carried out by the International Teaching Centre shows that, in some fifty advanced clusters surveyed, the quality of the Nineteen Day Feast has improved. Other reports indicate that contributions to the Fund have increased as consciousness of its spiritual significance expands and the need for material means is better understood. Reflection meetings at the cluster level are becoming a forum for the discussion of needs and plans, creating a collective identity and strengthening the collective will. Where such advanced clusters are flourishing, the influence they exert begins to spread beyond their own borders to enrich regional events, such as summer and winter schools.

35.13   As in the case of the individual, learning is the hallmark of this phase of the development of the community. You and your auxiliaries are urged to exert every effort in the coming years to ensure that, in cluster after cluster, learning is woven into the fabric of decision-making.

35.14   One of your primary concerns will be to strengthen appreciation for systematic action, already heightened by the successes it has brought. To arrive at a unified vision of growth based on a realistic assessment of possibilities and resources, to develop strategies that lend structure to it, to devise and implement plans of action commensurate with capacity, to make necessary adjustments while maintaining continuity, to build on accomplishments—these are some of the requisites of systematization that every community must learn and internalize.

35.15   By the same token, desire and willingness to open certain aspects of community life to the wider public should be integrated into a pattern of behavior that attracts souls and confirms them. Much has been achieved in this respect as the friends have adopted new ways of thinking and acting at a collective level. In welcoming large numbers into its embrace, the community is learning to see more readily the latent potentiality in people and to avoid setting artificial barriers for them based on preconceived notions. A nurturing environment is being cultivated in which each individual is encouraged to progress at his or her own pace without the pressure of unreasonable expectations. At the heart of such developments is a growing awareness of the implications of the universality and comprehensiveness of the Faith. Collective action is governed more and more by the principle that Bahá'u'lláh's message should be given liberally and unconditionally to humanity. Most gratifying are the endeavors being made to reach receptive populations with the teachings of the Faith. As unrelenting social and political forces continue to uproot people from their homelands and sweep them across continents, an uncompromising appreciation for a diversity of backgrounds and for the strength it confers on the whole will prove crucial to the expansion and consolidation of the community.

Perhaps the task that will occupy the attention of you and your auxiliaries above all others is to assist the community in its effort to maintain focus. This ability, slowly acquired through successive Plans, represents one of its most valuable assets, hard won through discipline, commitment and foresight as the friends and their institutions have learned to pursue the single aim of advancing the process of entry by troops. On the one hand, you will find it necessary to discourage the tendency to confuse focus with uniformity or exclusivity. To maintain focus does not imply that special needs and interests are neglected, much less that essential activities are dropped in order to accommodate others. Clearly, there are a host of elements that comprise Bahá'í community life, shaped over the decades, which must be further refined and developed. On the other hand, you will want to take every opportunity to reinforce the disposition to prioritize—one which recognizes that not all activities have the same importance at a given stage of growth, that some must necessarily take precedence over others, that even the most well-intentioned proposals can cause distraction, dissipate energy or impede progress. What should be plainly acknowledged is that the time available for the friends to serve the Faith in every community is not without limits. It is only natural to expect that the preponderating share of this limited resource would be expended in meeting the provisions of the Plan.

The Institutions

None of the accomplishments of the individual or the community could be sustained without the guidance, encouragement and support of the third participant in the Plan—the institutions of the Faith. It is heartening to see to what extent the institutions are promoting individual initiative, channeling energies into the teaching field, underscoring the value of systematic action, fostering the spiritual life of the community and nurturing a welcoming environment. In helping the community to remain focused on the aim of the Plan, they are learning in practical terms what it means to maintain unity of vision among the friends, to put mechanisms in place that facilitate their endeavors and to allocate resources in accordance with

35.16

35.17

priorities wisely set. These priorities include, of course, areas of activity that require the specialized skills of individuals. Worthy of particular mention in this category are the work of external affairs, which National Spiritual Assemblies are following diligently, and ventures of social and economic development, as, for example, undertaken by Bahá'í-inspired organizations. While tending to needs of this kind, the institutions find themselves increasingly capable of directing the thrust of the effort exerted by the generality of the believers towards the prosecution of the central tasks of the Plan.

35.18   Encouraging, too, are the determined steps being taken by National Spiritual Assemblies, in collaboration with the Counsellors, to respond to the administrative challenges brought by large-scale growth at the cluster level. Schemes that are emerging tend to call for one or more individuals named by the training institute to coordinate the delivery of courses in the main sequence, as well as programs for children and junior youth. An Area Teaching Committee appointed by the Regional Council, or by the National Assembly itself, is also required to administer other aspects of systematic effort to achieve accelerated expansion and consolidation. Auxiliary Board members work on both fronts to ensure that the two movements which have come to characterize the process of growth proceed unhampered. While these various components are being established in cluster after cluster, there is still much to be learned about the functions each is to perform and about the relationships among them. What is important is that the current degree of flexibility, which allows for the creation of new instruments as needed, not be compromised so that the scheme of coordination represents a response to the demands of growth itself. We count on you and National Assemblies to guide this learning process.

35.19   Throughout the Plan, we have watched with the keenest interest the effects of these developments on the functioning of Local Spiritual Assemblies. It gives us pleasure to note that two types of progress are being made in this respect. In those clusters where most of the Local Assemblies have been extremely weak, a growing number are gradually assuming their responsibilities as they learn to guide specific activities of the Plan in the areas under their jurisdiction. At the same time, long-standing Local Spiritual Assemblies are exhibiting signs of added strength as they have come to embrace a vision of systematic growth—this, often following a period of adjustment in which some struggled to understand the new realities being created at the cluster level.

What has brought us particular joy is to see that the process of growth unfolding around the world is gathering momentum in urban centers as well as rural areas. An important step taken in many large cities early in the current Plan was to divide them into sectors. This proved crucial to planning for sustained growth. As communities expand, however, it is not unreasonable to expect that cities will need to be divided into smaller areas—perhaps ultimately into neighborhoods—in each of which the Nineteen Day Feast is conducted. Maintaining a vision of the potential size of future communities is essential for the further development of Local Assemblies. To administer the affairs of communities whose membership will swell into the thousands, and to fulfill their purpose as the "trusted ones of the Merciful among men," those who serve on Spiritual Assemblies will necessarily undergo intense periods of learning in the years ahead. We intend to monitor the development of Local Spiritual Assemblies closely during the coming Plan and, as the size of the Bahá'í population and other circumstances in a locality demand, authorize a two-stage electoral process on a case-by-case basis, following the pattern developed in Ṭihrán during the ministry of the Guardian. 35.20

Intensive Programs of Growth

Sustained endeavor on the part of the individual, the community and the institutions to accelerate the institute process in a cluster, while contributing to its movement from one stage of development to another through well-proven means, culminates in the launching of an intensive program of growth. Indeed, the most significant advances in learning during the present Plan resulted from efforts in some two hundred clusters to implement such programs. We are convinced that this learning can now be systematically propagated in every continent, and at Riḍván 2006 we will call upon Bahá'ís worldwide to establish, during the next Plan, intensive programs of growth in no less than 1,500 clusters. 35.21

As currently conceived, an intensive program of growth is straightforward, simple and effective, but implies a level of exertion that tests the resolve of the friends. Conforming well 35.22

to the vision we presented five years ago, it employs a few measures that have proven to be indispensable to large-scale expansion and consolidation. It consists of cycles of activity, in general of three months' duration each, which proceed according to distinct phases of expansion, consolidation, reflection and planning.

35.23 The expansion phase, often a period of two weeks, demands the highest level of intensity. Its objective is to widen the circle of those interested in the Faith, to find receptive souls and to teach them. Although this phase might include some element of proclamation, it should not be seen as a time to hold a few events for this purpose or to undertake a set of activities that merely convey information. Experience suggests that the more closely teaching approaches and methods are aligned with the capacity acquired from the study of the institute courses the more rewarding the results.

35.24 Plans being devised for this phase invariably involve the implementation of carefully designed teaching projects and campaigns of home visits and firesides, often through the mobilization of teaching teams. The pattern of expansion that unfolds, however, varies from cluster to cluster. Where the population has traditionally shown a high degree of receptivity to the Faith, a rapid influx of new believers is to be expected. In one cluster of this kind, for example, the goal of enrolling fifty souls over a three-week period in a locality was surpassed by the second day, and the team wisely decided to end the expansion phase in anticipation of activities related to consolidation. One of the primary objectives of this next phase is to bring a percentage of the new believers into the institute process so that an adequate pool of human resources will be available in future cycles to sustain growth. Those not participating in study circles are nurtured through a series of home visits, and all are invited to devotional meetings, to the celebration of the Nineteen Day Feast and to Holy Day observances and are gradually introduced to the patterns of community life. Not infrequently, the consolidation phase gives rise to further enrollments as the family members and friends of new declarants accept the Faith.

35.25 In other clusters, enrollments during the expansion phase may not be high, especially in the first few cycles, and the goal is to augment the number of those willing to participate in core activities. This, then, defines the nature of the consolidation phase, which largely involves nurturing the interest of seekers and accompanying them in their spiritual search until they are confirmed in their faith. To the extent that these measures are vigorously followed, this phase can generate a considerable number of enrollments. It should be noted, however, that as learning advances and experience is gained, the ability not only to teach responsive souls, but also to identify segments of the general population with heightened receptivity, develops, and the totality of new believers increases from cycle to cycle.

Whatever the nature of the cluster, it is imperative to pay close attention to children and junior youth everywhere. Concern for the moral and spiritual education of young people is asserting itself forcefully on the consciousness of humanity, and no attempt at community building can afford to ignore it. What has become especially apparent during the current Five Year Plan is the efficacy of educational programs aimed at the spiritual empowerment of junior youth. When accompanied for three years through a program that enhances their spiritual perception, and encouraged to enter the main sequence of institute courses at the age of fifteen, they represent a vast reservoir of energy and talent that can be devoted to the advancement of spiritual and material civilization. So impressed are we by the results already achieved, and so compelling is the need, that we will urge all National Assemblies to consider the junior youth groups formed through programs implemented by their training institutes a fourth core activity in its own right and to promote its wide-scale multiplication. 35.26

Key to the progress of an intensive program of growth is the phase dedicated to reflection, in which the lessons learned in action are articulated and incorporated into plans for the next cycle of activity. Its principal feature is the reflection meeting—as much a time of joyous celebration as it is of serious consultation. Careful analysis of experience, through participatory discussions rather than overly complex and elaborate presentations, serves to maintain unity of vision, sharpen clarity of thought and heighten enthusiasm. Central to such an analysis is the review of vital statistics that suggest the next set of goals to be adopted. Plans are made that take into account increased capacity in terms of the human resources available at the end of the cycle to perform various tasks, on the one hand, and accumulated knowledge about the receptivity of the population and the dynamics of teaching, on the other. 35.27

When human resources increase in a manner proportionate to the rise in the overall Bahá'í population from cycle to cycle, it is possible not only to sustain but to accelerate growth.

35.28   To meet the ambitious goal of establishing 1,500 such intensive programs, the Bahá'í world will have to draw fully upon the experience gained and capacity built over the past ten years. Following your departure from the Holy Land, you will need to enter into thorough consultation with National Spiritual Assemblies and Regional Councils and together carefully assess conditions in each national community in order to identify the clusters that will receive focused attention and to map out strategic plans.

35.29   Implementation of these plans should begin as soon as possible after Riḍván 2006. Experience in advancing the movement of clusters from one stage to the next is now so widespread that the methods and instruments are well understood. The institute process must be strengthened so that a sizeable number of friends proceed through the main sequence of courses. Intensive institute campaigns that pay adequate attention to the practice component will be essential in this respect. The number of core activities should be steadily multiplied, and outreach to the wider community systematically extended. Meetings of reflection will have to be held periodically in order to monitor progress, maintain unity of thought and mobilize the energies of the friends. And schemes for administering the growth process should gradually be put in place, as circumstances demand. While capacity at the level of the cluster to sustain growth will remain the most compelling concern in the coming years, the ongoing development of regional and national structures to facilitate the flow of information and resources to and from the field of action cannot be neglected.

35.30   Equally important will be the support lent to a cluster through an influx of pioneers. The desire to pioneer arises naturally from deep within the heart of the individual believer as a response to the Divine summons. Whosoever forsakes his or her home for the purpose of teaching the Cause joins the ranks of those noble souls whose achievements down the decades have illumined the annals of Bahá'í pioneering. We cherish the hope that many will be moved to render this meritorious service during the next Plan, whether on the home front or in the international field—an act that, in itself, attracts untold blessings. The institutions, in turn, will have to exercise sound judgment to ensure that such friends are strategically placed. Priority should be given to settling short-term and long-term pioneers in those clusters that are the focus of systematic attention, whether as a means of reinforcing endeavors to lay the groundwork for accelerated growth or stabilizing cycles of activity under way. It is not unreasonable to assume that a concerted effort to build on strength will result in the eventual outflow of pioneers from such clusters to areas destined to become the theatre of future conquests.

Dear Friends: In the weeks and months ahead and over the course of the Plan, you and your auxiliaries will be a constant source of encouragement to the believers as they rise to the challenge being presented to them. We ask that you take every opportunity to convey to them our confidence in their capacity to overcome the obstacles that will inevitably appear in their path. They should not fail to recognize the scope of what they have achieved through the sustaining grace of Bahá'u'lláh over the past decade. In the course of the first four years, they created the institutional capacity throughout the planet to impart spiritual education to growing contingents of believers. Building on this accomplishment, they engaged in a rigorous process of learning that opened before their eyes vistas of great yet attainable possibilities. That the Bahá'í world has succeeded in multiplying the number of devotional meetings sixfold over the past five years, that classes for children and junior youth have increased more than threefold during the same period, that the number of study circles worldwide has surpassed eleven thousand—these provide a measure of the extraordinary strength the believers can draw upon in shouldering the responsibility entrusted to them. 35.31

Above all, the friends need to remain ever conscious of the magnitude of the spiritual forces that are at their disposition. They are members of a community "whose world-embracing, continually consolidating activities constitute the one integrating process in a world whose institutions, secular as well as religious, are for the most part dissolving." Of all the peoples of the world, "they alone can recognize, amidst the welter of a tempestuous age, the Hand of the Divine Redeemer that traces its course and controls its destinies. They alone are aware of the silent growth of that orderly world polity whose fabric they themselves are weaving." It is their institutions that "will come to be regarded as the hallmark and glory of the age" they have 35.32

been called upon to establish. The "building process," to which they are consecrated, is "the one hope of a stricken society." For, it is "actuated by the generating influence of God's change-less Purpose, and is evolving within the framework of the Administrative Order of His Faith." And remind them that they are the illumined souls envisioned by 'Abdu'l-Bahá in His prayer: "Heroes are they, O my Lord, lead them to the field of battle. Guides are they, make them to speak out with arguments and proofs. Ministering servants are they, cause them to pass round the cup that brimmeth with the wine of certitude. O my God, make them to be songsters that carol in fair gardens, make them lions that couch in the thickets, whales that plunge in the vasty deep."

THE UNIVERSAL HOUSE OF JUSTICE

36

To all National Spiritual Assemblies

Dear Bahá'í Friends,

In the coming weeks you will be engaged in consultations on the features of the next Five Year Plan as described in our message dated 27 December 2005 to the Conference of the Continental Boards of Counsellors. We feel that these deliberations will benefit from the following comments regarding the curriculum of the training institute. 36.1

When in our message dated 26 December 1995 we underscored the need for a formal program of training, we were aware that certain elements of a curriculum meeting the necessary requirements existed in the materials of the Ruhi Institute. It was our conviction, however, that the accumulated experience at that point did not justify our recommending a specific set of materials to be used by training institutes throughout the world. Therefore, the messages written by us and on our behalf in the early part of the Four Year Plan encouraged National Spiritual Assemblies and the Counsellors to open the way for training institutes to follow whatever curriculum they deemed appropriate. Yet, conscious of the inherent difficulty in creating comprehensive programs, we repeatedly expressed the view that the execution of plans should not await protracted decisions on the question of curriculum and that materials readily available should be used. The availability of such materials was limited worldwide, and National Spiritual Assemblies and institute boards began to adopt the books of the Ruhi Institute as they became aware of them, often through the Counsellors. By the time the Four Year Plan came to a close, it was all too apparent that national communities which had vigorously set out to implement the sequence of courses designed by the Ruhi Institute were far ahead of those who had attempted to develop their own program. 36.2

36.3   It was the Five Year Plan, however, that served to convince Counsellors, National Assemblies and boards everywhere of the merits of the Ruhi Institute curriculum. The introduction of the seventh book in the Institute's main sequence at the start of the Plan enabled many to appreciate more the intimate connection between the flow of individuals through a sequence of courses and the movement of clusters from one stage of growth to the next. Indeed, as progress was achieved in hundreds of clusters, it became clear to institutions at all levels that the content and order of the main sequence prepared the friends to carry out those acts of service required by the pattern of growth being established in a cluster. We have, in fact, described the dynamics of this relationship in our message of 27 December 2005.

36.4   We have now familiarized ourselves with the Ruhi Institute's present plans for curriculum development, which increasingly draw on experience worldwide in sustaining large-scale expansion and consolidation. We welcome the decision of the Institute, for example, to move the book currently occupying the fifth position in the sequence to a set of courses branching out from Book 3 for preparing Bahá'í children's class teachers and to insert in the fifth place a new book for raising up animators of junior youth groups. That the eighth book in the main sequence, initiating a series concerned with the institutional aspects of service to the Cause, will address the all-important question of the Covenant is noted with equal pleasure. With these thoughts in mind, we have reached the conclusion that the books of the Ruhi Institute should constitute the main sequence of courses for institutes everywhere, at least through the final years of the first century of the Formative Age when the Bahá'í community will be focused on advancing the process of entry by troops within the framework for action set forth in our 27 December message.

36.5   To select one curriculum to be used by training institutes worldwide for a certain period of time is not to ignore the variety of needs and interests of the friends as they endeavor to better equip themselves to understand and apply the teachings of Bahá'u'lláh. Nor does it in any way diminish the value of the efforts made to develop courses and materials to respond to these needs. It is not intended to suggest, either, that one curriculum should necessarily appeal to everyone. What this decision does imply, however, is that the present demands of the growth of the Faith are such that, for some years to come, training institutes should not attempt to meet all of the needs and interests of the friends.

The institutions of the Faith will continue to respect the wishes of those who, for whatever reason, do not feel inclined to participate in the study of the books of the Ruhi Institute. Those not so disposed should recognize that there are many avenues of service open to them, including, above all, individual teaching which is the paramount duty of every Bahá'í. Local deepening classes and summer and winter schools, which remain an important feature of Bahá'í community life, will provide ample opportunities for them to deepen their knowledge of the teachings. What we ask of such friends, as we have in the past, is that they not allow their personal preferences to hamper in any way the unfoldment of an educational process that has shown the potential to embrace millions of souls from divers backgrounds. Regarding the materials that have been developed in other contexts over the years, and which will continue to emerge, these surely have their proper place in the Bahá'í community. Some, for example, form the basis for deepening classes at the grassroots, while others, with the necessary modifications, can be situated along one of the branches of courses stemming out from the Ruhi Institute's main sequence.

36.6

In this connection, we feel that the subject of branch courses deserves a few words of explanation. In our message dated 9 January 2001 to the Conference of the Continental Boards of Counsellors, we indicated that the main sequence could be likened to the trunk of a tree, which supports other courses branching out from it, each branch addressing some specific area of action. A set of health materials being developed in Africa offers a good illustration of a few features of such courses. Following years of training community health workers in the late 1980s and early 1990s, several Bahá'í agencies decided to elaborate a series of modules aimed at preparing individuals to deal with progressively more complex health issues at the local level. By the time the first module began to be used in its initial form, the institute process had gained in strength, and it became evident that those who had studied Books 1 and 2 of the Ruhi Institute were better prepared to visit members of their extended families and friends and speak on health-related subjects. The design of the modules was modified so that they could constitute a branch after Book 2, which participants study while they continue along in the

36.7

main sequence. Efforts in this direction have met with definite success. This example illustrates that branch courses are not a disconnected collection of materials randomly placed at various points. Rather, they must emerge out of actual experience and adhere to a certain logic, both internally and in the context of the overall institute program, if they are to be pedagogically sound. Further, the very concept of a branch course suggests that it provides training for an area of service which will interest only some of those who are studying the books of the main sequence. We hope that the development of such courses to address specific needs, defined by action on the ground, will be a natural consequence of the endeavors of burgeoning communities which are avidly striving to translate into reality the teachings of Bahá'u'lláh and to use training materials as a means of systematizing their experience and sharing with increasing numbers the insights they gain.

THE UNIVERSAL HOUSE OF JUSTICE

37

31 December 2005

To the Bahá'ís of the World

Dearly loved Friends,

As the gathering of the Continental Counsellors in the Holy 37.1
Land draws to a close, we are moved to share with you the feelings of joy, triumph and confidence which have characterized
several days of focused deliberation on the present Five Year
Plan and on the global enterprise that will succeed it.

The Hand of the Cause of God 'Alí-Muḥammad Varqá 37.2
opened the conference with a stirring appeal for resolute
action, infusing the proceedings with a spirit of unwavering
determination. Stories poured forth of the inspiring activities of
the friends and the longing and responsiveness of the peoples of
the world, conveying assurances that the Faith of Bahá'u'lláh is
blossoming more abundantly in all parts of the globe. Persistent
questions of how to sustain the process of growth, of how to
achieve a balance between expansion and consolidation, that
have engaged the Bahá'í community for nearly half a century
found clear answers in the experiences shared from diverse
clusters on all continents. Accounts of obstacles surmounted,
fresh learning acquired, and creative insights discovered made it
evident that the Army of Light is prepared to advance towards
new horizons.

There can be no doubt that the Plan soon to end marks an 37.3
upturn in the fortunes of the Faith. We look to the next decade
and a half, the final years of the first century of the Formative
Age, with great expectations of what will be accomplished.
From this vantage point, the Bahá'í world can readily appreciate the significant extent to which the International Teaching
Centre provided the impetus so indispensable to blazing the
course set over these past few years and can, as well, discern
the rich possibilities that its consecrated endeavors portend for
the future.

37.4   Our message of 27 December addressed to the conference, which has already been transmitted to National Spiritual Assemblies, summarizes the learning about growth to date and delineates the priorities for the next Plan. Careful study of the message by all believers and institutions will be an essential requisite for the upcoming consultations that will take place at every level of the community upon the return home of the Counsellors.

THE UNIVERSAL HOUSE OF JUSTICE

38

Riḍván 2006

To the Bahá'ís of the World

Dearly loved Friends,

Riḍván 2006 is a moment charged with a spirit of triumph   38.1
and anticipation. The followers of Bahá'u'lláh everywhere can
take rightful pride in the magnitude of their accomplishments
during the Five Year Plan now drawing to a close. And towards
the future they can look with a confidence that is conferred
only on those whose resolve is steeled through experience. The
entire Bahá'í world is stirred at contemplating the scope of the
five-year enterprise that lies ahead, the depth of consecration
it will demand, and the results it is destined to achieve. Our
prayers join yours as you turn in gratitude to Bahá'u'lláh for
the privilege of witnessing the unfoldment of His purpose for
humanity.

In our message of 27 December 2005 to the Counsellors   38.2
gathered in the Holy Land, transmitted on that same day to
all National Spiritual Assemblies, we delineated the features
of the Five Year Plan that will stretch from 2006 to 2011. The
friends and their institutions were urged to study the message
thoroughly, and its content is no doubt well familiar to you.
We now call upon each and every one of you to bend your
energies towards ensuring that the goal of establishing over
the next five years intensive programs of growth in no less
than 1,500 clusters worldwide is successfully met. That in the
months following the Counsellors' departure from the World
Centre the groundwork for the Plan's launch was laid so rapidly and systematically in country after country is an indication
of the eagerness with which the Bahá'í community is taking up
the challenge presented to it. While there is no need for us to
elaborate further on the requirements of the Plan here, we feel
compelled to offer for your reflection a few comments on the

global context in which your individual and collective efforts will be pursued.

38.3   More than seventy years ago Shoghi Effendi penned his World Order letters in which he provided a penetrating analysis of the forces operating in the world. With an eloquence that was his alone, he described two great processes that have been set in motion by Bahá'u'lláh's Revelation, one destructive and the other integrative, both of which are propelling humanity towards the World Order He conceived. We were cautioned by the Guardian not to be "misled by the painful slowness characterizing the unfoldment of the civilization" being laboriously established or to be "deluded by the ephemeral manifestations of returning prosperity which at times appear to be capable of checking the disruptive influence of the chronic ills afflicting the institutions of a decaying age." No review of the course of events in recent decades can fail to acknowledge the gathering momentum of the processes he analyzed then with such precision.

38.4   One need only consider the deepening moral crisis engulfing humanity to appreciate the extent to which the forces of disintegration have rent the fabric of society. Have not the evidences of selfishness, of suspicion, of fear and of fraud, which the Guardian perceived with such clarity, become so widespread as to be readily apparent to even the casual observer? Does not the threat of terrorism of which he spoke loom so large on the international scene as to preoccupy the minds of young and old alike in every corner of the globe? Have not the unquenchable thirst for, and the feverish pursuit after, earthly vanities, riches and pleasures so consolidated their power and influence as to assume authority over such human values as happiness, fidelity and love? Have not the weakening of family solidarity and the irresponsible attitude towards marriage reached such proportions as to endanger the existence of this fundamental unit of society? "The perversion of human nature, the degradation of human conduct, the corruption and dissolution of human institutions," about which Shoghi Effendi forewarned, are sadly revealing themselves "in their worst and most revolting aspects."

38.5   The Guardian lays the greatest share of the blame for humanity's moral downfall on the decline of religion as a social force. "Should the lamp of religion be obscured," he draws our attention to the words of Bahá'u'lláh, "chaos and confusion will ensue, and the lights of fairness, of justice, of tranquility and peace cease to shine." The decades that followed the writing of his letters have seen not only a continued deterioration in the ability of religion to exercise moral influence, but also the betrayal of the masses through the unseemly conduct of religious institutions. Attempts at reinvigorating it have only given rise to a fanaticism that, if left unchecked, could destroy the foundation of civilized relationships among people. The persecution of the Bahá'ís in Iran, recently intensified, is ample evidence alone of the determination of the forces of darkness to quench the flame of faith wherever it burns brightly. Though confident in the ultimate triumph of the Cause, we dare not forget the warning of the Guardian that the Faith will have to contend with enemies more powerful and more insidious than those who have afflicted it in the past.

There is no need to comment extensively on the impotence 38.6 of statesmanship, another theme treated so masterfully by the Guardian in his World Order letters. The widening economic divide between the rich and the poor, the persistence of age-old animosities among nations, the swelling numbers of the displaced, the extraordinary rise in organized crime and violence, the pervasive sense of insecurity, the breakdown of basic services in so many regions, the indiscriminate exploitation of natural resources—these are but a few of the signs of the inability of world leaders to devise viable schemes to alleviate humanity's ills. This is not to say that sincere efforts have not been exerted, in fact, have not multiplied decade after decade. Yet these efforts, no matter how ingenious, fall well short of removing "the root cause of the evil that has so rudely upset the equilibrium of present-day society." "Not even," the Guardian asserted, "would the very act of devising the machinery required for the political and economic unification of the world . . . provide in itself the antidote against the poison that is steadily undermining the vigor of organized peoples and nations." "What else," he confidently affirmed, "but the unreserved acceptance of the Divine Program" enunciated by Bahá'u'lláh, "embodying in its essentials God's divinely appointed scheme for the unification of mankind in this age, coupled with an indomitable conviction in the unfailing efficacy of each and all of its provisions, is eventually capable of withstanding the forces of internal disintegration which, if unchecked, must needs continue to eat into the vitals of a despairing society."

38.7 Penetrating, indeed, is Shoghi Effendi's depiction of the process of disintegration accelerating in the world. Equally striking is the accuracy with which he analyzed the forces associated with the process of integration. He spoke of a "gradual diffusion of the spirit of world solidarity which is spontaneously arising out of the welter of a disorganized society" as an indirect manifestation of Bahá'u'lláh's conception of the principle of the oneness of humankind. This spirit of solidarity has continued to spread over the decades, and today its effect is apparent in a range of developments, from the rejection of deeply ingrained racial prejudices to the dawning consciousness of world citizenship, from heightened environmental awareness to collaborative efforts in the promotion of public health, from the concern for human rights to the systematic pursuit of universal education, from the establishment of interfaith activities to the efflorescence of hundreds of thousands of local, national and international organizations engaged in some form of social action.

38.8 Yet for the followers of Bahá'u'lláh the most significant developments in the process of integration are those directly related to the Faith, many of which were nurtured by the Guardian himself and which have advanced tremendously since their modest beginnings. From the small nucleus of believers to whom he imparted his first teaching plans has grown a worldwide community with a presence in thousands of localities, each following a well-established pattern of activity that embodies the Faith's principles and aspirations. Upon the foundation of the Administrative Order he so painstakingly laid during the early decades of his ministry has been raised a large, closely knit network of National and Local Spiritual Assemblies diligently administering the affairs of the Cause in more than one hundred and eighty countries. From the first contingents of Auxiliary Board members for the Protection and Propagation of the Faith brought into being by him has arisen a legion of nearly one thousand stalwart workers serving in the field under the direction of eighty-one Counsellors ably guided by the International Teaching Centre. The evolution of the World Administrative Center of the Faith, within the precincts of its World Spiritual Center, a process to which the Guardian consecrated so much energy, has crossed a crucial threshold with the occupation by the Universal House of Justice of its Seat on Mount Carmel and the subsequent completion of the

International Teaching Centre Building and the Centre for the Study of the Texts. The Institution of Ḥuqúqu'lláh has steadily progressed under the stewardship of the Hand of the Cause of God Dr. 'Alí-Muḥammad Varqá, appointed Trustee by Shoghi Effendi fifty years ago, culminating in the establishment in 2005 of an international board designed to promote the continued widespread application of this mighty law, a source of inestimable blessings for all humanity. The efforts of the Guardian to raise the profile of the Faith in international circles have developed into an extensive external affairs system, capable of both defending the interests of the Faith and proclaiming its universal message. The respect the Faith enjoys in international fora, whenever its representatives speak, is a most noteworthy accomplishment. The loyalty and devotion that the members of a community reflecting the diversity of the entire human race evince towards the Covenant of Bahá'u'lláh constitute a storehouse of strength the like of which no other organized group can claim.

The Guardian foresaw that, in succeeding epochs of the   38.9 Formative Age, the Universal House of Justice would launch a series of worldwide enterprises which would "symbolize the unity and coordinate and unify the activities" of National Spiritual Assemblies. Over the course of three successive epochs now, the Bahá'í community has labored assiduously within the framework of the global Plans issued by the House of Justice and has succeeded in establishing a pattern of Bahá'í life that promotes the spiritual development of the individual and channels the collective energies of its members towards the spiritual revival of society. It has acquired the capacity to reach large numbers of receptive souls with the message, to confirm them, and to deepen their understanding of the essentials of the Faith they have embraced. It has learned to translate the principle of consultation enunciated by its Founder into an effective tool for collective decision-making and to educate its members in its use. It has devised programs for the spiritual and moral education of its younger members and has extended them not only to its own children and junior youth but also to those of the wider community. With the pool of talent at its disposition, it has created a rich body of literature which includes volumes in scores of languages that address both its own needs and the interest of the general public. It has become increasingly involved in the affairs of society at large, undertaking a host of projects of social and economic development. Particularly since the opening of the fifth epoch in 2001, it has made significant strides in multiplying its human resources through a program of training that reaches the grassroots of the community and has discovered methods and instruments for establishing a sustainable pattern of growth.

38.10   It is in the context of the interplay of the forces described here that the imperative of advancing the process of entry by troops must be viewed. The Five Year Plan now opening requires that you concentrate your energies on this process and ensure that the two complementary movements at its heart are accelerated. This should be your dominant concern. As your efforts bear fruit and the dynamics of growth reach a new level of complexity, there will be challenges and opportunities for the World Centre itself to address in the coming five years in fields such as external affairs, social and economic development, administration, and the application of Bahá'í law. The growth of the community has already necessitated that new arrangements be put in place to double the number of pilgrims to four hundred in each group beginning in October 2007. There are several other projects that will also have to be pursued. Among these are the further development of the gardens surrounding the Shrine of Bahá'u'lláh, as well as the Riḍván Garden and Mazra'ih; the restoration of the International Archives Building; structural repairs to the Shrine of the Báb, the full extent of which are not yet clear; and the construction of the House of Worship in Chile as envisioned by the Guardian, the last of the continental Mashriqu'l-Adhkárs. As these endeavors advance, we will call on you from time to time for assistance, both in the form of financial support and specialized talents, mindful that the resources of the Faith should, to the greatest measure possible, be channeled to the requirements of the Plan.

38.11   Dear friends: That the forces of disintegration are gaining in range and power cannot be ignored. It is equally clear that the community of the Greatest Name has been guided from strength to strength by the Hand of Providence and must now increase in size and augment its resources. The course set by the Five Year Plan is straightforward. How can those of us aware of the plight of humanity, and conscious of the direction in which history is unfolding, not arise to the fullest of our capacity and dedicate ourselves to its aim? Do not the words of the Guardian that "the stage is set" hold as true for us today as they did when he wrote them during the first Seven Year Plan? Let his words ring in your ears: "There is no time to lose." "There is no room left for vacillation." "Such an opportunity is irreplaceable." "To try, to persevere, is to insure ultimate and complete victory." Be assured of our continued prayers at the Sacred Threshold for your guidance and protection.

THE UNIVERSAL HOUSE OF JUSTICE

PART II
Global Plans: Fundamental Concepts

A NUMBER OF CONCEPTS ARE INTEGRAL to understanding the recent global Plans of the Faith, and Part II consists of a document dated 29 October 2005 prepared by an ad hoc committee for a workshop presented as part of the Serving the Divine Plan Program at the Bahá'í World Centre. In the document, passages from letters written by or on behalf of the Guardian and the Universal House of Justice are used to explore a few of the most essential concepts such as advancing the process of entry by troops, two essential movements, and learning in action. The document also explores areas in which significant learning has taken place within the Bahá'í community from the start of the Four Year Plan at Riḍván 1996, through the Twelve Month and Five Year Plans, until the end of 2005, when the provisions of a new global enterprise were announced by the Universal House of Justice.

39

Advancing the Process
of Entry by Troops

In its message of 26 December 1995 to the Conference of   39.1
the Continental Boards of Counsellors, the Universal House
of Justice announced that the Bahá'í world would embark
upon a four-year global enterprise at Riḍván 1996 aiming at
a significant advance in the process of entry by troops. The
advance was to be achieved through marked progress in the
activity and development of the individual, the institutions, and
the local community—the three participants of the Four Year
Plan. The House of Justice went on to explain the significance
of this step:

> That an advance in this process depends on the progress   39.2
> of all three of these intimately connected participants is
> abundantly clear. The next four years must witness a dra-
> matic upsurge in effective teaching activities undertaken at
> the initiative of the individual. Thousands upon thousands
> of believers will need to be aided to express the vitality of
> their faith through constancy in teaching the Cause and by
> supporting the plans of their institutions and the endeavors
> of their communities. They should be helped to realize
> that their efforts will be sustained by the degree to which
> their inner life and private character "mirror forth in their
> manifold aspects the splendor of those eternal principles
> proclaimed by Bahá'u'lláh." An acceleration in the tempo
> of individual teaching must necessarily be complemented by
> a multiplication in the number of regional and local teach-
> ing projects. To this end the institutions should be assisted
> in increasing their ability to consult according to Bahá'í
> principles, to unify the friends in a common vision, and
> to use their talents in service to the Cause. Furthermore,
> those who enter the Faith must be integrated into vibrant

local communities, characterized by tolerance and love and guided by a strong sense of purpose and collective will, environments in which the capacities of all components—men, women, youth and children—are developed and their powers multiplied in unified action.[1]

39.3   The House of Justice indicated in November 1999 that advancing the process of entry by troops would continue to be the aim of the Plans through the first century of the Formative Age of the Faith:

39.4   The two stages in the unfoldment of the Divine Plan lying immediately ahead will last one year and five years respectively. At Riḍván 2000 the Bahá'í world will be asked to embark on the first of these two stages, a twelve-month effort aimed at concentrating the forces, the capacities and the insights that have so strongly emerged. The Five Year Plan that follows will initiate a series of worldwide enterprises that will carry the Bahá'í community through the final twenty years in the first century of the Faith's Formative Age. These global Plans will continue to focus on advancing the process of entry by troops and on its systematic acceleration.[2]

39.5   The House of Justice elaborated on the nature of this aim and the process it advances in its Riḍván 1996 message to the Bahá'ís of the world, stating that

39.6   The phrase "advance in the process of entry by troops" accommodates the concept that current circumstances demand and existing opportunities allow for a sustained growth of the Bahá'í world community on a large scale; that this upsurge is necessary in the face of world conditions; that the three constituent participants in the upbuilding of the Order of Bahá'u'lláh—the individual, the institutions, and the community—can foster such growth first by spiritually and mentally accepting the possibility of it, and then by working towards embracing masses of new believers, setting in motion the means for effecting their spiritual and administrative training and development, thereby multiplying the number of knowledgeable, active teachers and administrators whose involvement in the work of the Cause will ensure a constant influx of new adherents, an uninterrupted evolution of Bahá'í Assemblies, and a steady consolidation of the community.

Moreover, to advance the process implies that that   39.7
process is already in progress and that local and national communities are at different stages of it. All communities are now tasked to take steps and sustain efforts to achieve a level of expansion and consolidation commensurate with their possibilities. The individual and the institutions, while operating in distinctive spheres, are summoned to arise to meet the requirements of this crucial time in the life of our community and in the fortunes of all humankind.[3]

The process of entry by troops was described by the   39.8
House of Justice in a message dated 9 November 1993 in these terms:

... entry by troops is not merely a stage of the progress of   39.9
the Cause destined to occur in its own good time, depen-dent on the receptivity of the population as a whole—it is a phenomenon which the Bahá'í communities, by their own activities, can prepare for and help to bring about. It is also a process which, once started, can be sustained. By a wise allocation of resources and the energetic pursuit of simultaneous plans of expansion, deepening and consolida-tion, the process of entry by troops should bring about a rapidly increasing supply of active believers, soundly based local communities, and steadily evolving local and national Bahá'í institutions.[4]

Of course, it has been explained by the Guardian that entry   39.10
by troops is a stage in the growth of the Faith that presages the day when mass conversion on the part of the diverse peoples of the world will take place:

... winning to the Faith fresh recruits to the slowly yet   39.11
steadily advancing army of the Lord of Hosts, whose reinforcing strength is so essential to the safeguarding of the victories which the band of heroic Bahá'í conquerors are winning in the course of their several campaigns in all the continents of the globe.

Such a steady flow of reinforcements is absolutely   39.12
vital and is of extreme urgency, for nothing short of the vitalizing influx of new blood that will reanimate the world Bahá'í Community can safeguard the prizes which, at so

great a sacrifice, involving the expenditure of so much time, effort and treasure, are now being won in virgin territories by Bahá'u'lláh's valiant Knights, whose privilege is to constitute the spearhead of the onrushing battalions which, in divers theatres and in circumstances often adverse and extremely challenging, are vying with each other for the spiritual conquest of the unsurrendered territories and islands on the surface of the globe.

39.13   This flow, moreover, will presage and hasten the advent of the day which, as prophesied by 'Abdu'l-Bahá, will witness the entry by troops of peoples of divers nations and races into the Bahá'í world—a day which, viewed in its proper perspective, will be the prelude to that long-awaited hour when a mass conversion on the part of these same nations and races, and as a direct result of a chain of events, momentous and possibly catastrophic in nature and which cannot as yet be even dimly visualized, will suddenly revolutionize the fortunes of the Faith, derange the equilibrium of the world, and reinforce a thousandfold the numerical strength as well as the material power and the spiritual authority of the Faith of Bahá'u'lláh.[5]

Two Essential Movements

In a message to a conference held a few months into the Five   40.1
Year Plan in 2001, the Universal House of Justice first explicitly
referred to the concept of two essential movements:

> The Five Year Plan, which will undoubtedly be the   40.2
> focus of your consultations over the next few days, requires
> concentrated and sustained attention to two essential move-
> ments. The first is the steady flow of believers through the
> sequence of courses offered by training institutes, for the
> purpose of developing the human resources of the Cause.
> The second, which receives its impetus from the first, is the
> movement of geographic clusters from one stage of growth
> to the next.[1]

The first movement, then, is essentially an educational   40.3
process at the grassroots of the community. The following quotation from a letter written on behalf of the House of Justice to
a National Spiritual Assembly makes clear the responsibility of
the institute in overseeing this process:

> At this point in the growth of the Faith, the mandate   40.4
> of your training institute is fairly clear-cut: A sequence of
> courses has been adopted as the national program for the
> development of human resources. It is the job of the insti-
> tute, then, to help a steadily increasing number of youth
> and adults advance through that sequence. . . .[2]

A number of messages written by the House of Justice or   40.5
on its behalf explain that the sequence of courses adopted by
institutes should "endow growing contingents of believers with
the knowledge, spiritual qualities, and skills and abilities to
effectively carry out the many tasks of expansion and consolidation."[3] The following passage describes in the briefest way

how this educational process was set in motion at the outset of the Four Year Plan in 1996 and taken to the grassroots:

40.6   During the Four Year Plan, enormous effort was exerted in raising up training institutes in every part of the globe. To reach an increasing number of believers with their programs, institutes were encouraged to adopt a decentralized system for the delivery of courses. Study circles, guided by trained tutors, enabled the educational process to be taken to the local community. As more and more believers in each country entered the institute program in this way and advanced through its sequence of courses, the human resources of the Faith steadily grew at different levels of capacity.[4]

40.7   The establishment of this educational process was one of the major accomplishments of the Four Year Plan. The first movement was well under way, then, by the end of those four years. The concept of the second movement was introduced at the start of the Five Year Plan in 2001 when National Spiritual Assemblies were asked to divide their countries into small geographic areas that would enable the friends "to think about the growth of the Faith on a manageable scale and to design and implement plans close to the grassroots."[5] As a significant number of believers proceeded through the sequence of courses, they were now to be deployed at the level of the cluster to meet the needs of expansion and consolidation. "The educational process in which the friends have engaged over so many weeks and months," it has been explained, "should give shape to the individual and collective activities they now undertake."[6] The House of Justice underscored this point to the National Spiritual Assembly of Brazil in a letter written on its behalf:

40.8   . . . the [Regional Bahá'í] Council must ensure that, as the ranks of avowed supporters of the Faith swell through the institute process, they are deployed in the field of service, reinforcing the work of large-scale expansion and consolidation. This multiplication and deployment of human resources is to be carried out, of course, in the context of a regional plan to move each cluster in the region from its current stage of growth to the next advanced stage.[7]

40.9   From the above passage it is clear that the multiplication and deployment of human resources is carried out in the context of a plan to move a cluster from one stage of growth to the next. The 17 January 2003 message of the House of Justice to the Bahá'ís of the world further elaborates on this idea:

> During the initial months of the Plan, National Spiritual 40.10
> Assemblies proceeded with relative ease to divide the territo-
> ries under their jurisdiction into areas consisting of adjacent
> localities, called clusters, using criteria that were purely
> geographic and social and did not relate to the strength of
> local Bahá'í communities. Reports received at the World
> Centre indicate that there are now close to 17,000 clusters
> worldwide, excluding those countries where, for one reason
> or another, the operation of the Faith is restricted. The
> number of clusters per country varies widely—from India
> with its 1,580 to Singapore, which necessarily sees itself as
> one cluster. Some of the groupings are sparsely populated
> areas with only a few thousand inhabitants, while the
> boundaries of others encompass several million people. For
> the most part, large urban centers under the jurisdiction of
> one Local Spiritual Assembly have been designated single
> clusters, these in turn being divided into sectors, so as to
> facilitate planning and implementation.
>
> With the various countries and territories divided into 40.11
> manageable areas, national communities moved quickly
> ahead to categorize clusters according to the stages of the
> development of the Faith mentioned in our 9 January mes-
> sage. The exercise afforded a realistic means for viewing
> the prospects of the community, but the task of refining
> the criteria needed for valid assessments is proving to be
> an ongoing challenge to institutions. To assign a cluster
> to one or another category is not to make a statement
> about status. Rather, it is a way of evaluating its capacity
> for growth, in order that an approach compatible with its
> evolving development can be adopted. Rigid criteria are
> obviously counterproductive, but a well-defined scheme
> to carry out evaluation is essential. Two criteria seem
> especially important: the strength of the human resources
> raised up by the training institute for the expansion and
> consolidation of the Faith in the cluster, and the ability of
> the institutions to mobilize these resources in the field of
> service.[8]

Of course, the stages of growth mentioned in the 9 January 40.12
2001 message were defined as follows:

40.13   The areas into which a region divides will fall into various categories of development. Some will not yet be open to the Faith, while others will contain a few isolated localities and groups; in some, established communities will be gaining strength through a vigorous institute process; in a few, strong communities of deepened believers will be in a position to take on the challenges of systematic and accelerated expansion and consolidation.[9]

40.14   Here is how the Universal House of Justice described the movement of clusters in its 17 January message:

40.15   In most clusters, movement from one stage of growth to the next is being defined in terms of the multiplication of study circles, devotional meetings and children's classes, and the expansion they engender. Devotional meetings begin to flourish as consciousness of the spiritual dimension of human existence is raised among the believers in an area through institute courses. Children's classes, too, are a natural outgrowth of the training received early in the study of the main sequence. As both activities are made open to the wider community through a variety of well-conceived and imaginative means, they attract a growing number of seekers, who, more often than not, are eager to attend firesides and join study circles. Many go on subsequently to declare their faith in Bahá'u'lláh and, from the outset, view their role in the community as that of active participants in a dynamic process of growth. Individual and collective exertions in the teaching field intensify correspondingly, further fuelling the process. Established communities are revitalized, and newly formed ones soon gain the privilege of electing their Local Spiritual Assemblies.

40.16   The coherence thus achieved through the establishment of study circles, devotional meetings and children's classes provides the initial impulse for growth in a cluster, an impulse that gathers strength as these core activities multiply in number. Campaigns that help a sizeable group of believers advance far enough in the main sequence of courses to perform the necessary acts of service lend impetus to this multiplication of activity.[10]

40.17   In this connection, the House of Justice wrote: "The pattern of activity that is being established in clusters around the globe constitutes a proven means of accelerating expansion and consolidation."[11] It indicated, however, that this was "only a beginning":[12]

> In many parts of the world, bringing large numbers 40.18
> into the ranks of Bahá'u'lláh's followers has traditionally
> not been a formidable task. It is therefore encouraging to
> see that, in some of the more developed clusters, carefully
> designed projects are being added to the existing pattern
> of growth to reach receptive populations and lift the rate
> of expansion to a higher level. Such projects accelerate the
> tempo of teaching, already on the rise through the efforts of
> individuals. And, where large-scale enrollment is beginning
> to result, provision is being made to ensure that a certain
> percentage of the new believers immediately enter the insti-
> tute program, for, as we have emphasized in several mes-
> sages, these friends will be called upon to serve the needs of
> an ever-growing Bahá'í population. They help deepen the
> generality of the Bahá'ís by visiting them regularly; they
> teach children, arrange devotional meetings and form study
> circles, making it possible to sustain expansion.[13]

The above passage offers insight into how the two move- 40.19
ments interact with each other. In essence, one fuels the other,
as explained in the next passage:

> The challenge is not simply to have a certain percentage 40.20
> study one or two courses, but a sequence of several courses
> through an effective system of distance education. And if
> the institute succeeds in accomplishing this, there should be
> a corresponding increase in the tempo of the teaching work
> as more and more friends arise to serve the Faith. A steady
> stream of newly enrolled believers will, in turn, enter the
> institute's program, and in this way the system as a whole
> will be in a constant state of expansion.[14]

To maintain the system envisioned at the level of the cluster, 40.21
then, the ratio of believers in the sequence of courses to the
total Bahá'í population needs to be kept within a certain range.
Beyond the need to maintain proper ratios, however, there is the
question of tempo. The deployment of believers into the field of
service should lead to an intensification of teaching activities so
that the rate of the expansion of the overall Bahá'í population
steadily accelerates. This, in effect, is the idea underlying an

intensive program of growth, as explained in the 9 January message of the Universal House of Justice:

40.22   At the core of the program must lie a sound and steady process of expansion, matched by an equally strong process of human resource development. A range of teaching efforts needs to be carried out, involving both activities undertaken by the individual and campaigns promoted by the institutions. As the number of believers in the area rises, a significant percentage should receive training from the institute, and their capabilities be directed towards the development of local communities.[15]

40.23   What has become clear during the latter part of the Five Year Plan is that, if such programs are made up of a cycle of certain activities that is repeated every few months, it is possible to increase the rate of expansion, while at the same time maintaining the proper ratio of individuals in the sequence of courses to the total Bahá'í population. The Universal House of Justice in its Riḍván 2005 message wrote the following about such programs:

40.24   As the necessary conditions have thus been created, systematic programs for the expansion and consolidation of the Faith have been launched accordingly. A valuable body of knowledge about the nature of intensive programs of growth is accumulating, and certain features of these endeavors are now well understood. Such programs tend to consist of a series of cycles, each of several months' duration, devoted to planning, expansion, and consolidation. Human resource development proceeds uninterrupted from one cycle to the next, ensuring that the process of expansion not only is sustained but progressively gathers momentum. While undoubtedly many more lessons are still to be garnered, the experience already gained makes it possible to replicate the approach in an ever-increasing number of clusters around the world.[16]

41

Learning in Action

Referring to the global Plans, a letter written on behalf of the   41.1
Universal House of Justice to an individual believer in August
2002 indicated that the challenge before the friends everywhere
is "to study the guidance issued by the House of Justice, on the
one hand, and to learn from experience as they strive to put
that guidance into practice, on the other."[1] A letter written to
another believer not too long before expressed the hope of the
House of Justice that "the general messages it issues from time
to time, as well as its letters that shed light on certain specific
aspects of these new developments, will help the friends to
clarify issues in practice and move steadily toward unity of
thought and action."[2]

The above passages suggest that, at a most fundamental   41.2
level, the implementation of the global Plans of the Faith is
impelled by learning. Every global Plan represents a stage in
the unfoldment of the Divine Plan, which is leading humanity
towards the world civilization envisioned by Bahá'u'lláh. The
success of each stage of this historical enterprise depends on the
capacity of the Bahá'í community to respond to the provisions
set forth in the global Plan that defines that stage. It is in this
context that the aim of accelerating the process of entry by
troops, which will remain the focus of the global Plans until
2021,

> . . . identifies a necessity at this stage in the progress of the   41.3
> Cause and in the state of human society. With this perspec-
> tive, the three inseparable participants in the evolution of
> the new World Order—the individual, the institutions, and
> the community—must now demonstrate more tangibly than
> ever before their capacity and willingness to embrace masses
> of new adherents, to effect the spiritual and administrative
> transformation of thousands upon thousands, and, above
> all, to multiply the army of knowledgeable, consecrated

teachers of a Faith whose emergence from obscurity must be registered on the consciousness of countless multitudes throughout the earth.[3]

41.4   It is in learning to respond to the requirements of the global Plans, as set out in the messages of the House of Justice, that the capacity of the three participants increases. In this sense, learning is a "mode of operation." On various occasions, the House of Justice has explained that this mode of operation is characterized by action, reflection, and consultation:

41.5   If learning is to be the primary mode of operation in a community, then visions, strategies, goals and methods have to be re-examined time and again. As tasks are accomplished, obstacles removed, resources multiplied and lessons learned, modifications have to be made in goals and approaches, but in a way that continuity of action is maintained.[4]

41.6   The instrument that has allowed the process of action, reflection, and consultation to accelerate and the learning to occur at a fairly rapid rate at the grassroots is the reflection meeting. In its 17 January 2003 message to the Bahá'ís of the world, the House of Justice wrote,

41.7   It is especially gratifying to note the high degree of participation of believers in the various aspects of the growth process. In cluster after cluster, the number of those shouldering the responsibilities of expansion and consolidation is steadily increasing. Meetings of consultation held at the cluster level serve to raise awareness of possibilities and generate enthusiasm. Here, free from the demands of formal decision-making, participants reflect on experience gained, share insights, explore approaches and acquire a better understanding of how each can contribute to achieving the aim of the Plan. In many cases, such interaction leads to consensus on a set of short-term goals, both individual and collective. Learning in action is becoming the outstanding feature of the emerging mode of operation.[5]

41.8   What is important is that the experience gained in one part of the world does not remain isolated from the experiences elsewhere. Through the institution of the Counsellors, the lessons learned at the grassroots are systematized into a body of knowledge that can help the friends acquire a better understanding of the dynamics of promoting the process of entry by troops. This knowledge can then be diffused widely by the International Teaching Centre, the Counsellors and their auxiliaries, stimulating the work at the grassroots and accelerating the learning process further. The House of Justice has described this aspect of the Counsellors' work in the following way:

> A resource made available to the Counsellors by the International Teaching Centre and through them to the community at large is an accumulating store of wisdom born of experience—the experience of a highly diverse community dedicated to the creation of a new civilization. Through the network of Counsellors, Auxiliary Board members and assistants, the Teaching Centre can observe the workings of individual and collective endeavors, analyzing their methods and approaches, and introducing the conclusions it draws into the processes of the systematic growth of the Faith. Thus in the institution of the Counsellors we have a system through which the lessons learned in the remotest spots on the globe can be shared with the entire body of the believers, enriching consultation, stimulating experimentation and inspiring confidence that the great enterprise in which the Bahá'í world is engaged is assured of success.[6]

41.9

It was in this context that the House of Justice wrote to the Counsellors in 1998:

41.10

> You represent an army of able and highly motivated servants of the Cause throughout the world. Yours is an institution which, in one respect, has a particularly intimate relationship with the Universal House of Justice; in another, it is able to exercise an influence that penetrates the very grassroots of the community. Its nature fits it, uniquely, to serve as a river of encouragement, example and love whose waters can refresh and invigorate the spirit of every believer they touch.[7]

41.11

In the period covering the Four Year, Twelve Month and Five Year Plans, as the friends have learned to put into action the guidance of the Universal House of Justice, the changes in their habits of thoughts, modes of expression and patterns of behavior have become so widespread and so pervasive that there has been a marked shift in culture:

41.12

> Since the outset of the Four Year Plan, the entire Bahá'í world has been undergoing a profound change in culture

41.13

required by the single focus of the global Plans in this latter part of the first century of the Faith's Formative Age—advancing the process of entry by troops. It is important that the necessity of this change be fully appreciated by the friends and that new ideas not be measured by old modes of thinking, which, while valuable in many respects, have not been conducive to rapid growth.

41.14 When new and challenging ideas emerge, it is inevitable that differences of opinion would arise and levels of understanding vary. Not infrequently, extremes in thinking appear. It takes time for habits of thought and modes of expression to change and for patterns of action to be adjusted. What the Universal House of Justice finds encouraging is that the institutions of the Faith in . . . are making strides and are intensely engaged in trying to see how growth can be accelerated through such elements as study circles, devotional meetings and children's classes and that they can count on wise believers like you to help them in this essential process.[8]

41.15 An important aspect of the change in the culture of Bahá'í communities worldwide is a collective acknowledgement of what is needed to bring about entry by troops:

41.16 The central theme of the Four Year Plan—that of advancing the process of entry by troops—produced a high degree of integration of thought and action. . . . The thematic focus of the Plan bore implications for all categories of Bahá'í activity; it called for a clarity of understanding which made possible systematic and strategic planning as a prerequisite of individual and collective action. The members of the community came gradually to appreciate how systematization would facilitate the processes of growth and development. This raising of consciousness was a huge step that led to an upgrading of teaching activities and a change in the culture of the community.[9]

41.17 Collective consciousness of the requisites for advancing the process of entry by troops has given rise to new ways of thinking and acting, as the House of Justice explains in a letter written on its behalf:

41.18 A remapping of the Bahá'í community through the formation of clusters worldwide is an example of a change which is challenging the community to embrace new ways of thinking and acting, such as to mobilize a common effort among local institutions and individual believers that extends across contiguous borders within each cluster. As you will appreciate, this is a process which necessarily involves an initial period of adjustment and which will continue to unfold over a period of time into distinctive features of a dynamic community that is constantly evolving.[10]

As the Bahá'í community develops the habits of learning and meets the challenges of the Plans, unity of thought and action is becoming a tangible reality throughout the Bahá'í world.

41.19

42

Learning to Be Systematic

In the Riḍván 1998 message the Universal House of Justice 42.1 called on Bahá'ís to approach their work systematically, refer-ring to systematization as a "necessary mode of functioning animated by the urgency to act":

> Our hopes, our goals, our possibilities of moving 42.2 forward can all be realized through concentrating our endeavors on the major aim of the Divine Plan at its current stage—that is, to effect a significant advance in the process of entry by troops. This challenge can be met through persis-tent effort patiently pursued. Entry by troops is a possibility well within the grasp of our community. Unremitting faith, prayer, the promptings of the soul, Divine assistance—these are among the essentials of progress in any Bahá'í undertak-ing. But also of vital importance to bringing about entry by troops is a realistic approach, systematic action. There are no shortcuts. Systematization ensures consistency of lines of action based on well-conceived plans. In a general sense, it implies an orderliness of approach in all that pertains to Bahá'í service, whether in teaching or administration, in individual or collective endeavor. While allowing for individual initiative and spontaneity, it suggests the need to be clear-headed, methodical, efficient, constant, balanced and harmonious. Systematization is a necessary mode of functioning animated by the urgency to act.[1]

The message went on to highlight the essential role that 42.3 the training institute plays in systematically developing the human resources that will sustain and accelerate the expansion and consolidation of the Faith. In a sense, the development of human resources can be thought of as the first act of systematization on the part of Bahá'í communities. This step was initiated in December 1995 when the House of Justice introduced the concept of the training institute, related it to the earlier teaching institute and charged the Counsellors with assisting National Spiritual Assemblies everywhere in establishing training institutes at the national and regional levels. How this call for systematization came about is explained succinctly in the message of 26 December 1995 to the Counsellors:

42.4   During the Nine Year Plan, the Universal House of Justice called upon National Spiritual Assemblies in countries where large-scale expansion was taking place to establish teaching institutes to meet the deepening needs of the thousands who were entering the Faith. At that time, the emphasis was on acquiring a physical facility to which group after group of newly enrolled believers would be invited to attend deepening courses. Over the years, in conjunction with these institutes, and often independent of them, a number of courses—referred to, for example, as weekend institutes, five-day institutes, and nine-day institutes—were developed for the purpose of helping the friends gain an understanding of the fundamental verities of the Faith and arise to serve it. These efforts have contributed significantly to the enriching of the spiritual life of the believers and will undoubtedly continue in the future.

42.5   With the growth in the number of enrollments, it has become apparent that such occasional courses of instruction and the informal activities of community life, though important, are not sufficient as a means of human resource development, for they have resulted in only a relatively small band of active supporters of the Cause. These believers, no matter how dedicated, no matter how willing to make sacrifices, cannot attend to the needs of hundreds, much less thousands, of fledgling local communities. Systematic attention has to be given by Bahá'í institutions to training a significant number of believers and assisting them in serving the Cause according to their God-given talents and capacities.

42.6   The development of human resources on a large scale requires that the establishment of institutes be viewed in a new light. In many regions, it has become imperative to create institutes as organizational structures dedicated to systematic training. The purpose of such training is to endow ever-growing contingents of believers with the spiritual insights, the knowledge, and the skills needed to carry out the many tasks of accelerated expansion and consolidation, including the teaching and deepening of a large number of people—adults, youth and children. This purpose can best be achieved through well-organized, formal programs consisting of courses that follow appropriately designed curricula.[2]

An account of the historical developments leading up to the efforts to establish training institutes worldwide during the Four Year Plan is discussed in some detail in Chapter 9 of *Century of Light*. The chapter offers insight into why human resource development should have been the first area of Bahá'í activity to receive systematic attention. It will be helpful to quote from the document at length.   42.7

> As believers from urban centers set out on sustained campaigns to reach the mass of the world's peoples living in villages and rural areas, they encountered a receptivity to Bahá'u'lláh's message far beyond anything they had imagined possible. While the response usually took forms very different from the ones with which the teachers had been familiar, the new declarants were eagerly welcomed. . . .   42.8

> At the heart of the development, as has been the case in the life of the Cause from the outset, was the commitment made by the individual believer. Already, during the ministry of Shoghi Effendi, far-sighted persons had taken the initiative to reach indigenous populations in such countries as Uganda and Indonesia. During the Nine Year Plan, ever larger numbers of such teachers were drawn into the work, particularly in India, several countries in Africa, and most regions of Latin America, as well as in islands of the Pacific, Alaska and among the native peoples of Canada and the rural black population of the southern United States. . . .   42.9

> Even so, it soon became apparent that individual initiative alone, however inspired and energetic, could not respond adequately to the opportunities opening up. The result was to launch Bahá'í communities on a wide range of collective teaching and proclamation projects recalling the heroic days of the dawn-breakers. Teams of ardent teachers found that it was now possible to introduce the message of the Faith not merely to a succession of inquirers, but to entire groups and even whole communities. The tens of thousands became hundreds of thousands. The Faith's   42.10

growth meant that members of Spiritual Assemblies, whose experience had been limited to confirming the understanding of the Faith of individual applicants raised in cultures of doubt or religious fanaticism, had to adjust to expressions of belief on the part of whole groups of people to whom religious awareness and response were normal features of daily life.[3]

42.11 The chapter goes on to explain that the large influx of new believers during the period brought with it unprecedented challenges, not the least of which were deepening these friends and adapting to a wide range of cultures and modes of thought. It then continues by saying,

42.12 Initially, such problems proved stimulating as both Bahá'í institutions and individual believers struggled to find new ways of looking at situations—new ways, indeed, of understanding important passages in the Bahá'í Writings themselves. Determined efforts were made to respond to the guidance of the World Centre that expansion and consolidation are twin processes that must go hand in hand. Where hoped for results did not readily materialize, however, a measure of discouragement frequently set in. The initial rapid rise in enrollment rates slowed markedly in many countries, tempting some Bahá'í institutions and communities to turn back to more familiar activities and more accessible publics.

42.13 The principal effect of the setbacks, however, was that they brought home to communities that the high expectations of the early years were in some respects quite unrealistic. Although the easy successes of the initial teaching activities were encouraging, they did not, by themselves, build a Bahá'í community life that could meet the needs of its new members and be self-generating. Rather, pioneers and new believers alike faced questions for which Bahá'í experience in Western lands—or even Iran—offered few answers. How were Local Spiritual Assemblies to be established—and once established, how were they to function—in areas where large numbers of new believers had joined the Cause overnight, simply on the strength of their spiritual apprehension of its truth? How, in societies dominated by men since the dawn of time, were women to be accorded an equal voice? How was the education of large numbers of children to be systematically addressed in cultural situations where poverty and illiteracy prevailed? What priorities should guide Bahá'í moral teaching, and how could these objectives best be related to prevailing indigenous conventions? How could a vibrant community life be cultivated that would stimulate the spiritual growth of its members? What priorities, too, should be set with respect to the production of Bahá'í literature, particularly given the sudden explosion that had taken place in the number of languages represented in the community? How could the integrity of the Bahá'í institution of the Nineteen Day Feast be maintained, while opening this vital activity to the enriching influence of diverse cultures? And, in all areas of concern, how were the necessary resources to be recruited, funded, and coordinated?

The pressure of these urgent and interlocking challenges launched the Bahá'í world on a learning process that has proved to be as important as the expansion itself. It is safe to say that during these years there was virtually no type of teaching activity, no combination of expansion, consolidation and proclamation, no administrative option, no effort at cultural adaptation that was not being energetically tried in some part of the Bahá'í world. The net result of the experience was an intensive education of a great part of the Bahá'í community in the implications of the mass teaching work, an education that could have occurred in no other way. By its very nature, the process was largely local and regional in focus, qualitative rather than quantitative in its gains, and incremental rather than large-scale in the progress achieved. Had it not been for the painstaking, always difficult and often frustrating consolidation work pursued during these years, however, the subsequent strategy of systematizing the promotion of entry by troops would have had very little with which to work.[4] 42.14

This learning process took three decades to come to fruition. *Century of Light* describes the significance of this period in Bahá'í history: 42.15

The significance of these three decades of struggle, learning and sacrifice became apparent when the moment arrived to devise a global Plan that would capitalize on the insights gained and the resources that had been developed. 42.16

The Bahá'í community that set out on the Four Year Plan in 1996 was a very different one from the eager, but new and still inexperienced body of believers who, in 1964, had ventured out on the first of such undertakings that were no longer sustained by the guiding hand of Shoghi Effendi. By 1996, it had become possible to see all of the distinct strands of the enterprise as integral parts of one coherent whole.[5]

42.17 At the outset of the Four Year Plan, then, the Bahá'í world was able to capitalize on the insights it had gained during the preceding period as it focused on establishing a network of training institutes as a means of systematizing the work in the area of expansion and consolidation. Laying this foundation was the first act of systematization. Through it mechanisms were put in place to develop the human resources of the Faith. In its message of 26 November 1999 to the Bahá'ís of the world, the House of Justice praised the accomplishments that were achieved putting this network into place and alluded to the next area of Bahá'í activity to receive systematic attention, starting with the Twelve Month Plan:

42.18 It is essential that, during the one-year effort, national and regional institutes everywhere bring into full operation the programs and systems that they have now devised. National communities should enter the Five Year Plan confident that the acquisition of knowledge, qualities and skills of service by large contingents of believers, with the aid of a sequence of courses, will proceed unhindered. Ample attention must also be given to further systematization of teaching efforts, whether undertaken by the individual or directed by the institutions. In this respect, the International Teaching Centre has identified certain patterns of systematic expansion and consolidation for relatively small geographical areas consisting of a manageable number of localities.[6]

42.19 A letter dated 31 July 2002 written on behalf of the House of Justice to an individual believer described what this systemization entailed in concrete terms:

42.20 With institutes well positioned to address the challenges of human resource development, the stage was set to further systematize the teaching efforts worldwide. In its 9 January 2001 message regarding the Five Year Plan, the Universal

House of Justice asked that this systemization take place in the context of a "cluster"—a small geographic area that would enable the friends to think about the growth of the Faith on a manageable scale and to design and implement plans close to the grassroots of the community. As a first step in the execution of the Plan, Bahá'í institutions set out to map their countries with the aim of dividing them into clusters and categorizing them according to their current stage of development. Invariably, this undertaking served to galvanize the believers, for they were able to evaluate in realistic terms their strengths and weaknesses and to see with striking clarity a way forward. The resulting plans of action were thus able to envision the systematic deployment of the avowed supporters of the Faith, whose ranks were swelling through the efforts of the institute, to establish a pattern of growth based on three core activities—study circles, devotional meetings and children's classes. As this pattern has unfolded in clusters around the world, an increasing number are gradually reaching the stage where they are ready to launch intensive programs for the expansion and consolidation of the Faith.[7]

42.21 As indicated above, the concept of the cluster was introduced at the beginning of the Five Year Plan to assist in the systematization of teaching. Once communities had been divided into clusters, the institutions of the Faith were challenged to learn how to effectively deploy the human resources being generated by the training institute in the field of service. In this way, the systematization of teaching efforts, and before it of human resource development, has been a central feature of the global Plans of the Faith since the Four Year Plan.

42.22 And as the friends and institutions have proceeded earnestly along the path traced out by the Universal House of Justice, they have begun to internalize and integrate the lessons and experiences of systemization called for in the global Plans. They have come to realize, for instance, that an essential requirement of systematic action is to arrive at a unified vision of growth for their communities and regions. The House of Justice has noted in the statement "The Institution of the Counsellors,"

42.23 At the outset of the work of the year or at times when new plans are being formulated, it is often useful to arrange for consultations between the Auxiliary Board members and the National or Regional Teaching Committees or Regional Councils before these plans are given final definition. A highly fruitful practice has developed in many parts of the world whereby members of a number of institutions and agencies of a country, or a region thereof, come together in a meeting of consultation to reach a common vision for the growth of their community and discuss strategies for action. These "institutional meetings" help to steer the friends away from thinking merely in terms of the mechanics of projects and to infuse their plans and subsequent action with the spirit of the Faith. They do much to reinforce the confidence of the institutions in devising the teaching strategies that will best serve the needs of their respective regions and in mobilizing the support of the Local Assemblies and the believers.[8]

42.24   Further, it is becoming clearer, especially among Auxiliary Board members and their assistants, that a vision for the growth of a cluster or region can only emerge from a far-greater vision of such realities as the greatness of this Day, the power of divine assistance, the potential inherent in every human being, and the powers that become available to the believers when they truly unite and work in a spirit of oneness:

42.25   To labor in the arena of service, the individual draws upon his love for Bahá'u'lláh, the power of the Covenant, the dynamics of prayer, the inspiration and education derived from regular study of the Holy Texts, and the transformative forces that operate upon his soul as he strives to behave in accordance with the divine laws and principles. Therefore, these are all themes of an ongoing relationship between the Auxiliary Board members and the believers.[9]

42.26   Evolving a vision of growth, it is being recognized, is fundamentally a spiritual process, one that implies ever-increasing consciousness of the spiritual forces released by Bahá'u'lláh. What is more, the friends everywhere are coming to the understanding that, in developing a vision of growth and the strategies to bring structure to it, some knowledge of possibilities, resources and even methods is necessary. A natural consequence has been the increasing number of concrete plans of action that "take into account the particular resources of the believers" and "the capacity of the local Bahá'í communities."[10]

In this connection, the believers and their institutions have 42.27
also taken to heart the admonition of the House of Justice that
progress "cannot be achieved by a mere series of spasmodic,
uncoordinated exertions, no matter how enthusiastic"[11] and
have learned the value of continuity of action. The concept of
a line of action has proven particularly helpful in this respect.
The House of Justice has explained in the context of intensive
programs of growth: "The best approach is to formulate
plans for a few months at a time, beginning with one or two
lines of action and gradually growing in complexity."[12] A
line of action consists of a sequence of projects and activities,
each building on the previous one and preparing the way for
further advances. In this light, the role of periodic meetings of
consultation to "reflect on issues, consider adjustments, and
maintain enthusiasm and unity of thought"[13] has been crucial
to the friends' efforts to pursue lines of action and build on
their accomplishments:

> Arrangements can then be made for the lessons learned 42.28
> from this experience to be discussed with the active sup-
> porters of the Faith in each region, helping them to identify
> the approaches and methods applicable to their specific
> conditions and to set in motion a systematic process of
> community development. This process should be one in
> which the friends review their successes and difficulties,
> adjust and improve their methods accordingly, and learn,
> and move forward unhesitatingly.[14]

Towards the end of the Five Year Plan, this guidance finally 42.29
gave rise to the organization of intensive programs of growth in
terms of cycles of growth, a matter which is currently the object
of learning in cluster after cluster as an increasing number
around the world reach this stage in their development. The
following passage from a letter dated 19 October 2005 written
to one National Spiritual Assembly summarizes the overall
learning to date:

> The promising pattern of action emerging in clusters 42.30
> throughout the world integrates individual initiative and
> community endeavor in order to embrace an ever-wider
> circle of people and teach receptive souls. This pattern
> appears wherever a sizeable number of individuals who
> are moving through the sequence of institute courses make
> a conscious effort to translate what they are learning into

action, undertaking specific acts of service that challenge them to draw upon the knowledge and insights they are gaining and to sharpen the skills and abilities they are developing through the courses. One of the most noteworthy outcomes of the institute courses is the emergence of an ever-increasing number of tutors who, having themselves studied the courses and struggled to walk a path of service, engage others in the study of the sequence, instilling in them the same desire to arise and serve. In this way, a broad base is laid for universal participation, which remains one of the most fundamental goals of the Bahá'í community. You have, yourselves, witnessed this development in the few clusters that have reached an advanced stage of growth.

42.31　　You have, likewise, observed how the conditions thus created in such clusters have made it possible to launch intensive programs of growth, in which large numbers of friends eagerly participate in the learning that takes place through successive cycles of activity seeking to integrate well-coordinated collective action with effective individual initiative. And you are equally aware of how interaction among three entities—the institute, the Auxiliary Boards, and the Area Teaching Committee—in close collaboration with responsive Local Spiritual Assemblies, can help carry the friends from one cycle to another and accelerate the learning process.[15]

42.32　And the passage below written to another National Assembly points to some of the challenges ahead:

42.33　The pattern of activity that emerges from one cycle of the program to the next will, however, prove effective only if the tendency to fall into certain habits is avoided. Among these are an undue reliance on proclamation efforts in the intensive teaching phase; a proliferation of core activities that does not serve the purpose of involving a growing number of seekers; a disproportionate focus on increasing short-lived contacts that loses sight of the need to systematically teach those who have shown interest in the Faith; and an overemphasis on the administrative activities occupying veteran Bahá'ís as enthusiastic new believers are being introduced to the disciplines and functions of the community.

To ensure the successful unfoldment of the process   42.34
of action and reflection that should run throughout the
successive cycles, the friends will want to keep at least
two points in mind. First, having dedicated an enormous
amount of time and energy towards studying a sequence
of courses aimed at helping them carry out certain acts of
service, they should now strive to apply what they have
learned in the teaching field. Specifically, if the content of
the courses explores fundamental concepts related to direct
teaching, it is only natural that they would seek to translate
these into action. If a home visit, to take another example,
is defined in the courses as an opportunity to enter into a
deep conversation on spiritual matters, then it should not
be reduced to a mere social call in which the Faith may not
even be mentioned. In short, the educational process in
which the friends have engaged over so many weeks and
months should give shape to the individual and collective
activities they now undertake.

Second, the meetings of reflection called at various   42.35
intervals during the cycles should serve to reinforce an
attitude of learning among the participants in the program
so that any fear of failure or criticism gives way to the joy
of earnest striving. To achieve this, the friends involved
in organizing the meetings should recognize that guided,
participatory discussion can prove more instructive than
elaborate presentations and prolonged theoretical analyses.
A careful review of vital statistics, which highlight weaknesses that require remedial attention and point to strengths
that can be built upon in the next cycle of activity, will go
far in facilitating the planning process.[16]

43

Learning to Maintain Focus

For a twenty-five year period, from 1996 to 2021, the Bahá'í 43.1
world will focus its attention on one single aim, that is, "on
advancing the process of entry by troops and on its systematic acceleration."[1] First introduced in the message dated
26 December 1995 to the Conference of the Continental Boards
of Counsellors, this aim has required believers and their institutions to exercise a higher degree of discipline in their individual
and collective activities than previously called for. "There will
be challenges to face, difficulties to overcome and adjustments
to be made,"[2] the Universal House of Justice cautioned one
National Spiritual Assembly at the beginning of the Four Year
Plan in 1996. What would be important, the House of Justice
indicated, was for the institutions and the believers to set out
towards the realization of this aim in a "spirit of unity."[3]

Maintaining focus has proven to be one of the greatest 43.2
challenges to individuals and institutions in this regard. A letter
written to the National Assembly of Kenya explained,

> To help large numbers of believers go through a sequence 43.3
> of courses is a formidable task, involving systematic work
> with an increasing number of tutors, the establishment of
> study circles, and measures for monitoring the progress
> of the participants. The friends in charge of the process
> need to have clarity of vision and should be allowed to
> carry out their mission without distraction. To assign to
> the institute such tasks as visiting communities and helping
> Local Spiritual Assemblies in their functioning would only
> lead to confusion.[4]

The House of Justice advised one National Assembly in 1998 43.4
that

> . . . the time has come for attention to be focused on the 43.5
> task of raising up human resources for the work of the

Faith from among the believers in the [Dananè] region itself. If this implies that for some time the geographic expansion of the Faith through the opening of new localities has to come to a halt, it is entirely understandable. It would also be acceptable for the rate of expansion—that is, the number of fresh recruits—to drop dramatically for a period as a balanced process of expansion and consolidation is allowed to gather momentum. What is needed at this stage is to gradually expand the institute's coverage so that the many capable friends in the region can have access to a systematic program of training aimed at enhancing their capacity to perform the tasks that an accelerated process of growth demands.

43.6   Herein now lies the priority not only for Dananè, but for other regions of the country as well. A constant barrage of new activities and projects in the region, no matter how well-intentioned, will only distract attention away from this all-important task. An endless stream of invitations to individuals from other countries to participate in projects that are not well rooted in the community itself is counterproductive.[5]

43.7   These passages suggest that having an aim implies understanding that certain activities take precedence over others and that certain steps must precede others. "At various stages in the evolution of the Faith," a letter to an individual has indicated, "certain activities that assist with the pressing needs of the development of the Bahá'í community may receive emphasis in a particular global plan. The institute process is one such example and is concerned with raising up the needed human resources for this stage in the growth of the Faith."[6] It is clear, then, that not all activities have the same importance at a given stage of development. Some activities, while perhaps suitable at a later stage, will only serve as distractions at the present one. Such activities may divert human and financial resources away from pressing tasks and impede progress. One of the requisites of having an aim is to maintain a "clear vision of the steps"[7] that must be taken at each stage in order to reach it.

43.8   It took time, of course, for the friends to arrive at such an understanding. First it was necessary for them to realize that certain kinds of activities undertaken during previous Plans would not contribute to their aim. In the following passage

National Assemblies in Southeast Asia were advised early in the Four Year Plan against implementing a large-scale collaborative effort:

> The Universal House of Justice does not wish to discourage you in your endeavors. Nor should you feel that the efforts of those communities with more resources at their disposal to assist their sister communities are not appreciated. Yet there is so much to be achieved in each one of your countries, if the central aim of the Four Year Plan is to be realized, that you should be wary of introducing any extraneous regional projects, losing thereby focus on the execution of national plans.[8]

43.9

The friends and the institutions also came to realize they should guard against making their work overly complex:

43.10

> What is most important in Belarus at this stage is to develop a national institute program, which initially need not be complex, and to have a group of trained teachers who offer courses on a regular basis in different localities throughout the country.[9]

43.11

They began to see that "there is little need for lengthy and frequent consultations to set direction and devise and rethink fundamental plans"[10] and that they should avoid "excessive emphasis on the perfection of methods."[11] It became clear to them that "to train scores of facilitators in how to conduct the first few courses, so that they [could] offer them in the villages and towns throughout the country" was a formidable task that would "require tremendous focus and concentration."[12]

43.12

And as Bahá'ís devoted increasing attention to establishing training institutes for the development of human resources, they gradually understood that this step had implications for how they arranged their priorities, addressed other needs, and allocated resources:

43.13

> In the area of human resource development the most pressing need in Australia now is for the extension of institute programs across the entire country, as stated in our letter of 2 December 1998. The accomplishment of this vital objective will require a substantial expenditure of the limited resources available to you, as well as a concentration of effort. The Bahá'í Centers of Learning in each State will need to be strengthened and a sustained endeavor

43.14

carried out, in collaboration with the Counsellors and the Auxiliary Board members, to encourage the rank and file of the Australian Bahá'í community to participate in institute programs. The challenge before you is that of transforming the culture of the Bahá'í community to one of continual learning together with application of the Bahá'í teachings in activities designed to advance the interests of the Faith.

43.15 Giving priority to meeting this need does not mean that other initiatives which meet special needs or interests should be neglected. However, it does mean that the growth of such ventures should be restricted to such a degree as not to require an appreciable expenditure of the funds of the Faith.[13]

43.16 The friends also came to understand that even the most well-intentioned proposals could cause them to lose focus:

43.17 You seek guidance on the advisability of your distributing a deepening program to all Regional Bahá'í Councils for use by the friends, especially newly enrolled believers, in small groups or individually. It is, of course, important for deepening courses and study classes to flourish in local communities everywhere, and your desire to facilitate the multiplication of such activities is appreciated. Nonetheless, what you are suggesting would, in essence, constitute a national program that could distract the friends from the institute process and ultimately undermine the hard-earned progress that your community has achieved in recent years in that process.[14]

43.18 As appreciation for the work of the training institute grew, the friends eventually realized that it could not be used to address every need if it was to fulfill its purpose:

43.19 The House of Justice appreciates that there is a pressing need to continue to raise the awareness of the Bahá'í community concerning the significance of the Law of Ḥuqúqu'lláh. However, as you know, training institutes have been established as a means of developing human resources for the expansion and consolidation of the Faith. Naturally, the Law of Ḥuqúqu'lláh will have an appropriate place in a sequence of courses offered by an institute, as will the whole question of supporting the funds of the Faith. But to involve the training institutes in a specific endeavor to educate the friends in this Law would be a diversion from their main task. The Universal House of Justice feels that other means should be used for this purpose, for example, deepening sessions, seminars and occasional workshops.[15]

It also became clear with time that the work of the training institute could not accommodate every individual initiative:

43.20

> The House of Justice appreciates the sentiments of devotion and dedication that animate the messages from Mrs. . . . and her daughter. Regarding the introduction and guidelines for "story circles," in general, the House of Justice has no comment to make about the approach promoted by Mrs. . . . for sharing stories. However, as various institutes around the world, including the one serving . . . , strive to establish the concept of study circles, care should be taken to avoid attaching too many extraneous elements to it. The potential for complication is especially evident in this case where the "story circle" is intended to evolve into a study circle.[16]

43.21

And, most important, the friends learned that focus would require perseverance:

43.22

> By focusing the friends' attention on only two goals over the past year, you were able to make considerable advances in the establishment of ongoing training courses in both Yap and Palau, although in terms of the numerical growth of your community progress was negligible. Yet, you should not be discouraged. In the planning and execution of any set of activities, it is important to make sure that expectations are not raised unreasonably high. In the case of your institute program, those who have participated will have completed only the first course or two. If, as you say in your annual report, the results have been a firm acceptance of Bahá'í identity and heightened enthusiasm for service, then you should be heartened by your achievements.

43.23

> It is therefore imperative that you continue to vigorously pursue your plans to establish a training institute in each island group. Every effort should be made to expand the system for the delivery of courses so that more and more friends are able to enter your institute program. You should also make sure that many advance far enough along in the program to study courses directly designed to

43.24

increase their capacity to teach and to guide new souls to Bahá'u'lláh's Revelation.[17]

43.25   As the Five Year Plan opened, the question of deploying human resources in the context of clusters assumed prominence. "Concentrated and sustained attention"[18] was now focused on two movements. The concept of setting priorities was well understood by then, and most national communities soon identified two or three clusters "on which to focus special attention."[19] The House of Justice referred to the prioritization of clusters in its Riḍván 2004 message:

43.26   National Assemblies, while attending to the needs of all the clusters in their countries, have learned the value of concentrating special attention on certain priority clusters that show high promise, encouraging and developing them until the human resources they have raised up through the training institutes enable them to become centers of rapid, sustained growth.[20]

43.27   During this period National Assemblies were better able to distinguish activities that would contribute to the aim of the Plan from those which should be taken up at a later stage. It was in this light that the National Assembly of the Russian Federation was commended for its decision to forgo the implementation of a program related to social and economic development on a national scale:

43.28   The House of Justice noted with interest that the modules of the "My Home" program, prepared by the now defunct European Family Life Task Force, were well received by the believers and their friends in Russia. It is understood that, based on the recommendations of the Counsellors, a decision was made to suspend the implementation of this program, so that the limited human resources in your stronger clusters could pay adequate attention to the requirements of systematic expansion and consolidation. You should rest assured that your decision is well in keeping with the oft-repeated guidance of the House of Justice regarding the need to focus on the priorities of the Plan. The welcome acceleration of activities in several clusters in recent months, leading to the launching of two intensive programs of growth in Moscow and Ulan-Ude, is a clear vindication of your approach. As your communities expand and capacities increase, the institutions will be in a better position to assess the nature of social and economic development projects that need to be introduced.[21]

National Assemblies were helped to see how other types of activities related to the work of expansion and consolidation, on which the generality of the friends have been focused. For example, one Assembly was advised that 43.29

> The work of external affairs represents a very specialized field of service and is most commonly performed by a small group of believers in a national community. There is no reason to see it in competition with the activities of the generality of the friends for the expansion and consolidation of the Faith, vying, for example, for the human resources engaged in the teaching work and the institute process. It is suggested that you review the enclosed statement and, on that basis, adopt one or two lines of action that can be carried out by a small corps of believers with capacity in this area. As your experience increases over time, you can gradually expand the range of your endeavors in the field of external affairs.[22] 43.30

In this way, National Assemblies in Europe were counseled that the external affairs work "makes no widespread demand on the community, nor does it detract from, but is an essential contribution to, the processes of the Five Year Plan."[23] In addition to external affairs, the House of Justice would indicate that activities in other areas should be conducted within the context of the Plans. A letter written on its behalf acknowledging receipt of several reports on a conference of "young Bahá'ís interested in serious study of the Writings"[24] suggested the following: 43.31

> There certainly is great value in the initiative taken by individuals to engage in scholarly study of the Writings for its own sake; however, a greater value accrues to both the individual and the community when the motive for such study is prompted by a desire to serve the aim of the Plan in progress and, consequently, if relevant activities, such as the recent conference, are designed within the context of the Plan.[25] 43.32

In some instances, even the question of the purchase of properties should be addressed with the aim of the Plan in mind: 43.33

43.34   The House of Justice appreciates the desire of the friends to have a suitably located Bahá'í Center and recognizes the need for a reception center to serve both the friends in the metropolitan area and visitors from abroad. It feels, however, that the purchase of a building would not be appropriate at this juncture. Beside any financial considerations, the dispersed pattern of activity in the intensive program of growth now unfolding in London will undoubtedly influence future perceptions of the type of facilities required.[26]

43.35   There is clearly an increasing awareness among the friends of the need to maintain focus on the aim of advancing the process of entry by troops. They are beginning to see that the most effective way to pursue this aim is within the framework of the global Plans of the Faith. It is worth remembering in this regard how tenuous such focus can be and how easily it is lost. The following was recently written to one National Assembly:

43.36   . . . the plans for the teaching project adopted by the Spiritual Assembly appear to revert to a teaching mode that was used in the past and which proved not to be a sustainable approach to expansion and consolidation. Therefore, the House of Justice urges you to immediately consult with the Counsellors about finding ways to recast the project to bring it more closely into conformity with the priorities of the Five Year Plan.[27]

43.37   Of course, since the outset of the Four Year Plan there have been believers, some with the noblest of intentions, who have preferred to focus on other pursuits. In this regard it seems that the House of Justice has been anxious that they not feel compelled to do otherwise. One individual who wrote to the House of Justice to raise concerns about the format and content of study circles was offered the following in reply:

43.38   It is natural that any given educational program would not appeal to everyone, and clearly participating in the courses of an institute is not a requirement to be fulfilled by all believers. In no way, then, should those who do not wish to take part feel that they are disobeying the directives of the Universal House of Justice. It does ask, however, that everyone, even those not involved, support the institute process and not impede its steady progress.[28]

Another individual who expressed discomfort about the multi-   43.39
plication of core activities received this reply:

> You indicate that, despite your personal disapproval of   43.40
> the materials being used by institutes in . . . , you feel under
> an obligation to continue focusing your efforts on the core
> activities of the present Plan. The House of Justice believes
> that, given your views, there is no reason for you to feel
> such an obligation, and you are advised to determine, in the
> privacy of your own conscience, those ways in which you
> can most effectively serve the advancement of the Cause.[29]

Oftentimes the reason given for not wanting to participate   43.41
in the core activities is a feeling that the focus of the Bahá'í
world is giving rise to uniformity. This concern has been addressed in letters written on behalf of the House of Justice such
as the following:

> The House of Justice feels that you need to consider this   43.42
> issue in the larger context of the development of the train-
> ing institute as an element essential to the growth of the
> Faith, beginning with the Four Year Plan. Given the nature
> of this agency and the purpose defined for it by the House
> of Justice, it goes without saying that the emerging training
> institutes around the world would choose a sequence of
> courses and offer them to the friends in the territories they
> respectively serve. To have a large number of believers
> engaged in the study of these courses, far from a sign of
> uniformity, is part of the natural dynamics of a successful
> educational program. That at this point in the development
> of the Bahá'í community a significant percentage of the
> training institutes worldwide have opted to initiate their ac-
> tivities with a set of materials that has proven itself effective
> over many years of experience is a welcome phenomenon.
>
>   . . . the House of Justice feels that it would be beneficial   43.43
> for you to separate in your mind the training institute
> process, so intimately connected with the promotion of
> large-scale expansion and consolidation, from the many
> deepening classes, workshops and summer school courses
> that form a fundamental part of Bahá'í community life.
> Their number and diversity actually seem to be on the
> rise as a result of the institute process. Indeed, you will be
> reassured to know that, as the believers gain confidence
> in their capacity to serve through the institute process, a

much richer expression of the diverse talents of the friends is beginning to appear in the Bahá'í world—a richness that bodes well for the future progress of the Cause.[30]

43·44   Clearly, the unity of thought and action that results from maintaining focus is not to be confused with uniformity. The framework of the Five Year Plan—"a Plan designed to fit the requirements of these times"[31]—provides ample room for the exercise of individual initiative as well as collective action. Within this framework the friends are encouraged to carry out activities "aimed at advancing the process of entry by troops."[32] Each individual believer must decide for him or herself how to participate in this global enterprise. What is important is that his or her endeavors not go so far "beyond what the House of Justice had in mind when writing of encouraging individual initiative"[33] that they shatter focus and disrupt the work of the Plan. In this sense, by learning to work within the framework of the global Plans the friends are coming to a better understanding of how to contribute to the greater good: "The spirit of the approach to systematic programs of growth," a letter written on behalf of the House of Justice advised, "is that of believers working together effectively for the common good."[34] And another letter to an individual believer offered the following guidance:

43·45   Ultimately, the choice fruits of one's striving are manifested in selfless service to the Cause, surrendering all personal interests and desires for the things that pertain unto God, subordinating one's will to the common good and ever mindful of the pitfall of attachment to one's own service.[35]

43·46   And as institutions at all levels help the friends "to maintain a unity of vision"[36] and carry out individual and collective activities within the framework of the Plans, the believers are witnessing first hand what it means for their powers to be "multiplied in unified action":[37]

43·47   It would simplify and unify the efforts of the entire community if the friends would earnestly strive to follow the few but essential guidelines given for the operation of the Five Year Plan. The House of Justice has no doubt whatever that such strivings would intensify the dynamics for achieving entry by troops on an ever-widening scale.[38]

44

Learning to Develop Human Resources for Expansion and Consolidation

In its Riḍván 2000 message, the Universal House of Justice stated that "the system of training institutes established throughout the world with great rapidity" qualified as "the single greatest legacy of the Four Year Plan" in the field of expansion and consolidation.[1] Several months earlier in its 26 November 1999 message to the Bahá'ís of the world, the House of Justice had described this achievement in the following terms:

> The accomplishments during this period are encouraging indeed. An impressive network of training institutes on a scale but dimly imagined at the start of the Plan has been established throughout the world. These nascent centers of learning have made significant strides in developing formal programs and in putting into place effective systems for the delivery of courses. Reports indicate that the number of believers benefiting directly from training courses has climbed to nearly 100,000. Without question, the capacity of the worldwide community to develop its human resources has been distinctly enhanced.

> The effects of this systematic approach to human resource development are making themselves felt in the lives of all three protagonists of the Plan—the individual believer, the institutions, and the local community. There has been an upsurge in teaching activities undertaken at the initiative of the individual. Spiritual Assemblies, Councils, and committees have grown in their ability to guide the believers in their individual and collective endeavors. And community life has flourished, even in localities long dormant, as new patterns of thought and behavior have emerged.[2]

In this light, the House of Justice made the following remarks at the outset of the Five Year Plan in 2001 regarding the effects

44.1

44.2

44.3

44.4

of the institute on the individual, institutions, and community and its continued importance in the work of the Cause:

44.5   A searching analysis of the Four Year Plan recently prepared for us by the International Teaching Centre demonstrates that the training institute is effective not only in enhancing the powers of the individual, but also in vitalizing communities and institutions. The continued development of training institutes in the diverse countries and territories of the world, then, must be a central feature of the new Plan.[3]

44.6   The training institute has been defined by the House of Justice as an agency of the National Spiritual Assembly "charged with the task of developing human resources in all or part of country."[4] A letter written on behalf of the House of Justice explained that the growth of the Faith depends on a systematic process of human resource development:

44.7   In its message of 26 December 1995 to the Conference of the Continental Boards of Counsellors, the House of Justice clearly explained that occasional courses of instruction and the informal activities of community life, though important, had not proven sufficient as a means of human resource development. It indicated further that a systematic process for the development of human resources was essential to the sustained large-scale expansion of the Faith. To conceive and nurture an educational process of the magnitude envisioned by the Universal House of Justice is vastly different than thinking about one's own interests, which is not to say that personal study and spiritual growth are not legitimate and natural concerns of the individual.[5]

44.8   Creating the capacity within each national community to establish and administer such an educational process required an enormous amount of effort and a high degree of discipline on the part of the institutions of the Faith during the Four Year Plan. The Spiritual Assembly of Thailand was counseled at the start of the Plan:

44.9   Those engaged in this area of service—whether as teachers, coordinators, or members of the institute's board—will have to realize that there is much to be learned. How to offer the courses and how to attract the believers to them, which courses to offer at a central location and which ones to conduct in the towns and villages—these are among the many questions to which they will have to seek answers. They should never lose heart when difficulties appear, but should persevere in their endeavors, for only in this way will the institute acquire the capacity to develop the human resources of the Thai community.[6]

The methodology to be adopted in creating this capacity, the House of Justice advised, was one of action, reflection, and consultation. It encouraged the friends involved to approach their tasks with "an open attitude towards learning," fully cognizant of the need to "make decisions" about the work of the institute, "to implement them, to reflect on the results, and to make adjustments in the light of experience"[7] "Through such an approach," the House of Justice assured one National Assembly, "your institute will succeed in gradually increasing its capacity to develop the human resources"[8] of the community. 44.10

In this sense, in calling for the establishment of training institutes for the development of human resources, the House of Justice was also asking the Bahá'í world to learn what it means to work in a learning mode. And as the friends everywhere entered into this mode, they gradually came to better understand the nature of the institute and how to go about establishing it. "It is important to realize that the development of the institute in your national community, like everywhere else," it has been explained, "is a dynamic process in which all those involved gradually reach higher and higher levels of understanding as to the nature of the process itself."[9] The fact that the Bahá'í community worldwide has acquired a vocabulary necessary to speak on the subject indicates how successful it was both in creating capacity for developing human resources, on the one hand, and in adopting a posture of learning in all its affairs, on the other. Words and phrases such as "study circle," "sequence of courses," "institute campaigns," and "practice" are now commonplace. To speak about a "pyramid of human resources" or a "system of distance education" evokes a practical set of ideas in the minds of Bahá'ís everywhere. It is well understood by all when the training institute is referred to as the "engine for growth." 44.11

To reach this point required learning in two principal areas: in the nature of programs for the development of human resources and in the system for their delivery. This was 44.12

underscored in the message dated 9 January 2001 from the House of Justice:

44.13   Drawing on the wealth of experience now accumulated in this area of endeavor, institutes will have to provide their communities with a constant stream of human resources to serve the process of entry by troops. Elements of a system that can meet the training needs of large numbers of believers have already been tested worldwide and have proven themselves. Study circles, reinforced by extension courses and special campaigns, have shown their ability to lend structure to the process of spiritual education at the grassroots. The value of a sequence of courses, each one following the other in a logical pattern and each one building on the achievements of the previous ones, has become abundantly clear.[10]

44.14   As indicated in the above passage, it took time to come to an understanding of the role of a properly structured sequence of courses in enhancing the friends' capabilities of service. The document "Training Institutes," prepared for and approved by the House of Justice, had advised that "the complexity of the task of defining each sequence and elaborating the materials" should not be underestimated.[11] In this respect, many National Assemblies felt that the wisest course of action was "to make a start, using the tried and tested sequence of course materials" already available because of the pressing need to move forward.[12] It was in the light of such considerations that eventually more and more National Assemblies decided that their training institutes should adopt the materials of the Ruhi Institute for their courses:

44.15   When the concept of the training institute was introduced by the House of Justice, it left National Spiritual Assemblies free to adopt whatever kind of systematic training they felt best suited to their countries. Quite rapidly, however, it became evident, through experience, that the courses of the Ruhi Institute, developed over many years in Colombia, were far more effective than any other generally available. Some believers who did not have the experience of using the courses were of the opinion that they were too "elementary" for the people of their country, but, in one country after another, the Ruhi Institute courses have proved their effectiveness in virtually every environment. The House of Justice has still not limited National Assemblies in their choice of institute courses, but it has been pleased to note how most National Assemblies have recognized the effectiveness of the Ruhi Institute's main sequence of courses and have put it to full use—a use that in due time will enable them to develop additional materials suited to their specific environments, that supplement the books of the Ruhi Institute.[13]

Though born out of the experience of the Bahá'í community of Colombia in large-scale expansion and consolidation, the materials of the Ruhi Institute have clearly demonstrated their global applicability. The House of Justice has noted in a letter dated 26 July 2004 written on its behalf that those national communities which have adopted the materials "have increasingly shown the beneficial effect of this training on the expansion of the teaching work, the rise in the level of human resources, and the breaking down of the earlier barriers between Bahá'ís and others in worshipping together and in areas of service, including the education of children."[14] Further, with the spread in the use of its materials, the letter stated, "the Ruhi Institute has continued to evolve, incorporating the experiences and suggestions of friends in many parts of the world" into its materials.[15] 44.16

In communities where the materials of the Ruhi Institute have been adopted as the main sequence of the courses, training institutes are beginning to supplement these courses with others that are tailored to the specific needs of the populations they seek to serve. These other courses are generally offered after the completion of one or another course in the main sequence, which, in this case, can be thought of as a trunk of a tree with branches extending out from it. This model was of course discussed in the 9 January 2001 message of the House of Justice. "The main sequence," the message read, "much like the trunk of a tree, supports courses branching out from it, each branch dedicated to some specific area of training."[16] 44.17

With the majority of national communities adopting such a model, using the courses of the Ruhi Institute as the main sequence, they have begun to derive unexpected benefits from this arrangement. The letter dated 26 July quoted above went on to say that "a fortunate side effect of the choice of one set of materials by so many communities has been a commonality of experience in this vitally important Bahá'í activity throughout 44.18

the world."[17] The letter was referring to a statement from the Riḍván 2004 message of the House of Justice:

44.19   On assessing the opportunities and needs of their respective communities, the great majority of National Spiritual Assemblies have chosen to adopt the course materials devised by the Ruhi Institute, finding them most responsive to the Plan's needs. This has had the collateral benefit that the same materials have been translated into many languages and, wherever Bahá'ís travel, they find other friends following the same path and familiar with the same books and methods.[18]

44.20   Adopting a sequence of courses in this way has enabled the institutions to think more systematically about developing the human resources of their communities. For they could now set numerical goals "as to the number of believers who will pass through courses at various levels during a specified time period."[19] The metaphor of a "pyramid" of human resources is sometimes used in this respect, as explained in the passage below to one National Assembly:

44.21   In letters written on its behalf to other National Spiritual Assemblies, the House of Justice has stated that the development of human resources in a country may be likened to the building of an ever-expanding pyramid, whose base must be constantly broadened. An increasing number of friends are recruited to enter the first basic course, and relatively significant percentages are then helped to reach higher and higher courses, enhancing thereby their capacity for service.[20]

44.22   It is in this context that the system for the delivery of courses—the other principal area of learning—becomes important. In order to have "ever-growing contingents of believers" pass through the sequence of courses, training institutes soon came to realize that they would need to put in place a decentralized system of delivery. "The limitations of the approach in which institute courses are offered only to groups of believers at central facilities"[21] were all too apparent:

44.23   The primary challenge before you is to help hundreds and then thousands of the believers in Haiti to enter your institute program and study a well-defined sequence of courses.

Clearly, you cannot accomplish this by inviting them all to one central location.[22]

The idea that finally emerged was the study circle because it enabled the curriculum to reach large numbers. In this connection, the House of Justice noted that the approach that seems to be "most effective in reaching believers at the local level is the formation of study circles which are coordinated by a national institute. . . . In this case, a sequence of courses is offered to small groups of believers in a locality by tutors or teachers trained by the institute itself."[23] A letter to an individual dated 24 May 2001 elaborated on the theme: 44.24

> As you know, a study circle is not a structure in the Bahá'í Administrative Order. Rather, it is one element of a scheme of distance education that is showing great promise as it becomes more firmly established in Bahá'í communities throughout the world. From the reports received at the World Centre, it is clear that the success of this scheme depends on the degree to which the flexibility inherent to it is exploited. In many places a study circle will continue with the same tutor from course to course. Yet the membership of a study circle does not have to be fixed. Often the demands of life, especially the mobility of people today, prevent a person from studying the full sequence of courses with one group. Thus, after the completion of a course, one or two friends may find that they have to suspend their studies for a time and join another group for the next course when their circumstances allow. It is precisely because of this inherent flexibility that the scheme is proving to be so effective in moving a significant percentage of believers through a sequence of courses and in developing thereby the human resources of the community.[24]   44.25

Of course, some form of organizational structure is required in order to maintain a system of distance education in which a number of study circles are conducted throughout the year. This organizational structure does not need to be overly elaborate. A "national coordinator, assisted by regional coordinators if necessary, as well as a growing number of tutors in the country,"[25] is generally sufficient, in addition, of course, to the institute board appointed by the National Spiritual Assembly in consultation with the Counsellors. The following excerpt from a letter addresses the roles of the board and coordinator: 44.26

44.27   With such a focused aim, the roles of the respective participants are also clear. The coordinator needs to operate at the level of implementation, carrying out day-to-day plans and activities and ensuring that the basic function of the institute is performed—this, with the assistance of the tutors and any staff if necessary. The board oversees the institute process as a whole, largely through the periodic reports of the coordinator and through occasional consultations. It will want to make itself readily accessible to the coordinator, providing the atmosphere in which he or she can share ideas, seek the board's views on the possibilities and challenges facing the institute, and benefit from its advice. To carry out its role, the board does not need to meet frequently, as does a committee charged with undertaking a set of specific tasks.[26]

44.28   As mentioned in the 26 December 1995 message of the House of Justice, the structure of the organization in place in a community to oversee the development of human resources will depend to some extent upon the size of the community. National Assemblies with geographically large communities have chosen in consultation with the Counsellors to devolve responsibility for the implementation of courses on training institutes at the regional level, each with its own board and a regional coordinator. Regardless of the arrangements in place, the institutional capacity created in most national communities to impart spiritual education to growing numbers of believers was significant enough by 2001 for the House of Justice to make the following announcement:

44.29   . . . there are many countries in which the institute is the only structure developing the capacity to organize and maintain courses in locality after locality. As this approach is working well with youth and adults, and increasingly for junior youth, there is no reason why the training institute should not also shoulder similar responsibility with respect to children, where necessary. As a general rule, institutes do not take on the administration of plans and programs for expansion and consolidation. Conducting children's classes, however, is a unique enterprise, of special urgency. In those countries where the task is given to it, the institute becomes a center of learning intensely engaged in the spiritual education of the friends from the tenderest age through adulthood.[27]

The above offers a vision of a powerful educational institu-   44.30
tion offering a range of programs for children, junior youth, youth over 15, and adults—all carried out in the context of the expansion and consolidation of the Faith. As a means of ensuring that its programs keep current with the demands of growth at the level of the cluster, two additional mechanisms have proven to be important. One is the intensive institute campaign. Such campaigns, the House of Justice explained in its Riḍván 2005 message, when they pay due attention to the practice required, "have remained the vehicle for stimulating growth at the cluster level."[28] And when a cluster approaches the point where it is ready to launch an intensive program of growth, it is often necessary to have an institute coordinator at the level of the cluster—the other mechanism. Such a coordinator is "responsible for ensuring that the number of study circles, children's classes, and junior youth groups steadily multiplies."[29] He or she is "required to work with a growing contingent of tutors and children's class teachers in the cluster, maintaining their enthusiasm and helping them to improve the quality of their services."[30]

The above describes in the briefest terms the nature of the   44.31
institutional capacity that has been built through successive global Plans, beginning with the Four Year Plan, to develop the human resources needed for the expansion and consolidation of the Faith. As noted earlier, "the effects of this systematic approach to human resource development are making themselves felt in the lives of all three protagonists of the Plan—the individual believer, the institutions, and the local community." National Assemblies had to develop the capacity to encourage and empower the friends in their efforts to advance the institute process and to ensure that the institute had what it needed to succeed at its task:

> As for your National Assembly, what is needed most   44.32
> from you at this time is the kind of enthusiastic and ener-
> getic support for the institute process that comes from an
> ever-increasing understanding of the dynamics of growth in
> Ethiopia. Through constant encouragement, the judicious
> assignment of resources, and frequent consultations with
> the Counsellors, you can promote the learning called for

in the Five Year Plan and ensure that the creative energies of the many dedicated Ethiopian believers are channeled constructively and the vast potential of your community is realized.[31]

44.33   For the friends serving in the institute to be empowered in this way, they would need a wide degree of latitude to carry out their work:

44.34   Crucial to the future success of the institute will be the freedom of movement and action that it enjoys. The institute is, of course, an agency functioning under your aegis, and ultimately matters related to its operation rest with you. However, at this point in the growth of the Faith, the mandate of the institute is fairly clear-cut: A sequence of courses has been adopted as the national program for the development of human resources. It is the job of the institute, then, to help a steadily increasing number of youth and adults advance through that sequence and to carry out the concomitant task of organizing and maintaining classes for junior youth and children. There is little need for lengthy and frequent consultations to set direction and devise and rethink fundamental plans. Now is the time for action, and the central participants driving the institute process should be granted the latitude required to perform their functions effectively. Specifically, the national coordinator should be invested with enough authority to ensure that the basic purpose of the institute to raise up active supporters of the Faith is fulfilled.[32]

44.35   It also meant that National Assemblies would be challenged to find new approaches to overseeing the work of its agencies:

44.36   Your institute has been structured so as to accommodate a range of dynamic programs, including one in the area of mass media communications through the radio station. At the apex of its organizational structure is a board of directors that sets general policies, offers guidance as needed, and provides a forum for the executive director to share concerns and seek advice from time to time. Surely it is to be expected that such a complex organization would develop certain patterns and cycles in performing its operations, including phases for planning and budgeting. To halt the established rhythm to enable the National Spiritual

Assembly to carry out an evaluation of the institute's performance and give it instructions does not seem justified. This is not to say that the desire of the National Assembly to follow the progress of the institute is not a legitimate one. Indeed, at any time during the year or over the course of the Five Year Plan, you may wish to review the institute's work, along with the Counsellors, and provide guidance and encouragement. But this should not prevent the institute from proceeding with its programs, nor cause it to suffer from the lack of financial resources. Further, when adjustments are felt necessary, they should be done in a way that does not slacken the gathering momentum of the processes of growth in your community. You should remember that, in the final analysis, much of the success of your efforts to meet the requirements of the Five Year Plan will depend on the continued steady progress of your national agency for the development of human resources.[33]

National Assemblies gradually had to come to appreciate   44.37
that although having human resources in the field provided communities with the manpower needed to ensure that the growth of the Faith could move forward, this should never preclude the participation of all of the friends in its work. However, Assemblies also had to realize that certain positions would necessarily involve some formal preparation:

> Clearly the way should be open to all the friends to   44.38
> participate in the affairs of the Faith, to the extent that their personal circumstances and their desire to serve allow. In general, within the Bahá'í community, a distinction between "trained" and "untrained" believers is unwarranted. There do exist certain positions of service, however, that require specific qualifications, and an Assembly will naturally consider these qualifications in naming individual believers to fill them. In the case of a position responsible for coordinating courses offered according to a curriculum that has been adopted by the institutions, it seems only reasonable that the person called upon to perform this service would have a considerable degree of experience with the set of courses in question. Care should be taken, however, that such requirements are only brought into consideration when clearly necessary, for to have requisites for performing every kind of activity would have the harmful result of barring many

devoted and eager friends from contributing to the unfoldment of the Five Year Plan and, ultimately, the advancement of the Faith.[34]

44.39 The institutions also had to exercise the ability to help the friends to avoid creating false dichotomies on the basis of misunderstandings about the global Plans and to recognize that deepening and human resource development should not be held in opposition to each other:

44.40 National winter and summer schools, as well as deepening classes at the local level, are an integral aspect of community life in which the friends come together to deepen their knowledge of the Faith. Institutes were created as an instrument to develop the human resources necessary for the expansion and consolidation of the Faith. These two elements are complementary, and benefit from each other as they both flourish.[35]

44.41 For local communities, the effects of training institutes have been significant as well. The acts of service treated in the main sequence of the Ruhi Institute courses are intended to set in motion a process that will lead to the sound development of local communities or, as envisioned in the Five Year Plan, of clusters. A plan of growth for the cluster is, in some sense, embedded in the sequence of courses, as described in the passage below:

44.42 The training institute is intended to endow a certain percentage of the friends in a community with the spiritual insights, knowledge, and skills and abilities necessary to perform the various tasks that accelerated expansion and consolidation of the Faith demands. Through the deployment of such believers in the field of service, then, needs of the kind you have identified can gradually be met. In the sequence of courses adopted by your institute, for instance, those who have completed the first course often go on to initiate devotional meetings in their localities, an act of service that in many places constitutes the beginnings of a sustainable pattern of community life. This pattern is strengthened as participants in the courses gain the capacity to deepen their fellow believers in the fundamentals of the Faith through a program of home visits and to conduct classes for the spiritual education of children. As such efforts to deepen the generality of the believers and educate their children advance, the level of their participation in essential aspects of Bahá'í community life, for example, the Nineteen Day Feast and Holy Day observances, likewise increases.[36]

Communities, of course, are the collective expression of the individuals who compose them and who strive to promote their development. Ultimately, then, the purpose of the training institute is to build the capacity of individuals to meet the many needs of growing, vibrant communities. The content and order of the courses of the Ruhi Institute are based on a series of acts of service, the practice of which seeks to enhance such capacity. It views this process of capacity building in terms of "walking a path of service." On such a path the friends are assisted first in accomplishing relatively simple tasks and then in performing more complex and demanding acts of service. This is the nature of capacity building. Each is accompanied by another as he learns to walk the path on his own. "One of the most noteworthy outcomes of the institute courses," the Universal House of Justice has recently noted, "is the emergence of an ever-increasing number of tutors who, having themselves studied the courses and struggled to walk a path of service, engage others in the study of the sequence, instilling in them the same desire to arise and serve."[37] "Arise, then," it has urged, "to engage more and more trusted members of your families, friends, neighbors and coworkers in the sequence of courses and assist them to walk the path of service so that a sizeable expansion of the Bahá'í community is hastened and sustained."[38]

44.43

45

Learning to Open Aspects of
Bahá'í Community Life to Others

Referring to the development of communities at the level of   45.1
the cluster, the Universal House of Justice wrote the following
at the start of the Five Year Plan: "Among the initial goals for
every community should be the establishment of study circles,
children's classes, and devotional meetings, open to all the
inhabitants of the locality."[1] In its Riḍván 2002 message it
commented that significant progress had been made in opening
these activities to society at large, citing the training institute as
the means for this development:

> It is most encouraging to see that the progress of this   45.2
> work is being energized through the training institute
> process, which was considerably strengthened last year by
> the campaigns undertaken in many countries to increase
> the number of trained tutors. Where a training institute
> is well established and constantly functioning, three core
> activities—study circles, devotional meetings, and children's
> classes—have multiplied with relative ease. Indeed, the
> increasing participation of seekers in these activities, at the
> invitation of their Bahá'í friends, has lent a new dimension
> to their purposes, consequently effecting new enrollments.
> Here, surely, is a direction of great promise for the teaching
> work. These core activities, which at the outset were devised
> principally to benefit the believers themselves, are naturally
> becoming portals for entry by troops. By combining study
> circles, devotional meetings and children's classes within
> the framework of clusters, a model of coherence in lines
> of action has been put in place and is already producing
> welcome results. Worldwide application of this model, we
> feel confident, holds immense possibilities for the progress
> of the Cause in the years ahead.[2]

45.3   In the passage above the House of Justice encouraged the friends to fully exploit the possibilities for growth inherent in the three core activities. So successful was the Bahá'í community in doing so that the House of Justice could comment in its message of 17 January 2003 that the orientation of the Bahá'í world to society at large had undergone a significant change:

45.4   The coherence thus achieved through the establishment of study circles, devotional meetings and children's classes provides the initial impulse for growth in a cluster, an impulse that gathers strength as these core activities multiply in number. Campaigns that help a sizeable group of believers advance far enough in the main sequence of courses to perform the necessary acts of service lend impetus to this multiplication of activity.

45.5   It is evident, then, that a systematic approach to training has created a way for Bahá'ís to reach out to the surrounding society, share Bahá'u'lláh's message with friends, family, neighbors and coworkers, and expose them to the richness of His teachings. This outward-looking orientation is one of the finest fruits of the grassroots learning taking place.[3]

45.6   One obstacle believers had to overcome to achieve this change in orientation was the fear of introducing family and friends to educational programs whose content goes beyond the presentation of Bahá'í principles to speak about teachings that are explicitly religious in nature. A letter dated 25 September 2001 to a National Assembly encouraged the Assembly in this regard in the context of children's classes:

45.7   It is possible, of course, to create a program for children which is inspired by the Bahá'í teachings and conveys such topics as moral education, comparative religion, peace, concern for the environment, service to humanity, or world citizenship. Such programs might also convey practical subjects such as literacy, academic tutoring, or vocational training.

45.8   In its message dated 9 January 2001, however, the House of Justice refers specifically to Bahá'í children's classes as also being open to non-Bahá'í children. In the case of these classes, which are intended to address the complete spiritual education of Bahá'ís, it would not be possible to eliminate Bahá'í religious teachings, and topics such as Bahá'í history, Bahá'í laws, and the Covenant would be an integral part of these classes.

While Bahá'í religious teachings are part of the program of child education in Bahá'í classes, the design of the program, particularly the sequencing of content, may make it more attractive to non-Bahá'ís. For example, in the approach taken to child education in Ruhi Institute Book 3, the emphasis is placed initially on character development, and only later are specific aspects related to the life of Bahá'u'lláh and the Báb introduced. So too can we see the same principle at work in the main sequence of books in which many non-Bahá'í youth have participated. Book 1 addresses such broad topics as prayer and life and death (from a Bahá'í perspective, of course). It is in Book 4 that history is presented in detail. Thus a non-Bahá'í can feel welcome to participate and is not overwhelmed by new, purely religious teachings. Then, if attracted by the principles and general spiritual teachings, the non-Bahá'ís would not hesitate to engage in the full program; alternatively, they are free to withdraw or not participate in some segments.[4] 45.9

Since the beginning of the Four Year Plan, the House of Justice has envisioned that the educational process set in motion and the activities it would engender would be open to the community at large and serve as a means of teaching the Faith. In this way a letter dated 8 May 1997 written on behalf of the House of Justice encouraged the National Assembly of Bulgaria to open some of its institute courses to those who were not Bahá'ís, saying: "In addition to attracting thoughtful people to the Cause, such courses could also be a means of confirming them in the Faith and increasing the number of Bahá'u'lláh's faithful followers in your country."[5] Indeed, concern for the generality of humankind and its spiritual development has been at the heart of the call of the House of Justice to the Bahá'í world to focus its attention on advancing the process of entry by troops. "The community must become imbued with a sense of mission," the House of Justice wrote when announcing the Four Year Plan, "and the Assembly grow in awareness of its role as a channel of God's grace not only for the Bahá'ís but for the entire village, town or city in which it serves."[6] 45.10

Although significant progress has been made in opening the Bahá'í community to society at large, its orientation towards 45.11

those who have not yet declared their faith in Bahá'u'lláh will require continued adjustment. There seems to be a natural human tendency to draw a distinction between "us" and "them." A letter dated 27 April 2004 to an individual warns Bahá'ís not to allow their expectations to create unnecessary barriers for people:

45.12   From a careful reading of the messages regarding the Five Year Plan, it should be clear that the House of Justice is not calling on the friends to forgo all activities except devotional meetings, children's classes and study circles in their efforts to attract people to the Cause. Through a variety of endeavors, including regular firesides, seekers should be helped to reach the point where they eagerly embrace the Faith and join the Bahá'í community. Yet it is equally evident that the core activities of the Plan are proving to be an excellent means for the friends everywhere to widen their circle of influence and share Bahá'u'lláh's message with a growing number of people from different segments of society. Further, where such an open attitude exists among the believers, the distinction between those who are formally enrolled in the Faith and those who are drawing close to it does not define the level of their involvement in these core activities. Specifically, experience around the world suggests that many seekers, though certainly not all, welcome the opportunity to study the full sequence of institute courses and even engage in acts of service that contribute to Bahá'í community life, for instance hosting devotional meetings and teaching children's classes. Such participation has often been instrumental in the eventual confirmation of their faith and in their formal declaration. Care should be taken, therefore, that we do not allow our own expectations to set limits on people which, in reality, may not exist.[7]

45.13   Rather than simply categorizing people as "non-Bahá'ís," believers are encouraged, then, to see "each person who is drawn to explore Bahá'u'lláh's teachings" somewhere along a "never-ending continuum of spiritual search."[8] A letter dated 4 May 2005 written on behalf of the House of Justice to the National Assembly of Kazakhstan shows the extent to which this way of thinking should influence how we approach the question of teaching:

Most heartening to note are the plans to form six teams, some composed of family members, who will reach out to their friends, neighbors and relatives. The teams will work systematically to help an increasing number of seekers advance through the sequence of institute courses, nurturing in them the desire to begin core activities with their own family and friends. The intimate friendship that develops between team members and course participants will foster the resolve and capacity of the latter to reach out to other souls and assist them to arise, in turn, to carry out acts of service. In this way, a handful of believers can significantly extend the spiritual influence of the institute and lay a strong foundation for the accelerated expansion of the community.[9]   45.14

Central to this way of thinking seems to be the attitude   45.15
Bahá'ís adopt towards the teachings of the Faith. The House of Justice has said that "Bahá'ís should give the teachings of Bahá'u'lláh liberally and unconditionally to humanity so that people may apply them to pressing social issues and uplift themselves materially and spiritually."[10] It was this posture of giving to which the Guardian referred when he said,

We must be like the fountain or spring that is continu-   45.16
ally emptying itself of all that it has and is continually being refilled from an invisible source. To be continually giving out for the good of our fellows undeterred by fear of poverty and reliant on the unfailing bounty of the Source of all wealth and all good—this is the secret of right living.[11]

A posture of giving, it seems, is an essential attribute of   45.17
the intensive programs of growth that will continue to be the object of learning during the years to come. At the heart of these programs is the realization that the Faith is not intended for Bahá'ís alone but rather for all of humanity:

The friends who participate in these intensive programs   45.18
of growth should bear in mind that the purpose is to ensure that the Revelation of Bahá'u'lláh reaches the masses of humanity and enables them to achieve spiritual and material progress through the application of the Teachings. Vast numbers among the peoples of the world are ready, indeed yearn, for the bounties that Bahá'u'lláh alone can bestow upon them once they have committed themselves to building the new society He has envisioned. In learning

to systematize their large-scale teaching work, Bahá'í communities are becoming better equipped to respond to this longing. They cannot withhold whatever effort, whatever sacrifice, may be called for.[12]

46

Learning to Reach
Receptive Populations

In its message dated 17 January 2003, the Universal House   46.1
of Justice noted the effectiveness of the pattern of growth
established through the multiplication of core activities among
Bahá'ís and their families and friends. It then went on to
remark that

> In many parts of the world, bringing large numbers   46.2
> into the ranks of Bahá'u'lláh's followers has traditionally
> not been a formidable task. It is therefore encouraging to
> see that, in some of the more developed clusters, carefully
> designed projects are being added to the existing pattern
> of growth to reach receptive populations and lift the rate
> of expansion to a higher level. Such projects accelerate the
> tempo of teaching, already on the rise through the efforts
> of individuals.[1]

In this connection, it was explained to one National Spiritual   46.3
Assembly that "in general, focusing on receptive populations
is one of the strategies of the Five Year Plan for accelerating
growth."[2] On a number of occasions the House of Justice has
underscored the importance of focusing efforts on receptive
populations and systematically sharing Bahá'u'lláh's message
with them through appropriate methods and approaches. The
framework of the Five Year Plan, however, offered National
Assemblies a new way of addressing the question. In a letter
dated 20 March 2002, the National Assembly of Austria was
advised to select a cluster with a receptive minority population
for special attention:

> An important challenge now before you is to ensure   46.4
> that one or two clusters in Austria reach the level at which
> intensive growth programs can be established. This will
> involve, foremost, helping the institute in your country

develop to a more advanced stage, endowed with the capacity to accompany a significant percentage of individuals up to the point in its sequence of courses where they can be trained to act as tutors and multiply the number of study circles in the clusters selected. Given the receptivity displayed in the past by some of the minority groups in Austria, for example the Turkish, you would clearly do well to choose at least one cluster with a large representation of such a population.[3]

46.5   Every cluster, of course, has different demographic cross sections and will often have distinct social and ethnic groups. It is envisioned that, once the institute process in a cluster is well founded, activities will "move to the stage of reaching special populations."[4] The House of Justice, for instance, in a letter dated 5 August 2004 written on its behalf to the National Assembly of Canada, expressed the hope that the intensive program of growth launched in Vancouver would take advantage of the receptivity displayed among the Chinese-speaking population:

46.6   Your Assembly has no doubt already begun to give thought to how best to capitalize on the success. The House of Justice hopes that this development can be energetically exploited in pursuit of the teaching objectives of the Five Year Plan. Where clusters have advanced to such a degree that they are ready to take up the challenge of intensive growth, nothing is more promising than to encounter a significant opening among a minority population like the Chinese-speaking Canadians. Seizing such opportunities requires a major shift from the gradualist approach that meets the needs of clusters at earlier stages of progress.

46.7   The House of Justice is confident that, with your encouragement, the Regional Council will be able to devise an intensive program of activities focusing on the specific needs of Vancouver's Chinese population. Apart from taking advantage of Ms. . . . .'s very welcome willingness to lend assistance, it may also be wise for the Council to contact the Bahá'í Committee for China with respect to other human resources, teaching materials and practical suggestions.[5]

46.8   As the above passage suggests, the success of efforts to bring receptive populations into the Faith depends, to some degree, on the ability of teachers who can present the message in a suitable manner. The role of the institute, then, is crucial in this respect. "A major object of the recent emphasis on establishing training institutes," the House of Justice has advised, "is to increase the capacity of individuals to teach the Cause effectively."[6] An excerpt from the 9 January 2001 message of the House of Justice further explains the relationship between training and teaching:

> With the work of institutes growing in strength, attention has now to be given everywhere to systematizing teaching efforts. In the document "The Institution of the Counsellors" just issued, we emphasize the role that the Auxiliary Board members and their assistants play in helping the friends to meet this challenge, both at the level of individual initiative and of collective volition. As individuals progress through institute courses, they deepen their knowledge of the Faith, gain insights, and acquire skills of service. Some of the courses devoted to teaching will no doubt treat the subject in general terms. Others will focus on various means of sharing Bahá'u'lláh's message with specific segments of society, incorporating the wisdom gleaned from the teaching endeavors of the friends. This combined process of action, learning and training will endow communities with an ever-increasing number of capable and eager teachers of the Cause.[7]

46.9

This passage indicates that, as experience is gained in reaching out to a population, the learning that is acquired can then be systematized in courses that are offered by the training institute. As more and more individuals take part in the courses and gain the knowledge, spiritual insights and skills needed to bring people from among the population into the Cause, teaching activities multiply, enrollments increase, and further learning occurs which can be incorporated into the courses. "Training and teaching, then, become two parallel processes that fuel each other,"[8] explained the 1998 document "Training Institutes." "Training courses raise the enthusiasm of the friends for teaching and help them acquire the necessary skills. Increased experience in the teaching field is reflected in the constantly improving content of training courses."[9]

46.10

Such courses, then, can be regarded as the chronicles of the evolving experience of the Bahá'í community in sharing Bahá'u'lláh's message. They report what the community is

46.11

doing and learning. They systematize both the knowledge being generated through collective action and the results of that systematization. As endeavors to reach different populations and social groups intensify through programs of growth in the coming years, it is imagined that significant effort will be dedicated to developing branch courses in this way. A letter dated 26 June 2002 written on behalf of the House of Justice underscores the need for such courses:

46.12   The 9 January 2001 message of the Universal House of Justice likened an institute's main sequence of courses to the trunk of a tree, from which branch out other courses. One can already observe a degree of diversity emerging as branch courses begin to appear in some programs, designed to meet specific training needs. The elaboration of such courses will necessarily proceed in a gradual fashion since effective course content will depend on the amount of learning and experience acquired in the field of action.[10]

46.13   Training, however, will not be sufficient to raise the tempo of teaching, as explained in the 9 January message:

46.14   Training alone, of course, does not necessarily lead to an upsurge in teaching activity. In every avenue of service, the friends need sustained encouragement. Our expectation is that the Auxiliary Board members, together with their assistants, will give special thought to how individual initiative can be cultivated, particularly as it relates to teaching. When training and encouragement are effective, a culture of growth is nourished in which the believers see their duty to teach as a natural consequence of having accepted Bahá'u'lláh. They "raise high the sacred torch of faith," as was 'Abdu'l-Bahá's wish, "labor ceaselessly, by day and by night," and "consecrate every fleeting moment of their lives to the diffusion of the divine fragrance and the exaltation of God's holy Word." So enkindled do their hearts become with the fire of the love of God that whoever approaches them feels its warmth. They strive to be channels of the spirit, pure of heart, selfless and humble, possessing certitude and the courage that stems from reliance on God. In such a culture, teaching is the dominating passion of the lives of the believers. Fear of failure finds no place. Mutual support, commitment to learning, and appreciation of diversity of action are the prevailing norms.[11]

Clearly, much work remains to be done in this regard. 46.15
While a number of populations have been identified for special
attention in recent years, the Bahá'í community is still at the
initial stages of systematizing the knowledge it is acquiring in
teaching the Faith among them. These populations include "the
Sami and the other peoples of the arctic and sub-arctic areas
as far north as Spitsbergen," mentioned in the Riḍván 1996
message to the followers of Bahá'u'lláh in Europe, as well as the
inhabitants of "the islands of the Mediterranean, the Atlantic
and the North Sea" and "the Romany peoples, who have begun
to show such receptivity to the call of Bahá'u'lláh."[12] Arabic
speakers in North America have been urged to focus on "attracting souls from amongst the Arab population" within their
clusters,[13] and the National Assembly of the United States has
been advised that, among the Muslim population, Kurds and
Afghans may be particularly receptive.[14] In 2002 the National
Assembly of Uganda was asked to assist in spreading "the
spirit of the teachings among seeking and receptive souls" in
Sudanese refugee camps in the northern part of the country.[15]
And Bahá'í youth have been encouraged to "seek out receptive
souls" in "schools, at . . . universities, and in the workplace."[16]
Along these lines, the Riḍván 1996 message to the followers of
Bahá'u'lláh in Latin America and the Caribbean drew attention
to the fact that

> . . . the climate of search prevailing among both the lead- 46.16
> ers and the masses in your countries, which has emerged
> following the ideological upheaval of recent years, is of
> special significance. Two sectors have been particularly
> and differently affected and are athirst for the life-giving
> waters of Bahá'u'lláh's Revelation: on the one hand, the
> teachers in the national school systems and, on the other,
> university students and their professors. Historically, both
> have exerted widespread influence in your societies, and
> should you teach them systematically, you will certainly
> reap abundant fruits.[17]

These are only a few of the populations that, it is imag- 46.17
ined, will be the focus of the serious attention of the Bahá'í
community in the years to come as it pursues the aim of
advancing the process of entry by troops and strives to bring
together "the diverse members of the human race in ever closer
association."[18]

47

Learning to Exercise Disciplined Initiative and to Participate in Collective Action

"The power to act," the Universal House of Justice has stated, "resides primarily in the entire body of the believers. This power is unlocked at the level of individual initiative and at the level of collective volition."[1] "If the Cause is to realize Bahá'u'lláh's purpose for humankind," attention must be given to "the release of power in both these expressions."[2] In this light, the House of Justice has explained that "it is the duty and privilege of the individual" to take initiative "in teaching the Cause and in obtaining a deeper understanding of the purpose and requirements of the Faith."[3] "Parallel with the exercise of such initiative," it has indicated, "is the necessity of the individual's participation in collective endeavors, such as community functions and projects."[4]

At the start of the Four Year Plan, the Riḍván 1996 message described the role of the individual in the work of the Faith in these terms:

> The role of the individual is of unique importance in the work of the Cause. It is the individual who manifests the vitality of faith upon which the success of the teaching work and the development of the community depend. Bahá'u'lláh's command to each believer to teach His Faith confers an inescapable responsibility which cannot be transferred to, or assumed by, any institution of the Cause. The individual alone can exercise those capacities which include the ability to take initiative, to seize opportunities, to form friendships, to interact personally with others, to build relationships, to win the cooperation of others in common service to the Faith and society, and to convert into action the decisions made by consultative bodies. It is the individual's duty to "consider every avenue of approach

47.1

47.2

47.3

which he might utilize in his personal attempts to capture the attention, maintain the interest, and deepen the faith, of those whom he seeks to bring into the fold of his Faith."

47·4   To optimize the use of these capacities, the individual draws upon his love for Bahá'u'lláh, the power of the Covenant, the dynamics of prayer, the inspiration and education derived from regular reading and study of the Holy Texts, and the transformative forces that operate upon his soul as he strives to behave in accordance with the divine laws and principles. In addition to these, the individual, having been given the duty to teach the Cause, is endowed with the capacity to attract particular blessings promised by Bahá'u'lláh. "Whoso openeth his lips in this Day," the Blessed Beauty asserts, "and maketh mention of the name of his Lord, the hosts of Divine inspiration shall descend upon him from the heaven of My name, the All-Knowing, the All-Wise. On him shall also descend the Concourse on high, each bearing aloft a chalice of pure light."

47·5   Shoghi Effendi underscored the absolute necessity of individual initiative and action. He explained that without the support of the individual, "at once wholehearted, continuous and generous," every measure and plan of his National Spiritual Assembly is "foredoomed to failure," the purpose of the Master's Divine Plan is "impeded"; furthermore, the sustaining strength of Bahá'u'lláh Himself "will be withheld from every and each individual who fails in the long run to arise and play his part." Hence, at the very crux of any progress to be made is the individual believer, who possesses the power of execution which only he can release through his own initiative and sustained action. Regarding the sense of inadequacy that sometimes hampers individual initiative, a letter written on his behalf conveys the Guardian's advice: "Chief among these, you mention the lack of courage and of initiative on the part of the believers, and a feeling of inferiority which prevents them from addressing the public. It is precisely these weaknesses that he wishes the friends to overcome, for these do not only paralyze their efforts but actually serve to quench the flame of faith in their hearts. Not until all the friends come to realize that every one of them is able, in his own measure, to deliver the Message, can they ever hope to reach the goal that has been set before them by a loving and wise Master. . . . Everyone is a potential teacher. He has only to use what God has given him and thus prove that he is faithful to his trust."[5]

Two years into the Plan, at Riḍván 1998, the House of Justice made an assessment of the progress achieved. At that time the majority of communities were still developing the institutional capacity needed to raise up human resources called for at the beginning of the Plan. It was in this context that the Riḍván message emphasized the need for training and preparing the believers to meet the challenges before them: 47.6

> Towards ensuring an orderly evolution of the community, a function of Bahá'í institutions is to organize and maintain a process of developing human resources whereby Bahá'ís, new and veteran alike, can acquire the knowledge and capacity to sustain a continuous expansion and consolidation of the community. The establishment of training institutes is critical to such effort, since they are centers through which large numbers of individuals can acquire and improve their ability to teach and administer the Faith. Their existence underscores the importance of knowledge of the Faith as a source of power for invigorating the life of the Bahá'í community and of the individuals who compose it.[6] 47.7

In this way, participation in the courses of the institute would help the friends over the next few years to develop the capabilities they would need to respond to the requirements of the Plan. Equally important to the process of empowering the individual believer, the House of Justice explained in "The Institution of the Counsellors," would be the Auxiliary Board member: 47.8

> Stimulating individual initiative is one of the paramount duties of the Auxiliary Board members, a duty they can perform with the help of assistants they must carefully select, train and nurture. It involves constant encouragement of the friends, evoking the valor of the heroes of the Faith and bringing to their attention the importance of exemplifying in their lives the glory of the Teachings. It calls for fervent and moving appeals to the believers to be the cause of unity and harmony at all times, to attract receptive souls to the Cause, to teach them, nourish their faith and lead them to 47.9

the shores of certitude. It requires building confidence and changing fear and hesitation into courage and perseverance. It asks of the Board members and those they serve alike to forget their own weaknesses and fix their reliance on the power of divine confirmations. Further, it implies accompanying the friends in their endeavors as they develop the capabilities of effective service.

47.10   The role of the training institute in the development of these capabilities can hardly be overemphasized. The Auxiliary Board members are to use this powerful instrument to change passive acceptance of the Faith into a passion for teaching. As they generate enthusiasm, they need to help guide it into channels of systematic endeavor. It is in this context of systematic action that fostering sound individual initiative and promoting united collective action become two complementary aims ever engaging the Auxiliary Board member.[7]

47.11   With the launch of the Five Year Plan at Riḍván 2001, and the call to establish devotional meetings, children's classes and study circles in cluster after cluster, this process of spiritual empowerment began to reach fruition and the level of participation of the individual believer in the work of the Cause increased markedly. A letter dated 22 August 2002 written on behalf of the House of Justice noted,

47.12   The culture now emerging is one in which groups of Bahá'u'lláh's followers explore together the truths in His Teachings, freely open their study circles, devotional gatherings and children's classes to their friends and neighbors, and invest their efforts confidently in plans of action designed at the level of the cluster, that makes growth a manageable goal.[8]

47.13   In its 17 January 2003 message, the Universal House of Justice attributed "the rise in activity around the world" to the success of the institute courses "in evoking the spirit of enterprise required to carry out the divers actions that growth in a cluster, at whatever stage, demands."[9] "Particularly heartwarming to observe," it wrote, "is a growing sense of initiative and resourcefulness throughout the Bahá'í world, along with courage and audacity. Consecration, zeal, confidence and tenacity—these are among the qualities that are distinguishing the believers in every continent."[10] There was little doubt that the pattern of growth emerging in the Bahá'í world was the result of individual initiative. One letter commented that

> With the emphasis in the Five Year Plan on the multiplica- 47.14
> tion of devotional meetings, children's and junior youth
> classes, and study circles, the believers all over the world
> have learned to open their homes, or to use other suitable
> places in their localities, for holding these events.[11]

In some places, the effects on the life of the community have 47.15
been extraordinary. "The multiplication of the core activities
in the Five Year Plan," another letter indicated, "has created
a vibrant Bahá'í community life. In some clusters, a host of
individual initiatives have filled every night of the calendar with
one or more events."[12]

What is important to note is that the individual initiative 47.16
that has been exercised by the friends everywhere adheres to
certain requirements. It is not the kind of unrestricted indi-
vidualism that, if left free to reign in a community, results in
alienation and, eventually, stagnation:

> From its early days, the Bahá'í community in . . . has 47.17
> been blessed by having devoted, competent and energetic
> members, among both native believers and pioneers from
> abroad. Its potential was, and remains, very great. Alas, the
> sound development of the community has been repeatedly
> hampered by the upsurge of disunity, arising largely from
> the strong-mindedness of individual believers who had
> conflicting opinions of what was best for the community at
> any one time. Thus, a characteristic that can be a source of
> strength for the Faith in . . . has become, too easily, a source
> of division and thus of hindrance to the advancement of
> the Cause.[13]

Nor does the individual initiative that has character- 47.18
ized the Five Year Plan have anything to do with a sense of
superiority:

> In our Faith, as you know, individuals are allowed a reason- 47.19
> able latitude for initiative in this area [i.e., teaching] and
> are free to offer the Message to others in the manner best
> suited to their circumstances and opportunities. However,
> difficulties arise when individual views of a method or
> approach are seen to be the key for others to use in their

endeavors—a perception which all too frequently leads to debates that are endless, usually inducing inaction.[14]

47.20 It is an individual initiative that recognizes that "mistakes will be made" and is willing "to learn from these mistakes."[15] For it understands the intimate connection between *doing* and *being:*

47.21 As you know, taking to an extreme the exhortation that a teacher should, before all else, teach his own self can lead to a decline in the level of teaching activity, as more and more attention becomes focused on one's own perfection. There are, of course, numerous passages in the Writings which ask us to make daily effort so that our inner lives increasingly reflect the Teachings of the Faith. Moreover, it is evident that our inner state has a direct bearing on the success of our teaching efforts. But the Writings also tell us not to look at our own shortcomings, but to rely on the power of divine assistance in delivering His Message. The question of the development of one's inner life and its relation to teaching has to be viewed in this broader context. In doing so, we should remember that all Bahá'ís are called upon to teach the Cause, whatever their spiritual attainments may be. Furthermore, the act of sharing the Word of God with others profoundly affects the refinement of one's inner life.[16]

47.22 This individual initiative arises, not out of a reluctant sense of obligation, but from deep within one's being as a response to the Divine call:

47.23 In all of this great endeavor . . . you must be driven by a passion to teach the Faith. Let regular study of the Writings feed the flame of your enthusiasm. Let His Words so shape your thoughts that the most pressing obligation of your lives becomes the sharing of His Message with others.[17]

47.24 It is an individual initiative that is born out of the conviction that faith is conscious knowledge expressed in action:

47.25 Arise, then, to engage more and more trusted members of your families, friends, neighbors and coworkers in the sequence of courses and assist them to walk the path of service so that a sizeable expansion of the Bahá'í community is hastened and sustained. The time for action is now. . . .

Ultimately, success is assured by the faith in Bahá'u'lláh   47.26
that animates every conscientious believer. Faith is a state
of conscience imbued with a compulsion to express itself
in word and deed. Teaching combines these two aspects.
Your assistance and encouragement as tutors can foster in
the participants of study circles the spirit of initiative to
follow your example so that a stream of receptive souls may
find their home and haven in the Cause. Do your utmost to
carry out this noble and meritorious service with dispatch,
losing no opportunity. Surely, the forces of the Concourse
on high are ever ready to confirm your endeavors.[18]

This individual initiative does not find satisfaction in   47.27
pursuing whatever the heart desires. Nor is it characterized
by random motion according to some romantic notion about
creativity. It is an individual initiative that is sparked by a vision
of possibilities and moves in the direction of oneness. "Through
its messages on the global Plans," as one letter has explained,
"the Universal House of Justice provides a vision to the Bahá'í
world of the opportunities and possibilities open to the Faith.
The provisions of these Plans do not remain the same from one
to the next. They build on one another in order to move the
community forward to ever great accomplishments."[19] In the
case of the Five Year Plan, the exercise of dividing countries
into clusters and categorizing them according to stages of development helped the friends to proceed with unity of thought,
for it "served to galvanize the believers," who "were able to
evaluate in realistic terms their strengths and weaknesses and
to see with striking clarity a way forward."[20]

Perhaps above all else, then, it is an individual initiative   47.28
that appreciates the value of operating within a framework,
a framework that is derived from the messages of the House
of Justice outlining the global Plans. In this connection, it
understands that discipline is not something that is imposed
from without but rather comes from an inner conviction. This
inner conviction is not simply the result of willpower, however.
For the soul manifests its powers as it learns to submit to higher
authority, ultimately the laws that govern material and spiritual
existence. An understanding of these laws influences the conscience of the individual and gives meaning to the authority
conferred upon, and the course set by, the institutions. The
House of Justice has remarked in this regard that "even though
individuals may strive to be guided in their actions by their

personal understanding of the Divine Texts, and much can be accomplished thereby, such actions, untempered by the overall direction provided by authorized institutions, are incapable of attaining the thrust necessary for the unencumbered advancement of civilization."[21]

47.29   To date, the combined effect of the efforts of individuals within the framework provided by the House of Justice has been considerable. Efforts to engage in collective action, however, have yet to reach their full potential. It is only in the latter part of the Five Year Plan, as intensive programs of growth have become more widespread, that significant experience has been gained in participating in collective endeavors. Describing such programs of growth, the 9 January 2001 message of the House of Justice had indicated that "a range of teaching efforts" would need to be carried out "involving both activities undertaken by the individual and campaigns promoted by the institutions."[22] A recent letter dated 18 August 2005 to the National Assembly of Germany underscores this point:

47.30   Like their fellow believers in many clusters around the world, the friends in Frankfurt have labored systematically throughout the Five Year Plan to establish the conditions necessary for launching an intensive program of growth. Central to their efforts has been the goal of bringing more and more coworkers into the institute process so that a sufficient number would be prepared to perform the acts of service needed to sustain the accelerated expansion of the Faith. Now that the friends have crossed that threshold and stand ready to embark on an intensive program, they will be challenged to set in motion a pattern of activity which integrates individual initiative and community endeavor in order to embrace an ever-wider circle of people and teach receptive souls.[23]

47.31   No doubt it will take time for communities to learn the dynamics of such a pattern of activity. As this learning proceeds, the friends will see the confusion and the clash of opinions that can occasionally attend their efforts to promote intensive programs of growth recede and a new power come into focus:

47.32   Your sincere concerns regarding the unfoldment of the processes of the Five Year Plan in . . . are noted with appreciation. You are encouraged to have patience, recognizing that the friends have made a very rapid advance in their understanding and action in the past few years in that country. This has enabled them to launch intensive programs of growth in as many as seventeen clusters, more than ten percent of the total number in the entire country. It is not surprising, given such a dramatic transformation that encompasses the efforts of so many well-intentioned believers, that some additional time must pass and additional experience be gained before a further unity of thought and action in matters associated with the various aspects of administration, teaching, or the functioning of the institute becomes apparent. Confusion and the clash of opinion will gradually give way to a culture of learning in which the institutions serving the friends will be able to support the initiatives of individuals and merge diverse efforts into a powerful collective thrust.[24]

The attributes the friends have acquired throughout the Five Year Plan will surely assist them in meeting this new challenge. It is of course imperative that they do so, for while the present pattern of growth through the multiplication of core activities is sufficient to welcome individuals into the Faith and integrate them into community life, it is only through collective action that expansion and consolidation will occur on a large scale. And as the friends succeed in further acquiring the knowledge, qualities, skills and abilities needed to participate effectively in collective action, their communities will move closer to the vision presented by the House of Justice at the start of the Four Year Plan. In its 26 December 1995 message, it explained that 47.33

> ... those who enter the Faith must be integrated into vibrant local communities, characterized by tolerance and love and guided by a strong sense of purpose and collective will, environments in which the capacities of all components —men, women, youth and children—are developed and their powers multiplied in unified action.[25] 47.34

Though clearly a concern of the individual, the challenge of learning to exercise disciplined initiative and participate in collective action appears to be central to the question of community development. For, as suggested by the above quotation, the challenge is in reality to achieve universal participation in the work of the Cause. It seems to speak to the very nature of social organization envisioned by Bahá'u'lláh and to the welfare of society as a whole: 47.35

47.36   "Regard the world as the human body," wrote
Bahá'u'lláh to Queen Victoria. We can surely regard the
Bahá'í world, the army of God, in the same way. In the
human body, every cell, every organ, every nerve has its
part to play. When all do so the body is healthy, vigorous, radiant, ready for every call made upon it. No cell,
however humble, lives apart from the body, whether in
serving it or receiving from it. This is true of the body of
mankind in which God "has endowed each and all with
talents and faculties," and is supremely true of the body
of the Bahá'í world community, for this body is already an
organism, united in its aspirations, unified in its methods,
seeking assistance and confirmation from the same Source,
and illumined with the conscious knowledge of its unity.
Therefore, in this organic, divinely guided, blessed and
illumined body the participation of every believer is of the
utmost importance, and is a source of power and vitality as
yet unknown to us.[26]

48

Learning to Administer Growth

The message below addressed by the Universal House of Justice   48.1
to the National Spiritual Assembly of India in May 2004 highlights a fundamental challenge that the growth of the Faith
brought to the institutions everywhere:

> That a steadily growing number of the rank and file of the   48.2
> Indian Bahá'í community would, cognizant of their duties
> to the Cause, assume their rightful place in the forefront of
> Bahá'í activity was one of our most ardent aspirations at
> the outset of the Four Year Plan, and it has been a source
> of immeasurable joy to us to witness the progress that has
> been made towards the fulfillment of this cherished goal,
> especially over the last year. The processes that you set in
> motion, which have been vigorously pursued during the
> current Plan, are beginning to bear their long-awaited fruits.
> The challenge now falls on the institutions of the Faith to
> learn to administer the affairs of a community of active
> supporters of the Cause, and we have every confidence that,
> through the sustaining grace of Bahá'u'lláh, this important
> requirement will be met.[1]

As the two movements gathered momentum at the cluster   48.3
level during the Five Year Plan, it became clear that some kind
of scheme of coordination would need to be put in place to ensure continued progress. In its Riḍván 2004 message, the House
of Justice acknowledged the relationship between the growth
of the Faith at the cluster level and the need for administrative
structures:

> The movement of clusters from each level of activity to a   48.4
> higher one is well in hand and, as it proceeds, the kernel of
> avowed believers is being joined by a larger circle of people,
> still not Bahá'ís but enthusiastically involved in core activities

299

of the Plan. Structures for administering intensive growth are already appearing in certain advanced clusters.[2]

48.5   Such structures, then, began to emerge as a response to the demands of growth itself and became the object of learning in clusters where the two essential movements were well under way. The following letter dated 26 November 2003 written on behalf of the House of Justice to the National Assembly of India commended its efforts to find a suitable mechanism at the cluster level to coordinate the multiplication and deployment of human resources:

48.6   The House of Justice is greatly pleased to know that your Assembly is giving the question of growth at the level of the cluster such serious consideration. That you are, on the one hand, concerned to ensure that the institute process continues to gather momentum in each cluster and, on the other, eager to see the human resources thus generated systematically deployed in the field of service is a sign of the clarity with which you see the essential relationship between the various elements that sustain growth. The House of Justice will be interested to know how the efforts to establish appropriate structures at the cluster level progress and how the learning in the area advances.[3]

48.7   A letter written on behalf of the House of Justice to the National Assembly of Mexico goes further and describes the two principal elements of an effective scheme of coordination:

48.8   Meeting the challenge of fostering such growth will depend on the establishment and effective functioning of certain administrative mechanisms at the level of the cluster. It will require, on the one hand, an individual believer named by the institute in each priority cluster who would act as a coordinator, responsible for ensuring that the number of study circles, children's classes, and junior youth groups steadily multiplies. On the other hand, it will call for the formation of some kind of cluster-level committee with a capable secretary in charge of promoting the gradual increase in devotional meetings, arranging for systematic visits to the homes of newly enrolled believers, holding periodic reflection meetings, collecting vital statistics and encouraging the development of the Nineteen Day Feast and the strengthening of the Local Spiritual Assembly in each locality, with the help of the Auxiliary Board members and their assistants.[4]

A letter dated 16 September 2003 to the National Spiritual Assembly of the Philippines elaborates the scheme in more detail:

48.9

> From all reports received at the World Center, it is clear that there are now a few clusters in the Philippines primed for accelerated growth. However, for such growth to occur, administrative structures will need to be put into place at the level of the cluster to support the processes of expansion and consolidation. The Universal House of Justice is happy to know that consultations are giving rise to a scheme that identifies clearly the roles of the institute and Regional Councils. According to this scheme, the Dawnbreakers Foundation [the national agency responsible for human resource development] will, we understand, name a coordinator for each of the clusters selected who will be responsible for ensuring that the number of study circles for adults and older youth, Bahá'í children's classes and junior youth groups systematically multiplies. Such a coordinator would be required to work with a growing contingent of tutors and children's class teachers in the cluster, maintaining their enthusiasm and helping them to improve the quality of their services.

48.10

> As this educational process gains in strength, there will be a corresponding increase in the number of those eager to render service to the Cause, to share their newly acquired knowledge, and to put into practice what they have been studying. In order to facilitate the efforts of such friends and channel their energies into effective collective action, a strong committee with a highly capable secretary will, it is assumed, be named by the Regional Council to operate at the cluster level. This committee would be assigned tasks such as promoting the spread of short-term teaching projects and devotional meetings in the cluster, in addition to overseeing a program of visits to the homes of newly enrolled believers and those less active in the community in order to deepen them in the fundamentals of the Faith. The establishment of the Nineteen Day Feast and the strengthening of the Local Spiritual Assemblies in the localities would also constitute one of the committee's

48.11

primary concerns, as would the collection of statistical information. The latter will be vital to the efforts to monitor the growth process not only at the cluster level, but also at the regional and national levels, and in this connection, the House of Justice welcomes the news that your member Mrs. . . . has been asked to assume the responsibility for encouraging the implementation of the Statistical Report Program throughout the country.

48.12   It is to be expected that much of the committee's work could be carried out by its secretary, but it would also be possible for a few designated believers to discharge certain administrative functions. While maintaining clearly defined spheres of service, the institute coordinator and committee would collaborate closely to ensure that activities are synchronized effectively. For instance, an intensive campaign to raise the number of those who have completed the second course in the institute's main sequence, which prepares them to share deepening themes, might well be followed by an equally intensive campaign of home visits. Similarly, although the committee would be charged with the task of arranging periodic meetings of consultations to reflect on progress in the cluster, the timing and the program of such events would be fully discussed with the institute coordinator. In the performance of all their functions, the committee and the institute coordinator would, of course, receive the unflagging support of the Auxiliary Board members and their assistants.[5]

48.13   Of course, at the outset of the Five Year Plan, the House of Justice explained that the implementation of intensive programs of growth would "require the close collaboration of the institute, the Auxiliary Board members and their assistants, and an Area Teaching Committee."[6] It was not until a sufficient number of clusters around the world began to reach the stage where they were ready to launch such programs, however, that the implications of this statement came to be realized. Some of these implications have been described by the House of Justice in "The Institution of the Counsellors":

48.14   The involvement of the Auxiliary Board members in this process of design and implementation is multifaceted. They contribute to deliberations in which the worldwide aims and accomplishments of the Faith are analyzed, the condition of society and the forces operating within it are examined, opportunities and needs are detected. They bring their knowledge of the Faith to bear on consultations that generate shared vision and strategies for growth. Their familiarity with the friends and their talents, particularly as these are developed through the efforts of the training institute, enables them to draw attention to the characteristics of plans of action that are realistic and within the grasp of the believers. The network of assistants they each can name provides them with the means for stimulating activity at the local level and following it to completion. And above all, the love and respect in which they are held create for them the opportunity to act as standard-bearers and lead the community in action.[7]

The House of Justice has further explained that "this challenging conception"[8] of the work of the Auxiliary Board members with local communities calls for   48.15

. . . a fundamental departure from limited assumptions about social order which, in the world today, determine administrative theory and practice. For it aspires to infuse every act, individual and collective, with spiritual meaning. It places the sacred at the heart of community life, making it the focus of all reflection on activity.[9]   48.16

Undoubtedly a great deal of learning about administering the affairs of communities made up of active supporters of the Cause will continue in the months and years ahead as expansion accelerates. Already, however, some of the challenges are beginning to emerge. The aforementioned letter to the National Assembly of the Philippines pointed to an important one: 48.17

As you can well imagine, if the gathering momentum in your community is to accelerate significantly, some of the friends will have to be called upon to dedicate a period of full-time service to the Faith at the level of the cluster. But a word of caution is in order. A system of the magnitude being considered will not come into existence and flourish if it depends primarily on the efforts of a cadre of remunerated workers. Such a system must receive its impetus from the spiritual energies of those steadfast and devoted souls who long to labor without expectation of financial reward in the path of God and experience the joy of contributing purely   48.18

as volunteers to plans to build His Kingdom on earth, whether by acting as tutors, holding devotional meetings or participating in a teaching project. It is such selfless joy that should distinguish your community.

48.19   This is not to say that material means are not necessary. Clearly some financial resources will have to be channeled into each cluster when it reaches a certain level of development, and some funds may need to go towards the subsidies of a few individual believers who are charged with duties related to administration and coordination, but are lacking the personal material means that would allow them to provide such full-time services without financial support. However, if such subsidies are given to perform the kinds of services that the institute process is preparing the generality of the believers to carry out as part of the natural unfoldment of Bahá'í community life, for example conducting devotional meetings and children's classes, confusion will set in and the promise for growth will remain unfulfilled. In general, the utmost wisdom and care will have to be exercised in channeling resources into the clusters; otherwise budgets will soon reach unsustainable proportions, and the entire enterprise will become prohibitively expensive.[10]

48.20   Not only is the flow of financial resources into the cluster an immediate concern. So, too, is the need to channel contributions from the cluster to the regional or state level and up to the national level. A letter written on behalf of the House of Justice warmly acknowledged the efforts of the National Assembly of India to think about this two-way flow:

48.21   Obviously only in those states that have attained a certain level of growth will you want to open up the possibility of having the State Treasurer appoint a trustworthy person in each of the more advanced clusters to serve as his or her assistant. It is understood from the document submitted to you by Mr. . . . that such an assistant would be primarily responsible for collecting and forwarding contributions to the State Council and for disbursing funds to the Cluster Growth Committee on behalf of the Treasurer. This is a promising idea, and you are advised to make sure the plan of action takes a systematic approach to its implementation. The House of Justice will look forward to learning about your experience in this regard.[11]

From the passage above it becomes clear that "related to 48.22
the judicious use of material resources at the cluster level is
the question of the administration of funds at all levels of the
community—the national level, including the National Spiritual
Assembly and its agency [for human resource development], the
regional level and the local level."[12] It is in this light that the
following was written on behalf of the House of Justice:

> As the growth of the Faith steadily gathers momentum 48.23
> in country after country, and provisions are put in place
> to sustain the processes of expansion and consolidation in
> clusters around the world, the question of sound financial
> management by National Spiritual Assemblies and their
> agencies assumes increasing importance. Specifically, it
> seems that, if some National Assemblies are to succeed
> in taking advantage of the tremendous opportunities
> now presenting themselves, they will require assistance in
> developing their capacity to manage their fiscal affairs and
> in refining a financial system which ensures efficiency, trans-
> parency and accountability at all levels of the community,
> from the national to the local.[13]

But the flow of material resources to and from the cluster 48.24
is not the only one requiring attention. Equally important is
the flow of information, largely in the form of statistics. The
following paragraph from a letter written by the Department
of Statistics at the World Centre to several National Assemblies
explains the nature of a computer application designed to assist
in maintaining this flow of information:

> The program, referred to as the "Statistical Report 48.25
> Program," is conceived on the premise that a country is
> divided into clusters, most of which consist of a number of
> local communities. When the program is fully operational in
> a country, the membership and other data for each locality
> will be collected and recorded at the cluster level, transmit-
> ted to the regional and national levels, and eventually to the
> Bahá'í World Centre, where it will be incorporated into the
> worldwide statistics on the Bahá'í community. It is hoped
> that adopting this system will foster a dynamic process in
> which membership and locality records are continually
> being updated and the information shared from one level to
> the next. In this sense, the program is intended to provide a
> picture of the current situation at a given date (a statistical

snapshot) in a locality, cluster, region, or country, and not a historical record. The program can generate a set of reports at every level and thus be used as a tool for monitoring and planning growth.[14]

48.26   In a recent letter written on behalf of the House of Justice to the National Assembly of Germany, the significance of this flow of information is underscored:

48.27   In this connection, the House of Justice understands that you are among a small number of National Spiritual Assemblies that have achieved an accurate baseline of data on their communities in the Statistical Report Program, the instrument designed here at the World Centre for collecting and maintaining statistics from the cluster to the national levels. You are commended for this achievement and are encouraged to ensure that the information provided by the program is used as a means for keeping abreast of the developments in the community at all levels and for guiding it accordingly.[15]

48.28   It is important to note from the above that the House of Justice views both the flow of material resources and information as a means of supporting the work of the Faith at the grass-roots. Further, what is becoming clear is that the administration at each level of the community is directly affected by the one below it. "It is quite likely that by looking to the requirements at the regional level," a letter written on behalf of the House of Justice has advised, "you will gain a better idea of how the practices and procedures at the national level should be established."[16] In this connection, the National Assembly of India was encouraged to proceed with plans to begin examining its administrative machinery at the cluster level and to observe

48.29   . . . the workings of the new structures you are putting in place to support the processes of expansion and consolidation, with the aim of determining their implications for the administrative affairs of the State Bahá'í Councils and then, of course, for the operation of your National Center and the functioning of your national agencies.[17]

48.30   Clearly, then, the refinement of the administrative machinery at the regional and national levels is another area of learning that will need to receive increasing attention. The passage below from a letter dated 27 May 2005 written on behalf of the House of Justice to the National Spiritual Assembly of the Russian Federation offers insights in this respect. Noting that "with the division of countries into small geographic areas, clusters have become a new arena of activity," the letter explains that "in practical terms, this means that many decisions having to do with the expansion and consolidation of the Faith are now made at that level." It goes on to state,

> With such far-reaching developments occurring at the cluster level, the strengthening of Regional Bahá'í Councils takes on special significance. You yourself have recognized that it would indeed be difficult in a country as widespread and diverse as Russia for your Assembly to be in close and continual contact with communities and believers. The Regional Councils, on the other hand, have an intimate knowledge of the resources of the believers in their regions, the capacity of the local Bahá'í communities, and the capabilities of the Local Spiritual Assemblies. As they assume increasing responsibility for the promotion of the Faith within their regions, they will continue to grow in their ability to analyze the strengths and needs in their areas and, based on this analysis, to devise ways to assist in the implementation of the Plan. It is thus in the effective functioning of the Regional Councils that the House of Justice feels the answers to your concerns lie.   48.31

> At the national level, your Assembly has the responsibility to reinforce the efforts of the Regional Bahá'í Councils to carry out their challenging duties. This will involve keeping a loving and watchful eye over them, providing encouragement and guidance when needed, ensuring the availability of basic literature, augmenting their financial resources to take care of their ever-expanding activities, and implementing an efficient system for the collection and dissemination of statistics—that is to say, serving the manifold needs of the Regional Councils with the aim of empowering them to act with confidence and efficiency. Regional Bahá'í Councils will, of course, go through various stages of development; some will initially require a greater degree of direction, while others can even now function with a wide degree of latitude.[18]   48.32

It is within the context of such weighty responsibilities that the Universal House of Justice described to one National   48.33

Spiritual Assembly some of the characteristics of those to be appointed as members of Regional Bahá'í Councils:

48.34
As you know, the [Regional] Bahá'í Councils have a crucial role to play in the effective prosecution of the Five Year Plan. Your greatly blessed community, standing among the front ranks of the supporters of Bahá'u'lláh in Africa, is already moving a sizeable number of clusters to the point where intensive programs of growth can be established and sustained. The next Plan must witness a further multiplication of this number. It is therefore vital that the National Assembly exercise wisdom in its selection of the members of the Councils from among the nominees, both those elected by members of Local Spiritual Assemblies and those recommended by the Auxiliary Board members. With the specific duties of the Councils in mind, you should choose those women and men who, through their proven experience in the activities of the Plan, their capacity to participate in the learning process, and their upright character and constructive attitudes, can best advance the process of entry by troops in the various provinces. Much will depend on the quality of your deliberations, which should be carried out in a true Bahá'í spirit, standing humbly in the presence of Bahá'u'lláh, forgoing self-interest and all partisan concerns, and thinking only of the best interests of the Faith that you all hold dear.[19]

48.35
Of course, not all countries have the conditions necessary to warrant the establishment of Regional Bahá'í Councils. Irrespective, it is the task of all National Spiritual Assemblies "to decide how to deploy the resources it has available to it at any time."[20] Whether a country is large or small, whether its current set of activities is relatively simple or complex, the National Assembly needs to give careful consideration to administrative arrangements at the national level. "While every Assembly must guard against over-administration," the House of Justice has explained, "it is essential for a degree of administrative work to be performed in order to coordinate and assist the work of expansion and consolidation and carry out other essential functions at the national level."[21] In this connection, the House of Justice provided the following comments to the National Spiritual Assembly of the United States:

Commitment to establishing sound intensive programs   48.36
of growth in a realistic number of clusters across the
nation should provide the basis for addressing the many
questions associated with the necessary adjustment of your
administrative and financial affairs to meet the challenges
of massive expansion. . . . In considering the nature of these
mechanisms, you will want to bear certain points in mind.

With learning about the nature of growth unfolding so   48.37
rapidly at the grassroots, programs related to the expansion
and consolidation of the Faith can best be managed at the
regional or cluster level to ensure they evolve in accordance
with practical experience. The efforts of national agencies
should be examined to determine whether they overlap
with the responsibilities granted to agencies at those levels.
Where redundancies occur, the programs of national agencies may need to be modified significantly, or perhaps be
eliminated altogether, so as to avoid creating confusion,
diffusing focus, or dividing participation among an array
of programs which, no matter how valuable in themselves,
would end up at cross purposes, competing for the limited
time and energies of the believers.[22]

49

Learning to Plan and to Mobilize

Referring to the planning process, the Universal House of Justice has stated that "at its core it is a spiritual process in which communities and institutions strive to align their pursuits with the Will of God."[1] The Major Plan and Minor Plan of God, it has explained, are "the two known ways in which His purpose for humankind is going forward. The Major Plan is associated with turbulence and calamity and proceeds with an apparent, random disorderliness, but is, in fact, inexorably driving humanity towards unity and maturity. Its agency for the most part is the people who are ignorant of its course and even antagonistic towards its aim. . . . Unlike His Major Plan, which works mysteriously, God's Minor Plan is clearly delineated, operates according to orderly and well-known processes, and has been given to us to execute. Its ultimate goal is the Most Great Peace."[2] The Minor Plan unfolds in stages, each of which is governed by a global Plan articulated by the Head of the Faith. "It is to the achievement of its purpose," the House of Justice has indicated, "that we must all devote our attention and energies."[3] In its 9 January 2001 message, the House of Justice referred specifically to the role of the institutions in ensuring that this purpose is achieved:

> The Major Plan of God is at work and the forces it generates impel humanity towards its destiny. In their own plans of action, the institutions of the Faith must seek to gain insight into the operation of these great forces, explore the potentialities of the people they serve, measure the resources and strengths of their communities, and take practical steps to enlist the unreserved participation of the believers.[4]

The planning process, in this sense, begins with the global Plans delineated by the Universal House of Justice. These global Plans set the direction for the Bahá'í world and provide the basis for the formulation of national plans by National Spiritual Assemblies in consultation with the Counsellors. Planning then moves down to the regional, cluster and local levels, as explained in "The Institution of the Counsellors":

49.4   With the opening of the fourth epoch of the Formative Age, a procedure was activated whereby national plans are formulated in joint consultation between National Spiritual Assemblies and Continental Counsellors. This development ensures two significant benefits: It enables each institution to draw on the experience and insight particular to the other, thereby making available to the planning process two distinct channels of information from two levels of Bahá'í administration; and it also assures to the Counsellors a necessary familiarity with the background, rationale, and content of national plans, which as a matter of principle they are expected to support.

49.5   Creating a national plan involves far more than consultation between the Counsellors and the National Assembly. Excellent results can be achieved, for example, by holding consultative meetings among the various institutions in a country and with the active supporters of the Faith to discuss fully the possible provisions of the plan and their implications. Once the major elements of the national plan have been identified, it is desirable for the planning process to move quickly to the regional level, and subsequently to the level of smaller areas and finally to the local community. The balance that can be achieved in this process between nationally sponsored campaigns and grassroots efforts is a necessary condition for success.

49.6   National plans, formulated in the context of the global plans of the Faith, serve as the framework within which the friends can undertake action. Through them, National Assemblies not only set goals to be pursued by themselves and their agencies, but also give direction to the believers, define for them priorities and areas of action, and elicit from them wholehearted response to the directives of the Universal House of Justice. Accordingly, they adopt measures to provide resources—literature, pioneers and traveling teachers, regional and national events, and funds as required—to support the initiatives of the friends.

49.7   The plans of action that Regional Councils, Area Teaching Committees and Local Spiritual Assemblies devise in the ensuing process need to go beyond the mere enumeration of goals to include an analysis of approaches to be adopted and lines of action to be followed. Indeed, at this level, planning and implementation must go hand in hand. If learning is to be the primary mode of operation in a community, then visions, strategies, goals and methods have to be reexamined time and again. As tasks are accomplished, obstacles removed, resources multiplied and lessons learned, modifications have to be made in goals and approaches, but in a way that continuity of action is maintained.[5]

In a letter dated 12 December 2001 written on its behalf to the National Spiritual Assembly of the United States, the House of Justice described, in the specific context of the Five Year Plan, how the plan formulated at a given level is embedded in the plan above it:

49.8

> Plans for the growth of the Faith are required at several distinct levels, each embedded in the level above it and each serving a specific purpose. A national plan is elaborated in the context of the global plan, whose features are set forth by the Universal House of Justice. Through it, the National Spiritual Assembly provides an overall vision of the tasks to be accomplished, defines the areas of action to be pursued, and elicits from the believers wholehearted response to the directives of the Universal House of Justice. In its letter to you of 28 June 2001, the House of Justice expressed its pleasure at reading your national plan, which offers a clear framework within which the various components of the community can carry out their activities during the Five Year Plan.

49.9

> It would, of course, be counterproductive for a Regional Council to design a plan of a similar kind, or to operate outside the context of the national plan. Here what is required is an analysis of the specific approaches to be adopted and a determination of the lines of action to be followed. In the case of the Five Year Plan, a regional plan consists essentially of those provisions needed to help each cluster in the region move from its current stage of growth to the next advanced stage. Such a plan identifies priorities and sets objectives for a given period of time—certain clusters to be opened to the Faith, others to be strengthened,

49.10

and, in those deemed ready, intensive growth programs to be established. This implies that the Regional Council will base its plan on a categorization of the clusters in the region according to their current stage of development. Such a categorization should not be misconstrued as a judgment on the quality of local communities. It should be regarded, rather, as a means through which realistic strategies for growth can be devised and executed.

49.11 Detailed plans of action, with specific goals and the corresponding methods, rightly belong to the level of the cluster. While the institute process will constitute the engine for growth in all clusters, a diversity of action is bound to appear at this level. This diversity will be a natural outcome of plans of action that take into account the particular resources of the believers, the capacity of the local Bahá'í communities, and the strength of the Local Spiritual Assemblies.[6]

49.12 Clearly, plans devised at each level serve different purposes and have different elements. Those closest to the grassroots are concerned as much with implementation and action as they are with planning. Of course, the concept of the cluster was introduced during the Five Year Plan precisely with this in mind. "It should be remembered," a letter written on behalf of the House of Justice noted, "that 'clusters' are only a construct—albeit a highly useful one—that enables the friends to think about the growth of the Faith on a manageable scale and to design and implement plans close to the grassroots of the community."[7] At the current stage of development of the Bahá'í world, then, the cluster has proven to be a useful unit, in terms of size, for organizing the work of the Faith and mobilizing the believers so that growth can be realized:

49.13 With the division of countries into small geographic areas, clusters have become a new arena of activity, within which the training institutes are enhancing the capacity of an increasing number of believers to promote expansion and consolidation to the point where they are able to launch intensive programs of growth. One of the welcome outcomes of this process has been the sense of ownership exercised by the believers and institutions serving within the cluster. In practical terms, this means that many decisions having to do with the expansion and consolidation of the Faith are now made at that level.[8]

Plans of action at the level of the cluster, then, are able   49.14
to take into account conditions on the ground. Central to the
success of such plans is, of course, the question of human resources. As indicated in the above passage, the training institute
is an important element in mobilizing the friends. A message
written by the House of Justice at the start of the Four Year
Plan underscored the part the training institute would need to
play in this mobilization:

> Your past exploits were largely the result of the inces-   49.15
> sant labors of a comparatively few consecrated believers
> who devoted their time and resources to the spread of
> the Cause in locality after locality. If you are to sustain
> rapid expansion and consolidation in the coming years, it is
> imperative that far greater numbers of dedicated and com-
> mitted souls arise to promote these twin processes. Training
> courses—widespread, regular and well-organized—consti-
> tute the most effective means to mobilize believers on the
> scale required.[9]

Another message indicated that "plans focusing on these   49.16
areas of large-scale expansion will necessarily seek to mobilize
an appreciable number of believers within each population
not only to labor diligently in their own local communities,
but also to serve as long- and short-term pioneers and visiting
teachers in other localities." "Training programs," the message
went on to say, "constitute a most potent instrument for the
accomplishment of such a vast mobilization."[10] It is of course
the institutions of the Faith that are charged with directing this
mobilization and deploying the human resources developed by
the training institute:

> As the believers advance through the sequence of   49.17
> courses and their skills and abilities are enhanced, the
> responsibility will then fall on you and your other agencies
> to see that their energies and talents are channeled in some
> form of active service to the Faith. Ample opportunities
> should be given to them to put into practice what they
> have learned, and in this connection, you will need to cre-
> ate within your community an encouraging environment,
> one in which the friends feel empowered to step forward,
> whatever their capacities may be, and take up the work of
> the Faith.[11]

49.18   In addition to capitalizing on the capacities and talents of the friends, the institutions must, then, encourage them and help them to maintain clarity of vision if they are to successfully marshal their forces. Several National Spiritual Assemblies were counseled during the Four Year Plan:

49.19   What each of you must now ensure is that your community presses onward with clarity of vision and undiminished zeal. You should make every effort to see that, through the operation of your training institutes, the base of the human resources of each of your communities is steadily extended. While the number of those entering your institute programs increases, so too must the number of friends reaching the higher courses in the sequences you each have chosen. Cultivate an atmosphere of love in your communities and help the friends to become a source of encouragement to one another. Take every opportunity to focus the believers on the aim of the Four Year Plan. Do all within your powers to assist them in the field of action.[12]

49.20   Likewise, the institutions need to maintain enthusiasm and help the friends to set goals for themselves:

49.21   As a growing number of believers progress through the institute courses, the responsibility will fall on your Assembly, as well as the Local Spiritual Assemblies, to see that their enthusiasm is maintained. They will need to be assisted in setting goals for themselves and be encouraged to persevere in their endeavors until teaching becomes the dominating passion of their lives and they gain confidence in their ability to make a distinctive contribution towards the achievement of the central aim of the Four Year Plan.[13]

49.22   Bringing these elements together to mobilize the friends in the field of service, then, is a capacity that must be developed in the institutions. What has become apparent during the Five Year Plan is that the reflection meeting provides the institutions with the instrument they need to mobilize the friends in this way, as explained in the 17 January 2003 message of the Universal House of Justice:

49.23   Meetings of consultation held at the cluster level serve to raise awareness of possibilities and generate enthusiasm. Here, free from the demands of formal decision-making, participants reflect on experience gained, share insights, explore approaches and acquire a better understanding of how each can contribute to achieving the aim of the Plan. In many cases, such interaction leads to consensus on a set of short-term goals, both individual and collective.[14]

As the above passage suggests, the reflection meeting at the cluster level serves a twofold purpose. Not only does it provide a means for mobilizing the believers, but it also contributes greatly to the planning process. This is true whether the cluster is in an early stage of development or whether it has reached an advanced stage, in which cycles of activities are carried out as part of an intensive program of growth: 49.24

> . . . the meetings of reflection called at various intervals during the cycles should serve to reinforce an attitude of learning among the participants in the program so that any fear of failure or criticism gives way to the joy of earnest striving. To achieve this, the friends involved in organizing the meetings should recognize that guided, participatory discussion can prove more instructive than elaborate presentations and prolonged theoretical analyses. A careful review of vital statistics, which highlight weaknesses that require remedial attention and point to strengths that can be built upon in the next cycle of activity, will go far in facilitating the planning process.[15] 49.25

In this way, planning is a flexible process that is able to take advantage of rapidly changing circumstances. With so much organization being done in reflection meetings at the cluster level, one question that has arisen is whether "the plans arrived at through such consultations require ratification by the Local Assemblies before implementation can begin."[16] To this question, the House of Justice provided the following answer in a letter dated 9 December 2001: 49.26

> As a matter of principle, any plans carried out in the jurisdiction of a Local Spiritual Assembly should meet with its approval. That being said, we are asked to point out that the planning process called for during the Five Year Plan, with its emphasis on the development of small geographic areas, allows for a great deal of flexibility. The Universal House of Justice hopes that the consultations which take place in periodic meetings at the level of the cluster will generate such unity of thought about the growth of the Faith 49.27

that, in those cases where the lines of action affect localities with Local Assemblies, the requirement of receiving their approval will easily be met. It should be remembered that the aim of such consultations, beyond addressing certain practical considerations, is to maintain a high level of enthusiasm and to create a spirit of service and fellowship among those present. Discussions should not become bogged down by undue concern for procedural issues, but should focus on what can be achieved and on the joy of witnessing the fruits of hard work and diligent effort.[17]

49.28   In another letter dated 11 April 2005 written on its behalf, the Universal House of Justice has given this further clarification:

49.29   Activity at the level of the cluster is instilling a sense of unity and a spirit of service among the friends within units larger than the local community. Reflection meetings, which are an essential element of this endeavor, should certainly not be seen to exclude Local Spiritual Assemblies or to minimize the role of their designated functions, but, it is hoped, to include them in a highly collective enterprise, developing a more comprehensive sense of movement on a wide scale that is motivated by a greater understanding of the broad vision of the Faith.[18]

49.30   In this light, the work at the cluster level serves to reinforce the efforts of well-functioning, strong Local Spiritual Assemblies:

49.31   All of this opens thrilling opportunities for Local Spiritual Assemblies. Theirs is the challenge, in collaboration with the Auxiliary Board members who counsel and assist them, to utilize the energies and talents of the swelling human resources available in their respective areas of jurisdiction both to create a vibrant community life and to begin influencing the society around them.[19]

49.32   Auxiliary Board members are called upon "to work closely with these Assemblies, both in the formulation of plans and in their execution, helping them to shoulder the responsibility of systematic growth in their own communities and in localities adopted as extension goals."[20] It is this collaborative relationship that provides inspiration to the friends and elicits from them wholehearted response to plans:

Acting in their respective roles, the two institutions of 49.33
the Counsellors and the Spiritual Assemblies share responsibility for the protection and propagation of the Faith. The
harmonious interaction between them ensures the constant
flow of guidance, love and encouragement to the believers
and invigorates their individual and collective endeavors to
advance the Cause.[21]

Since Board members also work intimately with the train- 49.34
ing institute and Area Teaching Committee, they can ensure
that the endeavors of such well-functioning Local Spiritual
Assemblies are in accordance with plans of action at the level
of the cluster. This is especially critical in the case of clusters
that have become the focus of intensive programs of growth,
through which all the institutions must learn "to support the
initiatives of individuals and merge diverse efforts into a powerful collective thrust."[22] Of course, in most cases the work of the
Board members is "not carried out in the context of communities that enjoy the leadership of a mature Spiritual Assembly."[23]
Rather they work, with the help of their assistants, in localities
where the Assemblies are not yet functioning at the necessary
level, as described by the House of Justice in "The Institution
of the Counsellors":

> In a community where the Local Assembly is at the very 49.35
> early stages of its development, the role of the assistants in
> promoting the establishment of study groups, devotional
> meetings, classes for the spiritual education of children, and
> the Nineteen Day Feast is even more crucial. Further, the
> Auxiliary Board members give attention to strengthening
> the Local Spiritual Assemblies, helping them to master the
> art of consultation, to gain confidence in making decisions,
> to adhere courageously to principle, and to learn how to
> mobilize the friends in unified action.[24]

Whatever stage of growth the localities in a cluster have 49.36
reached, the Auxiliary Board members "play a vital part in
encouraging the friends"[25] and "take it upon themselves to
ensure that proper attention is devoted to the various components of the community,"[26] that is, to every man, woman,
youth and child. The latter two offer a special challenge. Board
members "keep before everyone's eyes the imperative of the
spiritual education of children and do everything in their power
to help establish and maintain regular classes for the children.

And, with complete confidence in the capacity of youth for heroic service to the Cause, they assist them in realizing their full potential as vital agents for the expansion of the Faith and the transformation of society."[27] The Universal House of Justice has repeatedly called upon the institutions to "give consistent attention to involving the youth in the expansion and consolidation work."[28] In this connection, it stressed at the start of the Four Year Plan:

49.37   Youth will undoubtedly be the most enthusiastic supporters of the programs of your institutes. They are eager to make a significant contribution to the progress of their communities and have shown, time and again, their capacity to respond to the call to service. They can be trained to help shoulder the manifold responsibilities demanded by rapid expansion and consolidation. But it is especially important for large numbers of them to become capable teachers of Bahá'í children's classes. As you are well aware, without the education of children it is impossible to maintain victories from one generation to the next.[29]

49.38   With this in mind, the House of Justice has advised that "strategies to advance the process of entry by troops cannot ignore children and junior youth."[30] Junior youth, of course, "represent a special group with special needs as they are somewhat in between childhood and youth when many changes are occurring within them."[31] The Bahá'í world will be focused on the aim of advancing the process of entry by troops until the end of the first century of the Faith's Formative Age, when today's children and junior youth will be young adults—the future teachers and administrators of the Faith. Auxiliary Board members have been urged to ensure that the friends raised up by training institutes are mobilized "to meet the spiritual requirements of children and junior youth."[32] "The youth, in particular, constitute a vast reservoir of energy and talent,"[33] the House of Justice has indicated. "Developing and utilizing this immensely valuable resource"[34] to meet the needs of children and junior youth, specifically, and to further the aim of the global Plans, in general, is surely one of the most pressing challenges ahead.

PART III
Additional Documents

IN ITS MESSAGE DATED 27 DECEMBER 2005, the Universal House of Justice indicated that, with the launch of the Four Year Plan at Riḍván 1996, the Bahá'í world set out on "a path of intense learning about the sustained, rapid growth of the Faith." At different points along the way since then, effort has been made at the international level of the community to distill the learning taking place at the grassroots and to diffuse the knowledge thus acquired in documents widely circulated to the friends. Part III includes four documents of this kind. The first, entitled "Training Institutes," was prepared for and approved by the Universal House of Justice in 1998. The next two, both similar to the first, were written by the International Teaching Centre at the instruction of the House of Justice. "Training Institutes and Systematic Growth" was released in 2000 and "Building Momentum: A Coherent Approach to Growth" in 2003. The final document presents an analysis by the Teaching Centre of the experience of the Bahá'í world in meeting the administrative challenges associated with large-scale expansion. Entitled "Impact of Growth on Administration Processes," it was prepared in July 2005.

50

Training Institutes

a document prepared for and approved
by the Universal House of Justice

April 1998

The Four Year Plan calls for a significant advance in the process 50.1 of entry by troops to be supported and sustained by the systematic development of human resources. In the messages of the Universal House of Justice on the Plan, the training institute is envisaged as an instrument crucial to this development.

The purpose of the present document is twofold. On the 50.2 one hand, it offers an overview of the efforts thus far made by the worldwide Bahá'í community to establish institutes; on the other, it reviews their accomplishments to date and explores their possibilities for further development and potential effect on the process of entry by troops. Passages from the relevant guidance given by the House of Justice provide the framework for the study undertaken. The document is divided into three sections:

1. Awareness of the Importance of Training

2. Enhancement of Institutional Capacity
    2.1   Institutes in small communities with a large
          percentage of knowledgeable believers
          ▪ Teacher training programs
          ▪ Instruments of teaching
    2.2   Institutes in communities which witnessed large-
          scale expansion prior to the Plan, but whose
          human resources remained exceedingly low
    2.3   Institutes in communities which, having experienced
          large-scale expansion, had already acquired
          some capacity for training prior to the Plan
          ▪ Sequence of courses
          ▪ Study circles

1. Awareness of the Importance of Training

50.3   In the two years since the launching of the Four Year Plan, considerable progress has been made in raising the friends' awareness of the need for training. As a result, the rigorous and methodical study of the writings, a habit that required reinforcement in many communities, has assumed prominence. This is a welcome development, but more has to be accomplished before the implications of systematic training are fully grasped. The Universal House of Justice explains:

50.4   With the growth in the number of enrollments, it has become apparent that such occasional courses of instruction and the informal activities of community life, though important, are not sufficient as a means of human resource development, for they have resulted in only a relatively small band of active supporters of the Cause. These believers, no matter how dedicated, no matter how willing to make sacrifices, cannot attend to the needs of hundreds, much less thousands, of fledgling local communities. Systematic attention has to be given by Bahá'í institutions to training a significant number of believers and assisting them in serving the Cause according to their God-given talents and capacities.[1]

50.5   In many parts of the world, attention is focused largely on gaining an understanding of the fundamental verities of the Faith. The corresponding institute programs cover a wide range of subjects aimed at deepening the friends' knowledge of various aspects of the teachings. To be effective in developing human resources, these programs need to impart knowledge, provide spiritual insights, and endow the participants with skills and abilities of service. In the messages on the Four Year

Plan, the House of Justice has made a number of statements on the nature of training, and the variations in wording lend perspective on this complex matter:

> The purpose of such training is to endow ever-growing contingents of believers with the spiritual insights, the knowledge, and the skills needed to carry out the many tasks of accelerated expansion and consolidation, including the teaching and deepening of a large number of people—adults, youth and children.[2]

50.6

> It is therefore of paramount importance that systematic attention be given to devising methods for educating large numbers of believers in the fundamental verities of the Faith and for training and assisting them to serve the Cause as their God-given talents allow.[3]

50.7

> They [training institutes] will help to develop in each participant a deep love for Bahá'u'lláh, a good understanding of His essential Teachings and an awareness of the importance of developing the spiritual life of each individual through prayer, meditation and immersion in the Sacred Writings. They will also cover such practical matters as how to teach the Faith, for there are too many who, for lack of confidence in their ability to do so, are hesitant to convey the Message.[4]

50.8

> Your participation in institute programs, through which you will deepen your knowledge of the Faith, cultivate your inner spiritual lives and develop abilities of service, will enable you to intensify your individual and collective exertions in the teaching field and will result in a commensurate acceleration in the expansion of your communities.[5]

50.9

> They [institute programs] should seek to develop in the participants a good understanding of Bahá'u'lláh's essential Teachings and to help them acquire those skills and abilities that will enable them to serve the Faith effectively. They should also strive to imbue their hearts with a deep love for Bahá'u'lláh—a love from which stems a desire to submit oneself to His Will, to obey His laws, to heed His exhortations and to promote His Faith.[6]

50.10

> These centers of Bahá'í learning will have as their goal one very practical outcome, namely, the raising up of large

50.11

numbers of believers who are trained to foster and facilitate the process of entry by troops with efficiency and love.[7]

50.12   Passages such as these define a clear purpose for training institutes. The experience of the past two years indicates that when institute programs fulfill this purpose through curricula that properly integrate the various components of training, the number of those who dedicate themselves to the work of the Faith increases dramatically.

2. Enhancement of Institutional Capacity

50.13   Most national communities have taken the necessary initial steps to establish one or more training institutes in their countries. Boards or committees to oversee the operation of the institutes have been appointed. Patterns of cooperation between the Counsellors and the National Spiritual Assemblies in this vital area of activity have been adopted. Working relationships between Auxiliary Board members and the institutes have not proven difficult to build. By now, institutes in almost all countries have successfully conducted a few training sessions. Some are at the stage of offering regular courses to relatively small groups, while others have gone further to establish elaborate systems to reach large numbers. To significantly enhance the institutional capacity of each national community so as to impart spiritual education to ever-increasing contingents of believers is a challenge that requires persistent attention. In a memorandum to the International Teaching Centre, the House of Justice explains:

50.14   From the various reports received at the World Centre, it is clear that a great deal of institutional capacity needs to be created in most national communities for training on a large scale. In many countries, offering regular courses to relatively small groups of believers is a formidable challenge. The Counsellors with the encouragement of the International Teaching Centre will need to devote considerable energy to helping national communities progress step by step along the way, if the believers of capacity in the villages and towns of the world are to receive training and we are to witness the kind of development in the Faith for which we hope.[8]

The greatest progress in this direction has been made in those national communities which have concentrated on the execution of programs, not allowing themselves to be diverted from action by lengthy discussions of theoretical matters. Their institutes have expeditiously chosen a series of courses with the best methods and materials available to them, trained teachers, and set out to build their systems of delivery in the process of implementation: 50.15

> In this connection, it brought the House of Justice much satisfaction to note in the program proposal for the development of human resources, sent to the World Centre in December, that a sequence of a few basic courses had already been defined, which would be conducted using available materials. In this way, emphasis could be placed on the execution of the program. The House of Justice is concerned that much time will be lost if the program coordinator is now asked to devote attention to ensuring that the institute offers courses to cover a wide range of training requirements. What is needed at this stage is to train scores of facilitators in how to conduct the first few courses, so that they can offer them in the villages and towns throughout the country, enabling thereby hundreds and eventually thousands to enter the institute's program. Such a task is, in and of itself, formidable and will require tremendous focus and concentration on the part of the institute.[9] 50.16

The following extract from a letter written on behalf of the House of Justice to an individual believer also addresses this point: 50.17

> That after so many years of constant effort throughout the Bahá'í world methods and approaches have been found to train at least a certain number of believers enrolled from among the receptive masses themselves—to deepen their knowledge of the Teachings of the Faith and to help them acquire skills and abilities to serve it effectively—is no small accomplishment, and these methods and approaches should now be fully exploited and utilized more extensively. Therefore, the emphasis on the establishment and operation of training institutes in the Four Year Plan is not only the expression of a great need in the Faith but also an acknowledgement of the capacity within the worldwide Bahá'í community to meet it on a large scale.[10] 50.18

50.19   Three patterns can be discerned according to which institutional capacity for training seems to be developing in the Bahá'í world.

2.1 Small communities with a large percentage of knowledgeable believers

50.20   One pattern is generally associated with countries where the number of knowledgeable believers in a rather small Bahá'í population is relatively high. Most of the communities in Western Europe fall into this category. The approach adopted by their institutes is for the boards to determine what courses should be offered and call upon individuals to design and deliver them. Depending on the size of the country, courses are held in a central place or repeated in various localities.

50.21   There is no doubt that this pattern, if carefully applied, will lead to a significant increase in human resources. To gradually develop an educational organization which offers a variety of courses to a larger and larger student body clearly enhances institutional capacity in any national community. Like institutes everywhere, those in this category will become strengthened as they learn how to motivate, guide and assist their teachers; to attract a steadily growing number of students; and to administer their courses with efficiency. For this development to be meaningful, however, a great deal of work has to be done on program content. The purpose of training, as outlined in the messages of the House of Justice, is not realized by simply making it possible for some of the friends to offer courses on their favorite subjects to groups of interested believers.

TEACHER TRAINING PROGRAMS

50.22   What is required of these institutes, then, is to identify in consultation with a group of collaborators the real needs of their national communities and address these in well-designed programs. Given the aim of the Plan, such needs are intimately related to opportunities for growth in the country. A letter written on behalf of the House of Justice underscores the role of such institutes in the promotion of teaching:

50.23   The House of Justice was heartened to note your goals related to teaching and hopes that you will give special consideration to the measures which can immediately be taken towards the achievement of a progressive increase in the number of individual enrollments. In this regard, it will be of particular importance that the friends are encouraged to arise and teach the Faith with ever greater determination and courage, and the continued development of your national training institute will be instrumental in this effort. At this stage in the growth of your community, the institute should consider as its primary task the offering of courses that seek to endow the friends with the knowledge, spiritual insights, and skills needed not only to proclaim the Cause, but to guide new souls to Bahá'u'lláh's Revelation.[11]

As they strive to work in this way, these institutes face a difficulty inherent in their communities' lack of experience in large-scale expansion, experience upon which they could draw to design appropriate curricular elements. While their present strength enables them to formulate with relative ease courses which impart knowledge of the Faith or examine spiritual and social issues, they struggle with the content of teacher training programs that would offer practical advice and insights. Utilizing materials developed in other parts of the world, where such experience exists, helps overcome this difficulty. The long-term solution, however, is for the appropriate institutions to establish systematic teaching plans that are approached with an attitude of learning. Training and teaching, then, become two parallel processes that fuel each other: Training courses raise the enthusiasm of the friends for teaching and help them acquire the necessary skills. Increased experience in the teaching field is reflected in the constantly improving content of training courses. 50.24

INSTRUMENTS OF TEACHING

Another dimension of institutional capacity that needs to be explored more vigorously by these institutes is their role as direct instruments of teaching: 50.25

The Universal House of Justice received with great pleasure a copy of the first quarterly report of the board of directors of your national training institute. It was particularly heartened to note that the board is approaching its tasks with an open attitude towards learning, fully cognizant of the need to make decisions about the content and methods of the institute program, to implement them, to reflect on the results, and to make adjustments in the light 50.26

of experience. Through such an approach, your institute will succeed in gradually increasing its capacity to develop the human resources of the Bulgarian community.

50.27   Since your community is relatively small, the board may wish to consider, as it continues to learn from experience, designing some courses which could be open to Bahá'ís and non-Bahá'ís alike. In addition to attracting thoughtful people to the Cause, such courses could also be a means of confirming them in the Faith and increasing the number of Bahá'u'lláh's faithful followers in your country.[12]

50.28   Given the growing interest among the public in social and spiritual issues, courses open to non-Bahá'ís could easily address such topics as the meaning of spirituality in a modern world, moral leadership, the spiritual education of children and youth, the dynamics of prayer, the nature of the soul and the afterlife.

2.2 Communities of large-scale expansion with extremely limited human resources

50.29   A second pattern is emerging mostly in countries which witnessed large-scale expansion prior to the Four Year Plan, but whose human resources remained exceedingly low. Here, the focus of institutes is on conducting courses of fixed duration, running from a few days up to several weeks, covering a set of basic deepening topics and assisting the participants in acquiring some skills. Groups of 20 to 30 are usually brought to a central place and trained, in the hope that they will return and strengthen their local communities. For these institutes, learning how to offer a course to group after group and to keep them enthusiastic day after day is in itself a significant step. It is heartening to see that a number of them are rapidly acquiring the capacity to accomplish this task.

50.30   In the context of entry by troops, however, institutes that conduct courses only at a central location have clear limitations. In a country of several thousand believers where a small group carries much of the weight of the work of the Faith, an institute course of a few weeks' duration, repeated four or five times a year, may double or triple the number of workers in the field. But this does not provide the human resources to set in motion a sustainable process of accelerated growth. Once an institute passes through such a first stage, then, it must face the challenge of reaching a greater number of believers. In several countries in this category, the friends are already aware of this need, but for them to acquire the necessary level of institutional capacity is not proving to be easy. In this connection, the following guidance was offered by the Universal House of Justice to the International Teaching Centre:

> Now that many institutes have passed through the initial stage of establishment, the Counsellors can help increase their efficiency by bringing to their attention the need to reach larger and larger numbers of students with their courses. It would be a poor use of limited financial resources for an institute with a budget which includes remuneration for several full-time staff to offer a few courses to a handful of believers year after year. But even in this case, an indicator such as the cost per student per course would have to be used carefully. Early on, as institutes are learning how to attract students and offer courses, it is to be expected that such costs would run relatively high.[13]

50.31

Since bringing a very large number of believers to one central location for the purpose of training would be unmanageable, other alternatives have to be found. One option is for the institute to establish branches in different regions, a possibility mentioned in the messages on the Four Year Plan. For some institutes, the creation of one or two branches is feasible at this stage. To operate many such centers, each with its own facilities and administrative structure, however, would be beyond the financial means of most communities:

50.32

> The primary challenge before you is to help hundreds and then thousands of the believers in Haiti to enter your institute program and study a well-defined sequence of courses. Clearly, you cannot accomplish this by inviting them all to one central location. Of course, it would be possible to establish one or more branches of your national institute. However, any scheme designed to reach a significant number of students by establishing many such centers, each with its own facilities and administrative structure, would be prohibitively expensive.[14]

50.33

It is becoming clear, then, that these institutes need to find more innovative ways to expand their coverage.

50.34

2.3 Communities of large-scale expansion with some prior capacity for training

50.35   A third notable pattern is unfolding in several national communities which, having experienced large-scale expansion, had already acquired some capacity for training prior to the Four Year Plan. The system being established in these communities, either by a national institute or a nationally coordinated network of regional institutes, has four components: a sequence of courses with well-prepared material distributed to every student, a small study circle usually composed of eight to ten people, a facilitator or tutor trained to teach the courses, and some scheme of coordination, both at the national and regional levels.

SEQUENCE OF COURSES

50.36   As experience is gained worldwide, various sequences of courses will undoubtedly be developed responding to the requirements of divers sectors of society. No one should underestimate the complexity of the task of defining each sequence and elaborating the materials. These have to adhere to some logic, if they are to succeed in raising up the needed human resources. Simply to compile a list of topics the friends should study, in the light of the guidance available in the writings, is not difficult. The order in which these topics should be presented, their correlation with the acquisition of skills to perform acts of service, and the way their study should be combined with the cultivation of inner perfection are matters of pedagogy that can best be discovered through systematic educational experience. For example, understanding the principles that govern the establishment and functioning of the Local Spiritual Assembly is of the utmost importance for every Bahá'í. One must ask, however, whether a course on this subject is effective when offered to believers whose knowledge of the Faith is extremely limited and who have not yet studied those spiritual truths that shape Bahá'í identity. It is noteworthy that, in practice, when institutes ignore the relevant pedagogical principles they fail to maintain the interest of the students, and the level of attendance in their courses falls.

STUDY CIRCLES

Before the second component of the system, namely, the 50.37
study circle, is examined, it should be noted that training institutes are not in charge of deepening the entire community; their
task is to focus on a percentage of the believers who are eager
to learn and willing to teach and deepen others. In response to
an institute proposal which included goals aimed at reaching
the majority of the believers, the following was stated in a letter
written on behalf of the House of Justice:

> The House of Justice was particularly heartened to see 50.38
> from your proposal that you intend to form "study circles"
> of six to ten believers in the towns and villages throughout
> the country, who will go through a series of basic courses
> together with a tutor. Through such an approach, you hope
> to reach large numbers with your institute program. It
> feels, however, that the numerical goals that you have set,
> beginning with the third year of the institute's operation,
> are too high. It should be remembered that the purpose of
> the institute is to raise up a certain percentage of the friends
> as human resources, who, in turn, will teach and deepen the
> majority of the believers. Once you have attained the goals
> for the first two years, which are themselves ambitious but
> achievable, then you can evaluate the situation and set
> realistic goals for the third and fourth years.[15]

Institutes in this category try to identify in each locality 50.39
eight to ten of the more capable believers, usually young people
with some formal education, and then to help them progress
through the selected sequence of courses. This has proven
possible, even when the generality of the believers are illiterate.
In working with such groups, institutes have learned to avoid
two extremes: underestimating the abilities of the friends and
sacrificing depth to an inordinate desire for simplicity, on the
one hand, and, on the other, expecting too much and overlook-
ing the need to adjust the pace of the courses to the educational
level of the participants.

In those countries where the system described here is 50.40
taking shape, much is being learnt about how to motivate
and maintain study circles over an extended period of time.
It is becoming clear, for example, that they must undertake
extra-curricular activities, particularly in the realm of cultural
enrichment. Further, although a group may continue to study

with the same tutor through the entire sequence of courses, it seems best for each course to have an official beginning and an event celebrating its successful completion. Some formality is proving to be essential, but the degree of it varies from country to country. In some parts of the world, for instance, the culture seems to respond to, and even demand, examinations and grades.

50.41   An important point to bear in mind is that these study groups are not local deepening classes or local institutes, but elements of a system of distance-education administered by a national or regional institute. The concept of "local institutes" created some confusion at the beginning of the Four Year Plan, and the House of Justice offered the following clarification:

50.42   For the establishment of a training institute to be a viable and worthwhile enterprise, it would clearly have to serve an area with a reasonably large number of believers. Moreover, the development of effective curricula to raise up human resources to carry forward the process of entry by troops is not, in reality, a task that small local Bahá'í communities can undertake. Generally speaking, the resources of a national community, or at least a sizeable region, need to be drawn upon in devising well-organized, formally conducted programs. Although it is likely that as local communities grow, there will be those large enough to have their own independent institutes, at this point, such institutes run the danger, as you have surmised, of turning into deepening classes, which are, of course, of critical importance themselves and an activity every local community should carry out.

50.43   This does not mean, however, that the courses of a national or regional institute would not be offered at the local level. In fact, a significant percentage of the national and regional institutes emerging around the world are organizing their programs in such a way that many of their courses are conducted in local communities by believers trained as teachers or facilitators.[16]

50.44   As a study group advances through the sequence of courses, the capacity of each member to serve the Faith increases, and various institutions and agencies step in and help the participants to put into practice what they have learned. The following passage from a letter written on behalf of the House of Justice commends one such effort:

> The plan of action you have devised for the coming months   50.45
> and the numerical goals you have set, closely correlated
> and well-measured, are clear evidence that you have gained
> valuable experience during this past year. If you continue
> unabated in your efforts, you will steadily increase the
> capacity within your national community to accompany
> large numbers of believers through a well-defined sequence
> of courses, helping them to acquire the needed capabilities
> of service. Since the first course in the sequence emphasizes
> spiritual identity and prayer, the House of Justice applauds
> your decision to increase, parallel to the formation of study
> circles, the number of local communities holding regular
> devotional meetings. Even in communities where the Local
> Spiritual Assembly is not functioning, it should be possible
> to establish such meetings through the initiative of those
> taking part in the study circles.[17]

TUTORS

The third component of the system under consideration is   50.46
the tutor (or facilitator). Such institutes begin their programs by
training several believers, already knowledgeable in the Faith,
as tutors. This makes it possible for them to form study groups
and establish their programs on a firm foundation. Yet the
expansion of the system depends on raising up an ever-growing number of tutors from among the participants themselves.
Here again, the challenge is to strike the right balance. It is
counter-productive to demand so high a quality of work from
tutors that only a few are able to meet the standard, resulting
in a system with inadequate coverage. On the other hand, an
indiscriminate selection of tutors, in which everyone is asked to
form a study group the moment he or she finishes one or two
courses, also proves to be ineffective and leads to the collapse
of the system:

> Crucial to the success of the institute's endeavors will   50.47
> be the effectiveness of its tutors. They themselves will
> require training, both in how to facilitate the courses and
> maintain the cohesion of the groups studying in the towns
> and villages across the country. The institute will need to
> make concerted effort, therefore, to build its own capacity

to supervise a growing number of tutors and train them, constantly improving the quality of their teaching.[18]

COORDINATION

50.48   The fourth component, namely, efficient coordination, is developed at two levels. At the national level, concern is for the efficacy of the courses, the fostering of enthusiasm for training in the country, and the compilation and dissemination of information regarding the institute, including the number of participants in the system and the record of their achievements. At the regional level, closer to the study groups themselves, the duties of the coordinators include training tutors, following their progress in the villages and towns, ensuring the availability of materials, and organizing conferences and seminars for the exchange of experience. With respect to coordination at the national level, the House of Justice states:

50.49   It is of the utmost importance, then, that you continue with unabated zeal and painstaking care to develop the capacity of your institutes to train growing contingents of believers. In this regard, you will need to ensure that your vision for the multiplication of human resources in that vast land is understood and shared by all those involved in this vital enterprise and that through various means, such as the regular dissemination of news of the accomplishments of your institutes, the friends' enthusiasm is heightened and maintained.[19]

INTEGRATING THE SYSTEM

50.50   It should be noted at this point that such a system is not necessarily put into place at the outset in the way it is described here. In several countries, the initial strategy has been to deploy a band of institute teachers in a particular region, assigning to each a number of towns and villages. The first course of the institute program is, then, conducted with a group of interested believers over a period of four or five consecutive days. Upon its completion, the teacher moves to another locality and repeats the course with a new group. When the number of those who have completed the first course is significant, the teachers go back again to help them study the second course. As the process advances, capable believers arise from the towns and villages themselves to act as tutors and form study groups of more permanence which meet regularly over an extended period.

These four components, methodically developed and properly integrated, create a system which has proven able to reach a large number of people at an affordable cost per student. The following statement from a letter written on behalf of the House of Justice provides a vision of the growth of such a system:

50.51

> The House of Justice was heartened to note that by the month of October 1997, over 900 believers in Tamil Nadu had gone through the first course of the national institute program, and some 200 had succeeded in completing the second one. It is assumed that a percentage of these will go on to study the third course, while the number entering the program will continue to grow. This is indeed a most promising process of human resource development for a rapidly expanding community. For the development of human resources in India may be likened to the building of an ever-expanding pyramid, whose base must be constantly broadened. An increasing number of friends are recruited to enter the first basic course, and relatively significant percentages are then helped to reach higher and higher courses, acquiring thereby the needed capabilities of service.[20]

50.52

2.4 *Social and economic development*

It is worth mentioning that, in keeping with the directives of the House of Justice, the Office of Social and Economic Development is helping some institutes to add another dimension to their operations, namely, training in the area of development and even the administration of development projects. For the present, this assistance is limited to a few countries. It entails raising the institutional capacity of an institute to a new level, one at which it has a much greater degree of autonomy:

50.53

> Now that the foundations for the next stage of the institute's work have been laid, the House of Justice urges your Assembly to grant the institute the autonomy needed to function properly. The development of human resources for expansion and consolidation and for social and economic development, and the effective management of development-related projects, are not simple tasks, and

50.54

the institute will require freedom of action to learn from its endeavors in order to consistently improve its work.[21]

50.55   The addition of this new dimension to the work of institutes is being carried out with great care. Since development-related activities often involve funds from non-Bahá'í sources, a financial system has to be in place to meticulously track various lines of expenditure. Further, once an institute becomes engaged in development, it needs to interact with government agencies and organizations of civil society, often entering into collaborative relationships with them. All of this demands a degree of maturity that is achieved only through consistent effort and experience. In those places where the work is moving in this direction, the profile of an institution capable of pursuing a highly complex set of activities is beginning to emerge, and an exciting vision of a dynamic center of learning is taking shape.

3. Advancing the Process of Entry by Troops

50.56   A pressing question at the mid-point of the Four Year Plan is what effect this impressive and rapid development of institutional capacity for the spiritual education of the friends will have on the process of entry by troops worldwide. Ultimately, the efficacy of an institute program has to be measured by the growth of the community being served. But expectations should remain within reason while the potential of the institute is being systematically realized. If national communities set their sights too low and are content with offering a few courses to a limited number of believers year after year, the required dynamics of growth will not develop. Yet placing unreasonable demands on training institutes and those who participate in their programs, especially at the early stage, would be counter-productive. What is needed is unrelenting resolve to steadily multiply human resources, combined with determination to take advantage of every opportunity for expansion.

3.1 *Increasing human resources*

50.57   Clearly measurable results will be achieved only as institutes succeed in training teachers of the Cause and active workers in large numbers. What constitutes a significant increase in human resources, of course, will vary from country to country. In the largest Bahá'í community, India, already more than 10,000 believers have studied the first course in the national institute program. Although this is an extraordinary accomplishment, the institutions of the Faith in the country are well aware that to train even ten percent of the total Bahá'í population will require involving some 200,000 people. While not comparable to India in size, many national communities throughout the world have tens of thousands of Bahá'ís, of whom only a small fraction can at present be counted among the active promoters of the Faith. For each community to help a relatively significant number of believers progress through a sequence of courses represents an enormous challenge. The House of Justice makes the important point that meeting this challenge—and thus increasing the number of believers who have a strong Bahá'í identity and a commitment to teaching the Cause—in itself constitutes an advance in the process of entry by troops:

> . . . if you are to realize your aspirations for the Cause in   50.58
> Guyana during the Four Year Plan, you will need to give
> further consideration, in consultation with the Counsellors,
> to what it means for your community to make a significant
> advance in the process of entry by troops. It is understand-
> able that you may not wish to repeat the pattern whereby
> you achieved large-scale expansion in the past. Yet, what-
> ever form entry by troops takes in your country in the
> future, it is clear that the development of your capacity to
> train a certain percentage of the believers for service to the
> Cause will be an inescapable imperative. Indeed, given that
> only a small fraction of the some 56,000 Bahá'ís in Guyana
> can be considered active supporters of the Faith, the very
> act of training a few thousand believers, and thus increasing
> the number who have a strong Bahá'í identity and a com-
> mitment to teaching the Cause, would in itself constitute an
> advance in the process of entry by troops.[22]

3.2 *Accelerating expansion*

An extraordinary opportunity to multiply its human   50.59
resources on a vast scale is now clearly within the grasp of the
Bahá'í community. Seizing it will call for added vigilance on
the part of the institutions—the National Spiritual Assemblies
and their agencies, on the one hand, and the Counsellors and
their auxiliaries, on the other—to ensure that the energies of

the friends are channeled into some form of active service to the Faith:

50.60   . . . as the friends steadily progress through a series of systematic courses, increasing their knowledge and skills, the responsibility will fall on your Assembly to see that their energies and talents are channeled in some form of active service to the Faith. This will have to be done in such a way that they are neither overburdened with responsibilities nor under challenged, but are allowed to gradually gain confidence in their ability to serve and to make a distinctive contribution towards the achievement of the central aim of the Four Year Plan.[23]

50.61   The immediate result of this multiplication of human resources will undoubtedly be an increase in teaching activity undertaken at the initiative of the individual believer, initiative that needs to be nurtured by the institutions:

50.62   For your community to grow at a pace commensurate with the receptivity of the people of Panama, your Assembly will need to pay close attention to certain fundamental areas of Bahá'í activity throughout the country. One of the primary forces that propels growth is teaching undertaken by the friends on their own initiative. To properly flourish, however, personal teaching requires stimulation from the institutions; it must be fostered by National and Local Spiritual Assemblies, on the one hand, and the Counsellors and their auxiliaries, on the other. The friends everywhere need encouragement. Regular gatherings, at various levels, need to be held to maintain and heighten their enthusiasm for teaching. Opportunities have to be created for them to share stories of the successes they have achieved and the methods they have used, so that they can learn from one another. Literature and teaching materials must be made available to them in abundance. Without concerted efforts of this kind, it is difficult to increase continually the number of believers arising to discharge their sacred duty to teach.[24]

50.63   Local teaching projects constitute yet another channel into which the energies of the friends benefiting from institute programs can be directed:

Of equal importance to the promotion of personal teaching in Peru is the development of local communities, particularly the enhancement of their capacity to carry out teaching plans. Working in close collaboration with the Counsellors, you will need to consider how you can consistently increase the number of Local Spiritual Assemblies that can design and execute plans which utilize the diverse talents of the friends, thus multiplying their powers as they unite in collective action.[25]   50.64

Essential as local teaching projects are, however, it should be realized that, at this point in the history of the Faith, most believers reside in communities in which the Local Spiritual Assemblies are but nascent institutions. Therefore, emphasis has now to be placed, in many countries, on implementing projects that concentrate on a small region, usually a cluster of villages with one or two towns. Even though most institutes have barely begun their work, in more than a few regions the effects of human resource development are already noticeable in the enthusiasm for service of groups who have been attending courses. Without doubt, the number of such regions will multiply rapidly in the months ahead, and it is crucial that teaching projects be promptly established in any region where the institute is exerting influence.   50.65

For a number of years, the International Teaching Centre has promoted projects of this kind under the designation "Long-Term Teaching Project." As a result, there is now ample experience in the Bahá'í world which can be readily shared among national communities through the Counsellors. While such projects aim at bringing large numbers into the Faith at an accelerating pace, they are not concerned merely with enrollments; nor is teaching carried out superficially. These projects involve a complex set of interrelated activities for expansion and consolidation which, together, result in a steady influx of new believers. Specifically, every effort is made to incorporate a significant percentage of the newly enrolled friends immediately into the institute program, extending thereby the human resource base in the region.   50.66

The tasks before the Counsellors and the National Spiritual Assemblies are multiple and urgent. On the one hand, they will continue to strengthen the institutes and ensure that an increasing number of believers benefit from their programs. On the other, they will support and encourage the friends in their   50.67

individual teaching endeavors, assist Local Spiritual Assemblies in executing teaching plans, and establish long-term teaching projects in region after region. All the necessary elements are in place. The stage is set. There is every reason to believe that the combined effect of all these efforts will lead to the fulfillment of the major thrust of the Four Year Plan.

51

Training Institutes and Systematic Growth

a document prepared by
the International Teaching Centre

February 2000

In its Riḍván message of 153 [1996] the Universal House of 51.1
Justice placed the establishment and development of training
institutes in the context of the far-reaching changes that would
characterize the progress of the Faith in this period of Bahá'í
history.

> The next four years will represent an extraordinary period 51.2
> in the history of our Faith, a turning point of epochal
> magnitude. What the friends throughout the world are now
> being asked to do is to commit themselves, their material
> resources, their abilities and their time to the development
> of a network of training institutes on a scale never before
> attempted.[1]

As we survey the development of training institutes during 51.3
the Four Year Plan, we are struck by the degree to which this
vision has been realized. The network of training institutes
encircling the globe numbers some 350 in 170 countries, with
nearly 100,000 believers having benefited from at least one
institute course. The magnitude of this achievement is rivaled
only by the "untold potential" that it augurs for the advancement of the process of entry by troops.

The purpose of training institutes was clarified and 51.4
elaborated in the April 1998 publication entitled "Training
Institutes," a document prepared for and approved by the
Universal House of Justice. On the basis of this elucidation of
the institute process, national communities began to refocus
their efforts, emphasizing a sequence of courses that would create capacity and commitment on the part of the friends to carry
out acts of service. Greater stress was placed on decentralizing

343

the institute process so as to reach ever-growing numbers of believers. The past two years have seen not only the expansion of training institutes worldwide but a deeper appreciation throughout the Bahá'í world of the unique and vital role training institutes must play in promoting systematic growth.

51.5   This paper presents an overview of the advancement of the institute process since the release of the April 1998 document. The analysis is framed in the guidance the House of Justice has given to National Spiritual Assemblies during the past two years in relation to training institutes. It is divided into four sections:

1. Experience with the Institute Process
    1.1   Administrative structure
    1.2   Collaboration
    1.3   Curriculum
        1.3.1   A systematic approach
        1.3.2   Sequence of courses
    1.4   Delivery systems
        1.4.1   Distance education
        1.4.2   Study circles
        1.4.3   Tutors and tutor training

2. Institutes in Action
    2.1   Creating human resources
    2.2   Impact on teaching and growth
    2.3   Direct instruments of teaching

3. Systematization of Teaching (Area Growth Programs)

4. Challenges for Training Institutes
    4.1   Quality and effectiveness
    4.2   Illiteracy
    4.3   Resource persons
    4.4   Infrastructure
    4.5   Deputization of institute staff

1. Experience with the Institute Process

51.6   In its Riḍván message of 156 [1999] the Universal House of Justice referred to the "demonstrated efficacy of training institutes." In order to better understand the long-range potential of the institutes and their impact on the progress of the Faith, it may be worthwhile to consider the elements that characterize an effective training institute. What administrative structures have served well in implementing institute programs? What level of collaboration between the institutions of the Faith has helped to foster the institute process? Are there any principles of curriculum development that have been learned? Has any type of delivery system proved especially effective? To answer these questions, and others, we offer the experience of national communities around the world that have, under the guidance of the House of Justice, moved the development of training institutes forward with extraordinary rapidity and impressive results.

The document "Training Institutes," released by the House of Justice at the 1998 International Bahá'í Convention, described the variations in national communities and how the training institute might emerge differently according to the characteristics of different countries and the nature and size of their Bahá'í communities. However, the most striking observation that can be made when surveying the growth of training institutes around the world during the past two years is that there are important parallels among the most successful programs and there is a convergence of thought and practice about the development of training institutes that has emerged from implementation of the careful guidance given by the House of Justice to this worldwide enterprise. 51.7

1.1 *Administrative structure*

In most countries of the world the basic administrative structure for the training institutes has been to establish a national institute with an institute board. In a few national communities that have large Bahá'í populations or that cover large geographical areas, and generally where Regional Bahá'í Councils exist, regional institutes have been established with their own boards. In the majority of these cases, National Spiritual Assemblies have decided that the institute boards report to the Regional Councils, while the National Assemblies themselves set broad policy and guide the overall development of the institute process. 51.8

In all parts of the world the boards of training institutes have taken up their responsibilities with vigor, carrying out their tasks either under the supervision of the National Assembly or the appropriate Regional Council. They seem to have 51.9

understood well the nature of their functions. Individuals who are appointed to the institute boards should have a readiness to learn about the challenges and promise of human resource development, be aware of the need to focus on training, and be able to work effectively in a small team. The collaboration of both arms of the Administrative Order in the appointment process has proved essential.

51.10   If a board of directors is named, its membership should be decided upon by the National Spiritual Assembly in consultation with the Counsellors and with their full support. . . .[2]

51.11   As Counsellors, National Assemblies, and the institute boards consider how to present courses to a growing number of believers, questions about the necessary administrative structures generally arise. The House of Justice has cautioned against an elaborate system of regional branches, which can be costly and generally still require believers to come to a central location:

51.12   . . . at this stage in your efforts to raise up human resources it is not necessary to establish regional branches, which generally involve high costs, including maintenance of facilities, equipment, and expenses for participants, such as transportation, food and housing.[3]

51.13   Rather than regional branches, an effective structure has been to appoint regional coordinators who oversee the extension of the institute courses to local communities within a region. As the number of study circles in an area increases, regional coordinators are needed to encourage and support the efforts of the tutors, to promote the further multiplication of study circles, and to coordinate the work of the institute with institutions in the area.

51.14   In some national communities there had been a proliferation of activities referred to as "institutes." It was necessary to clarify that these local initiatives, largely focused on deepening, while praiseworthy, were not "institutes" as called for by the House of Justice. In this connection, it is important to draw a distinction between such initiatives and the extension of institute courses to the local level as part of a national or regional program to provide training to ever-larger numbers of believers. The House of Justice explains:

As the friends gain a clearer understanding of the intent 51.15 of the House of Justice in calling for the establishment of institutes, these local efforts will gradually become associated, as branches or study groups, with a regional institute serving a much larger population. In this context, what defines a region will necessarily vary. . . . Regardless, with the strengthening of regional institutes, the concept of a training institute will become more and more separated in the minds of the friends from that of a local deepening class or a teaching group.[4]

1.2 *Collaboration*

In its Riḍván 153 [1996] message and other letters, the 51.16 House of Justice called for close collaboration between the two arms of the Administration in the development of institutes. In analyzing the growth and progress of training institutes during the Four Year Plan, one of the most compelling conclusions has been the importance of consultation between the Counsellors and National Assemblies about the direction and operation of the training institutes. To the degree to which close collaboration was achieved, there was a corresponding likelihood that the training institute process would be firmly grounded in the guidance of the House of Justice and would experience success in creating a body of confirmed and active supporters of the Faith.

In a national community there must exist a common vision 51.17 between the Counsellors and the National Spiritual Assembly about the character and direction of the institute process. This has been achieved where there has been "intimate involvement in institute operations" by the Counsellors and their auxiliaries. Furthermore, the collaboration of Counsellors with those Regional Bahá'í Councils that have responsibility for administering regional training institutes, and of Counsellors and Auxiliary Board members with training institute boards, has provided the opportunity for this arm of the Administration to further its sacred purpose of diffusing the Divine Fragrances and promoting learning. As explained in the Riḍván 153 [1996] message, the character of institutes "harmonizes with, and provides scope for the exercise of, the educational responsibilities of the Auxiliary Board members."[5]

51.18   The House of Justice has emphasized in several instances the necessity of the ongoing collaboration between the two arms of the Administration:

51.19   This matter calls for an intensification of the collaboration between the Continental Counsellors and National Spiritual Assemblies. For the success of these training institutes will depend in very large measure on the active involvement of the Continental Counsellors and the Auxiliary Board members in their operation. Particularly will it be necessary for Auxiliary Board members to have a close working relationship with institutes. . . .[6]

51.20   A process of decision-making must be arrived at, in consultation between you and the Counsellors, regarding the preparation and approval of the annual plans and budgets for the institutes. This would involve in each case, of course, close interaction between the Counsellors and the institutes or institute boards. . . .[7]

51.21   In the functioning of the training institute boards we have witnessed the close cooperation of the two arms of the Administration, particularly the participation of Auxiliary Board members, fulfilling the House of Justice's expectation that the "intimate involvement in institute operations should now become a part of the evolving functions of these officers of the Faith."[8]

51.22   From these guidelines, you can see that it is entirely acceptable for Auxiliary Board members to be appointed by the National Assembly in agreement with the Counsellors to the board of an institute. Of course, their participation in the institute work is not limited to membership on boards of directors. As mentioned in your letter, many will also serve as coordinators and act as teachers. Whether they take up these responsibilities on a full-time basis is a matter for them to decide in consultation with the Counsellors concerned.[9]

51.23   In most countries Auxiliary Board members are serving on institute boards. However, it is in those places where the guidance of the House of Justice on the critical role of the Board members in the development of the institute process has been fully implemented that one can observe the greatest progress.

In countries where Regional Bahá'í Councils exist, close interaction between the Councils and the training institutes is vitally important and can create "a galvanic coherence of the processes effecting expansion and consolidation in a region," and "the practical matching of the training services of institutes to the developmental needs of local communities."[10] — 51.24

1.3 *Curriculum*

At the heart of the training institute is the curriculum selected by the institute board, in consultation with the National Spiritual Assembly and the Counsellors. — 51.25

> In view of the experience gained thus far, you are urged to outline, in consultation with Counsellors and the boards, a sequence of a few courses designed to endow the friends in your community with the spiritual insights, knowledge and skills needed to serve the Faith with increasing effectiveness.[11] — 51.26

Since any curriculum is a vehicle for achieving educational goals, the most effective curriculum for institutes has proved to be one that truly trains the believers for service in the fields of expansion and consolidation. Early on in the Four Year Plan it became apparent in many countries that although deepening was essential and must continue, the in-depth study of a book or specialized subject in the institutes would not necessarily result in mobilizing large numbers of Bahá'ís to become active teachers. There are, of course, many important subjects in which believers need to deepen, but the House of Justice in several letters has discouraged training institutes from incorporating specialized topics into their programs at the expense of a focus on a basic sequence of courses. — 51.27

> The House of Justice has reservations, however, on the desirability of involving the Training Institutes in this program. The Training Institutes should be developing and applying a coherent, systematic program for increasing the human resources of the Bahá'í community. Naturally, as part of such a curriculum there will be place for including reference to the law of Ḥuqúqu'lláh and the whole matter of supporting the funds of the Faith as a part of the individual life of the believer and an essential element of Bahá'í community life. However, to involve the Training Institutes in a specific project of educating the members of — 51.28

the community in the law of Ḥuqúqu'lláh, or in preparing training materials, would seem to be a diversion of their main task.[12]

51.29   In designing the program for the education of the members of the Bahá'í community in the Teachings, and in selecting the curricula of summer schools and similar occasions, a National Spiritual Assembly should include all aspects of life, including the choosing of a spouse, but the House of Justice feels that it is important for this to be done in context. It is not felt, however, that this specialized subject is one which would be suitable for training institutes, which have their own clearly defined purpose.[13]

1.3.1 A SYSTEMATIC APPROACH

51.30   The April 1998 document on training institutes indicates that it is a complex task to design curriculum materials that combine the acquisition of knowledge and skills with the cultivation of inner qualities in a sequence that gradually prepares believers for higher and higher levels of service. For this reason national communities were encouraged to utilize materials already prepared in other parts of the world that employed a systematic approach and were designed to empower believers to arise and serve.

51.31   The House of Justice is greatly encouraged by the proposed plan of activities of your institute and is particularly pleased to note that it is concentrating on the execution of its program, which draws upon readily available materials, and has not allowed its energies to be consumed in planning and design.[14]

51.32   As part of its mandate to assess institute curricula that are available in the Bahá'í world, the International Teaching Centre has found the Ruhi Institute materials to be particularly appropriate. Many national communities are using the Ruhi Institute curriculum either as the focus of their training institute or as one of its tracks of study.

51.33   The Ruhi Institute curriculum had been tested and adapted over many years. It has enabled the friends in different countries to get the institute system up and running in a short time. Rather than having the participants be passive listeners to a wide array of unconnected talks, the Ruhi Institute materials seek to engage the friends fully in the process of learning.

Bahá'ís with diverse cultural and educational backgrounds have found the curriculum's deceptively simple approach, based heavily on connecting the believers to the Creative Word, both appealing and empowering.

Even in those countries where the Ruhi Institute materials have been chosen as the main curriculum or as one of the institute tracks, modifications and adaptations for local conditions have occasionally been made. In a few countries a beginning course has been developed for new believers which precedes Book 1. In some areas the Ruhi Institute books have been supplemented with other materials to suit the local requirements. Over time, through systematic educational experience, other sequential curricula will be developed in various parts of the world that display the same coherence that the Ruhi Institute materials have achieved but are derived from the experience of different national communities. 51.34

1.3.2 SEQUENCE OF COURSES

The Universal House of Justice has stressed the importance of a sequence of courses in preparing the friends for the expansion and consolidation work: 51.35

> ... it may be timely for you to consider introducing another component into your institute program. Unlike the courses designed for deepening the generality of the believers, this component would be concerned with helping a certain percentage of the friends, especially young people with some formal education, enhance their capacity to perform the tasks associated with an accelerated process of expansion and consolidation. It would entail choosing a sequence of courses which, building on one another, gradually endow the students with the knowledge, skills and qualities needed to serve the Faith with increasing effectiveness.[15] 51.36

Great strides have been made in involving the friends in training institute courses, but more attention needs to be given to ensure that they systematically proceed through a sequence of courses. 51.37

Once the sequence has been selected, a steadily increasing number of believers are recruited to enter the first basic course, and relatively significant percentages are then helped 51.38

to reach higher and higher courses, enhancing thereby their capacity for service.[16]

51.39   In countries with small Bahá'í populations a large number of the friends have taken not only one course but completed successive courses in a sequence. However, experience has shown that in countries with large Bahá'í populations, most participants study only the first level course. In a community like India, where about 34,000 believers have completed level one, this is undoubtedly a great achievement. Nevertheless, as the number of those entering the institute program steadily increases, so too should the percentage of believers who go on to study the subsequent courses in the sequence. In this way, the development of human resources is characterized by the image of an ever-expanding pyramid. The size of the "pyramid" is an indication of a national community's success in creating human resources to meet its needs for the tasks of expansion and consolidation.

51.40   In countries where the human resources are growing, other tracks of study, in addition to the basic sequence of courses, have been introduced. These tracks may focus on such areas as children's education, literacy training, or health.

1.4 Delivery systems

51.41   Worldwide, the Bahá'ís have experimented with different types of delivery systems in order to extend the reach of their national or regional training institutes. In addition to courses in central locations, several distance education delivery systems have been successfully implemented in a number of countries. These include extension courses, where the program of the national institute is held in an area that can draw on Bahá'ís from a cluster of villages or towns; institute campaigns, where an intensive series of classes is given at the local level over a period of a few weeks; and study circles, where a small group of believers come together on a regular basis in their own locality with a trained tutor who helps them to progress through a selected sequence of courses.

1.4.1 DISTANCE EDUCATION

51.42   During the first two years of the Four Year Plan, in the early stages in the establishment of many institutes, groups of believers were brought to one central facility, either in the capital or in a regional center, for a week or a few weekends to attend training courses and then returned to their home communities. It became apparent, however, that the number of believers who would be able to obtain training with this approach soon reaches a limit. Whether because of the sheer numbers of friends that must pass through the training or because of the cost and inconvenience of traveling and staying in a residential program, distance education has proved to be an effective delivery system. In many instances the House of Justice has stressed the value of this decentralized approach:

> What can expand the institute's coverage is for a sequence   51.43
> of a few well-conceived courses to be selected and a band of
> tutors trained, who then offer the courses at the local level
> throughout the region to groups of eager believers. In this
> way, the number of those studying in the institute program
> at various levels steadily increases.[17]

A decentralized approach to the delivery of courses does   51.44
not transfer responsibility for training to the local institutions
but is a system adopted by the national or regional institute
to extend its program to the grassroots. In several cases, the
House of Justice has clarified the intent of decentralization as
described in the April 1998 document "Training Institutes":

> The solution does not seem to be the establishment of local   51.45
> institutes, independent of the national institute. . . . these
> run the danger of turning into deepening classes. This is not
> to say that every local community should not continue to
> conduct regular deepening programs. But, as far as human
> resource development is concerned, the methodology that
> seems to be most effective in reaching believers at the local
> level is the formation of study circles which are coordinated
> by a national institute or one of its branches.[18]

1.4.2 STUDY CIRCLES

Of the three above-mentioned delivery systems, the most   51.46
widely practiced on all continents is the study circle, sometimes
called a study group, a circle of study, or a circle of learning.
The House of Justice has encouraged this flexible, low cost
form of distance education:

> Initially, such courses might need to be offered at the insti-   51.47
> tute sites, but, as a growing number of tutors are trained,

study circles could eventually be formed throughout the country. Such a system of distance-education seems particularly well suited to the geographical makeup of Papua New Guinea.[19]

51.48   ... the system of delivery of courses through study circles, a system which we understand the national institute of Bolivia is attempting to gradually establish throughout the country, is designed to bring the institute courses to the level of each locality. In this case, a sequence of courses is offered to small groups of believers in villages and towns by tutors trained by the institute itself or a branch operating in the region. Efforts to put into place such a vast system can only flourish in an environment characterized by a spirit of unity and collaboration among all the institutions of the Faith.[20]

51.49   A distinguishing feature of study circles is that in many countries, and across diverse cultures, they have created a new dynamic within the community and have become nuclei of community life and catalysts for teaching, service, and community development. In addition to study of the institute courses, the members of the study circle, both Bahá'ís and non-Bahá'ís, often participate in service and extracurricular activities that bind the group together in fellowship and attract others to this mode of learning. Having experienced the participatory learning style of the courses, the members of the study circle gradually take on a stronger commitment to actively serve and apply the knowledge and skills they are gaining to the work of the Faith. Some members of study circles are eventually trained as tutors and then initiate their own study circles.

51.50   After studying one course, many of the members of a study circle will stay together to go on to the next course, but some may drop out until they are ready and able to pursue a subsequent course. As friends move on to higher level courses, and other friends join at various points in the sequence, the membership of a study circle can gradually change. Although members of study circles will often engage in social and service activities together, no feelings of exclusivity should be allowed to develop among them. Furthermore, the study circles should be guided by the spirit of consultation in planning recreation, teaching, and service activities.

51.51   Since a key purpose of the study circle is to raise human resources that are to be utilized in the community, the Local

Spiritual Assemblies, the area teaching committees, and the Auxiliary Board members will need to know where they are located and draw on their members for the tasks of teaching and consolidation. Several letters written on behalf of the House of Justice address the importance of collaboration in supporting the friends in their teaching endeavors:

> . . . in a locality where the Local Spiritual Assembly is functioning, it would collaborate with the national institute or its branch in supporting the work of the study circles, while pursuing its own plans for the expansion and consolidation of the Cause.[21]

51.52

Personal teaching requires stimulation from the institutions; it must be fostered by National and Local Spiritual Assemblies, on the one hand, and the Counsellors and their auxiliaries, on the other. The institutions should also nurture and support the members of study circles and other individuals in the community in acts of service that come about through personal initiative.

51.53

1.4.3 TUTORS AND TUTOR TRAINING

The experience of the past few years has shown that the selection and training of tutors are crucial for the extension of the institute process to the grassroots and for the success of the study circles. In many parts of the world this realization has led to a focus on raising up an ever-growing number of tutors, either from among the participants in the study circles or, initially, from experienced believers who take part in events that combine institute courses with tutor training.

51.54

Since the effectiveness of the tutors is critical to the success of the institute process, more and more attention has been given to the content of the training, the skills needed to organize a study circle and lead the participants through the courses, and the attitudes necessary both to nurture the participants in their learning and maintain the cohesion of the group. Tutors require training in how to keep the participants focused on the material, how to formulate questions that stimulate reflection, and how to foster active participation within the group. They need to combine the qualities of love, humility, and patience, with the dedication, perseverance, and commitment required to create a spiritual atmosphere conducive to learning. It should be emphasized that tutor training is not a one-time event but

51.55

an ongoing activity where tutors come together periodically to share experiences and ideas. In many countries educated youth have proved to be an excellent source for institute tutors.

51.56 Regional coordinators, who often come from the ranks of tutors, will need these same abilities, plus some administrative capacity to maintain records, track the progress of the study circles, organize training programs, supervise tutors, and coordinate the work of the institute with the activities of the institutions in the area.

2. Institutes in Action

2.1 *Creating human resources*

51.57 As believers in each country advance through a sequence of courses and their skills and abilities are enhanced, the responsibility then falls on the institutions of the Faith to see that the energies, talents, and newly acquired skills of these friends are channeled in some form of active service to the Cause. In this regard, the House of Justice has pointed out:

51.58 Ample opportunities should be given to them to put into practice what they have learned, and in this connection, you will need to create within your community an encouraging environment, one in which the friends feel empowered to step forward, whatever their capacities may be, and take up the work of the Faith.[22]

51.59 One of the most exciting aspects of a review of the accomplishments of the Four Year Plan has been to survey the development of the training institutes worldwide and to take note of the successes national communities have reported in advancing the process of entry by troops. Each continent has had its own challenges and record of achievements in the growth of training institutes. Overall, however, a pattern of the institute process has emerged that is not confined to one country or part of the world but represents a common direction for the Bahá'í world in its development of human resources.

51.60 Previously Africa had several years of experience with institutes, but a shift had to be made from offering deepening courses to establishing training programs. In order to implement this new orientation, a focus was placed on tutor training and the translation of institute materials into French and Portuguese, as well as many local languages. Training institutes in several national communities in Africa have made significant advances, extending the reach of the institute process throughout each country while also initiating social and economic development activities. The Uganda Bahá'í Institute for Development has an impressive delivery system of courses; more than 1,500 friends have completed a level one course and 35 percent of them have gone through higher level courses. In Zambia the training institute has had similar success. Nearly 1,000 individuals have completed the first course and one-third of these participants have completed higher courses in the sequence. Both Uganda and Zambia have systematically trained tutors—185 and 144 respectively—in order to support their delivery systems.

The Americas have witnessed a tremendous acceleration   51.61
in the creation of human resources. There are more than 500 study circles in Latin America, and nearly 1,000 tutors have been trained. In Brazil alone the development of human resources has been impressive: there are 568 tutors and 260 study circles, with more than 5,000 believers participating in the institute process of which some 400 are junior youth. The Ruhi Institute, located in Colombia, has provided training to more than 40 members of National Assemblies and institute boards and has prepared a group of 16 resource persons who can advise institutes in different countries about their programs. In the United States, training in the methodology of the Core Curriculum, one of the tracks of the institutes in that country, has been provided to Bahá'ís from more than 52 countries.

In all 39 countries of Asia that have National Assemblies,   51.62
training institutes have been established and have recorded the highest levels of participation, in terms of absolute numbers as well as percentages. Approximately 60,000 friends have attended at least one training institute course, and of those, some 34,000 were in India. Nepal has shown a high degree of participation with approximately 20 percent of the Bahá'ís having completed the level one course. In Russia and the other countries of the Commonwealth of Independent States a large percentage of the national communities have attended at least one institute course—for example, 60 percent of the Bahá'ís in Armenia and 35 percent of the friends in Kazakhstan. In the Arabian countries, partly because of the small size of their communities, the percentages rise even higher—76 percent in Bahrain, 43 percent in Kuwait, and 36 percent in Oman.

51.63   This widespread involvement of the believers in the institutes is reflected in the achievements the national communities have made in the translation of curriculum into local languages—14 in India, 10 in Southeast Asia, and 5 in Central Asia. Most of the institutes in Asia, as in Africa, have also developed distinct tracks in their institutes so that in addition to a basic sequence, there are programs for literacy training, moral classes, and in some cases "higher learning" courses.

51.64   Like the institutes in Africa, those in Australasia are focusing their energies increasingly on the offering of training programs, rather than deepening courses alone. Outside resource persons are being utilized to train English- and French-speaking tutors for Australia, New Zealand, and 10 Pacific islands. A sequence of courses and study circles have been established in several states of Australia and on the major islands of Hawaii. In Papua New Guinea the institute organized an efficient network for delivering courses, mostly deepening in nature, to nearly two-thirds of the believers. Now the institute is focusing on delivering a sequence of courses that will train a percentage of these friends in the tasks of expansion and consolidation.

51.65   Europe refocused its training institutes on a sequence of courses and a decentralized delivery system. From the Baltics to the Balkans a host of 125 tutors has been trained and continent-wide resource persons are also being identified to assist national communities with training institutes. Over a nine-month period 12 regional tutor training seminars were held in England, France, Germany, Spain, Sweden, the Czech Republic, Albania, Romania, and Belarus. Out of this effort scores of study circles have been launched in country after country.

2.2 Impact on teaching and growth

51.66   Although there is always a range of factors that contribute to growth in a community, reports of achievements in the teaching field from Counsellors and National Assemblies indicate that these developments are increasingly influenced, either directly or indirectly, by the institute process.

51.67   In Bangladesh, where the training institute process is well established, over 11,000 believers entered the Faith in the third year of the Four Year Plan. A survey carried out by members of the institutions in that country determined that nearly 8,000 of these enrollments were the result of individual teaching by institute participants, particularly the tutors. In South

Africa, it has been reported that between the first two years of the Four Year Plan and the third year of the Plan, when the institute process was well under way, there was an increase of 40 percent in the number of new enrollments. The National Spiritual Assembly has concluded that this level of growth is due primarily to individual initiative stimulated by the training institute courses.

Local teaching projects and teaching campaigns have been 51.68 taken up with increasing vigor and have provided a major avenue of service for institute participants. In addition to the 30 percent increase since 1998 in the number of teaching projects funded by the Teaching Centre, news of several hundred locally initiated projects, many of them self-supporting, demonstrated the upswing in the tempo of teaching in different parts of the world.

Reports also suggest that there has been a marked increase 51.69 in the number of firesides around the world, an indication of the level of teaching undertaken at the initiative of the individual. In Ireland a national program entitled "Core Project," whose goal is to establish 20 firesides, has been operating in conjunction with a series of training institute courses. A similar trend has been noted in Slovakia, which launched a national fireside campaign during the last year of the Four Year Plan. In the southern region of the United States individual initiative has manifested itself in a growing number of firesides, particularly by institute participants. There has also been a notable rise in the number of firesides across the southern part of Australia in Victoria, New South Wales, and Western Australia, as well as in some island communities of the Pacific, such as Tonga, where over 660 souls have entered the Faith in the last three years. The National Spiritual Assembly of Japan has far exceeded its fireside goal for the Four Year Plan.

Parallel to this, and contributing to the overall spiritual 51.70 atmosphere needed for teaching and growth, is the dramatic increase in the number of devotional meetings worldwide. The April 1998 document on training institutes mentions the establishment of devotional meetings as one of the first acts of service that those who have completed institute courses can carry out. Such meetings have been initiated in several countries of Asia, where hundreds exist in India alone, and in many countries of Latin America.

2.3 Direct instruments of teaching

51.71   In the same document on training institutes it was suggested that Bahá'í communities that are small in size but have a large percentage of knowledgeable believers consider having their institutes open courses to non-Bahá'ís. A number of enrollments directly resulting from institute courses have been reported in countries such as France, Greece, Korea, and Nepal, as well as in countries with larger Bahá'í populations such as Ethiopia, Taiwan, Turkey, and the United States. In addition, the Baltic States, Belarus, Finland, and the Ukraine are opening some of their courses to non-Bahá'ís. Countries that have experienced large-scale expansion, such as India, Bangladesh, and the Philippines, are also benefiting from this approach to teaching. These countries have found that the majority of non-Bahá'ís who participate in the institute programs accept the Faith by the completion of the first course.

3. Systematization of Teaching
   (Area Growth Programs)

51.72   In order to realize the potential for growth that the training of human resources has brought about, attention must be given to the systematization of teaching efforts. In its message to the Bahá'ís of the world announcing the Twelve Month Plan and the Five Year Plan, the House of Justice presented this challenge to communities:

51.73   It is essential that, during the one-year effort, national and regional institutes everywhere bring into full operation the programs and systems that they have now devised. National communities should enter the Five Year Plan confident that the acquisition of knowledge, qualities and skills of service by large contingents of believers, with the aid of a sequence of courses, will proceed unhindered. Ample attention must also be given to further systematization of teaching efforts, whether undertaken by the individual or directed by the institutions.[23]

51.74   With the further systematization of teaching efforts in mind, the International Teaching Centre has identified certain patterns of expansion and consolidation that lead to a process of accelerated and sustained growth. This approach to systematized teaching is being developed in the context of an "Area Growth

Program," which focuses on a relatively small geographical area with a manageable number of localities. At the heart of the Area Growth Program is a systematic institute process under the direction of the national or regional institute. As a growing number of believers pass through the courses of the training institute, the pool of human resources for various expansion and consolidation undertakings increases. Auxiliary Board members and their assistants will encourage these believers to utilize their newly acquired capabilities in teaching the Faith and in acts of service, such as holding devotional meetings, deepening one's fellow believers, and conducting children's classes. Grassroots involvement, where the local believers consult together, take action, and support one another in individual or group activities, is a fundamental characteristic of an Area Growth Program.

Institute participants, as well as other local believers, will   51.75
take part in area-wide seminars and conferences, regional teaching campaigns, and small socio-economic development projects. Gradually, local collective endeavors will emerge, area committees and Local Spiritual Assemblies will formulate their own plans for expansion and consolidation, and the friends will begin to shoulder the responsibilities of systematic growth in their communities.

The process of learning about growth that was launched   51.76
with the Four Year Plan has confirmed the vision the House of Justice gave in its Riḍván message of 153 [1996] that advancing the process of entry by troops depends on raising up large numbers of trained believers. As increasing numbers of Bahá'ís go through the institute courses and, in so doing, develop a stronger Bahá'í identity and desire to serve, a dynamic for growth is created in our communities. Even if only a fraction of the participants become active teachers, having more and more Bahá'ís proceed through a sequence of courses generates a spirit that motivates the believers and revitalizes the community. For this reason the strategy of the Area Growth Programs is to have the teaching and expansion work revolve around the institutes.

4. Challenges for Training Institutes

The extraordinary growth of institutes around the world   51.77
has brought with it a number of challenges. Some of these are general issues that many communities face while others are

specific to continents or individual countries. A general priority is for national communities to reflect on the achievements of their institutes, to assess the efficacy of their approaches, and to modify certain elements in light of experience or new circumstances. This analysis and reflection should take place periodically between National Assemblies and Counsellors and by institute boards, Auxiliary Board members, and Regional Councils where applicable.

4.1 *Quality and effectiveness*

51.78 During the Four Year Plan, most national communities worked on the establishment and initial functioning of the institute process. At the start, a focus on generating institutional capacity to deliver a few basic courses generally took precedence over a concern with program quality. Gradually, increasing attention is being given to the challenge of striking a balance between quantity and quality. While it remains a priority to think in terms of reaching large numbers of friends with the institute program, attention at the same time must be given to improving its overall effectiveness. As institutes strive to upgrade the quality of training and the delivery of courses, they will come closer to fulfilling the aim of raising up "large numbers of believers who are trained to foster and facilitate the process of entry by troops with efficiency and love."[24]

4.2 *Illiteracy*

51.79 A great number of countries suffer from low literacy rates. In some populations or areas, the rate is so low as to pose a challenge to the institute process. The House of Justice has stressed that institutes need not be held back at the outset because of this concern.

51.80 It should be remembered that not every believer in Tanzania will necessarily participate in your institute program. Rather, a certain percentage of the friends will need to receive training in order to enhance their capacity to carry out the tasks of expansion and consolidation, including the teaching and deepening of the generality of the believers. At this early stage in the establishment of the institute, then, the question of illiteracy should not be a central concern. The immediate challenge before you is to help a large number of the many capable members of your community, especially young people with some formal education, progress through a sequence of a few basic courses. Once this has been accomplished, it may be possible for the institute to expand its program to include a second track of courses for the development of human resources in the area of social and economic development, including literacy.[25]

Although the present institute courses are geared to believers with basic education, efforts to address problems of illiteracy can be given more attention as the institute develops, possibly through offering a literacy course in a track for social and economic development. This would ensure that there will continue to be a ready population to undergo training and also guarantee that certain groups with a high degree of illiteracy, such as women, are not left behind in the process of developing human resources.

51.81

4.3 *Resource persons*

Institute resource persons are Bahá'ís who have had substantial training and national level experience in the development of training institutes. The last two years of the Four Year Plan witnessed a greater appreciation by the institutions of the Faith of the use of resource persons. Deployed at the discretion of the Continental Boards of Counsellors, they have played a significant and beneficial role in consulting with national and regional institutions about the institute process and in the training of coordinators and tutors. Excellent results have been achieved from such training programs on all five continents. The Teaching Centre would like to see a core of such individuals on every continent, available to assist institutions with clarifying concepts, training tutors, and enhancing the capacity of institutes. These outside consultants, however, are no substitute for the process of evaluation and reflection that National Assemblies, together with the Counsellors, must undertake and sustain in order for the training institutes to become fully indigenous and institutionalized.

51.82

4.4 *Infrastructure*

In the initial stages in the growth of an institute there has not been an emphasis on acquiring buildings for the program. In this respect the House of Justice has indicated:

51.83

51.84   With regard to the permanent training institute, you will need office space to maintain the files and administration of this organization, but the institute courses will need to reach a widely spread Bahá'í population. Access to physical facilities for institute courses will of course be necessary, but should probably not require the acquisition of permanent institute buildings. . . . The House of Justice is concerned that matters related to the acquisition and maintenance of a new institute building . . . would require resources which would be better used for the development of the institute program itself.[26]

51.85   During the past four years similar advice from the House of Justice has also been given to national communities with extensive institute programs. However, as the 26 December 1995 message to the Conference of the Continental Boards of Counsellors indicated, the institute, "at some stage of its development, may require a building of its own."[27] No doubt the question of infrastructure will soon need to be considered carefully, particularly in countries where large numbers of friends are moving through a sequence of courses.

51.86   The question of infrastructure is related not only to buildings but also to arrangements needed to maintain records and statistics, to stay in contact with students, and to put in place an efficient tracking system. The House of Justice has commented on such developments:

51.87   It now wishes us to commend you on the steps you have taken to create a Desk at your National Office dedicated to the systematization and dissemination of information on human resource development. Keeping the community informed of the status of your institute program and the accomplishments of those taking part in it will help you considerably to maintain enthusiasm among the friends for training. In this and many other ways, the Human Resource Desk will undoubtedly be of great assistance to you.[28]

4.5 *Deputization of institute staff*

51.88   In addition to collaborating with National Assemblies on the areas of budget, management, curriculum, and course delivery, Counsellors and Auxiliary Board members have been called upon to arouse the commitment of the friends to promote the teaching work through the deputization of institute staff, an opportunity introduced by the Universal House of Justice in its Riḍván 153 [1996] message. This new measure has given the friends yet another avenue to fulfill Bahá'u'lláh's injunction to propagate the Faith of God and that "Whoso is unable, it is his duty to appoint him who will, in his stead, proclaim this Revelation. . . ." The House of Justice has explained how the call for deputization falls within the framework of teaching and depends on individual response:

> With the creation of training institutes across the globe, an added opportunity for a more direct involvement in deputization presents itself to the individual; the House of Justice trusts therefore that the friends can be helped to feel some connection with the specific centers of teaching activity to which their offerings for deputization are sent.[29]   51.89

Although local, regional and national institutions are informing the friends of the importance of their sacred teaching obligation and of the opportunities for deputization, the Counsellors and Auxiliary Board members are in an advantageous position to reach individuals at the grassroots and summon forth their interest and commitment to this worldwide enterprise. The House of Justice has explained: 51.90

> It is for this reason that the Continental Counsellors and their auxiliaries have been called upon to play a distinctive role in this matter as officers bearing a particular responsibility for propagation, for the Auxiliary Board members and their assistants operate at the grassroots of the community and are able readily not only to stimulate individuals to teach but also to urge them, if their material circumstances allow, to respond to the need for deputization.[30]   51.91

It is up to the Counsellors and Board members to provide the friends with detailed information about current needs for deputization, including the level of support required by institute teachers in various parts of the world.   51.92

* * *

In conclusion, it might be said that the "dynamic state of transformation" referred to in the Riḍván 156 [1999] message aptly describes the impact of training institutes on our communities during the Four Year Plan. The institute has become central to the life of the community and is beginning to generate human resources to a degree that was not imagined   51.93

at the outset of the Plan. Clearly it is the institute process that is at the core of the coherent vision that is guiding us in advancing the process of entry by troops. As the House of Justice expressed in the same message: "Understanding of the necessity for systematization in the development of human resources is everywhere taking hold."[31] It is also understood that the process upon which we have embarked through the training institutes is a long-term one.

51.94   The learning that has taken place about the systematic development of human resources will now be extended to the process of learning about the systematization of teaching. Through the implementation of Area Growth Programs around the world a new body of experience will emerge that will inform our approach to teaching and our strategies about growth for the next two decades. These efforts at systematic and unabated action represent the deep desire and commitment of every Bahá'í "to fulfill the intentions of a Plan whose major aim is to accelerate that process which will make it possible for growing numbers of the world's people to find the Object of their quest and thus to build a united, peaceful and prosperous life."[32]

52

Building Momentum
A Coherent Approach to Growth

a document prepared by
the International Teaching Centre

April 2003

In its message of 17 January 2003 to the Bahá'ís of the world, the Universal House of Justice presents a cogent analysis of the progress of the Bahá'í world in advancing the process of entry by troops since the beginning of the Five Year Plan. Utilizing the 17 January message as the framework for reflecting on our "collective experience," this document reviews the learning which underlies that experience and offers further perspectives on the challenges of promoting systematic growth. The document is divided into five sections:

52.1

1. A Vision of Growth
    1.1   Categorizing clusters
    1.2   Establishing priorities
    1.3   Proceeding through a sequence of courses
    1.4   "Evoking the spirit of enterprise"

2. Movement of Clusters from One Stage of Growth to the Next
    2.1   Opening virgin areas
    2.2   Establishing the institute process in emerging clusters
    2.3   Advancing clusters with a vigorous institute process
    2.4   Accelerating expansion and consolidation in advanced clusters

3. Enhancing Institutional Capacity
    3.1   Managing the process of growth
    3.2   Reexamining administrative approaches
    3.3   Facilitating individual initiative
    3.4   Serving large numbers

4. Change in the Culture of the Bahá'í Community
   4.1 Learning and planning at the grassroots
   4.2 Maintaining a focus
   4.3 Empowering the rank and file
   4.4 An "outward-looking orientation"

5. The Movement of Humanity toward Bahá'u'lláh

* * *

Building Momentum
A Coherent Approach to Growth

1. A Vision of Growth

52.2 During the past two years the believers and institutions worldwide have focused their efforts on implementing the fundamental strategy of the Five Year Plan for creating a culture of growth, a strategy succinctly described in a message from the Universal House of Justice:

52.3 The Five Year Plan . . . requires concentrated and sustained attention to two essential movements. The first is the steady flow of believers through the sequence of courses offered by training institutes, for the purpose of developing the human resources of the Cause. The second, which receives its impetus from the first, is the movement of geographic clusters from one stage of growth to the next.[1]

52.4 These two movements have been at the heart of the learning experience of the Bahá'í world and are the focus of this analysis. The first movement had its beginnings with the establishment of a network of training institutes during the Four Year Plan. The second got under way only in the Five Year Plan, when national communities, in response to the guidance of the House of Justice, began by mapping their territories into geographic clusters.

52.5 . . . National Spiritual Assemblies proceeded with relative ease to divide the territories under their jurisdiction into areas consisting of adjacent localities, called clusters, using criteria that were purely geographic and social and did not relate to the strength of local Bahá'í communities.[2]

In its Riḍván 2002 message the House of Justice described 52.6 how the exercise of clustering and categorizing has given the institutions and believers a vision of systematic growth: "Such a mapping . . . makes it possible to realize a pattern of well-ordered expansion and consolidation."

1.1 *Categorizing clusters*

Acknowledging that in some cases cluster boundaries 52.7 would be only a "reasonable approximation,"[3] which might be modified through experience, National Spiritual Assemblies categorized the clusters according to broad stages of the development of the Faith as outlined in the message of 9 January 2001 from the House of Justice. In this connection the House of Justice has stressed the following point:

> To assign a cluster to one or another category is not to make 52.8 a statement about status. Rather, it is a way of evaluating its capacity for growth, in order that an approach compatible with its evolving development can be adopted.[4]

In order to systematically advance the growth process, 52.9 National Assemblies and Regional Bahá'í Councils sought to establish criteria for determining when a cluster would move from one category to the next. In some cases such criteria were expressed in numerical goals, while in others a qualitative description was adopted. Defining minimum criteria for each category is a process that grows principally out of experience. In its message of 17 January 2003 the House of Justice described the importance of this task:

> . . . the task of refining the criteria needed for valid 52.10 assessments is proving to be an ongoing challenge to institutions. . . . Rigid criteria are obviously counterproductive, but a well-defined scheme to carry out evaluation is essential.[5]

Wherever Regional Councils exist, they are generally in the 52.11 best position to determine the current categories of the clusters within their jurisdiction; Auxiliary Board members and agencies at the cluster level can also provide indispensable input. According to the House of Justice, "two criteria seem especially important" in this evaluation:

> . . . the strength of the human resources raised up by the 52.12 training institute for the expansion and consolidation of

the Faith in the cluster, and the ability of the institutions to mobilize these resources in the field of service.[6]

52.13 What is essential is that the institutions periodically assess the progress that has been made so that the strategies being applied in a cluster are "compatible with its evolving development."[7] When warranted, the classification of a cluster is changed and new priorities are set.

1.2 *Establishing priorities*

52.14 In addition to classifying clusters according to their capacity for growth, national and regional institutions set priorities as to which clusters would receive greater focus early in the Plan. At times this involved opening a few virgin clusters and advancing some weak ones, but generally, concentration was on the well-developed clusters in a country. Once the institutions came to understand the types of strategies needed to advance each category of clusters, it became apparent that it was advantageous to select a few promising clusters where the conditions for accelerated growth were the most favorable and then work toward establishing an intensive program of growth. The following guidance in a letter written on behalf of the House of Justice to a National Assembly reflects the advice given in such instances:

52.15 An important challenge now before you is to ensure that one or two clusters in Austria reach the level at which intensive growth programs can be established. This will involve, foremost, helping the institute in your country develop to a more advanced stage, endowed with the capacity to accompany a significant percentage of individuals up to the point in its sequence of courses where they can be trained to act as tutors and multiply the number of study circles in the clusters selected. Given the receptivity displayed in the past by some of the minority groups in Austria . . . you would clearly do well to choose at least one cluster with a large representation of such a population.[8]

52.16 And to another National Assembly, the House of Justice explained the need for focus on a few advanced areas of high potential:

52.17 In consultation with the Councils and the Counsellors, you have identified several small geographic areas in which the local communities are gaining strength through a strong institute process. As the second year of the Plan fast approaches, the House of Justice hopes that, if it has not already been done, two or three of these clusters will be selected to receive special attention in the coming months so that they will soon reach the point where it will be possible to consider launching an intensive program of growth in each.[9]

1.3 *Proceeding through a sequence of courses*

In its 17 January message the House of Justice addresses the effort in which the believers are currently and principally engaged: 52.18

> Focus in almost every country has now turned to stimulating the movement of its priority clusters from their current stage of growth to the next. What has become strikingly clear is that progress in this respect depends largely on the efficacy of the parallel process aimed at helping an ever-increasing number of friends to move through the main sequence of courses offered by the institute serving the area.[10] 52.19

The impetus given to the institute process in the past two years and, in particular, to having the believers proceed through a sequence of courses was felt on all continents. The number of participants who have completed at least one institute course in the basic sequence continues to rise, but the most significant achievement is that a swelling stream of friends has proceeded through higher level courses. For example, 18 months into the Five Year Plan, more than 10,000 believers had completed Ruhi Institute Book 6, accounting for an increase of over 500 percent since April 2001, and more than 8,000 had completed Ruhi Institute Book 7, resulting in a dramatically enlarged pool of trained tutors. 52.20

Gradually most national communities around the world adopted for their basic sequence of courses the Ruhi Institute curriculum, which had been developed over many years specifically in response to large-scale expansion. In light of the focus and energy being devoted to furthering the institute process in every national community, concerns were expressed by some believers about the emphasis on training and the use of a uniform curriculum. In such a wide-scale enterprise of taking 52.21

great numbers of friends through a set curriculum, it is to be expected that some individuals might not find the materials suited to their learning style. Responding to this circumstance, the House of Justice made the following comment in a letter written on its behalf to an individual believer:

52.22   . . . reports from countries of diverse backgrounds suggest that many national Bahá'í communities which have adopted the books of the Ruhi Institute are finding them highly effective. It is natural that any given educational program would not appeal to everyone and that some would not wish to participate. . . . Nevertheless, a choice has been made by the institutions in your country to offer certain courses to the believers in the context of their plans to advance the process of entry by troops. The House of Justice is happy to see from your letter that you respect this decision and do not want to make your own evaluation of the program a cause for disunity.[11]

52.23   In another letter written on behalf of the House of Justice, the relationship of the individual believer to the institute process is given further clarification:

52.24   To say that the institute is only useful for newly enrolled believers and those who read little is not correct. Many mature and deepened believers are participating in the institute process, both as students and as teachers of various courses, in an effort to contribute directly to the promotion of entry by troops in their respective countries. Through such participation they have furthered their understanding of the requisites of growth and of the action required to maintain it, have caught fresh glimpses of spiritual truths, and have developed their skills and abilities of service. Far from interfering with their own study of the Writings, each according to his or her own capacity and needs, their association with a training institute has enhanced the process. Yet clearly such participation is not a requirement for every Bahá'í, who, in the final analysis, can choose the manner in which he or she will serve the Faith. What is essential is that the institute process be supported even by those who do not wish to take part in it.[12]

52.25   At the same time the House of Justice has explained that no special designation should be accorded to those who are studying in the institute or serving as tutors, nor should the friends feel any demarcation based on participation in the institute:

> It is quite reasonable to expect that, as far as training 52.26
> by the institute is concerned, certain courses would have
> as their prerequisite the completion of other courses.
> However, this notion should not be carried over into
> other Bahá'í activities, and clearly no distinction should be
> made between "trained" and "untrained" believers in the
> country. That for certain types of service the qualifications
> of the believers would need to be taken into account is
> natural. Yet the way should be open for all the friends, ir-
> respective of the degree of their knowledge and experience,
> to participate in the affairs of the Faith. . . .[13]

Those communities that did not become absorbed with 52.27
issues of curriculum but turned their attention to putting a
system in place were able to learn more quickly how to deliver
their courses to large numbers of believers and to consolidate
the institute process. Nevertheless, by the outset of the Five
Year Plan the believers in most countries had not proceeded
beyond the first few courses of the institute. The challenge
for National Spiritual Assemblies of furthering the institute
process and maintaining a clear focus was aptly described in a
letter written on behalf of the House of Justice to a National
Assembly:

> To help large numbers of believers go through a sequence 52.28
> of courses is a formidable task, involving systematic work
> with an increasing number of tutors, the establishment of
> study circles, and measures for monitoring the progress of
> the participants. The friends in charge of the process need
> to have clarity of vision and should be allowed to carry out
> their mission without distraction.[14]

1.4 *"Evoking the spirit of enterprise"*

During the Four Year Plan, guidance from the House of 52.29
Justice had stressed that as the believers completed higher
courses in the sequence, their capacity to serve the Cause would
be enhanced. In its message of 17 January this dynamic was
confirmed:

> The rise in activity around the world testifies to the success 52.30
> of these courses in evoking the spirit of enterprise required

to carry out the divers actions that growth in a cluster, at whatever stage, demands.[15]

52.31   Nowhere was this "rise in activity" more evidenced than in the increase in study circles and other core activities. According to the data available at the Bahá'í World Centre, the number of study circles worldwide increased from 3,600 in April 2001 to almost 9,000 in October 2002. The participation of individuals in devotional gatherings and children's classes increased by 80 and 63 percent respectively in the same period, with the highest percentage rise in both categories registered by countries in Asia. For the most part this proliferation of community activities was the expression of individual initiative by believers who translated into action what they had internalized from their training institute courses.

2. Movement of Clusters from One Stage of Growth to the Next

2.1 Opening virgin areas

52.32   The newfound zeal and initiative of the believers have been manifested at one level in the opening of virgin clusters. Although in the first two years of the Five Year Plan most countries have focused on advancing well-developed clusters toward intensive programs of growth, whenever virgin areas were opened to the Faith, a concentrated effort was made to lay a solid foundation for systematic expansion. Cognizant of the advice from the House of Justice of the value of pioneers being "experienced in institute programs,"[16] National Assemblies encouraged homefront pioneers (short- and long-term) who settled in unopened clusters to promote the institute process. In general, study circles represented a principal means of teaching in these areas, along with devotional gatherings and firesides, as human resources began to emerge. This met with a warm response from the House of Justice:

52.33   As we had hoped, goals for the opening of virgin clusters are being readily met by enthusiastic participants of institute programs who, equipped with the knowledge and skills acquired through training courses, set out to establish the Faith in a new area and bring a fledgling community into being.[17]

In Canada, the National Assembly announced the goal   52.34
of settling homefront pioneers in all of the country's nine
unopened clusters by Riḍván 2002. To this end the Assembly
organized two national institute campaigns of five weeks each
whereby a total of 39 believers completed the books in their
institute's sequence. By Riḍván 2002, six of the nine goal areas
had been filled, and five of the pioneers were trained tutors. As
of September 2002, all the homefront goals were achieved.

Foremost among the strategies for virgin clusters, therefore,   52.35
have been encouraging homefront pioneers to become trained
as tutors and implementing homefront pioneering projects that
emphasize the establishment of the institute process in these
areas. It has sometimes proved advantageous to identify goal
areas adjacent to well-developed clusters, as these are more
accessible to believers who can facilitate study circles. In fact,
with a growing number of tutors being trained in the well-
developed clusters, homefront goals can increasingly be met
when such friends come forward to offer this kind of service.
Reports on pioneer movement during the first year of the Five
Year Plan indicate that about 725 believers arose to pioneer on
the home front, nearly half of them in the Americas.

2.2 *Establishing the institute process in emerging clusters*

Clusters at the next level of development, characterized in   52.36
the 9 January message as having "a few isolated localities and
groups," often encompass a broad spectrum of Bahá'í activity,
depending on the country, the history of growth in the cluster,
and whether the area is rural or urban.

Two different conditions have predominated in this   52.37
category. There are a number of clusters that experienced large-
scale growth in the past but had no functioning Local Spiritual
Assemblies and very few active believers. Also prevalent are
clusters that had, in addition to isolated localities and groups,
functioning Local Assemblies, some with only basic capacity
and others with longstanding experience and active communities, but with minimal or no institute activity. The general
approach in both these types of clusters has been to strengthen
the institute process, but the means and pace have differed
according to their particular circumstances.

In clusters that have experienced large-scale expansion,   52.38
an approach that has proved effective is for a teaching team
to reestablish contact with responsive friends and gradually

introduce institute courses in the area. In recommending such an approach to a National Assembly that faced the challenge of having areas with great numbers of believers who had not been contacted for years, the House of Justice explained:

52.39 In many countries of the world, meeting this challenge requires that attention be concentrated on those localities for which long lists of believers often exist, but which, with the passage of time, have ceased to have any Bahá'í activity. In your case you would do well to establish a specific program according to which teams of able teachers would visit such communities one after another, spend time with the believers they can locate, and teach receptive souls until the conditions become favorable for the institute to enter and offer its courses.[18]

52.40 In several national communities in Asia, believers who had completed their institutes' second book in the sequence undertook visits of this kind. In Bangladesh, India, and the Philippines, this effort resulted in a number of believers' joining institute courses and devotional gatherings and becoming reactivated after many years. In the letter cited above, the House of Justice elaborated further on this approach:

52.41 ... the purpose of such campaigns in local communities which have been dormant for years would not be to find every Bahá'í whose name appears on the membership list and verify his or her status. The list of names should be considered, rather, as a starting point, leading to opportunities to meet individuals who are willing to engage in meaningful conversation, exploring spiritual realities and learning more and more about the Faith.[19]

52.42 In clusters that had active communities but lacked a strong presence of the institute, a first requirement has been for the institutions and believers in such areas to acquire a clear vision of the pivotal role of the training institute in the implementation of the Plan and to commit themselves to this priority. Once this is grasped, these clusters can progress fairly rapidly to develop the institute process.

52.43 In practical terms, advancing the institute process in this category of clusters has meant increasing the number of tutors and study circles so that more believers become involved in the institute process. This objective can be achieved in a number of ways, depending on the level of human resources in the cluster—for example, by short-term homefront pioneers serving as tutors, by tutors from a nearby cluster facilitating study circles, or by friends from these emerging clusters participating in centralized training courses or extension courses in their area.

As more study circles have been established in these clusters, a growing number of friends have become engaged in the study of the first one or two books of the institute. However, the House of Justice highlighted the value of putting in place a system for taking believers through a full sequence of courses and the potential impact of this arrangement: 52.44

> The challenge is not simply to have a certain percentage study one or two courses, but a sequence of several courses through an effective system of distance education. And if the institute succeeds in accomplishing this, there should be a corresponding increase in the tempo of the teaching work as more and more friends arise to serve the Faith. A steady stream of newly enrolled believers will, in turn, enter the institute's program, and in this way the system as a whole will be in a constant state of expansion.[20] 52.45

2.3 *Advancing clusters with a vigorous institute process*

In order "to ensure that one or two clusters . . . reach the level at which intensive growth programs can be established,"[21] a great deal of attention has been directed toward further developing strong clusters and preparing them for intensive growth. The principal means to advance these clusters have been institute campaigns, reflection meetings, and a gradual multiplication of core activities. This latter objective is most easily fulfilled by inviting seekers to these activities. The experience of the institutions and believers in this category of clusters has been substantial and instructive. 52.46

2.3.1 INSTITUTE CAMPAIGNS

Although the meaning of a "vigorous" institute process was interpreted in a variety of ways, efforts to further the institute process in the more well-developed clusters have involved taking significant numbers of friends through the sequence of courses and rapidly increasing the number of trained tutors. In some instances this has been swiftly and effectively accomplished 52.47

through institute campaigns, which have augmented ongoing efforts to expand the number of study circles. In most instances these campaigns have been designed to enable the believers who have already completed the first few books in the sequence, and preferably have served as tutors, to move in an accelerated manner through the remaining books. This process has generated a great deal of enthusiasm and helped create a sizable group of capable believers who have begun to understand "the prerequisites for sustainable growth."[22]

52.48   In Asiatic Russia an institute campaign in the first few months of the Five Year Plan resulted in 76 believers completing all six books of the institute and becoming prepared to act as tutors for any of the books in the sequence. Urban clusters such as Perth, Australia; Minsk, Belarus; Vancouver, Canada; Ulaanbaatar, Mongolia; Karachi, Pakistan; and Los Angeles, the United States; and well-developed rural or semi-urban clusters in, for example, Cameroon, the Central African Republic, Kenya, India, and Italy undertook such campaigns and registered immediate gains in the number of study circles in the clusters. The House of Justice commented on this type of endeavor:

52.49   It is most encouraging to see that the progress of this work [the internal development of the clusters] is being energized through the training institute process, which was considerably strengthened . . . by the campaigns undertaken in many countries to increase the number of trained tutors.[23]

52.50   In areas with active, deepened believers, the progression of individuals through the sequence of courses has moved quickly, once the community members committed themselves to the process. A good example of this dynamic is evidenced in the experience of Western Australia. A concentrated focus in this state on involving increasing numbers of friends in the institute, aided by a series of campaigns, resulted in more than half of its 1,500 believers participating in institute courses. In less than three months the number of study circles, which included seekers, doubled from 52 to 103 and as a consequence of this "increase in the tempo of the teaching work," 36 new believers entered the Faith. This was three times the number of new enrollments recorded for each of the previous two years.

2.3.2 MULTIPLICATION OF CORE ACTIVITIES

Movement of the cluster toward the next stage of development is directly associated with "the multiplication of study circles, devotional meetings and children's classes, and the expansion they engender."[24] As the pool of trained human resources grows, an increase in these and other activities occurs naturally. As indicated, the attention given in the past two years to training more tutors has had a measurable impact on the number of study circles worldwide. Not only has this figure now reached 10,000, but one-third of the participants are studying the higher books in the institute's sequence. Efforts to bring new believers and seekers into the institute process have created a fresh dynamic in clusters. As more and more new declarants join institute courses, "the system as a whole will be in a constant state of expansion."[25]   52.51

The growing pool of human resources generated by the institute process has made it possible to establish an increasing number of two other core activities: devotional gatherings and children's classes.   52.52

Devotional meetings begin to flourish as consciousness of the spiritual dimension of human existence is raised among the believers in an area through institute courses.[26]   52.53

In various parts of the world, special endeavors to increase the number of devotional meetings often begin with encouraging believers inspired by their institute course on spiritual life to undertake such meetings on their own. Another approach that has resulted in an expansion in number previously not contemplated has been to hold devotional gatherings in the homes of non-Bahá'ís, who sometimes organize the meetings themselves. Employing this arrangement over a six-month period, the believers in Malaysia were able to increase tenfold the devotional meetings in their advanced clusters and the level of participation by 40 percent.   52.54

The multiplication of devotional gatherings has taken place with seeming ease in both rural and urban areas. In only 18 months, the number of individuals participating in devotional gatherings in Asia grew by nearly 200 percent and in the Americas and Europe by about 50 percent.   52.55

A marked increase in children's classes has been reported on all continents, confirming that they are also "a natural outgrowth of the training received early in the study of the main   52.56

sequence."[27] Efforts to multiply the number of children's classes in a strong cluster are predicated on training a sizable cadre of children's class teachers, and usually require a concerted outreach to the community at large, as the Bahá'í children may be few in number. Africa recorded the most significant rise in children's classes, with the number nearly doubling between April 2001 and October 2002.

52.57   The multiplication of core activities in well-developed clusters, growing out of increased individual initiative, has been identified as an important step in advancing toward a program of intensive growth. As the House of Justice wrote:

52.58   The coherence thus achieved through the establishment of study circles, devotional meetings and children's classes provides the initial impulse for growth in a cluster, an impulse that gathers strength as these core activities multiply in number.[28]

2.3.3 REFLECTION MEETINGS

52.59   A natural vehicle for multiplying core activities has been reflection meetings. These meetings at the cluster level have been particularly effective in well-established areas where an expanding pool of human resources exists. In such gatherings the institutions and the believers, many of whom are involved in the institute process, study the relevant Five Year Plan documents, share experiences, and consult on the achievements and strengths within the cluster. Avoiding "grandiose and elaborate plans,"[29] the friends reach a consensus on short-term goals which reflect the pledges of individual initiatives and collective actions that have emerged from the consultation. These goals are generally incorporated into a calendar of activities that becomes the framework for the subsequent two- to three-month period. In many clusters around the world, how to hold productive and enjoyable reflection meetings has become an important area for learning.

2.3.4 REACHING OUT TO ALL INHABITANTS

52.60   What has helped clusters with a strong institute process move toward the next stage of development has been the efforts of Bahá'ís to open their communities to the public at large and guide ready souls to the Cause in progressively increasing numbers. In some of these advanced clusters, most

of the participants in the first course of the institute have been
seekers.

> It is evident, then, that a systematic approach to train-   52.61
> ing has created a way for Bahá'ís to reach out to the sur-
> rounding society, share Bahá'u'lláh's message with friends,
> family, neighbors and coworkers, and expose them to the
> richness of His teachings. This outward-looking orientation
> is one of the finest fruits of the grassroots learning taking
> place.[30]

In this regard the House of Justice calls attention to the   52.62
promising opportunities offered by devotional gatherings and
children's classes:

> As both activities are made open to the wider community   52.63
> through a variety of well-conceived and imaginative means,
> they attract a growing number of seekers, who, more
> often than not, are eager to attend firesides and join study
> circles. Many go on subsequently to declare their faith in
> Bahá'u'lláh and, from the outset, view their role in the com-
> munity as that of active participants in a dynamic process
> of growth.[31]

Bahá'ís from Alaska to Australia, from Ireland to India,   52.64
have prepared imaginative brochures to attract seekers to their
devotional meetings. Family members, neighbors, and even
respondents to newspaper advertisements have been joining
the Bahá'ís for prayer and readings from the Scriptures, often
enhanced by music and followed by refreshments. Reports
from 75 percent of the national communities reveal that as of
October 2002, approximately 12,000 of the participants in
devotional meetings—20 percent—were non-Bahá'ís.

An equally effective form of outreach has been the active   52.65
extension of Bahá'í children's classes to the greater community.
Parents of all backgrounds and strata of society are united in
their desire to guide their children to a better life. The response
to offers by Bahá'ís to provide children in an area with spiritual education has been extremely encouraging. According to
reports from two-thirds of the national communities, more
than 27,000, or 40 percent, of the children attending Bahá'í
classes at the present time are from non-Bahá'í families. In
such countries as Botswana, Lesotho, the Dominican Republic,
Nicaragua, Panama, Paraguay, Puerto Rico, the Andaman and

Nicobar Islands, Myanmar, Nepal, Thailand, the Mariana Islands, Albania, and Romania, as of October 2002, 75 percent or more of the participants in their children's classes were from families of non-Bahá'ís.

52.66   The experience in the state of Tamil Nadu in India offers an example of a successful approach. Bahá'ís who had completed institute training for children's class teachers visited selected villages in their cluster and held public meetings at which they presented to the public, through the use of skits and posters, the dangers facing children in today's society and the importance of spiritual education. Scores of parents enrolled their children in Bahá'í classes, resulting in an unprecedented increase in children's classes in each of the target clusters. In five clusters where previously there had been 28 classes, the total rose to 136.

52.67   Wherever systematic efforts were made to invite receptive parents who had children in Bahá'í classes or individuals who were attending devotional meetings to join study circles, the results were also encouraging. For these souls, their introduction to the Bahá'í Faith has been first and foremost the Word of God. Connecting the seekers immediately with the Writings of Bahá'u'lláh has been a uniformly effective approach, one that recalls advice from the Guardian: "we are enjoined to constantly refer the seeker to the Word itself."[32]

52.68   It has also been reassuring to note that when non-Bahá'ís realize there is no pressure or proselytizing involved, but rather a genuine desire on the part of Bahá'ís to share the spiritual sustenance in the Teachings of Bahá'u'lláh, they respond positively and readily return to Bahá'í gatherings on their own. A program recently conducted in Medchal, India, offers a striking example of such a response. A presentation on the Bahá'í Faith's perspective on moral education was delivered to 80 teachers and students at the Government Industrial Training Institute. As a result of this event, more than half of those present chose to enroll in a study circle. Similarly, in Luxembourg at the end of a public meeting organized by the Bahá'ís on the spiritual education of children, 10 local residents registered for a Bahá'í study circle.

2.4 *Accelerating expansion and consolidation in advanced clusters*

2.4.1 PREREQUISITES FOR INTENSIVE GROWTH

As the second year of the Five Year Plan draws to a close, approximately 150 clusters worldwide have been identified as having attained conditions propitious for intensive growth. In many of these clusters the acceleration of the institute process has resulted in 50 to 60 percent of the believers being fully involved in institute courses, with a significant number having completed the current sequence. These highly motivated friends, stimulated and nurtured by the encouragement of the Local Spiritual Assemblies and Auxiliary Board members, have undertaken more and more individual initiatives in the teaching field. The number of core activities within these clusters has increased at a seemingly exponential rate, and these "portals for entry by troops" have become the channels for most of the new enrollments in Bahá'í communities.   52.69

A high degree of enthusiasm and a strong sense of ownership are also characteristics of clusters ready to embark on an intensive program of growth. Reflection meetings are well attended and participation is lively. The feeling of ownership of the process has been manifested in, among other ways, greater contributions to the Fund. Though facing serious economic difficulties, the friends in the well-developed clusters in Moldova and the Ukraine are contributing more generously than ever to all the funds of the Faith. In an advanced priority cluster in Nepal, the contributions of the believers to the National Fund increased by 100 percent over the previous year.   52.70

2.4.2 INTENSIFICATION OF TEACHING EFFORTS

The House of Justice stated in its message of 9 January 2001 that at the core of an intensive program of growth "must lie a sound and steady process of expansion, matched by an equally strong process of human resource development." The teaching work will include "a range of teaching efforts . . . involving both activities undertaken by the individual and campaigns promoted by the institutions."[33]   52.71

In a letter to a National Assembly, the House of Justice explained that the implementation of well-conceived teaching projects,   52.72

52.73   which are linked with the systematic training of a large number of believers for service to the Faith, . . . is an important step towards invigorating and sustaining the growth of the Cause.[34]

52.74   In its 17 January message the House of Justice has specifically identified teaching projects as a step toward intensive growth:

52.75   . . . carefully designed projects are being added to the existing pattern of growth to reach receptive populations and lift the rate of expansion to a higher level.[35]

52.76   In many parts of the world, "bringing large numbers into the ranks of Bahá'u'lláh's followers has traditionally not been a formidable task."[36] With the institute system in advanced clusters ready to absorb a periodic influx of new declarants, it is now timely in such areas to initiate short-term, direct teaching projects in order to "lift the rate of expansion to a higher level." A recent five-day teaching campaign in the Medak cluster in Andhra Pradesh, India, led to 194 individuals' embracing the Faith, of which 114 immediately joined a first level institute course. The House of Justice, in its 17 January message, praised this course of action for the more developed clusters:

52.77   Such projects accelerate the tempo of teaching, already on the rise through the efforts of individuals. And, where large-scale enrollment is beginning to result, provision is being made to ensure that a certain percentage of the new believers immediately enter the institute program, for, as we have emphasized in several messages, these friends will be called upon to serve the needs of an ever-growing Bahá'í population.[37]

52.78   After a sizable percentage of the new believers who have enrolled through teaching projects join institute courses and become integrated into core activities, another similar project can soon be undertaken. Not only will periodic teaching projects act as a catalyst for growth but continuing this cycle of expansion and consolidation will help accelerate and sustain the growth process.

52.79   Teaching projects will be especially effective if they are "carefully designed" and reach specific segments of the population in a cluster. Teaching approaches and materials may be tailored to persons, for example, of particular occupations (schoolteachers, university students, lawyers), ethnicities

(Aborigines, Chinese, Roma), and religions (animist, Buddhist, Christian, Muslim), or to women and youth. After substantial experience accumulates in the field as to the appropriate methods and contexts for teaching special populations, Bahá'ís involved in this work can assist the institute by designing a course that is specific to a particular group; such a course could be offered as a branch of the basic institute course on becoming an effective teacher.

2.4.3 THE DYNAMICS OF INTENSIVE GROWTH

A question often asked by the friends is how they will know when their cluster is ready for an intensive program of growth. One indicator that cannot be overlooked is growth itself—an increase in the number of Bahá'ís in the cluster. A vigorous institute process, the multiplication of core activities and their integration, a successful outreach to local inhabitants, an ever-growing number of individual and collective teaching initiatives, a vibrant community life, and a commitment to an ongoing learning process will result in growth. This includes new enrollments as well as reactivated Bahá'ís who have been roused by the newfound spirit and activity in their area. These elements will also naturally lead to and foster the conditions for intensive programs of growth identified by the House of Justice in its message of 9 January 2001, such as the "pronounced spirit of collaboration" among the institutions and "a reasonable degree of administrative capacity." 52.80

An intensive program of growth suggests just that—intensification—an intensification of activity that contributes to systematic growth. The friends in advanced clusters will become aware of a perceptible change in the intensity of activity in their area, and this will be reflected in the growth pattern. An intensive program of growth implies a pattern that is progressively accelerated and fully sustained. 52.81

3. Enhancing Institutional Capacity

The process of dividing a country into clusters undertaken in the first year of the Five Year Plan has made it possible for the institutions of the Faith "to realize a pattern of well-ordered expansion and consolidation."[38] National Assemblies and Regional Councils have formulated their plans of action, supported by a system for training the necessary human 52.82

resources, with an eye toward moving clusters from one stage of development to the next. And when an active cluster has the necessary elements in place and is registering new enrollments, it is the institutions that confirm its readiness to embark on an intensive program of growth.

52.83   Achieving and sustaining intensive growth demand a variety of capabilities and new approaches on the part of Bahá'í institutions. Reports indicate that the building of capacity, though gradual, takes place more readily when members of institutions have had first-hand experience with the dynamics of cluster development and the processes that contribute to growth.

3.1 *Managing the process of growth*

52.84   In promoting and overseeing the process of growth, Bahá'í institutions have been demonstrating a range of motivational and organizational capacities. These skills are enhanced when an attitude of learning prevails and an appreciation of the essential harmony between individual initiative and collective action exists.

3.1.1 FOSTERING AN ENCOURAGING ENVIRONMENT

52.85   Chief among the requirements for motivating believers and nurturing a culture of growth is the capacity to foster an encouraging environment where, as the Universal House of Justice wrote in its 9 January message, "teaching is the dominating passion of the lives of the believers" and "mutual support, commitment to learning, and appreciation of diversity of action are the prevailing norms." In the same message, the House of Justice also stated that an upsurge in teaching activity depends on "sustained encouragement."

52.86   In clusters preparing for intensive growth, it has been observed that the collaborating institutions have demonstrated the ability to create an atmosphere of mutual trust with the friends, utilize their talents, praise their accomplishments, and overlook minor mistakes. These are hallmarks of the emerging Bahá'í culture, and the success of this Plan depends in no small measure on the extent to which the institutions and individuals alike demonstrate these capacities. In a letter written on his behalf to a National Assembly, Shoghi Effendi made a comment about encouragement that is relevant to institutions at all levels of the Cause:

... the National Body is like the beating of a healthy heart in the midst of the Community, pumping spiritual love, energy and encouragement out to all the members.[39]

52.87

3.1.2 COORDINATION AT THE CLUSTER LEVEL

The actual work of promoting the process of growth in the clusters requires skills of organization and coordination. These functions are being carried out within a new framework of collaboration, as described by the House of Justice:

52.88

> The implementation of such a program [of intensive growth] will require the close collaboration of the institute, the Auxiliary Board members and their assistants, and an Area Teaching Committee.[40]

52.89

To the extent that these institutions, through effective collaboration, have been able to systematically enlarge the pool of human resources in a cluster and mobilize these resources for teaching and other acts of service, they have been successful in advancing the cluster toward a program of intensive growth. Underlying their efforts has been the realization that success would depend "on the manner in which lines of action are integrated and on the attitude of learning that is adopted."[41]

52.90

In clusters where well-functioning Local Spiritual Assemblies exist, a coordinating committee has at times replaced the role of an Area Teaching or Growth Committee as the agency collaborating with the Auxiliary Board members and the institute. In either case, meeting the challenges of furthering the institute process and promoting systematic growth have required increasing administrative capacities, not the least of which is effective consultation. The ability to organize productive and enjoyable reflection meetings has also been a feature of well-developed clusters.

52.91

3.1.3 THE ONGOING COLLECTION OF STATISTICS

Managing the growth process necessitates certain practical skills such as collecting statistics, because to monitor growth it is essential to be able to measure it. The friends are learning to maintain an accurate database at the grassroots by recording on a regular basis such information as the number of individuals going through the institute's sequence of courses, the number of core activities, the number of persons who attend these

52.92

activities, and the number of new enrollments. Special training in collecting statistics has often been necessary for the friends at the cluster level. This task needs to be carried out in such a way that it does not overburden communities but provides data sufficient for planning and for identifying measures to accelerate growth. Particular emphasis has been given to tracking the statistics in the most promising clusters at about three-month intervals, so that appropriate steps can be taken to move these clusters toward intensive growth.

3.2 *Reexamining administrative approaches*

52.93   Gradually National Spiritual Assemblies are coming to recognize that the administrative structures they put in place in their national communities should reflect and support the primary aim of the Plan. While in earlier years national committees and task forces were established for an array of local and national activities and proclamation events, the current focus on promoting systematic growth has influenced the nature and number of committees a National Assembly may wish to appoint. Some Assemblies, particularly in countries with small national communities, have found it useful to reduce the number of national committees to allow more time and energy for the priorities of the Five Year Plan. Eliminating or consolidating less vital committees has also enabled National Assemblies to better fulfill their responsibilities for monitoring the overall growth of the Faith in their countries and has freed up the believers for teaching activities.

52.94   A significant development that has made it possible for a number of National Spiritual Assemblies to modify the approach to their work was the establishment of Regional Bahá'í Councils. Under the guidance of the House of Justice, these National Assemblies are gradually learning to delegate responsibilities and authority to this new institution. Charged with overseeing the plans for expansion and consolidation in their regions, the Councils are able to analyze specific approaches to be adopted in the execution of the Five Year Plan, and design plans of action consisting "essentially of those provisions needed to help each cluster in the region move from its current stage of growth to the next advanced stage."[42] Again, the result has been that the National Assemblies are free to focus on larger strategic issues and other pressing matters, and the teaching plans and priorities have become more responsive to the conditions and resources at the grassroots. In countries where the organization of the teaching work has been carried out by Regional Teaching Committees, under the supervision of a National Teaching Committee, the benefits of this principle of decentralization are evident as well.

Delegation of authority has also been exercised by National Assemblies and Regional Councils with respect to Institute Boards. In a letter written on its behalf, the House of Justice has given the following advice on the delegation of responsibilities and the administration of the institute process: 52.95

> In the case of the boards of the regional institutes . . . one of the challenges before the Regional Bahá'í Councils is to delegate to them the functions that are properly theirs and to give them the freedom needed to discharge those functions. The boards, likewise, have to provide enough latitude to the coordinators of the institutes, and invest them with enough authority, for them to perform their daily work effectively. . . . 52.96

> . . . The coordinator needs to operate at the level of implementation, carrying out day-to-day plans and activities and ensuring that the basic function of the institute is performed—this, with the assistance of the tutors and any staff if necessary. The board oversees the institute process as a whole, largely through the periodic reports of the coordinator and through occasional consultations. It will want to make itself readily accessible to the coordinator, providing the atmosphere in which he or she can share ideas, seek the board's views on the possibilities and challenges facing the institute, and benefit from its advice. To carry out its role, the board does not need to meet frequently, as does a committee charged with undertaking a set of specific tasks. 52.97

> As for the Regional Council, it is, naturally, interested to know that such an important agency under its aegis as the institute is accomplishing the tasks for which it was created and is functioning in full capacity. Even more important, the Council must ensure that, as the ranks of avowed supporters of the Faith swell through the institute process, they are deployed in the field of service, reinforcing the work of large-scale expansion and consolidation. This multiplication and deployment of human resources is to be carried out, of course, in the context of a regional plan to 52.98

move each cluster in the region from its current stage of growth to the next advanced stage.[43]

52.99   Experience has indicated that when Institute Boards have been given a sufficient degree of autonomy to administer their work, they have been more effective in advancing the institute process than those in countries where the Assemblies or Councils have attempted to retain the process tightly within their control.

3.3 Facilitating individual initiative

52.100   The growing contingents of friends eager to find their paths of service have had implications for the role of Local Spiritual Assemblies in the Five Year Plan and beyond. The House of Justice calls attention to the challenge:

52.101   All of this opens thrilling opportunities for Local Spiritual Assemblies. Theirs is the challenge, in collaboration with the Auxiliary Board members who counsel and assist them, to utilize the energies and talents of the swelling human resources available in their respective areas of jurisdiction both to create a vibrant community life and to begin influencing the society around them.[44]

52.102   Intensive growth depends upon encouraging individuals to carry out a rapidly increasing number of core activities and other endeavors, and Local Assemblies have been instrumental in this process. Through their inspiration and support, a host of individual and collective actions have resulted. By recognizing and facilitating the initiatives of the many friends proceeding through the institute courses, as well as of other devoted servants in their communities, the Assemblies are assuming a style of leadership urged by the Guardian:

52.103   The first quality for leadership, both among individuals and Assemblies, is the capacity to use the energy and competence that exists in the rank and file of its followers.[45]

52.104   Because the planning environment has now broadened to the level of the cluster, often involving several Local Assemblies and the active participation of the believers in formulating short-term goals, an Assembly's scope of interest has begun to stretch beyond its boundaries. Its vision is expanded, its resources magnified, and its opportunities enlarged. In describing

the character of cluster meetings, the House of Justice alludes
to features of this wider perspective:

> The Universal House of Justice hopes that the consultations   52.105
> which take place in periodic meetings at the level of the
> cluster will generate such unity of thought about the growth
> of the Faith that, in those cases where the lines of action
> affect localities with Local Assemblies, the requirement
> of receiving their approval will easily be met. It should be
> remembered that the aim of such consultations, beyond
> addressing certain practical considerations, is to maintain
> a high level of enthusiasm and to create a spirit of service
> and fellowship among those present. Discussions should
> not become bogged down by undue concern for procedural
> issues, but should focus on what can be achieved and on
> the joy of witnessing the fruits of hard work and diligent
> effort.[46]

3.4 *Serving large numbers*

The challenges of growth will test and develop the capacities   52.106
of our institutions at all levels, but ultimately these bodies were
designed to serve large numbers of people. Indeed, "so much
of the ability of the Faith to develop capacity for community
building depends upon the size of our membership."[47] Shoghi
Effendi has assured us that growth is the answer to fulfilling the
potentialities of our Administrative Order:

> The problems which confront the believers at the   52.107
> present time, whether social, spiritual, economic or ad-
> ministrative, will be gradually solved as the number and
> the resources of the friends multiply and their capacity for
> service . . . develops.[48]

And in the same vein, the Universal House of Justice states: 52.108

> A massive expansion of the Bahá'í community must be   52.109
> achieved far beyond all past records. . . . The need for this
> is critical, for without it the laboriously erected agencies of
> the Administrative Order will not be provided the scope to
> be able to develop and adequately demonstrate their inher-
> ent capacity to minister to the crying needs of humanity in
> its hour of deepening despair.[49]

The ability to guide and sustain a growth process will   52.110
contribute toward the capacity and maturation of institutions

at all levels. The House of Justice highlighted this point in its Riḍván message at the beginning of the Four Year Plan:

52.111 ... the maturity of the Spiritual Assembly must be measured not only by the regularity of its meetings and the efficiency of its functioning, but also by the continuity of the growth of Bahá'í membership.[50]

52.112 This maturation comes about through the enhancement of the capabilities of Bahá'í institutions as they are involved in promoting growth, responding to the needs of increasing numbers of believers, and facilitating their service to the Cause.

4. Change in the Culture of the Bahá'í Community

52.113 At the end of the Four Year Plan the Universal House of Justice wrote that "the culture of the Bahá'í community [had] experienced a change."[51] The "new patterns of thought and action"[52] introduced by the training institutes were having a profound impact on individuals, institutions, and communities. Fundamental to this new orientation was an attitude of learning, along with an appreciation of systematization and focus, a commitment to enlisting a greater number of believers in the work of the Cause, and a conscious outreach to society at large.

52.114 At the level of the cluster and the community, where the culture of learning is taking root, a new dynamic has emerged whereby the friends are engaged in actions that are purposeful, systematic, and energizing.

4.1 Learning and planning at the grassroots

52.115 Two observations that are important to the ongoing prosecution of the Five Year Plan can be made about the experience of working in clusters. First, reflection meetings have become the learning matrix of the clusters. These periodic consultations have enabled the believers to "reflect on issues, consider adjustments, and maintain enthusiasm and unity of thought."[53] The value of short-term goals is immediately recognized, as accomplishments and challenges can regularly be evaluated, "obstacles removed, resources multiplied and lessons learned,"[54] and modifications in the goals made without losing continuity of action. Flexibility and patience are encouraged, as essential prerequisites of the learning process. The friends have begun to appreciate that not all answers can be tied down in advance but are garnered through experience. In describing this process, the House of Justice wrote:

> Meetings of consultation held at the cluster level serve to raise awareness of possibilities and generate enthusiasm. Here, free from the demands of formal decision-making, participants reflect on experience gained, share insights, explore approaches and acquire a better understanding of how each can contribute to achieving the aim of the Plan. In many cases, such interaction leads to consensus on a set of short-term goals, both individual and collective. Learning in action is becoming the outstanding feature of the emerging mode of operation.[55]

52.116

A second critical feature of working in clusters is the shift to planning at the grassroots. The House of Justice described this as one of the purposes of the clustering exercise, but its implications for the roles of individuals and local institutions in implementing the Plan are only beginning to be felt. Rather than "the mere enumeration of goals,"[56] often unconnected to the realities of the resources in an area, planning at reflection gatherings is based on the human resources actually available. The impact of the training institute on the planning process and the stimulation of individual initiative has been widely seen. Armed with new insights, skills, and abilities, individuals have arisen in cluster after cluster to take up tasks in support of their area plan. Through the encouragement of the institutions, particularly the Auxiliary Board members, enthusiasm for service has been generated and guided "into channels of systematic endeavor."[57]

52.117

4.2 *Maintaining a focus*

At Bahá'í institutional meetings and other gatherings in every country of the world, one is struck by the clear and common focus demonstrated by the friends in their efforts to advance the process of entry by troops. The House of Justice associated this development with the change in culture:

52.118

> ... since the beginning of the Four Year Plan, the entire Bahá'í world has been undergoing a profound change in culture required by the single focus of the global Plans in this latter part of the first century of the Faith's Formative Age—advancing the process of entry by troops.[58]

52.119

52.120 Accustomed to pursuing a wide range of goals at the national and local levels, many Bahá'ís faced the challenge of focusing their teaching and other forms of service more directly on advancing this overriding aim of the Plan. While a "diversity of action" was expected, the guidance of the House of Justice provided an explicit framework for that action, and the believers became aware that "old modes of thinking, which, while valuable in many respects, have not been conducive to rapid growth."[59]

52.121 Coupled with the focus on advancing the process of entry by troops is a growing appreciation of the need to be systematic in action. Growth should not be explosive and short-lived but steady and sustained. By definition, a process means a systematic series of actions directed toward a specific end. A systematic approach to training human resources is already yielding substantial results, and the systematization of the teaching work through the movement of clusters is demonstrating its efficacy. As stated at the outset of this document, it is "concentrated and sustained attention" to these two movements that will lead to the fulfillment of the aim of the Five Year Plan.

4.3 *Empowering the rank and file*

52.122 Referred to as the "chief propellant" of the change in culture, the training institutes, with their ability to produce an expanding number of human resources, have fundamentally altered the approach of the Bahá'í community to the tasks at hand. More than ever the rank and file of the believers are involved in meaningful and vital service to the Cause. Whether by holding devotional meetings, facilitating study circles, or teaching children's classes, a greater number of friends have found paths of service that do not depend on public-speaking prowess. The training institutes have imparted the necessary "spiritual insights," "knowledge," and "skills" that have enabled the believers to "facilitate the process of entry by troops with efficiency and love."[60] The House of Justice has remarked on this accomplishment:

52.123 It is especially gratifying to note the high degree of participation of believers in the various aspects of the growth process. In cluster after cluster, the number of those shouldering the responsibilities of expansion and consolidation is steadily increasing.[61]

The growing confidence and commitment of the believers, 52.124
which have been reflected "in the thrust of individual initiatives,"[62] are gathering momentum in the Five Year Plan. In this
regard the House of Justice has reassured the friends that

> as the believers gain confidence in their capacity to serve 52.125
> through the institute process, a much richer expression of
> the diverse talents of the friends is beginning to appear in
> the Bahá'í world—a richness that bodes well for the future
> progress of the Cause.[63]

4.4 *An "outward-looking orientation"*

When the Universal House of Justice called on the Bahá'ís 52.126
at the beginning of the Five Year Plan to open their study
circles, children's classes, and devotional meetings "to all the
inhabitants of the locality," that phrase signalized a change in
the culture of Bahá'í communities, a change that is intimately
linked with the efforts of the Faith to grow and to embrace
humankind.

In reaching out to all inhabitants of a locality we are 52.127
inspired by the words of Bahá'u'lláh: "This Day a door is open
wider than both heaven and earth."[64] Making a concerted effort
to open the portals of our community life to the outside world
requires both courage and imagination. Stories abound of the
creative measures Bahá'í communities around the globe are
employing to attract seekers to their activities.

Beyond opening the doors of the Bahá'í community to the 52.128
outside world, the believers are also exerting themselves to
reach out. Bahá'ís are striving to expand their social circles and
ultimately their friendships, as friendship is the surest foundation for touching the hearts. To pursue these aims, individuals
have begun to examine their priorities, including the services
they are rendering the Faith, and to reorder their lives so as to
allow themselves more time for interaction with their relatives,
friends, and coworkers. Ultimately, what is the point of striving
to become more effective teachers if we are not meeting people
to teach?

Having an "outward-looking orientation" also suggests 52.129
that it is important for Bahá'ís to understand more deeply the
forces operating on the world stage and the solutions offered
by the Revelation of Bahá'u'lláh. Our task is to convey to
seekers that we are all living in the same world, facing common

trials, and striving to fulfill similar, long-held aspirations for the human race. Our expressions of solidarity with our fellow human beings must be sincerely voiced and genuinely felt.

5. The Movement of Humanity toward Bahá'u'lláh

52.130   A premise underlying our current teaching efforts is the realization that all humanity is moving toward Bahá'u'lláh.

52.131   Let there be no doubt that what we are witnessing is the gathering momentum of that process of the entry of humanity into the Cause by troops, foreshadowed in Bahá'u'lláh's Tablet to the King of Persia, eagerly anticipated by the Master, and described by the Guardian as the necessary prelude to mass conversion.[65]

52.132   Not everyone learns or responds at the same rate but the path to Him is wide enough to accommodate one and all regardless of their pace. "The Cause of God has room for all"[66] suggests that not only are divers peoples welcome but that individuals may be at different points in their understanding and acceptance of the Faith. Adopting an attitude of openness and inclusion will help diminish the sharp line that believers have sometimes tended to draw between themselves and the public at large.

52.133   Bahá'ís everywhere are also acutely aware that events outside the Faith are serving, as the Universal House of Justice wrote, "to awaken in the hearts of those who share this planet with us a longing for unity and justice that can be met only by the Cause of God."[67] All of the plans, campaigns, and reflection meetings are aimed at finding ways to share the Divine Message with the waiting masses. Above all, the friends should be encouraged to remember Bahá'u'lláh's call "This is the day in which to speak,"[68] and 'Abdu'l-Bahá's exhortation that we "should strive with our whole hearts to offer ourselves up, guide others to His path, and train the souls of men."[69]

53

Impact of Growth on Administration Processes

a document prepared by
the International Teaching Centre

July 2005

The dramatic progress achieved on all continents in the course   53.1
of the Five Year Plan has been reflected in many aspects of the
life of the Bahá'í community. The training institute process has
continued to enhance the capacity of an increasing number of
believers to promote the processes of expansion and consolidation. The enhanced sense of ownership and enthusiasm thus
generated, reflected in a marked increase in individual initiative,
has been especially evident in advanced clusters where the
renewed teaching fervor of the friends is directed towards
intensive programs of growth.

One of the welcome results of this new vibrancy is that   53.2
there is a growing contingent of believers involved in the
work of the Cause, serving in numerous capacities within the
framework of the Plan. Meanwhile an expanding community of
interest is challenging the Bahá'í community to re-conceptualize
its boundaries and cater to the requirements of an ever-swelling body of individuals walking together the path towards
Bahá'u'lláh. The progress made has been reinforced by the
emergence of a new culture of growth in the community.

As these developments have continued at an accelerating   53.3
pace, several national communities have taken steps to reframe
their administrative arrangements, so as to align them with the
new requirements. Below is a review of some of the most salient
aspects of the developments which impinge on the administration of the processes of growth. This review reflects the experiences of communities in the advance guard of these processes.
Whereas in some instances the changes have been relatively

minor and adjustments easily made, in other cases they have necessitated a major rethinking of structures and practices.

Administering the Process of Growth at the Cluster Level

53.4   With the division of countries into small geographic areas, the cluster construct has created a new arena within which the teaching work can be organized on a manageable scale. Large-scale expansion in the past had proven difficult to sustain. Whilst this was principally owing to lack of a systematic process for raising human resources, there was also limited experience with managing the process of growth at the grassroots. In this context, the learning that has been achieved about the administration of growth at the cluster level constitutes one of the major accomplishments in the current Plan.

53.5   In its 9 January 2001 letter, the Universal House of Justice placed the locus of the cluster planning work on three entities at the cluster level: "The implementation of such a program will require the close collaboration of the institute, the Auxiliary Board members and their assistants, and an Area Teaching Committee." In advanced clusters these entities are directly focused on the planning and execution of teaching plans, ensuring that the victories are immediately consolidated, learning is captured, and appropriate adjustments quickly made. Taken together, the three agencies constitute a strong infrastructure, making it possible for many decisions related to the process of growth to be made by those most intimately involved in their execution.

53.6   As the specific responsibilities of agencies operating at the cluster level became defined by the House of Justice, in several countries detailed documents that set out the scheme of coordination involving these agencies and their ancillary arms have been developed. Often modelled on the first such paper that was developed in India, these have assisted in clarifying roles and removing ambiguities. These documents have also formed the basis in these countries of the training and orientation of the members of the agencies, necessarily an ongoing process which continues to be refined in light of experience.

53.7   One instance of the training required by the Area Teaching Committee occurred in an advanced cluster in Mongolia. There, the sharp increase in new believers and the complexity of managing the consequent rise in consolidation activities highlighted the urgent need for training of the members of the Committee as well as of members of the Local Spiritual Assemblies in the cluster. The training included a range of important organizational capabilities—data collection and analysis, team building, and computer skills. The collaboration of the Committee, the institute coordinators, and the Auxiliary Board members has enabled this cluster to scale remarkable heights in expansion, consolidation, and human resource development.

A critically important aspect which cannot be deferred for long is the significant investment of time required from the cluster agencies, in particular the training institute coordinator and the secretary of the Area Teaching Committee—occasionally referred to as the cluster development facilitator. Experience is showing that where the number of core activities, the various campaigns related to the teaching work, and the tasks related to the collection of statistics, among other duties, reach a certain level of complexity, part- and eventually full-time workers are required. In such instances, institute coordinators and development facilitators, functioning with increasing effectiveness, are proving indispensable to the greater mobilization of the rank and file of the believers and the continuity of teaching and consolidation efforts.

53.8

The question is not initially related to whether such staff are remunerated—in many clusters the services of volunteers in these posts are being effectively harnessed. Rather, the issue is one of recognising that the management of the processes of growth requires intensive effort on the part of a dedicated team of individuals functioning in clearly defined spheres at the grassroots. Eventually, of course, it will not be possible for the work to be carried out on a purely voluntary basis and, in time, individuals will need to be employed. Where remuneration is required, new challenges arise related to the use of the funds, and the way in which they are to be generated within the cluster and augmented from outside as necessary. Another challenge is ensuring that a flexible approach is adopted to allow for various employment arrangements.

53.9

Another important consideration is that the sizeable enlargement of the community of interest is proving a spur to the friends and institutions to adopt approaches that minimize the demarcation between Bahá'ís and non-Bahá'ís. As core activities attract an increasing number of participants, the challenge is to meet their needs by making them feel at home

53.10

within a Bahá'í environment. To administer this new element of the community requires intimate knowledge of their needs and application of systematic attention. It involves regularly communicating with them, engaging them in a single discourse, readily utilising their services and learning how to guide them to an ever increasing commitment to the Cause. All this is greatly facilitated by having agencies that can function at the cluster level, for this is the arrowhead of learning about all aspects of the growth process. The cluster agencies can put in place the necessary elements such as creating a special newsletter aimed at the community of interest, engaging these new friends in the work of the cluster, or assisting Local Spiritual Assemblies to play their own part in this regard.

Involvement of Local Spiritual Assemblies

53.11   The role of the Local Spiritual Assembly is, like that of all other institutions, an evolutionary one, which will develop in relation to the processes of growth. Although observations in this area are still rather preliminary, certain broad conclusions are already discernible. Where Local Assemblies have acquired the new vision of growth and adjusted to the requirements of operating within the context of the cluster, they have greatly enhanced the teaching work. Conversely, where there has been resistance to the new realities, the process of growth has been adversely affected.

53.12   It is instructive to note the effective role that Local Spiritual Assemblies have played in many clusters. In several countries where Assemblies had a low level of functioning, a significant revival of Assemblies in advanced clusters has been observed. The believers are taking responsibility for the election of their Assembly and, once formed, the Assembly is assuming greater responsibility for the affairs of the Cause than ever before.

53.13   In other instances, particularly in the context of intensive programs of growth, Local Assemblies with a high level of functioning are rising to the challenges created by the program. Such Assemblies have effectively reinforced the cluster plan formulated by the cluster agencies and assumed responsibility for certain elements of the endeavor within their own area. Given that the geographic scope of the planning involved often extends to several localities, a useful practice in the initial stages of development has been for the cluster agencies to share the proposed plan with the Local Spiritual Assemblies in the area. This approach can enhance the Assemblies' ability to lend their support to the program, and encourages them to take steps to reinforce it in their localities. An example of where this is happening in many instances is the United States.

As teaching efforts and core activities have multiplied, Local Assemblies have been thrilled to see the opportunities created for serving the wider population. For example, an Assembly in whose area children's classes have multiplied in various neighbourhoods is delighted to know that the community in its charge is able to administer to a greater number of the children of the locality than it was ever possible before. Yet beyond the increased capacity for outreach, the positive effect on the quality of Bahá'í community life has also been reported and is reflected in the enhanced quality of its internal processes. 53.14

These conclusions are drawn in part from a survey conducted by the International Teaching Centre in about fifty advanced clusters throughout the world. The study which assessed the impact of the process of growth on several aspects of Bahá'í community life identified that 90 percent of the surveyed clusters had experienced improvements in the Nineteen Day Feast, with nearly two-thirds of them also recording a rise in participation levels. Insights gained from conducting devotional gatherings are increasingly reflected in the spiritual program of the Feast. According to the survey, even the consultative processes at all levels in the community—including Assembly meetings—have improved in efficacy, becoming more purposeful, united, and focused. It has also been observed that in many instances contributions to the Bahá'í Fund have been positively impacted as levels of commitment and consciousness about its spiritual significance have increased. These successes are owed to the effect of the institute process which, fostering a deep spiritual transformation, has proven more effective in dealing with great numbers of people than most efforts at community and Spiritual Assembly development. 53.15

The survey indicated that the most significant initial contribution of Local Assemblies to the processes of growth was providing encouragement to the believers. This was particularly effective when an expansion of vision had resulted from the participation of Assembly members in the institute process as well as the study of Five Year Plan documents. Interactions with the cluster agencies were also identified as enabling Assemblies 53.16

to make effective contributions. Such interactions often occur at the cluster level in the context of particular plans of action. Another effective approach to building unity of vision and action has been the convening of conferences for Local Assembly members. This approach has been employed in Canada where such gatherings held at the regional or cluster level by Regional Bahá'í Councils have done much to assist Local Assemblies to realign their administrative processes and priorities.

53.17 Beyond these considerations, the leadership role of the Spiritual Assemblies—be they national or local—is of profound importance. It has been observed in many clusters that the processes of growth are greatly enhanced where this leadership role is exercised through the Assemblies' constant effort to maintain the vision of growth before the believers, allowing for the two essential movements to impact priorities, avoiding unnecessary distractions, providing the necessary resources, and reinforcing the plans and initiatives at the cluster level. Further, the dynamic force of individual example as the members of Assemblies themselves become personally involved in the cluster activities, actively supporting the efforts of the cluster agencies, is imperative.

Decentralization and Regional Bahá'í Councils

53.18 Given the far-reaching developments occurring at the level of the cluster and as more intensive programs of growth are launched, decentralization of administrative processes becomes ever more important. Accordingly, the strengthening of Regional Bahá'í Councils, where these exist, takes on added significance. The main consideration is related to the devolution of the decision making process to the appropriate level of the Bahá'í administration. In practice, this principle applies both to the devolution of decision making by National Spiritual Assemblies to the regional level, and by the Regional Bahá'í Council to the cluster level. It is increasingly evident that where the framework of the Five Year Plan has been well understood by Regional Councils, through their stewardship of the expansion and consolidation processes in their regions, the aim of a significant advance in the process of entry by troops is becoming realized.

53.19 One approach to the question of decentralization would be to focus on the relationship of the Councils with the

Counsellors, the National Assembly, national committees, and offices of the National Center, looking at the hierarchy of the various entities involved. However, more relevant to the relation between decentralization and the aim of advancing the process of entry by troops would be a consideration of whether the administrative structures are consistent with and conducive to growth at the cluster level, particularly large-scale growth. What many countries are learning is to construct the vision of administrative processes that affect growth from the cluster upwards, asking at each stage what arrangements will best advance the process of entry by troops in this new arena of action.

What is being learnt, then, is that an effective administra-   53.20
tion with regard to the teaching work is one that aims to release the power of individual initiative, providing the flow of resources and freedom of operation to the coordinating structures at the cluster level. Indeed, one national community which is undertaking a wide-ranging review of its administrative processes, India, began by considering the reality at the level of the cluster, and considered what processes would most effectively ensure the promotion of growth. For this purpose, administration was conceptualized as constituting the channels to facilitate a series of necessary flows—flows of guidance, direction, encouragement, human resources, literature, and information, including statistics.

The challenge of gathering accurate statistics is being   53.21
addressed in many countries through the application of the Statistical Report Program (SRP) devised by the Department of Statistics at the Bahá'í World Centre. What this program facilitates is the gathering and analysis of key data that enable an accurate and timely picture of the development of the community to be built up. Aggregating the information at the cluster, region, and country levels, SRP provides an important tool for Bahá'í institutions in their decision making process, enabling the prioritization of resources and lines of action at each level of the administration. Although initially the program will require the investment of some effort to train a few individuals in its use and to enter the base data, once in place it is proving a valuable aid to the process of decentralization. Countries that are already implementing the SRP package include some with a substantial size of membership, such as Brazil, Colombia, Malaysia, and Zambia.

Impact on Administrative Processes at the National Level

53.22   The ongoing process of decentralization necessitated by the Five Year Plan carries with it profound implications for administration at the national and regional levels. As national communities review their administrative structures, it is heartening to note that in many instances they are doing so in anticipation of a community that is several fold larger in size. Such a perspective is necessitating a significant shift in resources to the regional and cluster levels, as well as inevitable concomitant changes in the size and structure of the National Office.

53.23   As stated above, in the vanguard of this administrative review is India where the institutions have, at the encouragement of the House of Justice, begun to reassess and modify the national administration in that country to become better equipped for sustaining and extending the remarkable growth that has been achieved. The challenge has been enthusiastically embraced and has already brought with it a reorganization of the national treasury office, a restructuring of some of the national agencies, and a streamlining of the flow of information, including statistics.

53.24   One area that has required a fresh perspective in many countries is how the national budget reflects and reinforces the priorities of the Plan: human resource development and the advancement of clusters. Where the expansion and consolidation work effectively devolves upon the Councils, in some communities a substantial transfer of funds to these bodies has occurred, as well as an assessment of the resources needed for sustaining intensive programs of growth at the cluster level. New budget analyses and formulations have taken into account the decentralization necessary to fulfill the singularly important aim of a significant advance in the process of entry by troops.

53.25   In the United Kingdom the National Assembly, responding to the demands of the Plan, reassessed its staffing situation at the national level and managed through streamlining of functions and consolidation of posts to release the necessary funds to substantially increase the financial support for regional institutions. This step, begun in 2002, made it possible to appoint the first full-time regional training institute coordinator, and later to fund a second post, as well as providing the financial support for positions at the cluster level as these become necessary—measures which are making a direct and decisive impact on the impressive development of the process of growth in that country.

The statement in the document "Building Momentum: A Coherent Approach to Growth" related to re-examining administrative approaches has led many national communities to undertake a process of reflection in light of the realities and requirements of promoting a culture of growth. In several cases the number of national committees has been radically reduced to ensure that the processes of growth receive the appropriate priority and that as many believers as possible are released to focus on the teaching work. Kenya and Germany are notable examples. 53.26

In several countries, the mandates of committees whose functions directly impinge on the processes of growth—such as the National Teaching Committee, the National Child Education Committee, and the National Youth Committee—have been carefully reviewed not only to ensure alignment with the aims of the Plan but also to examine whether any elements are already covered by other agencies, thus obviating the duplication of effort. In some cases these committees, once considered mandatory, have been deactivated where it has become clear that the essential aspects of their work are already being conducted by other agencies, such as Regional Bahá'í Councils, or training institutes. In Australia increased capacity at the grassroots made it possible for the responsibilities of the National Child Education Committee to be successfully devolved to the Regional Bahá'í Councils. 53.27

Clearly, questions related to the role of any particular committee must be decided on a case-by-case basis and no prescription can be provided that would fit every eventuality. Nevertheless, the principle that the new circumstances created by the Five Year Plan necessitate a reconsideration of administrative arrangements at the national level is increasingly being recognized in many countries. 53.28

* * *

The emerging experience in the Bahá'í world, reflected in the foregoing observations, is an impressive fruit of the learning mode increasingly evident in every department of the life of the community. As the processes of growth gather pace, there is every expectation that administrative processes and structures will continue to evolve in response to the particular exigencies of each new stage. 53.29

Notes

39 Advancing the Process of Entry by Troops

1 Message dated 26 December 1995 written by the Universal House of Justice to the Conference of the Continental Boards of Counsellors.

2 Message dated 26 November 1999 written by the Universal House of Justice to the Bahá'ís of the world.

3 Riḍván 153 [1996] message written by the Universal House of Justice to the Bahá'ís of the world.

4 Message dated 9 November 1993 written by the Universal House of Justice to all National Spiritual Assemblies.

5 Letter dated 25 June 1953 written on behalf of Shoghi Effendi to the National Spiritual Assembly of the United States, cited in *Citadel of Faith: Messages to America, 1947–1957* (Wilmette: Bahá'í Publishing Trust, 1965, 1995 printing), p. 117.

40 Two Essential Movements

1 Message dated 22 December 2001 written by the Universal House of Justice to the Friends gathered at the Eighth ASEAN Youth Conference in Thailand.

2 Letter dated 23 March 2003 written on behalf of the Universal House of Justice to the National Spiritual Assembly of Trinidad and Tobago.

3 Letter dated 31 July 2002 written on behalf of the Universal House of Justice to an individual believer.

4 Ibid.

5 Ibid.

6 Letter dated 18 August 2005 written on behalf of the Universal House of Justice to the National Spiritual Assembly of Germany.

7 Letter dated 23 December 2001 written on behalf of the Universal House of Justice to the National Spiritual Assembly of Brazil.

8 Message dated 17 January 2003 written by the Universal House of Justice to the Bahá'ís of the world.

9 Message dated 9 January 2001 written by the Universal House of Justice to the Conference of the Continental Boards of Counsellors.

10 Message dated 17 January 2003 written by the Universal House of Justice to the Bahá'ís of the world.

11 Ibid.

12 Ibid.

13 Ibid.

14 Letter dated 8 September 2000 written on behalf of the Universal House of Justice to the National Spiritual Assembly of Eritrea.

15 Message dated 9 January 2001 written by the Universal House of Justice to the Conference of the Continental Boards of Counsellors.

16 Riḍván 2005 message written by the Universal House of Justice to the Bahá'ís of the world.

41 Learning in Action

1 Letter dated 14 August 2002 written on behalf of the Universal House of Justice to an individual believer.

2 Letter dated 12 August 2002 written on behalf of the Universal House of Justice to an individual believer.

3 Message dated 31 December 1995 written by the Universal House of Justice to the Bahá'ís of the world.

4 *The Institution of the Counsellors*, a document prepared by the Universal House of Justice (Haifa: Bahá'í World Centre, 2001), p. 24.

5 Message dated 17 January 2003 written by the Universal House of Justice to the Bahá'ís of the world.

6 *The Institution of the Counsellors*, pp. 28–29.

7 Message dated 3 May 1998 written by the Universal House of Justice to the Conference of the Continental Counsellors.

8 Letter dated 14 August 2002 written on behalf of the Universal House of Justice to an individual believer.

9 Riḍván 2000 message written by the Universal House of Justice to the Bahá'ís of the world.

10 Letter dated 11 April 2005 written on behalf of the Universal House of Justice to an individual believer.

42 Learning to Be Systematic

1 Riḍván 155 [1998] message written by the Universal House of Justice to the Bahá'ís of the world.

2 Message dated 26 December 1995 written by the Universal House of Justice to the Conference of the Continental Boards of Counsellors.

3 *Century of Light,* a document prepared on behalf of the Universal House of Justice (Haifa: Bahá'í World Centre, 2001), pp. 99–100.

4 Ibid., pp. 101–108.

5 Ibid., p. 108.

6 Message dated 26 November 1999 written by the Universal House of Justice to the Bahá'ís of the world.

7 Letter dated 31 July 2002 written on behalf of the Universal House of Justice to an individual believer.

8 *The Institution of the Counsellors,* p. 18.

9 Ibid., pp. 19–20.

10 Letter dated 12 December 2001 written on behalf of the Universal House of Justice to the National Spiritual Assembly of the United States.

11 Riḍván 153 [1996] message written by the Universal House of Justice to the Followers of Bahá'u'lláh in Europe.

12 Message dated 9 January 2001 written by the Universal House of Justice to the Conference of the Continental Boards of Counsellors.

13 Ibid.

14 Message dated 26 December 1995 written by the Universal House of Justice to the Conference of the Continental Boards of Counsellors.

15 Letter dated 19 October 2005 written on behalf of the Universal House of Justice to the National Spiritual Assembly of the United States.

16 Letter dated 18 August 2005 written on behalf of the Universal House of Justice to the National Spiritual Assembly of Germany.

43 Learning to Maintain Focus

1 Message dated 26 November 1999 written by the Universal House of Justice to the Bahá'ís of the world.

2 Letter dated 16 September 1996 written on behalf of the Universal House of Justice to the National Spiritual Assembly of India.

3 Ibid.

4 Letter dated 23 October 2000 written on behalf of the Universal House of Justice to the National Spiritual Assembly of Kenya.

5 Letter dated 18 September 1998 written on behalf of the Universal House of Justice to the National Spiritual Assembly of Côte d'Ivoire.

6   Letter dated 17 May 2005 written on behalf of the Universal House of Justice to an individual believer.

7   Letter dated 11 July 2005 written on behalf of the Universal House of Justice to the Spiritual Assembly of Malaysia.

8   Letter dated 10 August 1997 written on behalf of the Universal House of Justice to the National Spiritual Assemblies represented at the Fourth Bahá'í ASEAN Forum.

9   Letter dated 7 April 1997 written on behalf of the Universal House of Justice to the National Spiritual Assembly of Belarus.

10 Letter dated 9 June 2002 written on behalf of the Universal House of Justice to the National Spiritual Assembly of Uganda.

11 Letter dated 6 July 1997 written on behalf of the Universal House of Justice to the National Spiritual Assembly of Guyana.

12 Letter dated 1 June 1997 written on behalf of the Universal House of Justice to the National Spiritual Assembly of Uganda.

13 Letter dated 25 December 2000 written on behalf of the Universal House of Justice to the National Spiritual Assembly of Australia.

14 Letter dated 13 August 2002 written on behalf of the Universal House of Justice to the National Spiritual Assembly of Brazil.

15 Letter dated 24 December 2001 written on behalf of the Universal House of Justice to the National Spiritual Assembly of the United States.

16 Letter dated 25 March 2001 written on behalf of the Universal House of Justice to a Bahá'í agency.

17 Letter dated 29 June 1997 written on behalf of the Universal House of Justice to the National Spiritual Assembly of the Western Caroline Islands.

18 Message dated 22 December 2001 written by the Universal House of Justice to the Friends gathered at the Eighth ASEAN Youth Conference in Thailand.

19 Letter dated 22 December 2004 written on behalf of the Universal House of Justice to the Administrative Committee of Burundi.

20 Riḍván 2004 message written by the Universal House of Justice to the Bahá'ís of the world.

21 Letter dated 4 July 2005 written on behalf of the Universal House of Justice to the National Spiritual Assembly of the Russian Federation.

22 Letter dated 2 September 2001 from the Department of the Secretariat of the Universal House of Justice to the National Spiritual Assembly of Paraguay.

23 Message dated 11 July 2005 written on behalf of the Universal House of Justice to the National Spiritual Assemblies in Europe.

24 Letter dated 15 May 2005 written on behalf of the Universal House of Justice to the National Spiritual Assembly of the United States.

25 Ibid.

26 Letter dated 18 August 2005 written on behalf of the Universal House of Justice to the National Spiritual Assembly of the United Kingdom.

27 Letter dated 31 May 2005 written on behalf of the Universal House of Justice to a National Spiritual Assembly.

28 Letter dated 26 June 2002 written on behalf of the Universal House of Justice to an individual believer.

29 Letter dated 22 August 2004 written on behalf of the Universal House of Justice to an individual believer.

30 Letter dated 26 June 2002 written on behalf of the Universal House of Justice to an individual believer.

31 Riḍván 2003 message written by the Universal House of Justice to the Bahá'ís of the world.

32 Letter dated 20 February 2003 written on behalf of the Universal House of Justice to an individual believer.

33 Letter dated 16 March 2004 written on behalf of the Universal House of Justice to an individual believer.

34 Letter dated 8 October 2001 written on behalf of the Universal House of Justice to the National Spiritual Assembly of New Zealand.

35 Letter dated 27 August 2002 written on behalf of the Universal House of Justice to an individual believer.

36 Letter dated 14 January 1999 written on behalf of the Universal House of Justice to the National Spiritual Assembly of the United States.

37 Message dated 26 December 1995 written by the Universal House of Justice to the Conference of the Continental Boards of Counsellors.

38 Letter dated 20 February 2003 written on behalf of the Universal House of Justice to an individual believer.

44 Learning to Develop Human Resources for Expansion and Consolidation

1 Riḍván 2000 message written by the Universal House of Justice to the Bahá'ís of the world.

2 Message dated 26 November 1999 written by the Universal House of Justice to the Bahá'ís of the world.

3 Message dated 9 January 2001 written by the Universal House of Justice to the Conference of the Continental Boards of Counsellors.

4 Message dated 26 December 1995 written by the Universal House of Justice to the Conference of the Continental Boards of Counsellors.

5 Letter dated 31 May 2001 written on behalf of the Universal House of Justice to an individual believer.

6 Letter dated 19 January 1997 written on behalf of the Universal House of Justice to the Spiritual Assembly of Thailand.

7 Letter dated 8 May 1997 written on behalf of the Universal House of Justice to the National Spiritual Assembly of Bulgaria.

8 Ibid.

9 Letter dated 19 November 2001 written on behalf of the Universal House of Justice to an individual believer.

10 Message dated 9 January 2001 written by the Universal House of Justice to the Conference of the Continental Boards of Counsellors.

11 "Training Institutes," a document prepared for and approved by the Universal House of Justice, April 1998, p. 7.

12 Letter dated 7 June 2001 written on behalf of the Universal House of Justice to the National Spiritual Assembly of Australia.

13 Letter dated 16 March 2004 written on behalf of the Universal House of Justice to the National Spiritual Assembly of the Czech Republic.

14 Letter dated 26 July 2004 written on behalf of the Universal House of Justice to an individual believer.

15 Ibid.

16 Message dated 9 January 2001 written by the Universal House of Justice to the Conference of the Continental Boards of Counsellors.

17 Letter dated 26 July 2004 written on behalf of the Universal House of Justice to an individual believer.

18 Riḍván 2004 message written by the Universal House of Justice to the Bahá'ís of the world.

19 Memorandum dated 7 November 1996 written by the Universal House of Justice to the International Teaching Centre.

20 Letter dated 14 April 1998 written on behalf of the Universal House of Justice to the National Spiritual Assembly of Côte d'Ivoire.

21 Letter dated 5 October 1998 written on behalf of the Universal House of Justice to an individual believer.

22 Letter dated 19 January 1998 written on behalf of the Universal House of Justice to the National Spiritual Assembly of Haiti.

23 Letter dated 5 October 1998 written on behalf of the Universal House of Justice to an individual believer.

24 Letter dated 24 May 2001 written on behalf of the Universal House of Justice to an individual believer.

25 Letter dated 23 March 2003 written on behalf of the Universal House of Justice to the National Spiritual Assembly of Trinidad and Tobago.

26 Letter dated 23 December 2001 written on behalf of the Universal House of Justice to the National Spiritual Assembly of Brazil.

27 Message dated 9 January 2001 written by the Universal House of Justice to the Conference of the Continental Boards of Counsellors.

28 Riḍván 2005 message written by the Universal House of Justice to the Bahá'ís of the world.

29 Letter dated 26 August 2003 written on behalf of the Universal House of Justice to the National Spiritual Assembly of Mexico.

30 Letter dated 16 September 2003 written on behalf of the Universal House of Justice to the National Spiritual Assembly of the Philippines.

31 Letter dated 11 May 2003 written on behalf of the Universal House of Justice to the National Spiritual Assembly of Ethiopia.

32 Letter dated 9 June 2002 written on behalf of the Universal House of Justice to the National Spiritual Assembly of Uganda.

33 Letter dated 19 May 2004 written on behalf of the Universal House of Justice to a National Spiritual Assembly.

34 Letter dated 17 May 2004 written on behalf of the Universal House of Justice to the National Spiritual Assembly of Sarawak.

35 Letter dated 18 June 2001 written on behalf of the Universal House of Justice to the National Spiritual Assembly of Finland.

36 Letter dated 23 April 2004 written on behalf of the Universal House of Justice to an individual believer.

37 Letter dated 19 October 2005 written on behalf of the Universal House of Justice to the National Spiritual Assembly of the United States.

38 Letter dated 11 September 2005 written on behalf of the Universal House of Justice to a National Spiritual Assembly.

45 Learning to Open Aspects of Bahá'í Community Life to Others

1 Message dated 9 January 2001 written by the Universal House of Justice to the Conference of the Continental Boards of Counsellors.

2 Riḍván 2002 message written by the Universal House of Justice to the Bahá'ís of the world.

3 Message dated 17 January 2003 written by the Universal House of Justice to the Bahá'ís of the world.

4 Letter dated 25 September 2001 written on behalf of the Universal House of Justice to the Spiritual Assembly of Argentina.

5 Letter dated 8 May 1997 written on behalf of the Universal House of Justice to the National Spiritual Assembly of Bulgaria.

6 Message dated 26 December 1995 written by the Universal House of Justice to the Conference of the Continental Boards of Counsellors.

7 Letter dated 27 April 2004 written on behalf of the Universal House of Justice to an individual believer.

8 *One Common Faith,* a document prepared for and approved by the Universal House of Justice (Haifa: Bahá'í World Centre, 2005), p. 52.

9 Letter dated 4 May 2005 written on behalf of the Universal House of Justice to the National Spiritual Assembly of Kazakhstan.

10 Memorandum dated 27 April 1998 written by the Universal House of Justice to the Office of Social and Economic Development.

11 Shoghi Effendi, published in *Bahá'í News,* no. 13, September 1926, p. 1, cited in *Principles of Bahá'í Administration: A Compilation* (London: Bahá'í Publishing Trust, 1976), p. 20.

12 Message dated 9 January 2001 written by the Universal House of Justice to the Conference of the Continental Boards of Counsellors.

46 Learning to Reach Receptive Populations

1 Message dated 17 January 2003 written by the Universal House of Justice to the Bahá'ís of the world.

2 Letter dated 28 May 2004 written on behalf of the Universal House of Justice to the National Spiritual Assembly of the United States.

3 Letter dated 20 March 2002 written on behalf of the Universal House of Justice to the National Spiritual Assembly of Austria.

4 Letter dated 28 May 2004 written on behalf of the Universal House of Justice to the National Spiritual Assembly of the United States.

5 Letter dated 5 August 2004 written on behalf of the Universal House of Justice to the National Spiritual Assembly of Canada.

6 Letter dated 31 October 2002 written on behalf of the Universal House of Justice to an individual believer.

7 Message dated 9 January 2001 written by the Universal House of Justice to the Conference of the Continental Boards of Counsellors.

8 "Training Institutes," p. 5.

9 Ibid.

10 Letter dated 26 June 2002 written on behalf of the Universal House of Justice to an individual believer.

11 Message dated 9 January 2001 written by the Universal House of Justice to the Conference of the Continental Boards of Counsellors.

12 Riḍván 153 [1996] message written by the Universal House of Justice to the Followers of Bahá'u'lláh in Europe.

13 Letter dated 22 June 2005 written by the Universal House of Justice to a conference of Arabic-speaking believers, July 2005.

14 Letter dated 28 May 2004 written on behalf of the Universal House of Justice to the National Spiritual Assembly of the United States.

15 Letter dated 25 March 2002 written on behalf of the Universal House of Justice to the National Spiritual Assembly of Uganda.

16 Message dated 10 April 2003 written by the Universal House of Justice to the Friends gathered at the series of youth forums called by the Regional Bahá'í Council of the Western States, U.S.A.

17 Riḍván 153 [1996] message written by the Universal House of Justice to the Followers of Bahá'u'lláh in Latin America and the Caribbean.

18 Message dated 10 January 2002 written by the Universal House of Justice to the Bahá'ís of the world.

47 Learning to Exercise Disciplined Initiative and to Participate in Collective Action

1 *The Institution of the Counsellors*, p. 19.

2 Ibid.

3 Riḍván 152 [1995] message written by the Universal House of Justice to the Bahá'ís of the world.

4 Ibid.

5   Riḍván 153 [1996] message written by the Universal House of Justice to the Bahá'ís of the world.

6   Riḍván 155 [1998] message written by the Universal House of Justice to the Bahá'ís of the world.

7   *The Institution of the Counsellors*, pp . 20–21.

8   Letter dated 22 August 2002 written on behalf of the Universal House of Justice to an individual believer.

9   Message dated 17 January 2003 written by the Universal House of Justice to the Bahá'ís of the world.

10 Ibid.

11 Letter dated 10 July 2005 from the Department of the Secretariat of the Universal House of Justice to an individual believer.

12 Letter dated 21 July 2005 written on behalf of the Universal House of Justice to the Local Spiritual Assembly of Guelph, Canada.

13 Letter dated 16 March 2004 written on behalf of the Universal House of Justice to a National Spiritual Assembly.

14 Letter dated 20 February 2003 written on behalf of the Universal House of Justice to an individual believer.

15 Riḍván 153 [1996] message written by the Universal House of Justice to the Followers of Bahá'u'lláh in Europe.

16 Memorandum dated 9 April 1996 written by the Universal House of Justice to the International Teaching Centre.

17 Riḍván 153 [1996] message written by the Universal House of Justice to the Followers of Bahá'u'lláh in Latin America and the Caribbean.

18 Letter dated 11 September 2005 written on behalf of the Universal House of Justice to a National Spiritual Assembly.

19 Letter dated 24 January 2003 written on behalf of the Universal House of Justice to two individual believers.

20 Letter dated 31 July 2002 written on behalf of the Universal House of Justice to an individual believer.

21 Letter dated 19 May 1994 written by the Universal House of Justice to the National Spiritual Assembly of the United States.

22 Message dated 9 January 2001 written by the Universal House of Justice to the Conference of the Continental Boards of Counsellors.

23 Letter dated 18 August 2005 written on behalf of the Universal House of Justice to the National Spiritual Assembly of Germany.

24 Letter dated 14 September 2005 written on behalf of the Universal House of Justice to an individual believer.

25 Message dated 26 December 1995 written by the Universal House of Justice to the Conference of the Continental Boards of Counsellors.

26 Message dated September 1964 written by the Universal House of Justice to the Bahá'ís of the world, cited in *Messages from the Universal House of Justice, 1963–1968* (Wilmette: Bahá'í Publishing Trust, 1996), pp. 42–43.

48 Learning to Administer Growth

1 Letter dated 7 May 2004 written by the Universal House of Justice to the National Spiritual Assembly of India.

2 Riḍván 2004 message written by the Universal House of Justice to the Bahá'ís of the world.

3 Letter dated 26 November 2003 written on behalf of the Universal House of Justice to the National Spiritual Assembly of India.

4 Letter dated 26 August 2003 written on behalf of the Universal House of Justice to the National Spiritual Assembly of Mexico.

5 Letter dated 16 September 2003 written on behalf of the Universal House of Justice to the National Spiritual Assembly of the Philippines.

6 Message dated 9 January 2001 written by the Universal House of Justice to the Conference of the Continental Boards of Counsellors.

7 *The Institution of the Counsellors,* p. 23.

8 Ibid., p. 22.

9 Ibid.

10 Letter dated 16 September 2003 written on behalf of the Universal House of Justice to the National Spiritual Assembly of the Philippines.

11 Letter dated 14 February 2005 written on behalf of the Universal House of Justice to the National Spiritual Assembly of India.

12 Letter dated 16 September 2003 written on behalf of the Universal House of Justice to the National Spiritual Assembly of the Philippines.

13 Letter dated 17 November 2004 written on behalf of the Universal House of Justice to an individual believer.

14 Letter dated 8 July 2005 from the Department of Statistics at the Bahá'í World Centre to the National Spiritual Assembly of Namibia.

15 Letter dated 18 August 2005 written on behalf of the Universal House of Justice to the National Spiritual Assembly of Germany.

16 Letter dated 15 January 2004 written on behalf of the Universal House of Justice to an individual believer.

17 Letter dated 21 November 2003 written on behalf of the Universal House of Justice to the National Spiritual Assembly of India.

18 Letter dated 27 May 2005 written on behalf of the Universal House of Justice to the National Spiritual Assembly of the Russian Federation.

19 Letter dated 27 October 2005 written on behalf of the Universal House of Justice to the National Spiritual Assembly of the Democratic Republic of the Congo.

20 Letter dated 15 December 2003 written on behalf of the Universal House of Justice to the National Spiritual Assembly of Moldova.

21 Ibid.

22 Letter dated 19 October 2005 written on behalf of the Universal House of Justice to the National Spiritual Assembly of the United States.

49 Learning to Plan and to Mobilize

1 Message dated 9 January 2001 written by the Universal House of Justice to the Conference of the Continental Boards of Counsellors.

2 Riḍván 155 [1998] message written by the Universal House of Justice to the Bahá'ís of the world.

3 Ibid.

4 Message dated 9 January 2001 written by the Universal House of Justice to the Conference of the Continental Boards of Counsellors.

5 *The Institution of the Counsellors*, pp. 23–24.

6 Letter dated 12 December 2001 written on behalf of the Universal House of Justice to the National Spiritual Assembly of the United States.

7 Letter dated 12 August 2001 written on behalf of the Universal House of Justice to the National Spiritual Assembly of the Philippines.

8 Letter dated 27 May 2005 written on behalf of the Universal House of Justice to the National Spiritual Assembly of the Russian Federation.

9 Riḍván 153 [1996] message written by the Universal House of Justice to the Followers of Bahá'u'lláh in the Andaman and Nicobar Islands, Bangladesh, India, Nepal and Sri Lanka.

10 Riḍván 153 [1996] message written by the Universal House of Justice to the Followers of Bahá'u'lláh in Latin America and the Caribbean.

11 Letter dated 3 March 1998 written on behalf of the Universal House of Justice to the Spiritual Assembly of Hong Kong.

12 Letter dated 3 March 1999 written on behalf of the Universal House of Justice to the National Spiritual Assemblies of Cambodia, the Lao People's Democratic Republic, Malaysia, Myanmar, the Philippines, Sabah, Sarawak, Singapore, and Thailand.

13 Letter dated 29 June 1997 written on behalf of the Universal House of Justice to the National Spiritual Assembly of the Western Caroline Islands.

14 Message dated 17 January 2003 written by the Universal House of Justice to the Bahá'ís of the world.

15 Letter dated 18 August 2005 written on behalf of the Universal House of Justice to the National Spiritual Assembly of Germany.

16 Letter dated 9 December 2001 written on behalf of the Universal House of Justice to the National Spiritual Assembly of Seychelles.

17 Ibid.

18 Letter dated 11 April 2005 written on behalf of the Universal House of Justice to an individual believer.

19 Message dated 17 January 2003 written by the Universal House of Justice to the Bahá'ís of the world.

20 Message dated 26 December 1995 written by the Universal House of Justice to the Conference of the Continental Boards of Counsellors.

21 Introduction to *The Institution of the Counsellors*, p. 2.

22 Letter dated 14 September 2005 written on behalf of the Universal House of Justice to an individual believer.

23 *The Institution of the Counsellors*, p. 22.

24 Ibid.

25 Introduction to *The Institution of the Counsellors*, p. 3.

26 *The Institution of the Counsellors*, pp. 21–22.

27 Ibid., p. 22.

28 Riḍván 153 [1996] message written by the Universal House of Justice to the Followers of Bahá'u'lláh in Africa.

29 Riḍván 153 [1996] message written by the Universal House of Justice to the Followers of Bahá'u'lláh in the Andaman and Nicobar Islands, Bangladesh, India, Nepal, and Sri Lanka.

30 Message dated 26 November 1999 written by the Universal House of Justice to the Bahá'ís of the world.

31 Riḍván 2000 message written by the Universal House of Justice to the Bahá'ís of the world.

32 Message dated 26 November 1999 written by the Universal House of Justice to the Bahá'ís of the world.

33 Letter dated 11 January 1995 written on behalf of the Universal House of Justice to the National Spiritual Assembly of Peru.

34 Ibid.

50 Training Institutes, a document prepared for and approved by the Universal House of Justice, April 1998

1 Message dated 26 December 1995 written by the Universal House of Justice to the Conference of the Continental Boards of Counsellors.

2 Ibid.

3 Riḍván 1996 message written by the Universal House of Justice to the Bahá'ís of the world.

4 Riḍván 1996 message written by the Universal House of Justice to the Followers of Bahá'u'lláh in Europe.

5 Riḍván 1996 message written by the Universal House of Justice to the Followers of Bahá'u'lláh in Cambodia, Hong Kong, Lao People's Democratic Republic, Macau, Malaysia, Mongolia, Myanmar, Singapore, Taiwan, Thailand, and Vietnam.

6 Riḍván 1996 message written by the Universal House of Justice to the Followers of Bahá'u'lláh in the Andaman and Nicobar Islands, Bangladesh, India, Nepal, and Sri Lanka.

7 Riḍván 1996 message written by the Universal House of Justice to the Bahá'ís of the world.

8 Memorandum dated 3 April 1997 written by the Universal House of Justice to the International Teaching Centre.

9 Letter dated 1 June 1997 written on behalf of the Universal House of Justice to the National Spiritual Assembly of Uganda.

10 Letter dated 29 August 1996 written on behalf of the Universal House of Justice to an individual believer.

11 Letter dated 29 July 1997 written on behalf of the Universal House of Justice to the National Spiritual Assembly of Sweden.

12 Letter dated 8 May 1997 written on behalf of the Universal House of Justice to the National Spiritual Assembly of Bulgaria.

13 Memorandum dated 10 July 1997 written by the Universal House of Justice to the International Teaching Centre.

14 Letter dated 19 January 1998 written on behalf of the Universal House of Justice to the National Spiritual Assembly of Haiti.

15 Letter dated 16 May 1997 written on behalf of the Universal House of Justice to the National Spiritual Assembly of Honduras.

16 Letter dated 5 February 1997 written on behalf of the Universal House of Justice to an individual believer.

17 Letter dated 21 January 1998 written on behalf of the Universal House of Justice to the National Spiritual Assembly of Brazil.

18 Letter dated 14 November 1997 written on behalf of the Universal House of Justice to the National Spiritual Assembly of El Salvador.

19 Letter dated 3 April 1997 written on behalf of the Universal House of Justice to the National Spiritual Assembly of Brazil.

20 Letter dated 24 December 1997 written on behalf of the Universal House of Justice to the National Spiritual Assembly of India.

21 Letter dated 5 December 1996 written on behalf of the Universal House of Justice to the National Spiritual Assembly of Uganda.

22 Letter dated 6 July 1997 written on behalf of the Universal House of Justice to the National Spiritual Assembly of Guyana.

23 Letter dated 9 January 1997 written on behalf of the Universal House of Justice to the National Spiritual Assembly of the Eastern Caroline Islands.

24 Letter dated 14 April 1995 written on behalf of the Universal House of Justice to the National Spiritual Assembly of Panama.

25 Letter dated 11 January 1995 written on behalf of the Universal House of Justice to the National Spiritual Assembly of Peru.

51 Training Institutes and Systematic Growth, a document prepared by the International Teaching Centre, February 2000

1 Riḍván 153 [1996] message written by the Universal House of Justice to the Bahá'ís of the world.

2 Message dated 26 December 1995 written by the Universal House of Justice to the Conference of the Continental Boards of Counsellors.

3 Letter dated 19 November 1998 written on behalf of the Universal House of Justice to the Spiritual Assembly of Chad.

4 Letter dated 10 August 1998 written on behalf of the Universal House of Justice to the National Spiritual Assembly of the United States.

5 Riḍván 153 [1996] message written by the Universal House of Justice to the Bahá'ís of the world.

6   Ibid.

7   Letter dated 9 December 1998 written on behalf of the Universal House of Justice to the National Spiritual Assembly of the Russian Federation.

8   Riḍván 153 [1996] message written by the Universal House of Justice to the Bahá'ís of the world.

9   Letter dated 19 October 1997 written on behalf of the Universal House of Justice to an individual believer.

10 Riḍván 156 [1999] message written by the Universal House of Justice to the Bahá'ís of the world.

11 Letter dated 27 March 1998 written on behalf of the Universal House of Justice to the National Spiritual Assembly of Vanuatu.

12 Letter dated 18 March 1999 written on behalf of the Universal House of Justice to the National Spiritual Assembly of the United Kingdom.

13 Letter dated 18 January 1999 written on behalf of the Universal House of Justice to an individual believer.

14 Letter dated 29 July 1998 written on behalf of the Universal House of Justice to the National Spiritual Assembly of Bolivia.

15 Letter dated 9 October 1998 written on behalf of the Universal House of Justice to the National Spiritual Assembly of Papua New Guinea.

16 Letter dated 16 March 1998 written on behalf of the Universal House of Justice to the National Spiritual Assembly of Tonga.

17 Letter dated 14 April 1998 written on behalf of the Universal House of Justice to the National Spiritual Assembly of Côte d'Ivoire.

18 Letter dated 5 October 1998 written on behalf of the Universal House of Justice to an individual believer.

19 Letter dated 9 October 1998 written on behalf of the Universal House of Justice to the National Spiritual Assembly of Papua New Guinea.

20 Letter dated 10 December 1998 written on behalf of the Universal House of Justice an individual believer.

21 Letter dated 5 October 1998 written on behalf of the Universal House of Justice to an individual believer.

22 Letter dated 3 March 1998 written on behalf of the Universal House of Justice to the Spiritual Assembly of Hong Kong.

23 Letter dated 26 November 1999 written by the Universal House of Justice to the Bahá'ís of the world.

24 Riḍván 153 [1996] message written by the Universal House of Justice to the Bahá'ís of the world.

25 Letter dated 20 May 1998 written on behalf of the Universal House of Justice to the National Spiritual Assembly of Tanzania.

26 Letter dated 22 September 1999 written on behalf of the Universal House of Justice to the National Spiritual Assembly of Norway.

27 Message dated 26 December 1995 written by the Universal House of Justice to the Conference of the Continental Boards of Counsellors.

28 Letter dated 10 April 1998 written on behalf of the Universal House of Justice to the National Spiritual Assembly of India.

29 Letter dated 24 August 1999 written on behalf of the Universal House of Justice to the National Spiritual Assembly of the United States.

30 Ibid.

31 Riḍván 156 [1999] message written by the Universal House of Justice to the Bahá'ís of the world.

32 Ibid.

52 Building Momentum: A Coherent Approach to Growth, a document prepared by the International Teaching Centre, April 2003

1 Message dated 22 December 2001 written by the Universal House of Justice to the friends gathered at the Eighth ASEAN Youth Conference in Thailand.

2 Message dated 17 January 2003 written by the Universal House of Justice to the Bahá'ís of the world.

3 Letter dated 12 December 2001 written on behalf of the Universal House of Justice to the National Spiritual Assembly of the United States.

4 Message dated 17 January 2003 written by the Universal House of Justice to the Bahá'ís of the world.

5 Ibid.

6 Ibid.

7 Ibid.

8 Letter dated 20 March 2002 written on behalf of the Universal House of Justice to the National Spiritual Assembly of Austria.

9 Letter dated 8 April 2002 written on behalf of the Universal House of Justice to the National Spiritual Assembly of Bolivia.

10 Message dated 17 January 2003 written by the Universal House of Justice to the Bahá'ís of the world.

11 Letter dated 3 June 2001 written on behalf of the Universal House of Justice to an individual believer.

12 Letter dated 31 May 2001 written on behalf of the Universal House of Justice to an individual believer.

13 Letter dated 4 October 2000 written on behalf of the Universal House of Justice to the Spiritual Assembly of the Andaman and Nicobar Islands.

14 Letter dated 23 October 2000 written on behalf of the Universal House of Justice to the National Spiritual Assembly of Kenya.

15 Message dated 17 January 2003 written by the Universal House of Justice to the Bahá'ís of the world.

16 Message dated 9 January 2001 written by the Universal House of Justice to the Conference of the Continental Boards of Counsellors.

17 Message dated 17 January 2003 written by the Universal House of Justice to the Bahá'ís of the world.

18 Letter dated 3 June 2001 written on behalf of the Universal House of Justice to the National Spiritual Assembly of the Union of Myanmar.

19 Ibid.

20 Letter dated 8 September 2000 written on behalf of the Universal House of Justice to the National Spiritual Assembly of Eritrea.

21 Letter dated 20 March 2002 written on behalf of the Universal House of Justice to the National Spiritual Assembly of Austria.

22 Message dated 9 January 2001 written by the Universal House of Justice to the Conference of the Continental Boards of Counsellors.

23 Riḍván 2002 message written by the Universal House of Justice to the Bahá'ís of the world.

24 Message dated 17 January 2003 written by the Universal House of Justice to the Bahá'ís of the world.

25 Letter dated 8 September 2000 written on behalf of the Universal House of Justice to the National Spiritual Assembly of Eritrea.

26 Message dated 17 January 2003 written by the Universal House of Justice to the Bahá'ís of the world.

27 Ibid.

28 Ibid.

29 Message dated 9 January 2001 written by the Universal House of Justice to the Conference of the Continental Boards of Counsellors.

30 Message dated 17 January 2003 written by the Universal House of Justice to the Bahá'ís of the world.

31 Ibid.

32 Letter dated 4 June 1957 written on behalf of Shoghi Effendi to the National Spiritual Assembly of Canada, published in *The Gift of Teaching* (England: Bahá'í Publishing Trust, 1977), p. 35.

33 Message dated 9 January 2001 written by the Universal House of Justice to the Conference of the Continental Boards of Counsellors.

34 Letter dated 3 April 2000 written on behalf of the Universal House of Justice to the National Spiritual Assembly of Guyana.

35 Message dated 17 January 2003 written by the Universal House of Justice to the Bahá'ís of the world.

36 Ibid.

37 Ibid.

38 Riḍván 2002 message written by the Universal House of Justice to the Bahá'ís of the world.

39 Letter dated 30 June 1957 written on behalf of Shoghi Effendi to the National Spiritual Assembly of Alaska, published in *High Endeavors* (n.p.: National Spiritual Assembly of the Bahá'ís of Alaska, 1976), pp. 35–36.

40 Message dated 9 January 2001 written by the Universal House of Justice to the Conference of the Continental Boards of Counsellors.

41 Ibid.

42 Letter dated 12 December 2001 written on behalf of the Universal House of Justice to the National Spiritual Assembly of the United States.

43 Letter dated 23 December 2001 written on behalf of the Universal House of Justice to the National Spiritual Assembly of Brazil.

44 Message dated 17 January 2003 written by the Universal House of Justice to the Bahá'ís of the world.

45 Letter dated 30 August 1930 written on behalf of Shoghi Effendi to the National Spiritual Assembly of the United States and Canada, published in *Lights of Guidance* (New Delhi: Bahá'í Publishing Trust, 1996), p. 19.

46 Letter dated 9 December 2001 written on behalf of the Universal House of Justice to the National Spiritual Assembly of Seychelles.

47 Letter dated 20 August 2002 written on behalf of the Universal House of Justice to an individual believer.

48 Handwritten note of Shoghi Effendi appended to a letter dated 11 March 1933 written on his behalf to an individual believer, cited in a message dated 20 October 1983 written by the Universal House of Justice to the Bahá'ís of the world, published in *Readings on Bahá'í Social and Economic Development* (Florida: Palabra Publications, 2000), p. 7.

49 Riḍván 150 [1993] message written by the Universal House of Justice to the Bahá'ís of the world.

50 Riḍván 153 [1996] message written by the Universal House of Justice to the Bahá'ís of the world.

51 Riḍván 2000 message written by the Universal House of Justice to the Bahá'ís of the world.

52 Ibid.

53 Message dated 9 January 2001 written by the Universal House of Justice to the Conference of the Continental Boards of Counsellors.

54 *The Institution of the Counsellors*, a document prepared by the Universal House of Justice (Haifa: Bahá'í World Centre, 2001), p. 24.

55 Message dated 17 January 2003 written by the Universal House of Justice to the Bahá'ís of the world.

56 *The Institution of the Counsellors*, p. 24.

57 Ibid, p. 20.

58 Letter dated 12 August 2002 written on behalf of the Universal House of Justice to an individual believer.

59 Letter dated 14 August 2002 written on behalf of the Universal House of Justice to an individual believer.

60 Riḍván 153 [1996] message written by the Universal House of Justice to the Bahá'ís of the world.

61 Message dated 17 January 2003 written by the Universal House of Justice to the Bahá'ís of the world.

62 Riḍván 2000 message written by the Universal House of Justice to the Bahá'ís of the world.

63 Letter dated 26 June 2002 written on behalf of the Universal House of Justice to an individual believer.

64 Bahá'u'lláh, quoted by Shoghi Effendi in *The Advent of Divine Justice* (Wilmette: Bahá'í Publishing Trust, 1990), p. 78.

65 Message dated 17 January 2003 written by the Universal House of Justice to the Bahá'ís of the world.

66 Letter dated 10 December 1942 written on behalf of Shoghi Effendi to two individual believers, published in *Lights of Guidance*, p. 67.

67 Message dated 24 May 2001 written by the Universal House of Justice to the believers gathered for the events marking the completion of the projects on Mount Carmel.

68 Bahá'u'lláh, quoted by Shoghi Effendi in *The Advent of Divine Justice*, p. 82.

69 *Selections from the Writings of 'Abdu'l-Bahá* (Wilmette: Bahá'í Publishing Trust, 1997), sec. 218.8.

Index